BARENTIN'S MANOR
Excavations of the Moated Manor at Harding's Field, Chalgrove, Oxfordshire 1976–9

by Philip Page, Kate Atherton and Alan Hardy

with contributions by

E. Allison, M. Archibald, J. Blair, J. Carlinge, P. Carstairs, J. Channer, B. Ellis, A.R. Goodall, I. Goodall, J. Haslam, J. Hind, B. Knight, P. Powell, M. Robinson, S. Robinson, C. Salter, S. Smithson, J. Steane, C. Storey, C. Tremolet, R. White, M. Wilkinson, B. Wilson.

Illustrations by

E. Beard, P. Hughes, W. Page, R. Read, A. Tucker and Swindon College School of Art and Design BA Archaeological Illustration students

Alan Hardy · Phil Page

K. Atherton

Oxford Archaeology

Thames Valley Landscapes Monograph No. 24

2005

The publication of this volume has been generously funded by English Heritage

Published for Oxford Archaeology by Oxford University School of Archaeology
as part of the Thames Valley Landscapes Monograph series

Designed by Oxford Archaeology Graphics Office

Edited by Anne Dodd

This book is part of a series of monographs about the Thames Valley Landscapes – which can be bought from all good bookshops and Internet Bookshops. For more information visit www.oxfordarch.co.uk

ISBN 0 947816 623

Typeset and Printed in Europe by The Alden Group, Oxford, UK

Dedicated to the memory of Jean Mary Cook FSA

Contents

Figures

CHAPTER 1

CHAPTER 2

CHAPTER 3

CHAPTER 4

CHAPTER 5

Plates

Tables

Summary

Archaeological investigations at Harding's Field, Chalgrove, revealed the remains of one of the most complete examples of a moated medieval manor yet excavated in England. Evidence of a pre-moat occupation dating from the first half of the 13th century, which may not have been seigneurial, was succeeded in the mid 13th century by the construction of the moated manor house. The documentary evidence indicates that this house belonged to the Barentins, a prominent Oxfordshire family.

The manor underwent considerable alterations and improvements during the following 200 years, particularly during the early part of the 14th century and, to a lesser extent, in the late 14th to early 15th century. It passed out of the hands of the Barentin family shortly before it was demolished in the late 15th century.

The artefacts included an assemblage of pottery that contained many fine wares and some examples of continental imports. Decorated floor tiles, coins, objects of metal, bone, ivory and stone, together with vessel and window glass and some slags were also recovered. A significant bone assemblage was recovered, including mammal, bird and fish remains.

Zusammenfassung

Bei Untersuchungen in Harding's Field, Chalgrove, stießen Archäologen auf Überreste einer der komplettesten mittelalterlichen Wasserburgen, die bislang in England ausgegraben wurden. Vor dem Ausheben des Grabens bestand in der ersten Hälfte des 13. Jh. eine möglicherweise nicht feudalherrschaftliche Siedlung, die Mitte des 13. Jh. durch den Bau der Wasserburg abgelöst wurde. Urkundliche Belege deuten darauf hin, dass das Gebäude den Barentins gehörte, einer angesehenen Familie aus Oxfordshire.

In den folgenden 200 Jahren wurden an dem Bau beträchtliche Änderungen und Verbesserungen vorgenommen, besonders im frühen 14. Jh. und – in geringerem Ausmaß – im späten 14. und frühen 15. Jh. Die Wasserburg ging kurz vor ihrer Zerstörung im späten 15. Jh. von der Familie Barentin in andere Hände über.

Unter den gefundenen Artefakten befand sich eine Keramiksammlung mit viel Feinware und einigen kontinentaleuropäischen Importen. Außerdem wurden verzierte Fußbodenziegel, Münzen, Gegenstände aus Metall, Knochen, Elfenbein und Stein, Hohlgläser und Fensterglas sowie einige Schlacken geborgen. Auch beachtliche Knochenfunde waren zu verzeichnen, etwa von Säugetieren, Vögeln und Fischen.

Résumé

Des recherches archéologiques à Harding's Field, Chalgrove, ont révélé les vestiges d'un manoir médiéval à douves, un des exemples les plus complets jusqu'alors fouillé en Angleterre. Des indices d'une occupation antérieure à la construction des douves et datant de la première moitié du XIIIème siècle, qui n'était peut-être pas seigneuriale, fut remplacée vers le milieu du XIIIème siècle par la construction d'un manoir à douves. Les témoignages documentaires indiquent que la demeure appartenait aux Barentins, une famille influente d'Oxfordshire.

Le manoir fut l'objet d'altérations et d'améliorations considérables aux cours des 200 ans qui suivirent, en particulier durant la première partie du XIVème siècle et, dans une moindre mesure, vers la fin du XIVème et début du XVème siècles. Il échappa aux mains de la famille Barentin peu de temps avant sa destruction vers la fin du XVème siècle.

Les artefacts retrouvés sur le site comprenaient un ensemble de poterie, qui contenait nombre de productions fines et quelques exemples d'imports continentaux. Des carreaux de pavés décorés, des pièces de monnaie, des objets métalliques, de l'os, de l'ivoire et de la pierre, ainsi que des récipients en verre, du verre de vitrage et des scories furent également découverts. Un ensemble significatif d'ossements animaux fut mis au jour, y compris des restes de mammifères, d'oiseaux et de poissons.

Acknowledgements

Many people have been involved in the project, during the excavation and through the succeeding years, and thanks are due to all of them. The authors would like to thank the owners of Harding's Field, Oxfordshire County Council Education Department, for their co-operation and for allowing access to the site. Mr Adrian Nixey and members of the Chalgrove Local History Society were particularly helpful in the initial stages of the excavation. The headmaster, Mr Bell, and staff of Chalgrove County Primary School gave us the use of their premises on numerous occasions. Finance was provided by the Manpower Services Commission and the Department of the Environment. English Heritage's financial contribution to the final phase of post-excavation made publication possible.

Philip Page would like to thank his supervisors Simon Palmer, Christopher Storey and Andrew Gilby, and finds supervisors Dianne Hofdahl, Francis Cox and Gwynne Oakley. A majority of the fieldwork team during the project consisted of individuals enlisted through the Manpower Services Commission, a government-sponsored job-creation scheme. Very few of these people had prior training in archaeology, and it speaks volumes for their commitment and ability, and that of their supervisors, that the standards of excavation and recording were never compromised. Many volunteers also participated during each season; their help is greatly appreciated.

OAU staff Eleanor Beard and Wendy Page produced the original illustrations and Paul Hughes produced later phase plans. Paul Hughes should also be thanked for his work on the original figures so that they could be included in this monograph. Kate Atherton would also like to thank Ian Scott for his guidance during the final preparation of the monograph.

John Blair wishes to thank Gerald Harriss (Archivist), Mr Christopher Woolgar and Mrs Brenda Parry-Jones (Assistant Archivist) for permission to use estate records at Magdalen College and help throughout all stages of the work. He would also like to thank Mr Alan Crossley and Dr Janet Cooper of the Victoria County History for allowing him to consult the unpublished draft manorial descent of Chalgrove, which was compiled by Mr M G Cook of the City Archives Office, Newcastle-on-Tyne. John Steane would like to acknowledge G Bussell (Oxford University Laboratory for Archaeology and Art), M Hammett (Brick Development Association) and J Bailey (Ancient Monuments Laboratory).

The authors are indebted to James Bond, John Steane and the late Jean Cook for providing invaluable advice and assistance during the life of the project.

Chapter 1: The Project and the History of the Site

INTRODUCTION

The site in Harding's Field, Chalgrove (SU 6350 9682) was discovered by Richard Chambers of Oxford Archaeological Unit (OAU) in July 1976, during aerial reconnaissance of the earthworks (Miles 1977, 60). Shortly afterwards he and James Bond, then of Oxfordshire County Council Department of Museum Services (ODMS), carried out an earthwork survey of the field and identified two moated islands. Disturbed ground and the presence of nettles marked the position of structures on the larger eastern island and the good preservation of the earthworks, together with the rich grass and flora, suggested that the area had not been ploughed since the demolition of the buildings. Oxfordshire County Council Education Department had acquired Harding's Field from Magdalen College, Oxford, in 1971, and Oxford Archaeological Unit (OAU, now Oxford Archaeology) began excavations in 1976 after the decision had been made to prepare the site for use as a playing field.

Site location, topography and geology
(Fig.1.1, Pl. 1.1)

The village of Chalgrove, in Ewelme Hundred, Oxfordshire, lies 15.3 km (9.5 miles) south-east of Oxford and 5.6 km (3.5 miles) to the north-west of Watlington, the nearest market town. The name 'Chalgrove' means 'at the chalk or limestone pit' (Gelling 1953, 122) and the village lies near the foot of the scarp slope of the Chilterns, in the valley of the river Thame. This is a relatively low-lying area and Chalgrove village has a maximum elevation of 72.7 m OD at its eastern end and falls to 64.1 m OD at its western end.

Chalgrove is situated on Gault clays at the south-western end of the Vale of Aylesbury. The Gault is drained transversely by many small streams and patches of gravels and outcrops of Upper Greensand (OS Geological Survey sheet 254) further interrupt its surface. The numerous streams around the south-west side of the village have deposited a band of alluvium, approximately 400 m wide, over the Gault clay. These alluvial soils tend to be poorly drained and are mostly under permanent meadow grass (Jarvis 1973, sheet 253).

The natural east-west drainage has been considerably interfered with by the construction, probably in the 18th century, of a dam across one of the streams at the west of the village to provide a head of water to drive a breastshot water mill (Mill House – Fig. 1.1). The result of this is that the village is prone to flooding, and Harding's Field lies in the floodplain of the dammed stream.

A cut has been taken off the stream, at the east end of the village, which is controlled by a sluice gate. This man-made water course runs along the north side of the main street before rejoining the stream at the western end of the High Street.

Harding's Field lies south of the High Street, 250 m to the north-west of St Mary's Church and adjacent to Frogmore Lane. This lane is one of the oldest rights of way in the village and links the moated site to the church and the High Street. The site name derives from Thomas Harding who farmed the land in the latter half of the 19th century (Chalgrove Local History Group 1980, 8); it is currently owned by Oxfordshire County Council.

At the time of the excavations only four other known moated sites in Oxfordshire had been investigated archaeologically. None had been the subject of large-scale open-area excavation. Harding's Field presented OAU with an opportunity which appeared to satisfy all the research criteria proposed by the Moated Sites Research Group (Le Patourel 1978a and 1978b). The field containing the two moated enclosures was under pasture and free of buildings and had not been ploughed in living memory. The moat survived as shallow earthworks and a significant part of it had not apparently been recut. Research by John Blair identified substantial documentary evidence relating to the site and to a second moated site within the village, Manor Farm, now known as Chalgrove Manor. His account of the documentary evidence is given below.

Archaeological and historical background
(Fig. 1.2, Pls. 1.2–4)
by Jill Hind

Prehistoric

Prehistoric activity in Oxfordshire was primarily concentrated on the limestone hills and the gravel terraces and floodplains of the major rivers where many of the sites have been identified from aerial photographs and cropmarks. No prehistoric sites are known in the vicinity of Chalgrove, possibly because early prehistoric settlers are thought to have avoided the heavy soil (Emery 1974, 35), although it should be remembered that buried features on clay seldom show up as cropmarks on aerial photographs. Nevertheless there have been some stray finds; a Neolithic polished axe (PRN 5158) about 1.3 km north east of the village and an Iron Age gold coin (PRN 2037) from Chalgrove Field, about 0.8 km to the north-east. A few sherds of Iron Age pottery were also recovered during the Harding's Field excavations.

Roman

Little evidence has been found of significant Roman occupation in the vicinity of Chalgrove, which lies

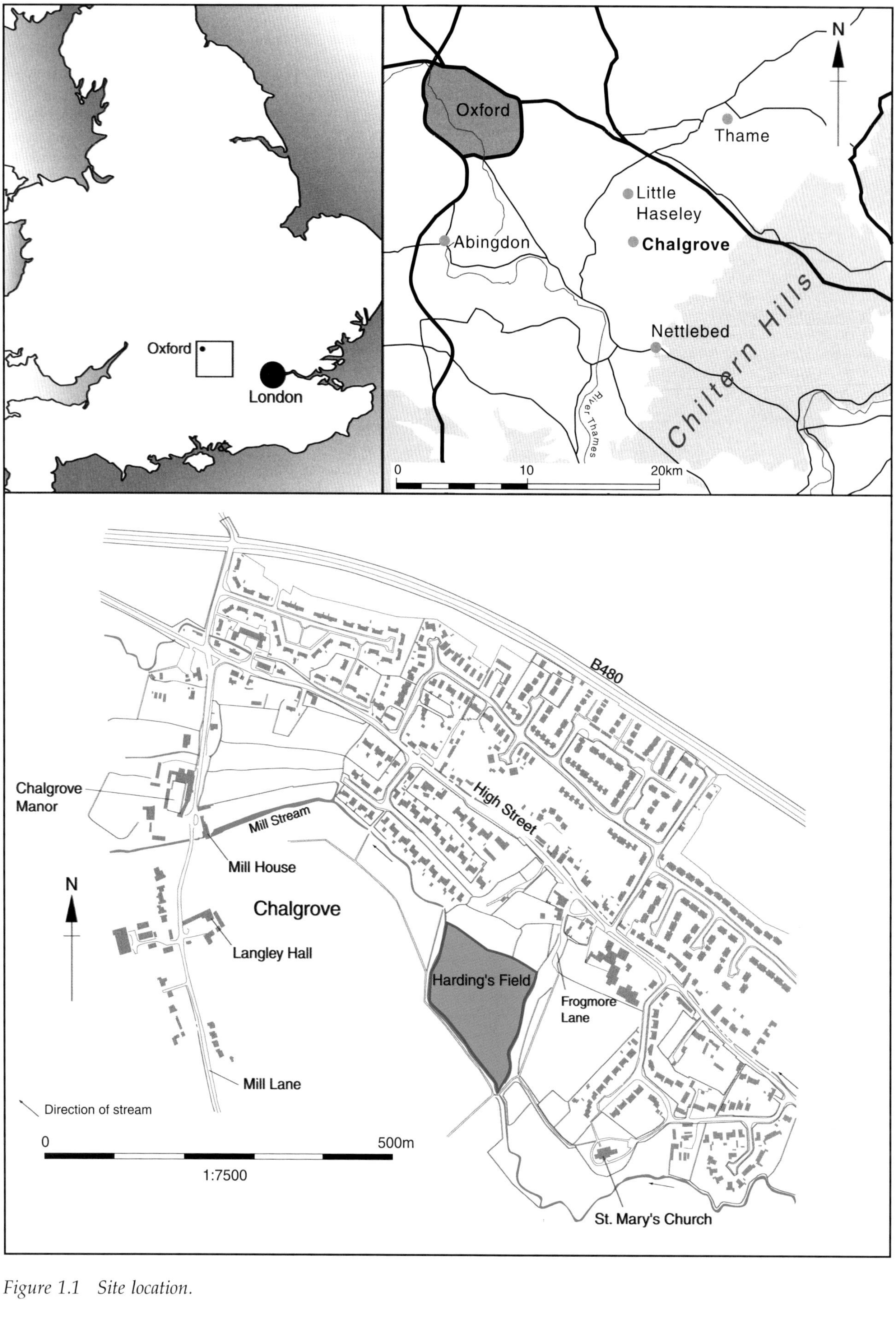

Figure 1.1 Site location.

Plate 1.1 Aerial view of Chalgrove in 1978 looking north-west, showing Harding's Field centre left.

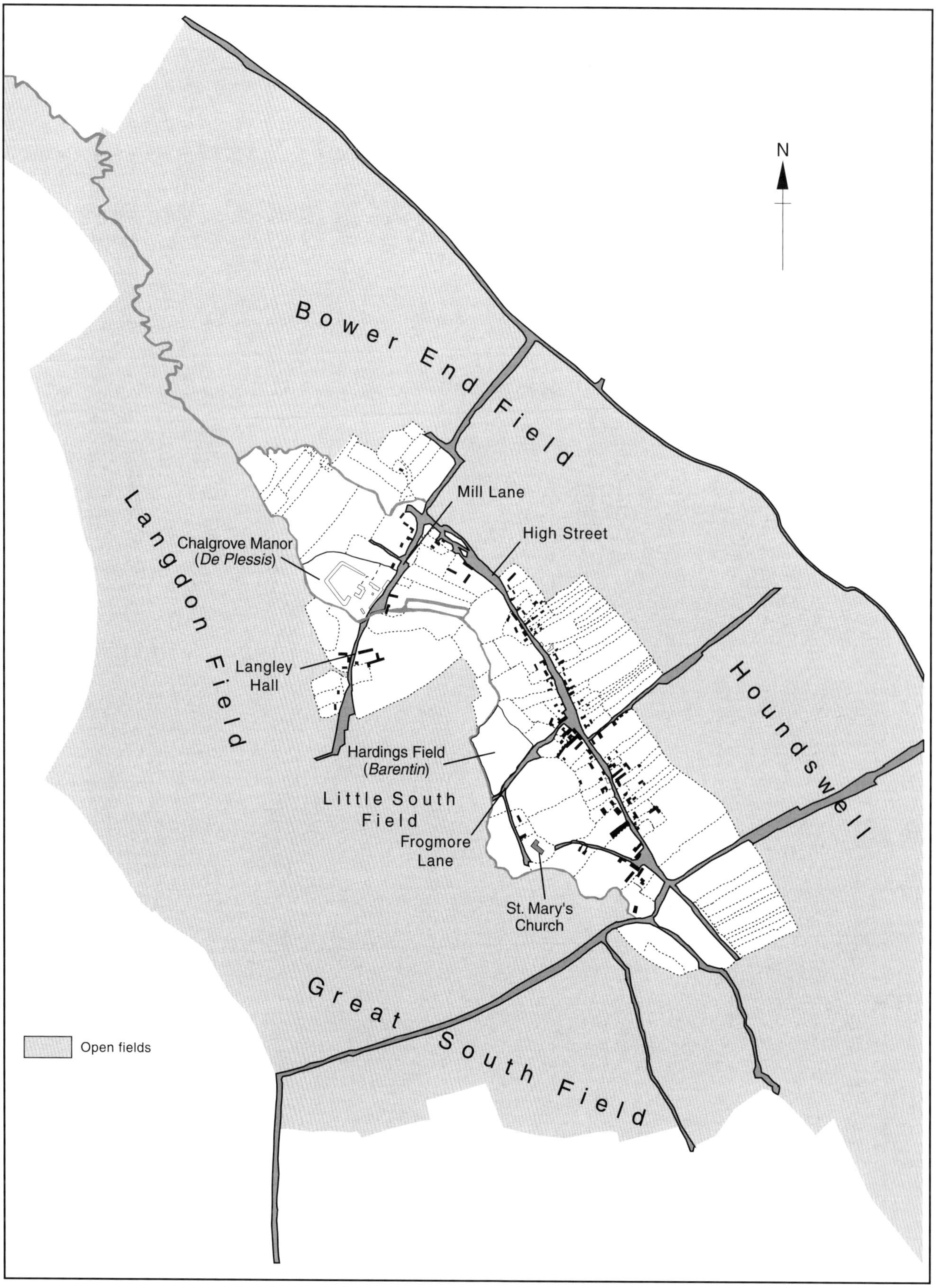

Figure 1.2 The village of Chalgrove from the 1822 estate map, showing the open field arrangement.

Plate 1.2 Aerial view of Harding's Field c 1970 showing cropmarks of moats, and relationship of manor site to the church (lower right).

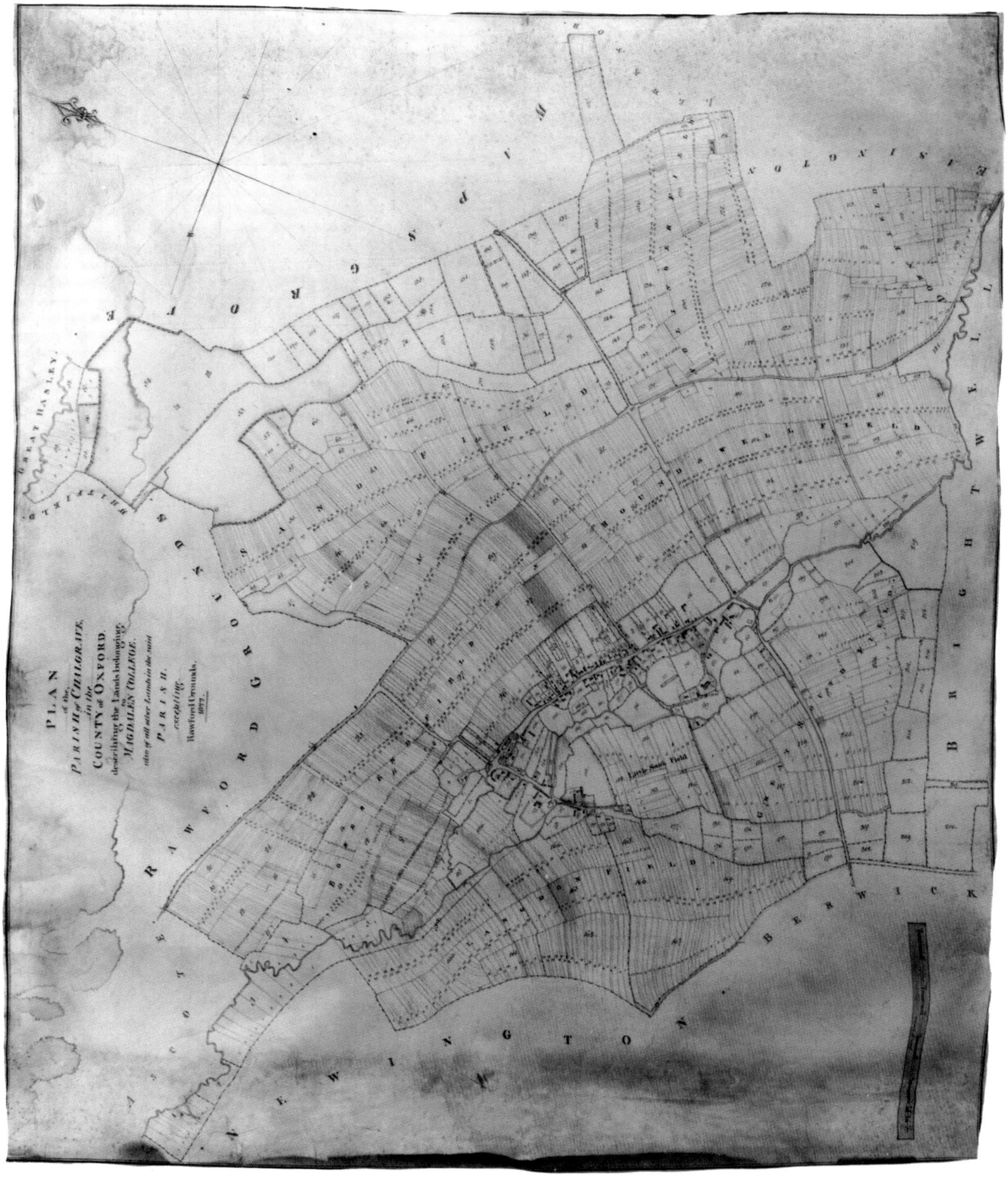

Plate 1.3 *Estate map of Chalgrove in 1822, showing Hardings Field, No. 96. Reproduced by kind permission of the President and Fellows of Magdalen College, Oxford.*

Plate 1.4 The 15th-century Barentin brasses in St Mary's Church, Chalgrove, depicting Reynold Barentin, and Drew Barentin III with his first and second wives Joan and Beatrice (by kind permission of St Mary's Church PCC).

only about 7 km east of the Roman small town of Dorchester on Thames. Small-scale settlement is suggested by two sets of cropmarks identified as Romano-British on the basis of associated pottery. The first (PRN 4490) lies west of Chalgrove Manor, in the moat of which has been found pottery, bone and charcoal (PRN 11133) of Roman date. Aerial survey in 1976 showed sub-rectangular and linear features (PRN 12491) between Mill Lane and the High Street, and fieldwalking of the area produced Romano-British pottery.

It is possible that a Roman road ran through the parish to the south of the village. The Lower Icknield Way, originally a prehistoric trackway, has been traced from Aston Clinton, Bucks, to Pyrton, 4 km east of Chalgrove, but its subsequent route is uncertain (Margary 1976, 183).

The excavations at Harding's Field produced a few pottery sherds and a spoon handle from this period. Plot recorded finds of a Roman glass jug and pottery (PRN 2300) from an area to the SE of the village (1677), although the exact location is not clear.

Anglo-Saxon

There is very little material evidence for Anglo-Saxon activity at Chalgrove. A single pottery rim sherd (PRN 11143) was found when a cottage about 170 m west of the church was demolished in 1977. During the Harding's Field excavations more sherds and two 9th-century strap ends were recovered. Such Saxon material as has been recovered has come from the area on the south side of the modern village and just west of the church. The church lies on the edge of the modern village, but the presence of earthworks around it suggests that it may have been surrounded by settlement at an earlier period (Pl.1.2). It seems likely that the nucleus of the late Saxon settlement could have been close to a church on, or near, the site of the present building.

Medieval

Domesday Book records that Miles Crispin held 10 hides in Chalgrove in 1086, and the manor had formerly been held by Thorkell (Morris 1978, 35–6). (This is a Scandinavian name, but there was a fashion among the English for using such names, and it does not necessarily signify that Thorkell was a Dane (Williams 1986, 11)). The Domesday entry lists 23 villagers and 10 smallholders, and mentions 5 mills. The number of mills in relation to the size of the manor is very striking, and suggests that the manor may have been of some significance in the late Saxon period. Aside from the known Mill House, it is not clear where these mills stood. An undated millstone was found at the Post Office (PRN 11132), which straddles the stream running parallel to the High Street and could conceivably have been the site of one of them.

The earliest feature of St Mary's church (PRN L/3996) is the late Norman south arcade in the nave, but the building was altered considerably during the medieval period (Sherwood & Pevsner 1974, 526). Its most significant interior features are a group of 14th-century wall paintings in the chancel, and the 15th-century brasses of the Barentin family. The excavation site at Harding's Field (PRN 4486) and a large rectangular pond or fish pond (PRN 11135), filled-in for a playing field in recent times, lie to the north-west, while immediately to the south-west of the church boundary ditches and another pond have been recorded. Plate 1.2 shows the cropmarks in Harding's Field, the tree-lined Frogmore Lane linking the site to the High Street to the north, and St Mary's church to the south-east.

Chalgrove was divided into two manors during the 13th century (see Blair, below), and this led to the creation of two separate manorial centres. One, belonging to the Barentin family, occupied the excavated site at Harding's Field. The other, held by the de Plessis and Bereford families, is probably to be identified with the site of the house now known as Chalgrove Manor (formerly Manor Farm), which is located on the west edge of the village, off Mill Lane (Fig. 1.1). Chalgrove Manor is a fine timber-framed house comprising a hall with two cross-wings, which in its present form dates from the 15th century. Behind the house are the remains of a roughly quadrilateral moat (PRN 1115; see Plate 1.3). It is clear from documentary evidence (Blair, below) that the Plessis/Bereford manor house stood within a moat, but the date of the moat at Chalgrove Manor has not been certainly established and it remains possible that it is substantially post-medieval, at least in its present form. The existence of the two manorial centres may explain the attenuated layout of the modern village; the focus of settlement has clearly shifted away from the church, and houses line the High Street and Mill Lane (Fig. 1.2; Plate 1.3).

Post-medieval

By 1487 most of the land within Chalgrove Parish was held by Magdalen College, Oxford. The post-medieval morphology of the village is clearly indicated by the early maps of the area. Davis' Map of 1793–4 shows most of the village arranged along two principal roads (Mill Lane and High Street) with a third road (Frogmore Lane) leading to the church to the south, a pattern which persisted until the second half of the 20th century. Davis shows several buildings along Mill Lane, south of the mill stream, and another group is shown along the south-western continuation of Frogmore Lane. The village is surrounded by a large area of open land, Chalgrove Field.

The settlement shift may have been further accentuated by the building of Langley Hall on Mill Lane in the early 16th century (Figs 1.1, 1.2). The house was occupied in the 17th century by members of the Quartermain family, and was altered in the 18th century and given a four-bay stuccoed facade.

The Magdalen College plan of Chalgrove Parish compiled in 1822 (Fig.1.2, Pl.1.3) shows the detail of the strip land allocation around the village, and the attenuated nature of the post-medieval settlement. Harding's Field (numbered 96 on the map) remains undivided, but interestingly there is no indication of earthwork relics of the moats. There are also indications of settlement shrinkage, away from the east end of the village, and its southern extremities. The buildings along Frogmore Lane, which are depicted on Davis' map, have disappeared, as has the line of the road south-west of the mill stream, and there are fewer buildings shown around Langley Hall. It is possible to see the walled garden to the south of the hall (PRN 11145) with the 17th-century brick lodge in the north-west corner. The moated enclosure to the rear of Chalgrove Manor can be seen clearly, as can the rectangular pond north-west of the church.

On the 1840 Tithe Map and 1845 Enclosure Maps the only changes are the effects of the enclosures themselves on the surrounding fields. The line of the track going south from Frogmore Lane, which persists to the present as a green lane, is visible again.

Only minor changes are visible on the 1st Edition Ordnance Survey Map 1872–80. Farm buildings cover the pond by the mill close to Chalgrove Manor and there are some new buildings along the High Street. These include the school and the Wesleyan Methodist Chapel built in 1869 (PRN 376). The site of the Civil War battle on Chalgrove Field (PRN 2048) to the north of the village is marked, together with the memorial erected to John Hampden in 1843, marking the 200th anniversary of the battle at which he was mortally wounded.

Modern development

Chalgrove remained largely unchanged throughout the post-medieval period, serving a small agricultural community. In the second half of the 20th century a large number of houses were built to serve Oxford commuters, but the area occupied by the village hardly changed. New development has filled in most of the open space behind plots fronting onto the High Street. A bypass now runs along the northern edge of the village, separating it from the disused World War II airfield. The Ordnance Survey maps of 1973–4 and 1999 show the progressive erosion of open space leaving only Harding's Field, the school grounds and the field south of the church undeveloped (compare open spaces in Plate 1.2 with infilling development in Plate 1.1).

THE MANORIAL HISTORY OF CHALGROVE

(FIG. 1.3, PL. 1.3 & 1.4)

by John Blair

The historical background

In 1086 Miles Crispin held ten hides in Chalgrove, a member of the great honour of Wallingford.[1] This estate, which probably corresponded to the modern parish excluding the hamlets of Rofford and Warpsgrove, was held by the Boterel family for three knights' fees from *c* 1100 until the death of Peter Boterel in 1165.[2] Tenure of the manor over the next 70 years was very unstable: assigned for the maintenance of a succession of royal servants, it reverted to the crown at frequent intervals.[3]

The division into two shares, which was so marked a feature of Chalgrove's later history, begins to appear at this date. In 1199 the king granted Chalgrove to Hugh Malaunay with the advowson and some additional properties, to be held, however, for only two fees.[4] By 1212 this Chalgrove property had reverted to the crown: 25 librates were held by Thomas Keret, while the rest remained in the king's hand and yielded £20 p.a.[5] Later that year the king's part was restored to Hugh de Malaunay.[6] Passing briefly on his death to his son Peter, it was granted in 1224 to Hugh de Plessis, Drew de Barentin and Nicholas de Boterel for their support in the king's service. Meanwhile Keret's part had returned to the crown, and was granted to Hugh le Despenser, again in 1224, as a moiety of the manor with the capital messuage.[7] It is clear from the Letters Close of 1224 that the divided manor still possessed only one manor house. Both parts were soon resumed by the crown, and in 1229 the whole manor was re-granted to Hugh de Plessis, John de Plessis and Drew de Barentin.[8] Hugh de Plessis's portion, described as a third of the manor with the capital messuage, was granted to William de Huntercombe in 1231 but shared out in 1233 between the other two parceners, John de Plessis and Drew de Barentin.[9]

John de Plessis and Drew de Barentin held two fees in Chalgrove in 1235–36, and henceforth Chalgrove descended as two separate fees in the Plessis and Barentin lines.[10] By 1279 the former had passed to Margaret de Plessis, while Drew had been succeeded by one William Barentin.[11] In that year the Hundred Rolls itemise the demesne, customary land and freeholds of both halves.[12] A remarkable feature of the demesne and customary holdings is the almost exact parity between the two manors. (The freeholds are a complex mixture of interrelated tenures and any original regularity has become obscured by 1279.) The Barentin demesne consisted of 311¾ acres arable, 30 acres meadow, 30 acres pasture and 2 mills; the Plessis demesne was 312½ acres arable, 30 acres meadow, 30 acres pasture and 1 mill. Unfree land comprised 5 virgates, 16 half-virgates (total 13 virgates) and 5 cottages on the Barentin fee, and 7 virgates, 11 half-virgates (total 12½ virgates) and 3 cottages on the Plessis fee. (This corresponds with the 1336 customal of the Plessis/Bereford fee except that two virgates had been divided, giving a total of 5 virgates, 15 half-virgates and 3 cottages.)[13] Customary rents and services were almost identical, and a fourth mill was held of the two lords jointly.

The only possible explanation for this is a systematic partition of Chalgrove into identical

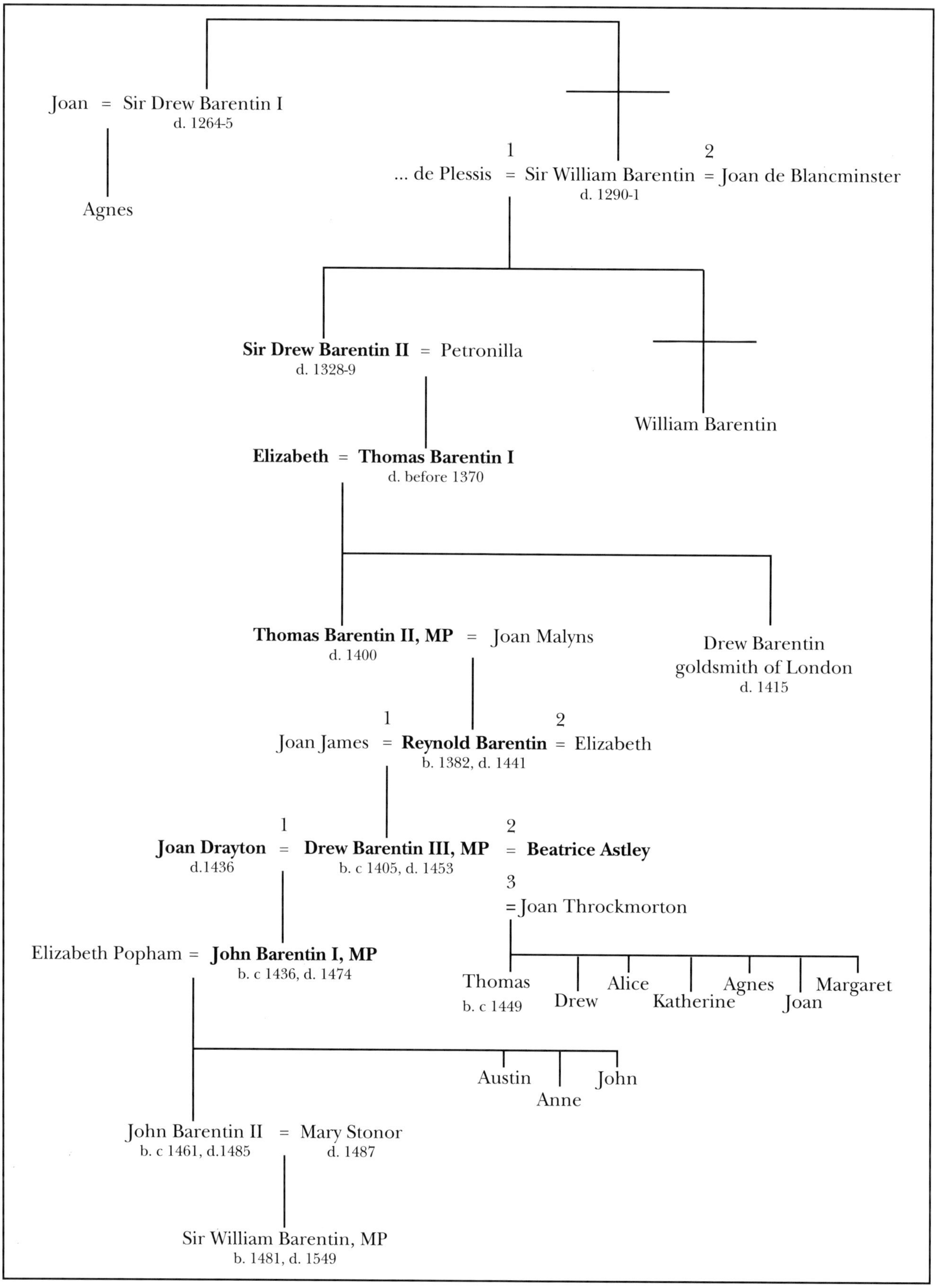

Figure 1.3 The family tree of the Barentin family. People whose names are in bold type are known to have been buried in the chancel of Chalgrove church.

half-shares, still sufficiently recent in 1279 for the similarities to remain conspicuous. It recalls the established 13th-century practice in cases of division between co-heirs, when it was normal to make a detailed survey for allocating the portions.[14] Under the 1229 grant the three parceners had evidently held Chalgrove in common, but in 1231 the sheriff was ordered to make an extent of the demesne, rents and villein holdings and put Huntercombe in seizin of one-third.[15] It may be conjectured that the manor was now parcelled out in three equal shares; two years later, the halving of Huntercombe's portion between Plessis and Barentin would produce the situation revealed in the Hundred Rolls.

This twofold division persisted through the 14th and 15th centuries. The Barentin moiety descended to the late 15th-century John Barentin II (see below). Beset by financial troubles, John sold the manor in 1485 to Thomas Danvers, Bishop Waynflete's agent, for endowing his newly-founded college. A survey of that year (see below) shows that 'Barentin's Manor' had retained its identity over the previous two centuries. But if the Barentin descent was straightforward, that of the Plessis moiety was complex. In the words of a manorial clerk writing in 1503 the Chalgrove demesnes were

> divided into 2 equall parts, whereof one part belongeth to the heyres of Barantine and so now to Mag[dalen] Coll[ege]. The other part is divided between 3 lords, whereof one is called Senclerise, the which Master Hampden of Woodstock hath. The 2nd was called sometyme the lands of Master Hoore, the which now Mr Darell hath. The 3rd part was called Argentines lands, the which now Mag[dalen] Coll[ege] hath. [16]

The Plessis manor remained unitary until the late 14th century. Margaret de Plessis was still holding it in 1284–5,[17] but by 1293 she had married the royal judge William de Bereford.[18] Between 1316 and 1335, their son Sir Edmund de Bereford succeeded to the moiety.[19] A magnificent survey of Edmund's Chalgrove property was compiled in 1336, giving a full rental and customal as well as a parcel-by-parcel description of the demesne in both measured and customary acres.[20] The list begins with the *'situs curie infra fossatum... in quo edificatur aula, boveria et stabula'*, an unusually clear contemporary description of a moated manor house.

Sir Edmund de Bereford died in 1354, to be followed only two years later by his son and heir.[21] The moiety was now fragmented between Edmund's three sisters, Margaret, Joan and Agnes, and his grandson Baldwin de Bereford.[22] Baldwin's fraction[23] seems to have become amalgamated with the share of Joan, one of Edmund's three heiresses and wife of Gilbert de Ellesfield. Baldwin's 1371–72 rental is stated to be that of 'Ellesfield's Manor'.[24] The property descended to William de Ellesfield, who died in 1398 leaving it to relatives named Hore.[25] Clearly these were the 'lands of Master Hoore' of the 1503 memorandum. Margaret de Bereford married James Audley; her fraction passed to her daughter Joan, wife of Philip St. Clare,[26] and was later known as 'St. Clare's'.[27] The third sister, Margaret, married Sir John Mautravers and later Sir John de Argentein, by whose name her share came to be known.[28] Passing through various hands,[29] 'Argentines lands' were bought for Magdalen by Thomas Danvers in 1487.[30] Thus Magdalen College held from its foundation the Barentin moiety of the entire manor, and the Argentein third of the Plessis/Bereford moiety.

Notwithstanding these separate lines of descent, some of the manors were held and administered jointly. A rental compiled in 1377[31] includes the inheritances of all three sisters, and in 1399 the Ellesfield manor was demised for a life to Thomas Barentin's widow.[32] In 1428 Reynold Barentin owed the feudal obligations for the former Bereford fee as well as his own, while a court roll of the same year deals with tenements held both *'de feodo Barentyn'* and *'de feodo Bereford'*.[33] During the 1430s courts seem to have been held jointly for the Barentin, St. Clare and Hore tenants.[34] Purchases by John Barentin of Argentein's manor in 1457 and St. Clare's in 1474 are recorded.[35] It is hard to establish the real effect of these involved transactions, which evidently placed most of Chalgrove under the immediate control of the Barentins for much of the 15th century. It is quite clear, however, that for administrative and accounting purposes the subdivisions were respected, the manors being consistently regarded as distinct entities. There is every reason to think that the symmetrical partition carried out before 1279 was still a tenurial reality two centuries later.

The identity of the site in Harding's Field

From this descent it will be clear that between *c* 1240 and *c* 1370 Chalgrove contained two capital messuages, serving respectively the Barentin and the Plessis/Bereford manors, and that the break-up of the Bereford half may have resulted in the appearance of subsidiary manor houses in the late 14th or early 15th century. Excavation has shown that the moated site in Harding's Field was occupied from the late 12th/early 13th century and extensively rebuilt in the 13th and early 14th centuries. Therefore it must be identified either with the chief messuage of the Barentins or with Sir Edmund de Bereford's moated house of 1336. To establish which, it is necessary to work backwards from late sources in which the site can be firmly identified.

A map and terrier drawn up in 1822 (Fig.1.2, Pl. 1.3) show the field as an old enclosure called Court Hays, copyhold of John King and late of Thomas King.[36] In 1675 Ralph Quartermain surrendered Court Heyes, a customary close of pasture, to the use of Thomas King.[37] A terrier of *c* 1600 includes 'the syte of the manour of Magdalen College in the tenure of Elisabeth Quartermayn, wherapon is a barne, a pigion house and an orcharde, Called Court Hayse'.[38] In 1520 John Quartermain owed 10s. rent for a former demesne close 'where the manour stood' and a further 10s. for 'a barn and a culver house', while in *c* 1500 John Quartermain the elder was paying 10s. *'pro claus[ura] voc[ata] Court Close'*.[39] It can hardly be doubted, especially in view of the highly suggestive name 'Court Hays', that all these entries refer to the same piece of land.

Luckily its history can be traced a little further back, to just before the Barentin and Argentein manors were permanently reunited under Magdalen College. The transfer of the Barentin manor to Danvers in 1485 occasioned the compilation of a new and very detailed survey.[40] Here the *'manerium vocatum Barantynes maner'* is firmly identified with the lands and tenements *'pro parte Thome Danvers'*. The names of the demesne closes (including Grassheys, Southparrok, Shrevemannysheys, Newclose, Luxe and Stratfords) correspond exactly with earlier rentals of the Barentin manor, such as that for 1405–6[41] which include the farmed-out demesne. The Barentin demesne, then, still remained distinct. Only a few months later than this survey, a list of rents owing to Danvers from the lands and tenements late of John Barentin for the financial year 1485–6 gives the same list of demesne closes, with one crucial addition: *'Et de v s*[half-yearly, ie. 10s pa] *de firma Johannis Quatermayn' pro scita manerii ibidem cum pastura, fructibus, stagnis et aliis proficuis ibidem, hoc anno sic dimissa'*.[42] Clearly this was identical with 'Court Close' which Quartermain held for the same rent only a few years later, and hence with the modern Harding's Field.

If the site was in Danvers's hands by 1485–6 it clearly cannot represent the capital messuage of the Argentein portion, which he did not acquire until 1488. At this date the other two shares of the original Plessis/Bereford moiety (St Clare and Hore/Pudsey) were still self-contained and independent manors. The only reasonable conclusion is that this was the Barentin manor house, demolished on the completion of the transfer from Barentin to Danvers in October 1485; hence the statement of 1485–6 that its vacant site had been 'thus demised this year'.

The Bereford 'court within a moat' of 1336 must therefore have been elsewhere, and it is not unlikely that it preceded the existing moated house now known as Chalgrove Manor (formerly Manor Farm). Chalgrove village consists essentially of two road axes, respectively High Street and Mill Lane, both of which are flanked by house plots. Hardings Field lies near the church and main axis, while Manor Farm adjoins the lesser axis. Is this a case of village morphology determined by tenurial factors? It is tempting to suggest that High Street, the church and the Harding's Field site represent the village and manorial curia as existing before 1233, whereas Manor Farm and the tofts on Mill Lane were created with the reorganisation of Chalgrove as two equal and self-contained manors. R A Dodgshon has drawn attention to the importance of symmetrical 'township splitting' in the development of British villages and field systems, and has noted that it seems common in Oxfordshire (1980, chapters 5–6). Unless there is another moated site within the village of which no trace remains, it also seems reasonable to suggest that the moat at Manor Farm is that described in the survey. The survey also gives the area of *'summa placia curie'* as 1 acre, 1 rood, 32 perches. If this is interpreted as the area *'infra fossatum'* it would correspond quite well to that of the moat as shown on the 1846 tithe award map. To date, limited excavation at this site has been within the 15th-century standing building and has confirmed the date of its construction while suggesting that this building stood on virgin ground. However, the trenches were located outside the line of the moat. It would seem possible that the south-eastern arm of that moat was partially back-filled by the time of the construction of the house or with the addition of its wings. But it is interesting to note the line of a boundary shown on the 1822 estate map that corresponds to the position of that moat arm. The most likely location of the remains of the Bereford Manor buildings would be in the area to the west of the present building, which may well represent a direct replacement for the medieval hall.

The Barentins and Chalgrove (Fig. 1.3 & Pl.1.4)

If it is disappointing to find that the Harding's Field site is not the moated house described in 1336, its firm association with the Barentins is ample compensation. For several generations this was the principal home of a leading county family, and the development of the site can be closely related to its owners' circumstances and social pretensions.[43]

The mid 13th-century co-tenants had both grown prosperous in the royal service. Like their predecessors over some decades, Plessis and Barentin were originally assigned Chalgrove for their maintenance on a short-term basis; it was only because their tenures became, in the event, permanent that the manorial division remained stable from 1233. John de Plessis first appears in the early 1220s and rose rapidly in the court circle after *c* 1230. Marrying the Warwick heiress, he was styled Earl of Warwick from 1247 until his death in 1263.[44] Drew de Barentin's career was not dissimilar.[45] From 1222 he received a yearly allowance of 10 marks,[46] and in 1232–3 he and John de Plessis were joint tenants of land in Jersey.[47] At this period the king began to employ Drew on administrative and diplomatic assignments. In 1235 he appears as Warden of the Channel Isles, where he is known to have built on a lavish scale.[48] Drew relinquished the post in 1252,[49] but in 1258 he was holding the Channel Isles against the Lord Edward.[50] He was Seneschal of Gascony from 1247,[51] and throughout his career he made frequent journeys abroad on the king's business.[52] He was with Henry III in France throughout 1254.[53] He steadily enlarged his holdings in the Channel Isles,[54] which may have been worth considerably more than his single Oxfordshire manor by his death in 1264–5.[55]

Did these two men take any active interest in Chalgrove? The excavated evidence for occupation from the early 13th century (Phase 1) supports the suggestion already made on topographical grounds that the Barentin house was the earlier of the two and a primary element in the village plan. Since the capital messuage had been assigned to Huntercombe's fraction in 1231, it must have passed to Drew de Barentin when this share was split between John de Plessis and himself two years later. Plessis would have needed a house also, so it can be inferred on prima facie grounds that a new curial complex is likely to have been created soon after 1233. On the Barentin site, the earliest fully excavated set of buildings (Phase 2) must date from Drew's time or not long after.

Thanks to Henry III's habit of bestowing goods in kind, some written evidence remains for this work. Between the 1230s and the 1260s the Close Rolls record a long series of royal gifts to John de Plessis and Drew de Barentin, mostly in the form of deer, wine, firewood and timber. In 1232 they were joint recipients of four oaks from Shotover Forest to make posts and wallplates,[56] presumably for some building needed as a result of the current tenurial rearrangements. In a series of later gifts, all the timber trees came from Bernwood Forest (including Brill and Panshill) on the Oxfordshire-Buckinghamshire border. (This excludes gifts to Plessis from forests in other parts of England, which are clearly nothing to do with Chalgrove.) From Bernwood Plessis received 30 trunks (*fusta*) in 1240 'in the places nearest to the land which he has in Chalgrove', followed by four timber oaks in 1248, five in 1255 and eight in 1259.[57] The more modest gifts to Barentin comprised seven timber-oaks in 1255 and a further ten in 1256.[58] Since Drew had no other recorded manors which were anywhere near Bernwood, it must be presumed that all this material was destined for Chalgrove.

The royal gifts need not, of course, have provided all the necessary timber, but they presumably met a specific need and reflect to some extent the scale of operations. The evidence suggests a major building campaign on the Plessis manor in *c* 1240 followed by lesser works over the next 20 years, and a campaign on the Barentin manor during 1255–6. It seems very likely that the 1240 works mark the creation of Sir Edmund de Bereford's '*situs curie infra fossatum*' of a century later. On the Barentin site, a date of 1255–6 agrees well with the excavated Phase 2 (see below), where the stone-rubble walling may help to explain why less timber was received from the king. Thus the aisled hall and associated buildings, with their encircling moat, can be attributed with some confidence to the later years of Sir Drew Barentin I, a house worthy of his status as a senior crown servant.

Drew I's heir (and perhaps nephew) Sir William Barentin first appears as a newly-made knight in 1260.[59] He was less notable politically and seems to have been often in debt,[60] though his second marriage, with a Blancminster heiress, added extensive Essex properties to the family estate.[61] His son Drew II had succeeded by 1291, when William's widow Joan pursued a claim in the Essex manors against Drew and his wife Petronilla.[62]

Sir Drew Barentin II retained both the family estates in the Channel Isles and his stepmother's inheritance.[63] In addition to this, he had substantial Kentish property and further manors in Suffolk, Buckinghamshire and Oxfordshire.[64] Like the first Drew he did occasional business for the king in Jersey and Guernsey, and acted there as Justice Itinerant in 1309–10.[65] He was recorded as non-resident on his Essex manors in 1296 and during 1322–5 he served as sheriff of Oxfordshire and Berkshire.[66] Oxfordshire was clearly his main focus of interests, and until his death in 1328–9 he performed the normal range of duties appropriate to a leading county gentleman.[67]

Sir Drew II's principal house was undoubtedly Chalgrove manor, where a neighbouring lord is said to have written to him in 1295 to announce the birth of a son.[68] Despite the fabulous nature of much of the circumstantial detail in such 'proofs of age', it seems reasonable to conclude from this statement that Sir Drew normally resided at Chalgrove. Probably attributable to him are the excavated Phases 3/1 and 3/2 (see below) of *c* 1300–30, which involved extending and modernising the buildings to meet rising standards of domestic comfort. An integrated service, solar and undercroft range was added to the hall, and a base-cruck probably replaced the central aisle truss. Architecturally the result must have been much more impressive than the hall of the 1250s, comparable to the surviving base-cruck hall at Sutton Courteney 'Abbey' in scale and internal effect.[69]

Significantly, Chalgrove now became the Barentins' established place of burial. During *c* 1310–30 the chancel of St Mary's church was lavishly rebuilt and decorated, perhaps by Sir Drew though more probably by Thame Abbey, which held the advowson from 1317.[70] A list compiled in *c* 1480 tells us that Sir Drew II and his successors for the next five generations were buried in this chancel, all but the last (John I, d. 1474) under 'marble stones'.[71] In the cases of Thomas II, Reynold and Drew III, these slabs survive (Pl. 1.4) and prove to be monumental brasses,[72] and it seems highly likely that Sir Drew II and his son were also commemorated by this newly fashionable type of memorial. Brasses were almost invariably set in Purbeck marble and in normal late medieval usage the term 'marble slab' carries a strong implication of brass inlays. Like the rebuilding of the manor house on more imposing lines, this creation of a 'family mausoleum' suggests a heightened sense of identity with the main residence and church, now a miniature *caput honoris*. In thus imitating 12th- and 13th-century noble dynasties, Sir Drew Barentin and his immediate successors were wholly typical of their age and class.

On Sir Drew's death his son Thomas Barentin I inherited Chalgrove and its nearby dependencies; the property in Essex and the Channel Isles passed to a nephew named William Barentin and never returned to the senior line.[73] It is clear that both Thomas and his son, a second Thomas, resided consistently at Chalgrove, where they executed several deeds between the 1340s and the 1390s.[74] Thomas II married Joan Malyns, a daughter of a neighbouring knightly family at Chinnor.[75] In 1370 he and Joan received episcopal licence for an oratory at Chalgrove,[76] and this could refer to either the possible stone chapel, Building A11 (see below), or an earlier timber building that was not located. Thomas was sheriff of Oxfordshire and Berkshire in 1378 and MP for Oxfordshire in 1387, thereafter serving frequently in both capacities.[77]

On his death in 1400 Thomas II held the single manor of Chalgrove, worth just under £27 pa net; the heir was his son Reynold, aged 20¾ in December 1402.[78] Reynold Barentin may have begun his occupation with the last major refurbishment of the manorial buildings (Phase 4). This included a new kitchen linked to the service passage, the partial flooring-in of the hall and the division of the farmyard into two courts (see below). However, in 1415 Reynold suddenly found himself master of a much finer house on the death of his wealthy uncle, the London goldsmith Drew Barentin. Drew is described as 'probably the only goldsmith of his day who could match men like the mercer, Richard Whittington, in wealth and influence'.[79] In 1391, with his brother Thomas Barentin II, Drew had bought the Oxfordshire manor of Little Haseley.[80] The sumptuous manor house at Haseley Court, much of which still remains, must have been built soon afterwards,[81] and Leland's statement that 'Barentyne the gold-smythe buylded the Manor Place at Litle Haseley' is easily accepted.[82] Drew died childless, and the heir to his numerous manors, including Little Haseley, was his nephew Reynold.[83]

This was a crucial event in the history of Chalgrove manor house, for within a few decades Little Haseley had displaced it as the main Barentin residence. In 1441 Reynold was succeeded by his son Drew Barentin III,[84] MP for Oxfordshire in 1445–6 and a prominent figure in local administration.[85] By 1451 he was dating deeds from Little Haseley,[86] and in 1453, the year of his death, he is described as 'of Little Haseley and Chalgrove'.[87] His will requests burial at Chalgrove beside his first wife Joan,[88] but it is significant that the ornaments of his chapel are left to a chapel in Chalgrove parish church, subject to his third wife's life-interest. There seems a clear implication here that services in the manorial chapel were expected to cease with the widow's death.

Drew was succeeded in his numerous Oxfordshire and Berkshire manors by his son John Barentin I,[89] sheriff in 1464–5 and MP in 1467–8.[90] Until his father's death he may have maintained a household at Chalgrove: he is called 'late of Chalgrove' in 1458,[91] and he enlarged his estate there by purchase (see above), but in later life his home was Haseley Court. On his death in 1474 he was buried with his ancestors at Chalgrove, but the customary bequest for forgotten tithes was made to Great Haseley church, 'where as I am paryshener'.[92] The will requests burial in Chalgrove chancel and the Barentin burial list notes John's grave there, though *'sine lapide'*.[93] His wife Elizabeth, who was jointly enfeoffed with him in the main family holdings, was to have custody until the majority of their heir, another John.[94] John's inquisition lists several manors but not Chalgrove or Little Haseley, presumably because they were in joint feoffment.[95]

Both before and after coming of age, John Barentin II and his wife Mary Stonor seem to have lived at Little Haseley.[96] Here their son William was born in December 1481,[97] and when part of the Chalgrove property was demised in 1478 the old Barentin demesne was stated to be in the hands of various farmers.[98] By now the manor house had probably been abandoned for residential use, and in this context it is interesting to note a petition by the Abbot of Abingdon which seems to date from the early 1480s.[99] The Abbot claims to have bought from John Barentin for £18 'the tymber of certeyn houses than sette in the towne of Chalgrave... and the tyles wych than covered the same houses', subsequently withheld by John on the pretext that the land had been in feoffees' hands at the time of the bargain. The sum is considerable, and it seems at least possible that this refers to the decaying manorial buildings, reprieved for a few more years by this calculated trickery.

This incident is one sign of growing financial problems. The Barentins sold off Argentein's and St Clare's in 1482,[100] and a series of protracted mortgage transactions culminated in 1485 in the final sale of the old family demesne to Thomas Danvers.[101] The infant heir, later Sir William Barentin MP, succeeded in that year to the remaining estates.[102] He lived his whole life at Haseley Court, where John Leland admired his 'right fair mansion place, and marvelus fair walkes topiarii operis, and orchardes and pooles'.[103] The Barentins' connection with Chalgrove ended on the death of John II in December 1485, within a few months of the destruction of his ancestral home.

MOATED SITES IN OXFORDSHIRE (FIG. 1.4)

[Editor's note. There was considerable interest at the time of the excavations in moated sites as a monument type. A survey of moats in Oxfordshire was drafted by Philip Page from data in the county Sites and Monuments Record around the time that the site at Harding's Field was first recognised (Page 1976) and this was subsequently incorporated into James Bond's general survey of the Oxford region in the Middle Ages (Bond 1986). It seems to have been the intention to include a version of the moat survey in the Harding's Field report, presumably in the expectation that this would appear in advance of the

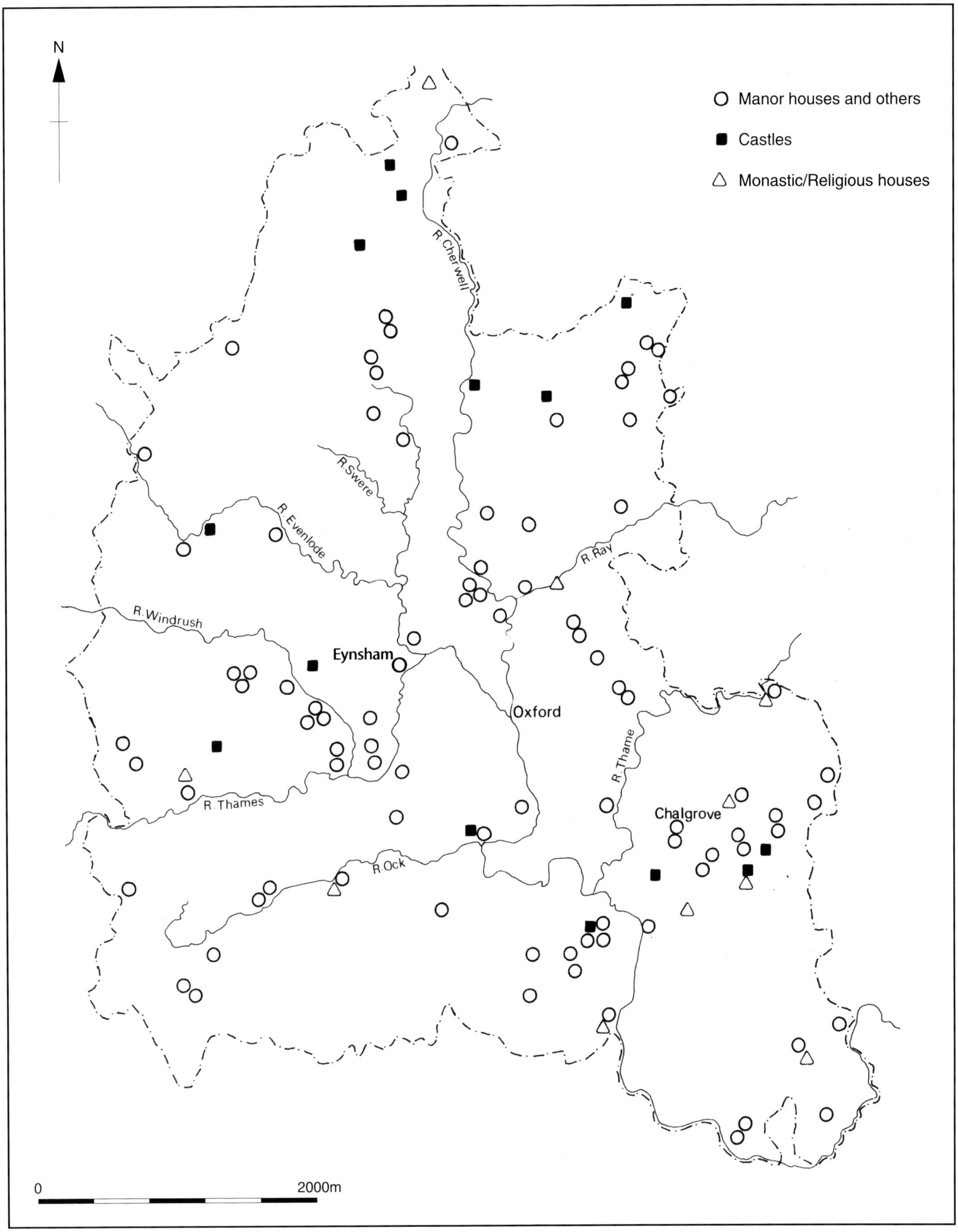

Figure 1.4 The distribution of moated sites in Oxfordshire.

countywide general survey. In the event, this was not the case. Despite the existence of the fuller published account, a summary of this survey has been included here since *The Archaeology of the Oxford Region* has long been out of print, and is now very hard to come by.]

A total of 96 moated sites had been identified in the county in 1986, suggesting that Oxfordshire lies somewhere in the middle of the range for the country as a whole. Of these, 75 could be identified with reasonable confidence and a further 21 were doubtful. In addition there were ten moated castles and six moated monastic sites or granges. The distribution of moated sites reflects the underlying geology (Fig. 1.4) and there is a particular concentration on the Gault and Kimmeridge Clay at the foot of the scarp slope of the Chilterns, which appears to take advantage of the spring line. This has been recorded in other counties, notably in Essex (Cook 1960). There are other concentrations on the Oxford Clay in the Upper Thames Valley and in north-east Oxfordshire. However, geology was not an absolute determinant of location and, if the desire for a moat was great enough, it could be overcome.

Approximately 48% of Oxfordshire moats are located within the boundaries of existing villages, and a further 23% are associated with deserted medieval villages; only some 28% could be described as isolated or distant from nucleated settlements. This suggests that the majority of moated sites in Oxfordshire may have belonged to sites of manorial rank, rather than being primarily associated with areas where assarting and colonisation of waste and forest was taking place. This may be linked to the fact that one of the largest areas of known assarts, Wychwood Forest (Emery 1974, 85), was situated on limestone.

The majority of moated sites in Oxfordshire appear to be single quadrilateral enclosures containing an area of 0.3 to 0.8 hectares. This shape also predominates in Worcestershire (Bond 1978a, 73) and Essex (Hedges 1978, 65). However, survey work by C C Taylor in Lincolnshire has shown that field investigation often reveals a more complex pattern of earthworks than may be discernible from a map (lecture for Moated Sites Research Group). This is probably also the case in Oxfordshire. A small proportion of moated sites in the county are known to have more than one island and, apart from Harding's Field, Sugarswell is an example of this. Concentric moats are rare and where they do occur they need not be contemporary with each other. The triple moats at Park Lodge, Beckley Park, appear from documentary evidence to have been excavated in at least two phases (Allen Brown *et al*. 1963, 899). Approximately 18% of sites appear to be incomplete but it is impossible without excavation or geophysical survey to determine whether any infilling has taken place (Page 1976).

Groups of two or more moats sometimes occur in close proximity. This may be the result of one site going out of use and being replaced by another, or it may indicate that the moated areas served different functions. Apart from the two moated sites at Chalgrove, there is a group of three physically separate moats at Curbridge, Oxfordshire: Black Moat, Caswell House and Lower Caswell Farm (Bond 1986, 151).

Excavation on moated sites in Oxfordshire has been limited and the most notable instances are at Lilley Farm, Mapledurham (Fowler 1971, 25), Moat Cottage, Kidlington (Chambers 1978b, 114–6; Chambers and Meadows 1981, 127–8), Manor Farm, Kingham (Bond 1981, 23–24) and the sub-manorial moated site within the Abbey precinct at Eynsham (Keevill, 1995) In addition limited work has been undertaken at Chalgrove Manor (formerly Manor Farm, Chalgrove; Bond 1981, 22–23). The excavation of the moated manor at Harding's Field, Chalgrove remains the most complete of any moated manorial site to date in Oxfordshire.

THE FIELDWORK (FIG. 1.5)

The earthworks survey

The earthworks survey by Chambers and Bond in 1976 revealed two moated islands (Fig. 1.5). The smaller one, to the west, was rectangular, some 30 m by 45 m and enclosed an area of 0.15 hectares (0.37 acres). A slight internal bank was evident around all four sides but otherwise there were no obvious internal features. There was the stub of a possible bridge abutment at its south-eastern corner. The larger, eastern island was roughly triangular in shape and measured 125 m by 75 m by 95 m and enclosed an area of 0.56 hectares (1.38 acres). A number of slight earthworks were identified (not illustrated) including a platform that measured *c* 25 m by 30 m in the north-eastern corner.

The excavation methodology (Fig. 1.5)

1976

In November 1976 Oxfordshire County Council decided to seal the earthworks with dumped topsoil to level up the ground for the creation of a playing field. In response, R A Chambers, with the help of Mr Adrian Nixey, a local farmer, evaluated the site with three trenches (OAU 1976, 1). Trenches IA and II confirmed the presence of building remains in the larger island but Trench III did not locate any archaeological features in the interior of the smaller island. The field to the north of the site was developed for housing during 1976 but no archaeological features were revealed during the watching brief. A resistivity survey was carried out in the field to the south of the moated islands in 1979 and this also recorded no archaeological activity.

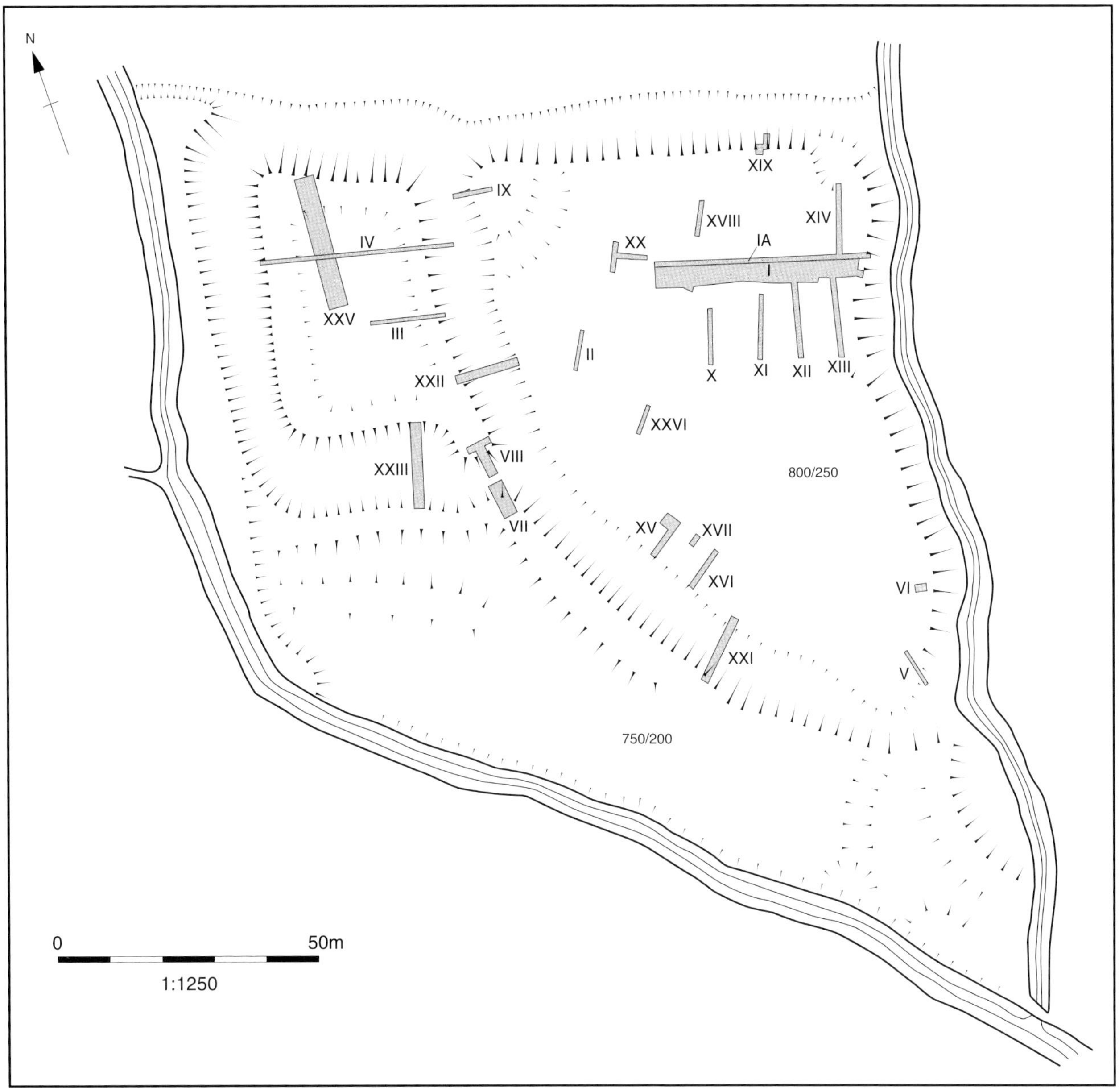

Figure 1.5 Earthwork plan, showing the locations of the trial trenches.

1977

The poor availability of topsoil meant that the County Council was forced to reconsider its plan during the spring of 1977 and it was decided to reduce the height of the earthworks in order to level and drain the site, with the potential effect of destroying much of the archaeological evidence. OAU and the ODMS believed that further excavation was desirable and, with limited resources, small-scale excavation was carried out in 1977. The initial objectives were to reveal the extent of the site and establish a chronological sequence for the remains. Initial trial trenches revealed that up to 0.60 m of stratigraphy survived in the northern part of the larger moated island and topsoil stripping by the County Council revealed the presence of both domestic and agricultural buildings.

Trench IA was expanded into a small area excavation (Trench I) and a further six trenches (IV to IX) were excavated mechanically. Trench I, located on the larger island, revealed the remains of a substantial building with rubble walls of mortared and coursed limestone, about 1.0 m thick set on clay-bonded foundations with a similar thickness. Evidence was found for internal rearrangements and for external additions to the building. Only earth floors were uncovered but medieval floor tiles were found in surface rubble to the north of the trench, suggesting that at least some of the floors had been tiled. Lime-washed wall plaster, some still *in situ*, and fragments of painted window glass were also found. This building, dated to the first half of the 14th century, sealed the clay floors of an earlier structure. Trenches III and IV (machine excavated) transected the smaller island but found no archaeological evidence for activity.

During the summer of 1977 the County Council recut the line of the northern moat with a narrow ditch and the entire field was stripped of its topsoil in September. This was done in extremely wet conditions and inevitably damage to archaeological features was caused. However, a watching brief by Chambers produced a partial plan of the outbuildings uncovered in the southern half of the island. Chambers identified an aisled barn erected on sill walls and the sill wall of another long, narrow outbuilding which had some pitched limestone paving on its north side. The site became waterlogged, prompting the postponement of further levelling until the following spring; over the winter the site remained open (Chambers 1978a, 110–112).

1978

The seven-month season of work that took place in 1978 was expected to be the last opportunity for excavation before the destruction of the site. The main objectives, therefore, were to obtain a plan and dating evidence for the buildings of the latest and most complete phase of occupation, to excavate the associated farm buildings and to determine if the small rectangular enclosure contained any evidence of occupation. It was decided to clarify the various phases of alterations to the manor house and its relationship to the moats and to obtain further dating evidence for the earliest use of the sites and the excavation of the moats. Excavation continued from May until December under the direction of Philip Page, using labour from the Manpower Services Commission job-creation scheme.

The excavation revealed a layer of general demolition debris, still mixed to some extent with the topsoil. This was removed as one layer and the finds recorded in a 5 m grid. After the removal of this layer some parts of the site were still covered by demolition debris and this was removed as a sequence of individual archaeological deposits.

Most of the trenching was mechanical but the moat was still full of water in places and the northern and eastern arms were used for drainage which made mechanical excavation unsuitable. However, a hand-dug section through the western edge of the eastern moat arm did revealed undisturbed deposits in the base of the moat, which were sampled for ecofactual analysis (see Chapter 5). Trenches XXI to XXIII provided complete sections of the moat profiles on the western side of the site, but no significant finds other than molluscs. Trenches XX and XXVI were also hand-excavated to the level of the natural, as part of the attempt to find evidence for the early phase of the site's occupation. These trenches were particularly helpful in defining the edges of the moat upcast which, in plan, could not easily be distinguished from the natural alluvium. The site was prone to flooding but, except in the bottom of the moats, there was no evidence for the survival of waterlogged deposits.

1979 onwards

The field was again left exposed over the winter and, in the spring of 1979, the Department of the Environment recommended the scheduling and preservation of the site. Negotiations began with the County Council for the burial of the site with the Department meeting a proportion of the costs and funding further limited excavation. Philip Page directed another season of work between July and October again making use of Manpower Services Commission labour. The objectives were specifically to complete the excavation of the farm buildings and to prepare the site for burial. At the Department's request the stone footings of the main building were levelled to the top of the surrounding stratigraphy, thereby restoring a level archaeological horizon.

In March 1981 the larger of the two islands was covered with a layer of gravel and, the following August, this was covered with topsoil and grass-seeded to provide space for two football pitches.

THE REPORT AND ARCHIVE

Editor's note on the history of the Harding's Field report

A programme of post-excavation analysis was undertaken in the years immediately following the fieldwork, under the direction of the excavator, Philip Page. This included the analysis of the stratigraphic evidence, the pottery and all other finds, the animal bone, and the environmental samples. The site and research archives were assembled and indexed, and the specialist contributions in Chapters 3–5 of the present volume, and the accompanying illustrations, were largely completed at that time. Philip Page left OAU in the early 1980s to pursue a career outside archaeology. A report was subsequently prepared for publication in *Oxoniensia* in a form that offered a highly abbreviated and synthesised account of the results, illustrated by phase plans, and with the detail of the specialist reports consigned to a fiche annexe. This was submitted to the project funders (by then English Heritage) for refereeing in 1991. All those who commented on the report at that time felt that the presentation of the evidence was unsatisfactory in a number of respects, and publication was not pursued.

Lack of resources meant that no further work was undertaken on the project until 1998, when John Steane and the late Jean Cook of OAU's Academic Advisory Panel arranged with English Heritage for limited funding to allow the necessary revisions to be undertaken. This work was started in 1999 by Kate Atherton, and completed by Alan Hardy who undertook a thorough review of the stratigraphic narrative and discussion. James Bond kindly provided extensive and most helpful comments. It was clear that the phase plans that had been produced to illustrate the stratigraphic narrative failed to convey the quality of the original record. As a result, a programme of work was commissioned to make the detailed building plans in the archive available for publication. This was undertaken, under the supervision of Robert Read, by students on the BA degree course in Archaeological Illustration at Swindon College of Art who have produced Figures 2.6–2.20 of the present volume. The length of the report meant that it was no longer appropriate for publication in *Oxoniensia*, and it was simultaneously revised for publication as a monograph in OA's Thames Valley Landscapes series, with the reintegration of the specialist reports into the main body of the text.

The revised report was submitted to English Heritage for review in 2003, and OA are grateful to English Heritage and the anonymous referee for their support for its publication. Over the winter of 2003, many of the specialist contributors to Chapters 3–5 reviewed their reports after a 25-year hiatus, and have kindly allowed us to publish with only the minimum of essential corrections. Unfortunately it was not possible to arrange for the coin, pottery, glass, tile, stone slate or plaster reports to be reviewed, and these reports have been published, with minor editorial amendments, in the form in which they were deposited in the research archive.

Inevitably, much has changed since the excavations at Harding's Field took place, and both the fieldwork and the report remain essentially a product of the late 1970s and early 1980s. The fortuitous nature of the site's discovery, the constant uncertainties about the excavation programme, the reliance on inexperienced temporary excavation staff and the goodwill of volunteers and landowners, and the familiar struggle to make a little funding stretch as far as humanly possible, are typical of their time. So too is the failure to see the post-excavation programme through to publication, as OAU's resources were diverted to new sites, many of them also under serious threat, and the funding and the excitement of discovery faded away. So, too, some of the approaches, methodologies and research aims of the project will now appear dated, and limited in scope, compared with what could be done on a similar site today.

Nevertheless, Chalgrove Harding's Field remains even today one of the country's most fully excavated examples of a medieval moated manor, and the range and quality of the information recovered remains unusual, and still holds considerable research value. It is for these reasons that the publication of this report has been pursued, despite all the shortcomings due to its age and history.

Location of the archive

All of the original artefacts and site records, together with material generated during post-excavation analysis, have been deposited with the Oxfordshire County Museums Service who have issued the site with the Accession Number: 1986.188. A master copy of the paper archive on microfilm has been lodged with the National Archaeological Record, Swindon.

Notes

1 *VCH* 1939, 418
2 Salter 1930, 305
3 Ibid; *Book of Fees*, 117–18
4 Salter 1930, 305; *Rot. Chart.* i, 11b
5 *Book of Fees*, 117
6 *Rot. Lit. Claus.* i, 127a
7 *Excerpt. Rot. Fin.* i, 77, 123; *Rot. Lit. Claus.* ii, 8
8 *Cal. Pat. R. 1225–32*, 313; *Cal. Chart. R.* i, 108
9 *Cal. Close R. 1231–34*, 13, 195, 198; *Cal. Close R. 1227–31*, 530, 540, 550
10 *Book of Fees*, 446, 555
11 *Rot. Hund.* ii, 31
12 Ibid., 768–70
13 Magdalen College Estate Papers 141/40–41
14 *cf.* Dodgshon 1975, 21–22
15 *Cal. Close R.* 1227–31, 530
16 Transcript in Magdalen College 1666 Rental Book, p. 158
17 *Feudal Aids*, iv, 154
18 *Cal. Pat. R. 1292–1302*, 108
19 *Feudal Aids* iv, 171, 177; *Cal. Chart. R.* iv, 339
20 Magdalen College Estate Papers 141/40–41
21 *Cal. Inq. P.M.* x, 211–13, 272–74
22 *Black Prince's Reg.* iv, 121
23 see *Cal. Chart. R.* v, 264
24 Magdalen College Estate Paper 141/39
25 *Cal. Close R. 1377–81*, 28; *Cal. Fine R.* xi, 233; Bodl. MS Oxon. Ch. 334
26 Dugdale revised Thomas 1730, 210a, 232a; *Cal. Close R. 1422–29*, 212; *Cal. Inq. P.M.* iv, 163, 192–93
27 Magdalen College Estate Paper 141/49 is a rental of the St Clare manor in 1462–3
28 Dugdale revised Thomas 1730, 210a, 232a; Carter 1936, 69–70
29 for example, Magdalen College Deeds Chalgrove 12A, 2B, 193
30 Magdalen College Deeds Chalgrove 22A, 168, 195
31 Magdalen College Estate Paper 141/38
32 PRO Anc. Deeds, C146/634
33 *Feudal Aids*, iv, 193; Magdalen College Estate Paper 123/6
34 Magdalen College Estate Papers 122/6, 86/17, 86/12
35 BL Add. Chs. 20319–23: Macray, 'Calendar of Magdalen College Deeds', transcript in Magdalen College Library, Oxon. III, 303, 305, V, 133
36 Magdalen College Archives
37 Magdalen College Court Book 49, p. 596
38 Magdalen College Adds. 61
39 Transcript of rental in Magdalen College 1666 Rental Book, p. 152; Magdalen College Estate Paper 86/13
40 Magdalen College Estate Paper 142/26
41 Magdalen College Estate Paper 142/17
42 Magdalen College Estate Paper 142/12
43 for an earlier account of the family see Greening Lamborn 1942, 190–92
44 *Complete Peerage*, x, 535–8
45 Moor 1929, 44
46 *Rot. Lit. Claus.* i, 500b, 599a; *Cal. Liberate R. 1226–40*, 28, 179
47 *Cal. Close R. 1231–34*, 41, 106–7
48 *Cal. Close R. 1234–37*, 73 and numerous later references; McCormack 2002, 113
49 *Cal. Pat. R. 1247–58*, 135

50 ibid., 640
51 *Cal. Close R. 1247–51*, 8 and many later references
52 for example *Cal. Close R. 1237–42*, 165; *Cal. Pat. R. 1247–58*, 413, 584
53 *Cal. Pat. R. 1247–58 passim*
54 for example *Cal. Close R. 1247–51*, 5; *Cal. Pat. R. 1247–58*, 184
55 *Cal. Pat. R. 1258–66*, 415, 506
56 *Cal. Close R. 1231–34*, 82: *ad postes et pannas facienda*
57 *Cal. Close R. 1237–42*, 202; *Cal. Close R. 1247–51*, 55; *Cal. Close R. 1254–56*, 114; *Cal. Close R. 1256–59*, 420, 424
58 *Cal. Close R. 1254–56*, 35, 266
59 *Cal. Close R. 1259–61*, 124; for Drew's nephew's see *Cal. Pat. R. 1247–58*, 459; for an outline biography see Moor 1929
60 *Cal. Close R. 1264–68*, 180; *Cal. Close R. 1272–79*, 124, 345
61 Salter 1930, 314; Essex Archaeological Society 1913–28, ii, 49; *Cal. Inq. P.M.* ii, 226, 318; for the first wife, a de Plessis heiress, see Magdalen College Deed Chalgrove 41A
62 *Cal. Close R. 1288–96*, 189
63 Outline biography in Moor 1929
64 For the Essex and Kent manors see *Cal. Close R. 1288–96*, 42, 189; *Cal. Inq. P.M.* ii, 501; *Cal. Pat. R. 1313–17*, 521–22
65 *Cal. Close R. 1296–1302*, 63; *Cal. Pat. R. 1307–13*, 112
66 Moor 1929
67 *Cal. Pat. R. 1327–20*, 335; *Cal. Close R. 1327–30*, 462
68 *Cal. Inq. P.M.* iv, 78
69 Parker 1853, 32, 272–74
70 *Cal. Pat. R. 1313–17*, 672; for the chancel and its paintings see Parker and Burges 1860, 431–8
71 Magdalen College Deed Chalgrove 41A, printed *Oxford Archaeological Society Report 1909*, 32
72 de Watteville 1897, 113–15
73 *Cal. Close R. 1327–30*, 462, 562
74 For deeds dated at Chalgrove see Bodl. MS Top. Oxon. d. 88 f.30; BL Add. Chs. 20384, 20311. Other references are in Magdalen College Deeds Chalgrove 47A, 48A, 209, 84, 147, 60, 72, 210. For the lost brass of Thomas I and his wife Elizabeth, and the extant brass inscription of Thomas II, see notes 71–2 above
75 Greening Lamborn 1942, 191
76 Gibbons 1888, 179
77 Greening Lamborn 1942, 191
78 Inquisition, PRO C137/34 (4): *Calendarium Inq. P.M. Sive Esceat.* iii, 273; for Reynold's two wives *cf.* Greening Lamborn 1942, 191
79 Reddaway and Walker 1975, 279–82
80 *Cal. Close R. 1389–92*, 334
81 Sherwood and Pevsner 1974, 685–87
82 Toulmin Smith 1910, 233
83 *Calendarium Inq. P.M. Sive Esceat.* iv, 23
84 Monumental brasses: see de Watteville 1897, 113–15
85 Wedgewood and Holt 1936, 40; corrections in Greening Lamborn 1942, 191
86 BL Add. Ch. 20316
87 *Cal. Pap. Reg.* x, 605
88 Gibbons 1888, 179; this lists his numerous children. For Drew's brass see de Watteville 1897, 113–15
89 Inquisition, *Calendarium Inq. P.M. Sive Esceat.* iv, 256, in which the heir's age is given as eighteen
90 Wedgewood and Holt 1936, 40–41
91 Wedgewood and Holt 1936, 41
92 Weaver and Beardwood 1958, 32–33
93 Magdalen College Deed Chalgrove 41A, printed *Ox. Arch. Soc. Report 1909*, 32
94 Will, in Weaver and Beardwood 1958, 32–33, which also lists their other children
95 *Cal. Inq. P.M. Sive Esceat.* iv, 368
96 for the younger John and his marriage, see Kingsford 1919, 128–29; Greening Lamborn 1942, 192
97 *Cal. Inq. P.M. Henry VII,* ii, 12
98 BL Add. Ch. 20324
99 PRO Anc. Petitions, C1/36/110
100 Bodl. MS Top. Oxon. d. 88; Macray, 'Calendar of Magdalen College Deeds': typescript in Magdalen College Library, Oxon. III, 36
101 BL Add. Chs. 20326–27; Bodl. MS Top. Oxon. d. 88 ff.29–33; Magdalen College Deed Chalgrove 228; Macray, *op. cit.* note 100, Oxon III, 317–25
102 *Cal. Inq. P.M. Henry VII*, i, 82; for Sir William see Greening Lamborn 1942, 192
103 Toulmin Smith 1907, 114

Chapter 2: Archaeological Description

INTRODUCTION

The site prior to excavation

Immediately prior to the excavation, the site was under rough pasture and undergrowth. The north and east arms of the moat were still extant and serving as drainage ditches/boundaries between Harding's Field and Frogmore Lane to the east and the new housing estate to the north, although some construction debris from the estate had encroached upon the northern edge of the large island. The curving western arm, and the small rectangular moat to the west, were visible only as very shallow depressions.

The phasing and chronology of the archaeology (Figs 2.1–2.5)

The phasing and its chronology have largely been determined on the basis of stratigraphy, supported by ceramic and other artefactual evidence. However, for various reasons the following phasing summary should be considered with caution. A number of buildings and a large part of the main island were not fully excavated, nor were all stratigraphic relationships investigated. Recourse in the construction of the phasing framework has been made to architectural or stylistic parallels, and to the historical context suggested by the documentary evidence. The following summary should be seen as an interpretative framework.

Phase 1 – Late 12th to early 13th century
Phase 2 – Mid to late 13th century
Phase 3/1 – Early 14th century
Phase 3/2 – Early to mid 14th century
Phase 4 – Late 14th to early 15th century
Phase 5 – Mid to late 15th century

The recording methodology

The focus of most of the excavation over the three seasons was the domestic range, eventually comprising several attached rooms or structures. The whole domestic range was labelled 'A', with each room, structure or attached building given a supplementary number. Discrete buildings, structures or functional areas, whether directly associated with the domestic range or not, were given identifying letters.

THE EXCAVATIONS

Phase 1 (Late 12th to early 13th century) (Fig. 2.1)

Summary

The earliest activity was represented by surfaces, features and wall footings partially revealed in the north-east corner of the site. Evidence of one definite and two possible structures was revealed, all apparently constructed upon the contemporary ground surface. No evidence of a buried topsoil was identified, although any such layer would most likely have degraded to silty clay indistinguishable from the alluvial clay natural. Such dating evidence as could be reliably associated with the Phase 1 structures suggested that they were standing in the late 12th or early 13th centuries.

The function of the structures revealed can only be tentatively suggested on the basis of the limited excavation evidence. The remains possibly represent a kitchen and/or hall, along with associated buildings and structures – all of which can be seen as part of a precursor to the moated manor.

Building P *(Figs 2.1, 2.6, 2.15)*

Building P was defined by the remains of cob walls and internal surfaces sealed below the Phase 2 levelling material that was derived from the moat construction (see below). Cob is a generic term for a mixture of clay, gravel and/or stone, and organic matter.

The structure was aligned NW-SE and measured *c* 11.3 m by 7.5 m externally, the dimensions extrapolated from the surviving parts of the walls seen in plan and section. The best preserved wall (402/1127/1128) survived as a linear block of mixed clay and small stone, up to 0.40 m high × 0.60 m wide. It represented the west wall of the structure, and was traceable across the width of Trench 1. A further small isolated fragment of the north wall was revealed in plan (967). The walls appeared to be built directly on the underlying natural surface, although immediately west of wall 1128 in section a deposit of limestone rubble (1201) was revealed which could represent a stone plinth (Fig. 2.15). Remains of an interior floor of the building were identified (1106, a mix of chalk and flint in a clay matrix), in part overlain by an occupation layer (1137) of silty clay with charcoal and ash inclusions (Fig. 2.15 section 51). A large hearth (372) was identified towards the western end of the building, and a section revealed up to eleven superimposed burnt clay and ash deposits, representing a significant amount of use. No other internal features were identified, nor was evidence found of the location or character of an entrance to the structure, although this is not surprising, given both the partial nature of the excavation and the degree of truncation by later activity. A total of 69 sherds of pottery were recovered from the floor deposits and the fabric of the walls, the date of which suggests construction and use of the building between the late 12th and early 13th centuries.

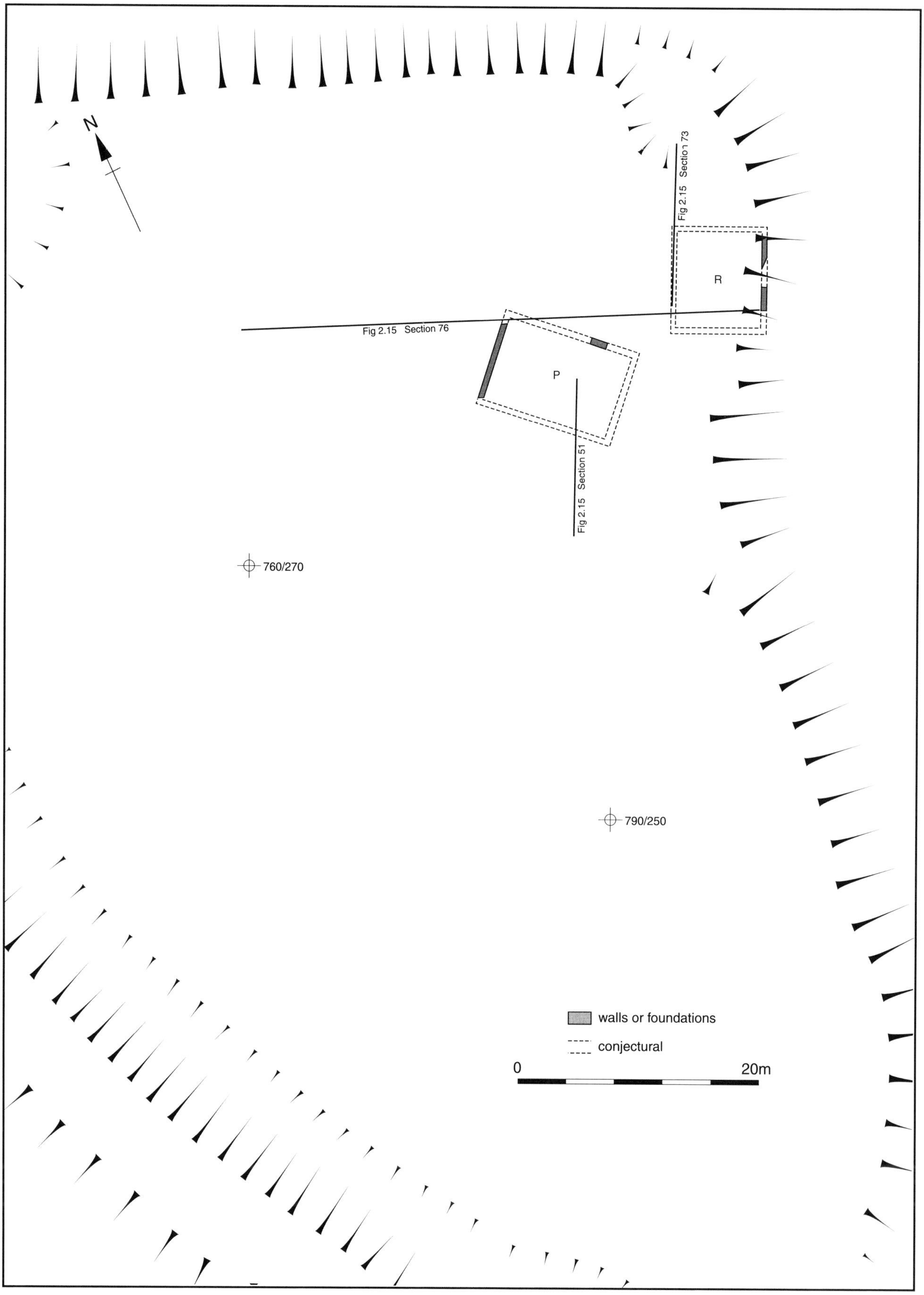

Figure 2.1 Plan of Phase 1.

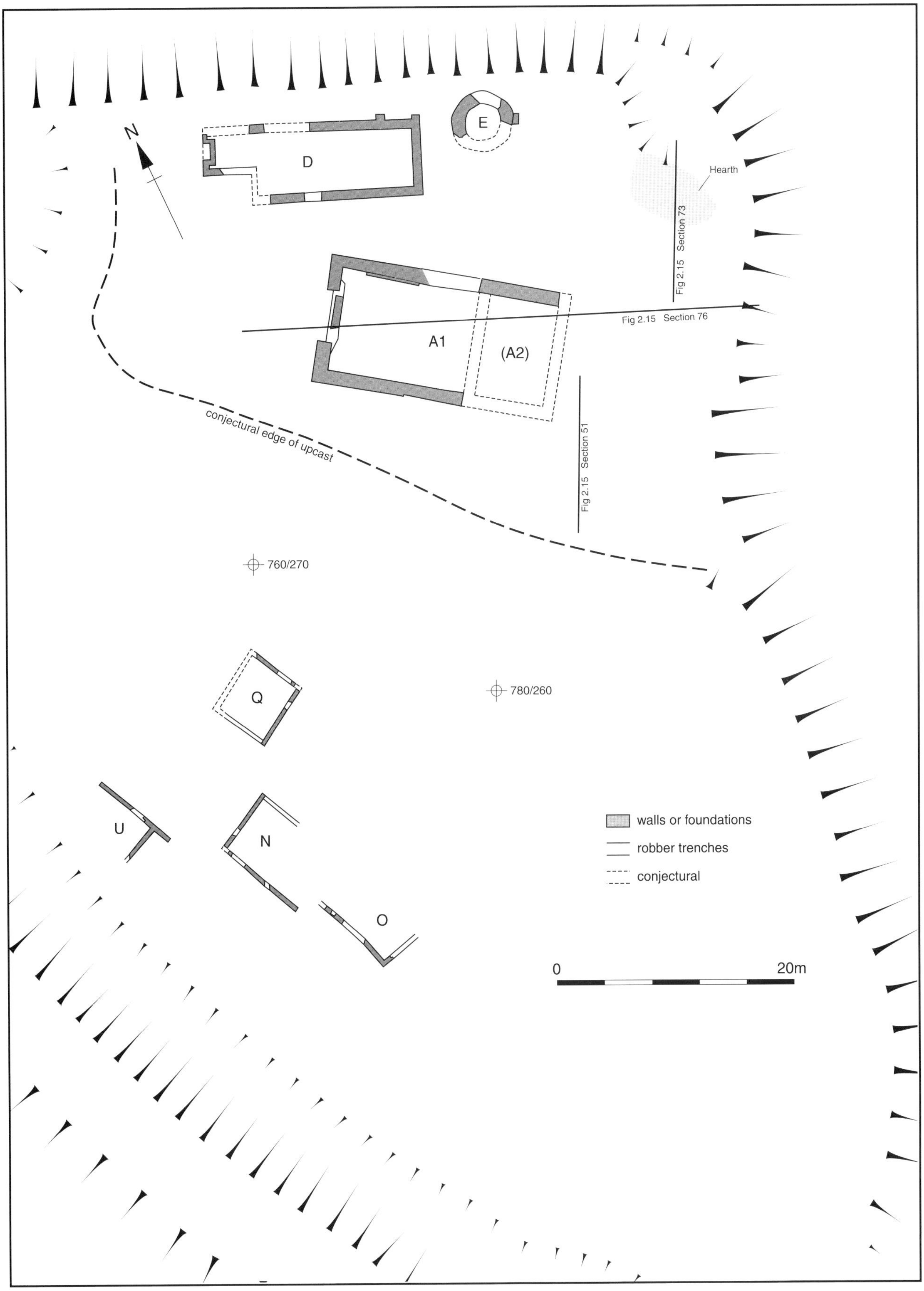

Figure 2.2 Plan of Phase 2.

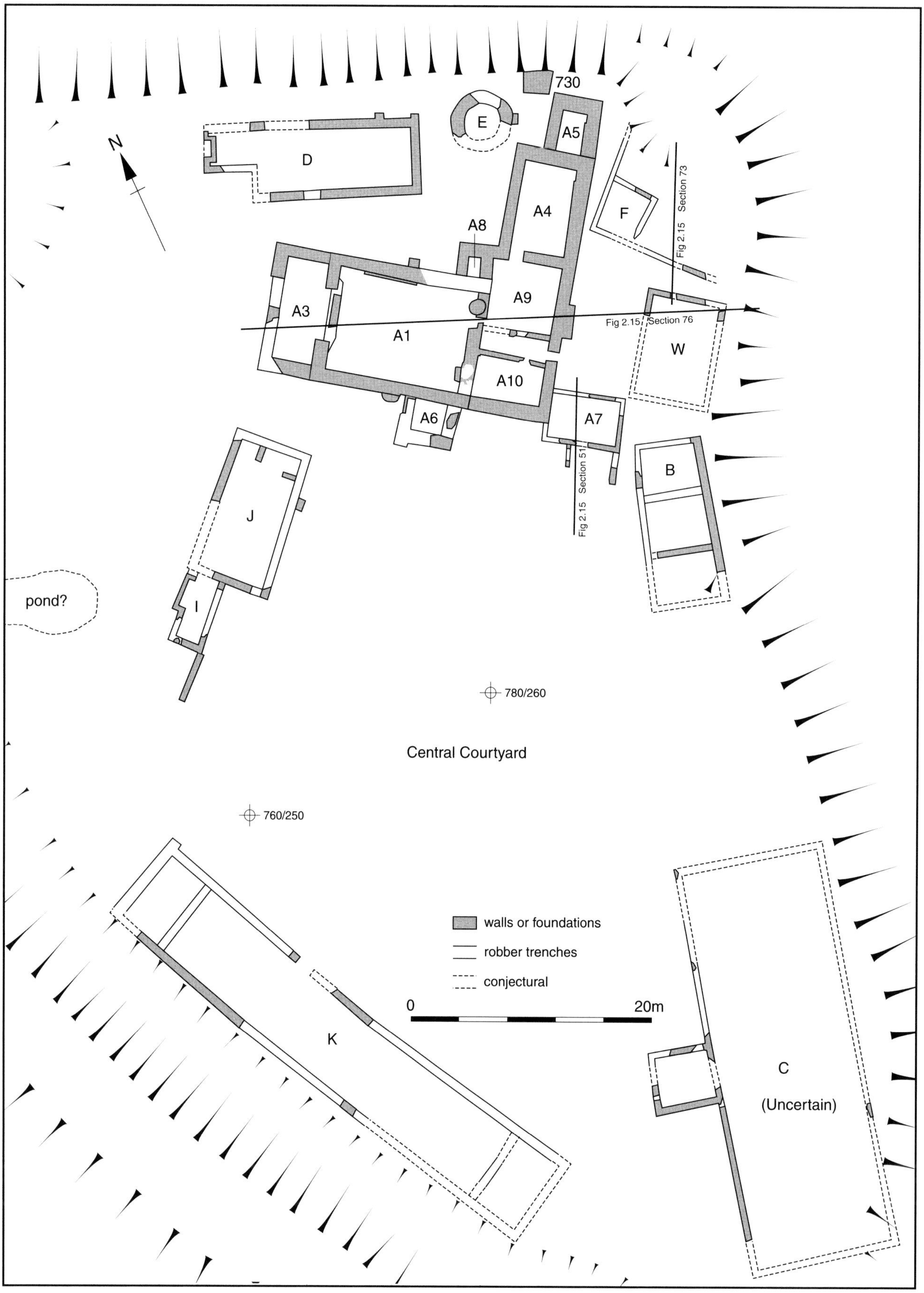

Figure 2.3 Plan of Phase 3.

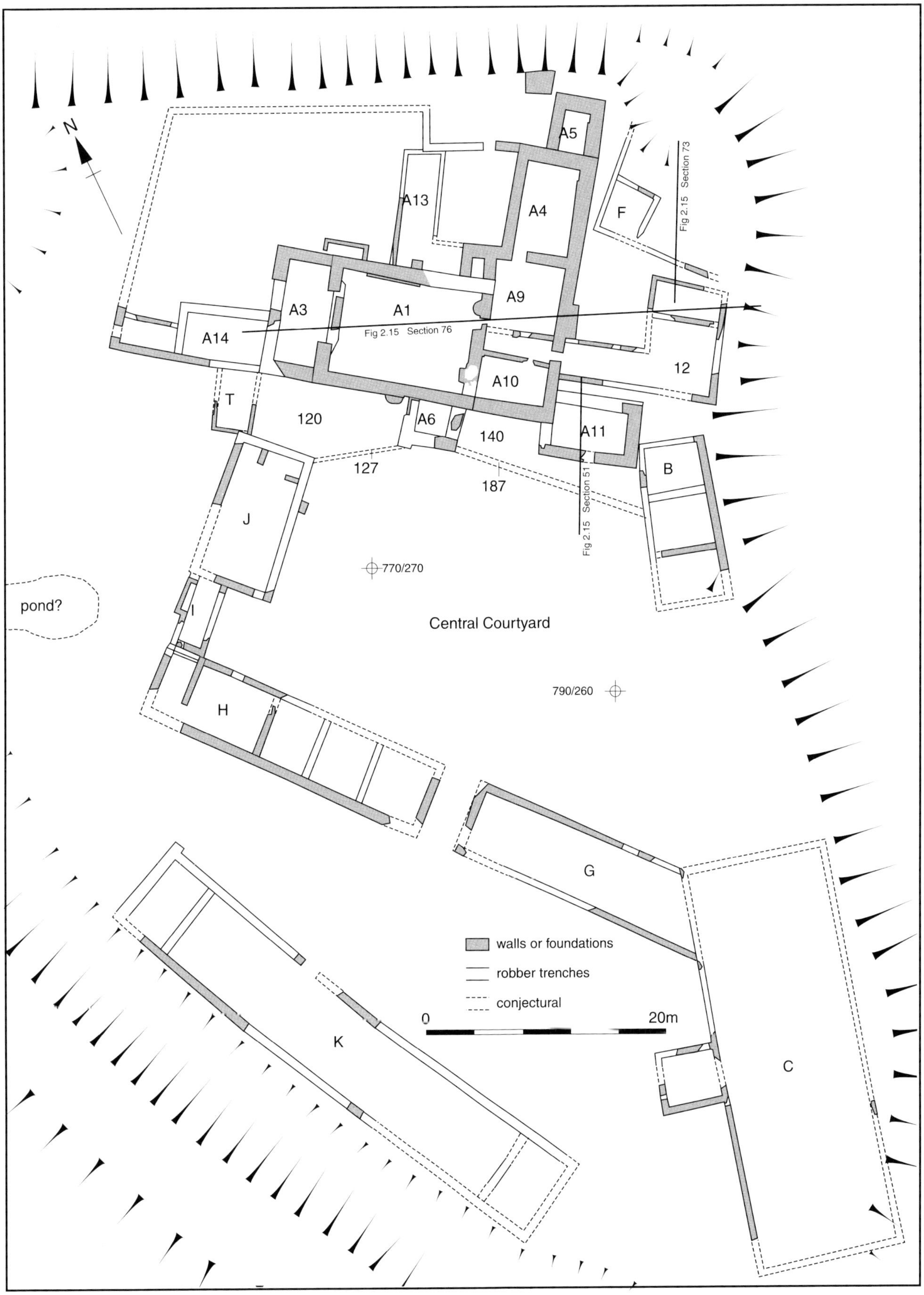

Figure 2.4 Plan of Phase 4.

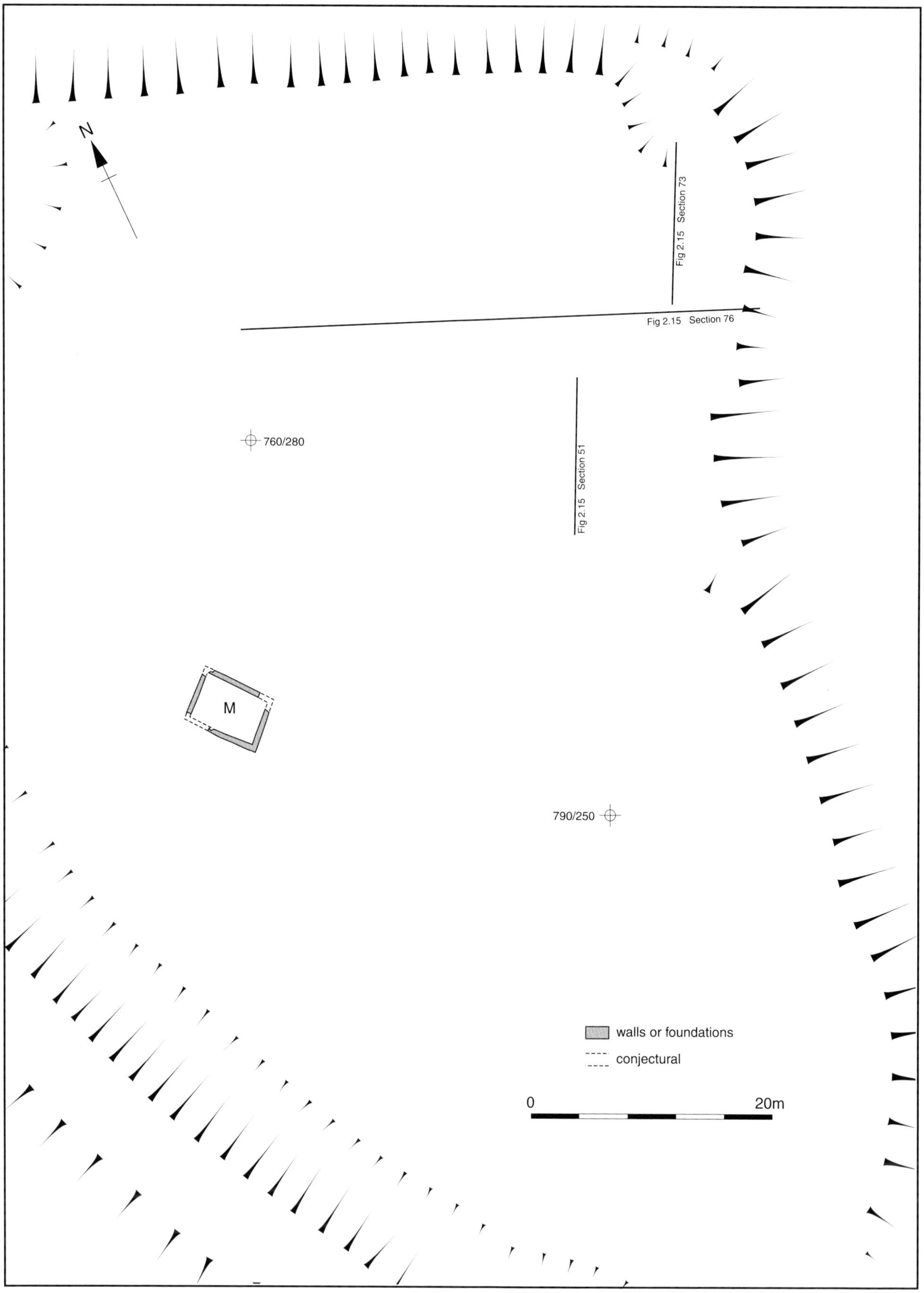

Figure 2.5 Plan of Phase 5.

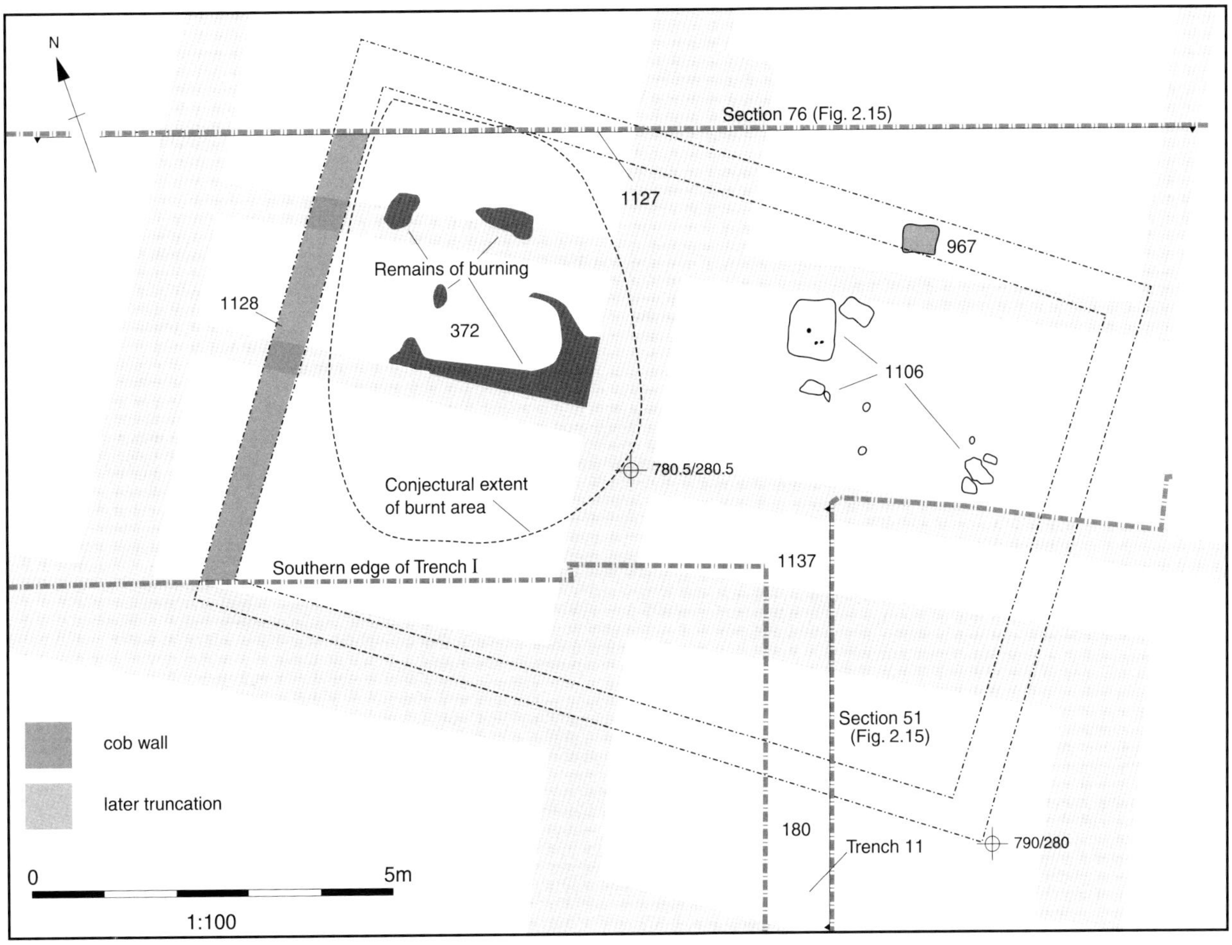

Figure 2.6 Detailed plan of Building P – Phase 1.

***Building R** (Figs. 2.1, 2.15)*

The structure was defined by a spread of chalk and clay floor (847 – see Fig. 2.15 section 73) edged on the eastern side by the disturbed remnants of a coursed rubble footing (1112 – Fig. 2.15 section 76), which measured approximately 0.70 m wide and survived to a depth of 0.10 m. The footing appeared to have slumped into the moat dug immediately to the east. The positions of the other three walls were inferred from the limits of the floor deposits, and what may represent a partition wall beamslot (848) (Fig. 2.15 section 73). No other internal features were identified. An iron hinge pivot (SF460: Fig. 3.18.42) was recovered from the floor surface, along with two sherds of pottery (Chapter 3 and Figs 3.1.4 and 3.1.7).

***Building S** (not illustrated)*

A possible structure or building, situated to the north-west of Building P, was indicated by a surviving length of rubble limestone footing (1215) noted in section in the robber trench of part of the north wall of Building A1. Possible floor or occupation layers (1216) were also identified abutting the footing. No dating material was recovered, so its association with Buildings P and R is suggested (but cannot be demonstrated) by the common overlying material (924) derived from the Phase 2 moat digging.

Other features

The remains of an isolated oven or kiln (692) found towards the west of the island may possibly belong to this phase (Fig. 2.19). The feature was revealed during the topsoil stripping of the site and was considerably disturbed, but was seen to consist of an irregular spread of burning with a circular concentration of daub, together with a quantity of pottery and bone, not apparently contained within any structure. Its stratigraphic relationship to the Phase 2 moat upcast material was uncertain, and its inclusion in Phase 1 is based upon the early to mid 13th-century pottery found in its vicinity.

A compacted flint and clay hardstanding (180, see Fig. 2.15 section 51) was identified to the south of Building P, apparently respecting the line of the conjectural south wall. The surface was revealed (in Trench XII) to extend at least 9.0 m to the south of the building. A single piece of worked limestone was recovered from the surface of the hardstanding (WS44).

A possible hearth (1211 – not illustrated) overlain by a mixed flint and gravel layer (1210) was revealed in Trench XX approximately 20.0 m west of Building P. Early 13th-century pottery and possible daub fragments were recovered from layer 1210.

Finds summary

A total of 69 pottery sherds were recovered from contexts assigned to Phase 1. Only a scatter of animal bone was recovered from securely dated Phase 1 contexts, and no significant bone assemblages were recovered.

Phase 2: (mid to late 13th century)

Summary (Figs 1.5 and 2.2)

The beginning of Phase 2 is represented by the demolition of the Phase 1 Building P and other possible structures in its vicinity, and the construction of the large moat. The description of the small moat is also included in this phase, although the dating of its construction cannot be confirmed by the archaeological record.

Two buildings in the northern part of the main island were defined and dated to this phase. Evidence of a group of buildings to the south-west was also recovered, although the buildings' definition is incomplete due to later building and to the selective excavation strategy.

This phase sees the establishment of the moated manor, with the main hall (Building A1) laid out in the northern part of the large island, on a platform created from the moat upcast. The hall will form the structural heart of the manor for the next 200 years. Truncation has made the two buildings D and E difficult to interpret, but it is suggested that the former is a bakehouse or brewhouse. Building E is somewhat enigmatic – it may have been associated with Building D, as a store for malted grain, although the possibility that it was a dovecote is also considered. The moats themselves were developed from existing watercourses and appear, from their modest depth, to have had no seriously defensive function. In the southern part of the main island a scatter of presumably agricultural buildings (N, O, Q, and U) were identified.

The moats (Figs 1.5, 2.2 and 2.7)

The line of the moats around both islands survived as slight earthworks and – in aerial photography (see Pl.1.2) – as distinct darker marks in the landscape. From earthwork measurements and sample sections it was seen that the width of the moats was generally between 9 m and 10 m although in some places a width of up to 13 m was apparent.

Two trenches (XXI and XXII) were cut across the infilled curving western arm of the large moat and one (XXIII) across the southern arm of the small moat. All revealed a similar shallow U-shaped profile with a flat bottom and a depth of between 1.0 m and 1.5 m. Section 36 (Fig. 2.7) depicts the fairly typical depositional sequence of the moat section in trench XXI. Silty clay layers 275/6 and 275/5 produced no dating evidence, and could have accumulated during the lifetime of the manor, although, with evidence elsewhere that the moat was regularly cleaned, these layers could have accumulated at the very end of the manor's occupation. Layer 275/4, against the 'island' side of the moat, contained broken roof tile and could represent the Phase 5 demolition, followed by the dark silty clay layer 275/3, representing an accumulating topsoil/turf line. The upper layers 275/2 and 275/1 represent modern disturbance/levelling. In none of the sections was there any evidence of stone or timber revetting of the channel. The fact that few finds were recovered from either moat has implications for their interpretation and function.

It was not possible to dig full sections of the north or east arms of the large moat, as these were serving as modern drainage. However, a section (Fig. 2.7 section 39) was hand-dug into the western edge of the eastern moat arm, close to the eastern end of Trench I. The lowest deposit revealed (279/2) was sampled for ecofactual evidence (see Robinson, Chapter 5). A small group of roof tile fragments was noted in the interface between layers 279/2 and 279/11.

The large island

The moat upcast (924) was identified at various points across the north and north-eastern part of the large island, being at its deepest (0.50 m) in the north-eastern corner, and petering out to the south-west (Fig. 2.2). No evidence was found to suggest that an internal bank was formed from the upcast material. The upcast material generally consisted of brown silty clay with inclusions of gravel and chalk, and contained a quantity of datable finds. A large assemblage of mainly domestic late 12th- and early 13th-century pottery was recovered, along with a few residual Romano-British sherds. Various iron and copper alloy objects were also recovered, mostly identifiable as 12th- to 13th-century artefacts, although the collection included a 9th-century Saxon strap end (SF 313: Fig. 3.8.15).

On the northern edge of the large island a length of substantial rubble limestone footing (736) with a width of *c* 0.80 m was partially exposed. Its stratigraphic relationship with the moat and the Phase 1 features to the south was unclear; it could represent a pre-moat structure truncated by the moat construction or equally possibly, an early bridge abutment, later rebuilt as 730 (Fig. 2.9 and Pl. 2.1).

The upcast from the moat construction and the material from the demolished walls was used to level up the northern half of the large island, in preparation for the construction of the new complex

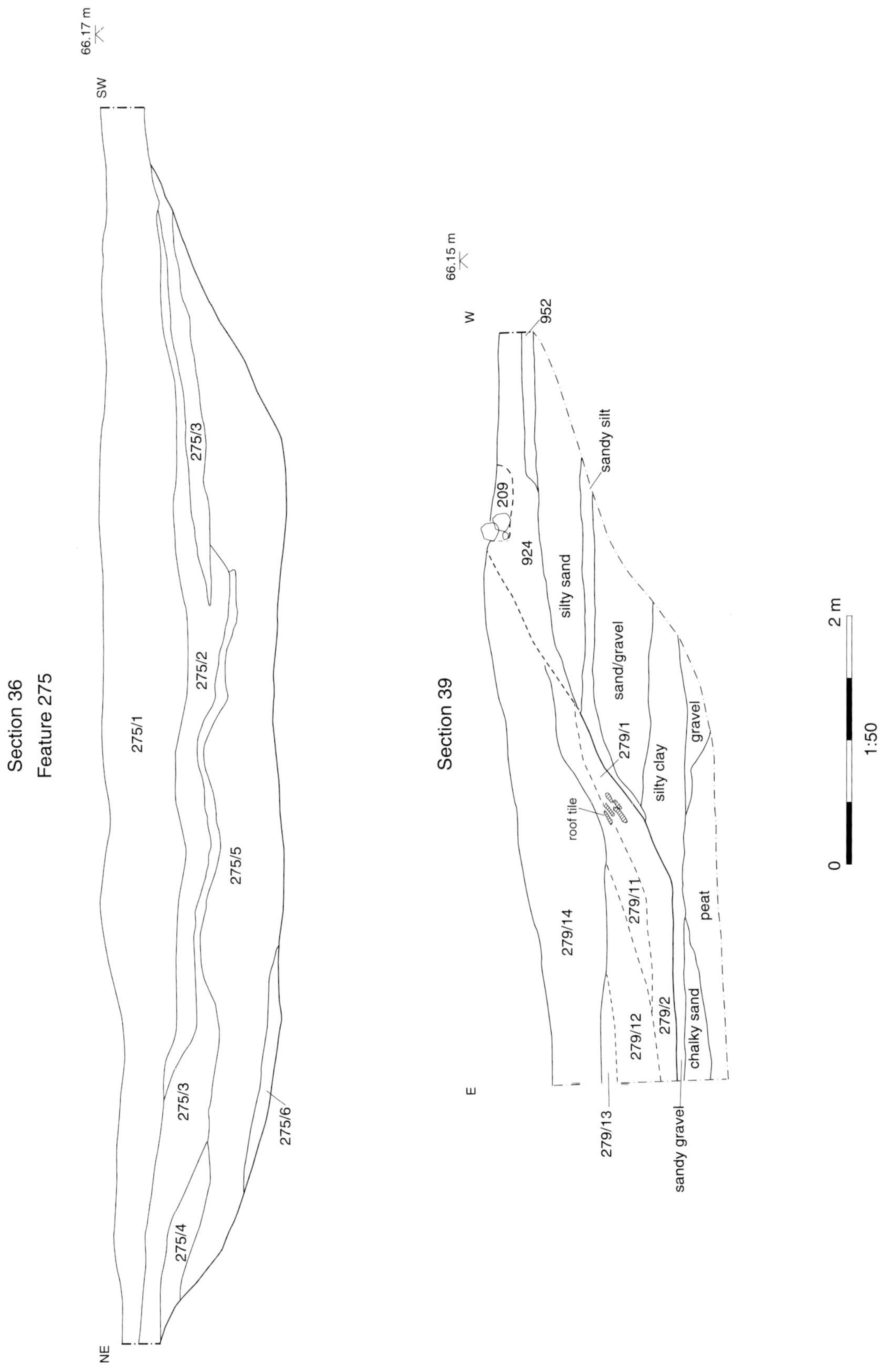

Figure 2.7 Sections across the large moat.

Plate 2.1 The northern moat, showing bridge abutment 730 and the edge of Building E.

of buildings. The extent of the spread of this material was defined in some of the trenches (see Fig. 2.15, section 51, context 353), and is conjecturally indicated on Figure 2.2.

The small island (Fig. 1.5)

Two trenches (III and IV) were initially cut across the platform of the small subrectangular island in 1977. In 1978 a larger trench (XXV) was machine-excavated down to the natural subsoil. No detailed section drawings or record of the stratigraphy have survived, although it was recorded that in none of the trenches was there any structural evidence, occupation layers or finds.

Building A1 (inc. A2) (Figs 2.2, 2.8, 2.15, Plate 2.2)

The building was defined by partially robbed rubble footings of a rectangular structure measuring 19.9 m × 10.12 m externally, orientated NW–SE. The surviving clay-bonded footings (10, 557, 625, 824) averaged 1.20 m wide × 0.50 m deep, set in shallow trenches cut into the platform of moat upcast material. In places the wall superstructure (0.80–0.85 m wide) survived as randomly coursed and roughly faced Portland limestone facing with a rubble core, set in a yellow clay matrix.

Fragments of ceramic roof tile found in a layer of demolition debris (144) belonging to the beginning of Phase 3 to the east of the building suggest a possible roof covering (see Chapter 6 and Fig. 2.15 section 51). Window glass fragments in the same debris suggest the presence of glazed windows (see Chapter 4).

A layer of silty clay and gravel (942) levelled the surface inside Building A1. This dump layer was almost indistinguishable from the underlying platform (Fig. 2.15 Section 76, cxt 1118) except that fragments of construction debris (decayed plaster and stone fragments) were sandwiched between them (Section 76; cxts 828, 891, 892, 940). Most of the pottery associated with the building came from the dump layer and could therefore have included residual material. However, a marked decline in the proportion of Fabric 20 compared with the Phase 1 pottery assemblage, and an increase in the proportion of Fabric 46 (mid 13th to 15th century) support a mid 13th-century date for the construction of Building A1.

Apart from one posthole (1045) sealed by Phase 3 layer 1017, there was no evidence for interior structural features. No remains of a contemporary floor surface survived; it is feasible that the top of the levelling represented the floor, although the possibility that the floor was flagged should not be ruled out – the flagstones could have been removed for re-use when the building was redeveloped.

The first in a sequence of hearths was identified near the west end of the building. The demolition debris (1075) from the first hearth (1077) suggests

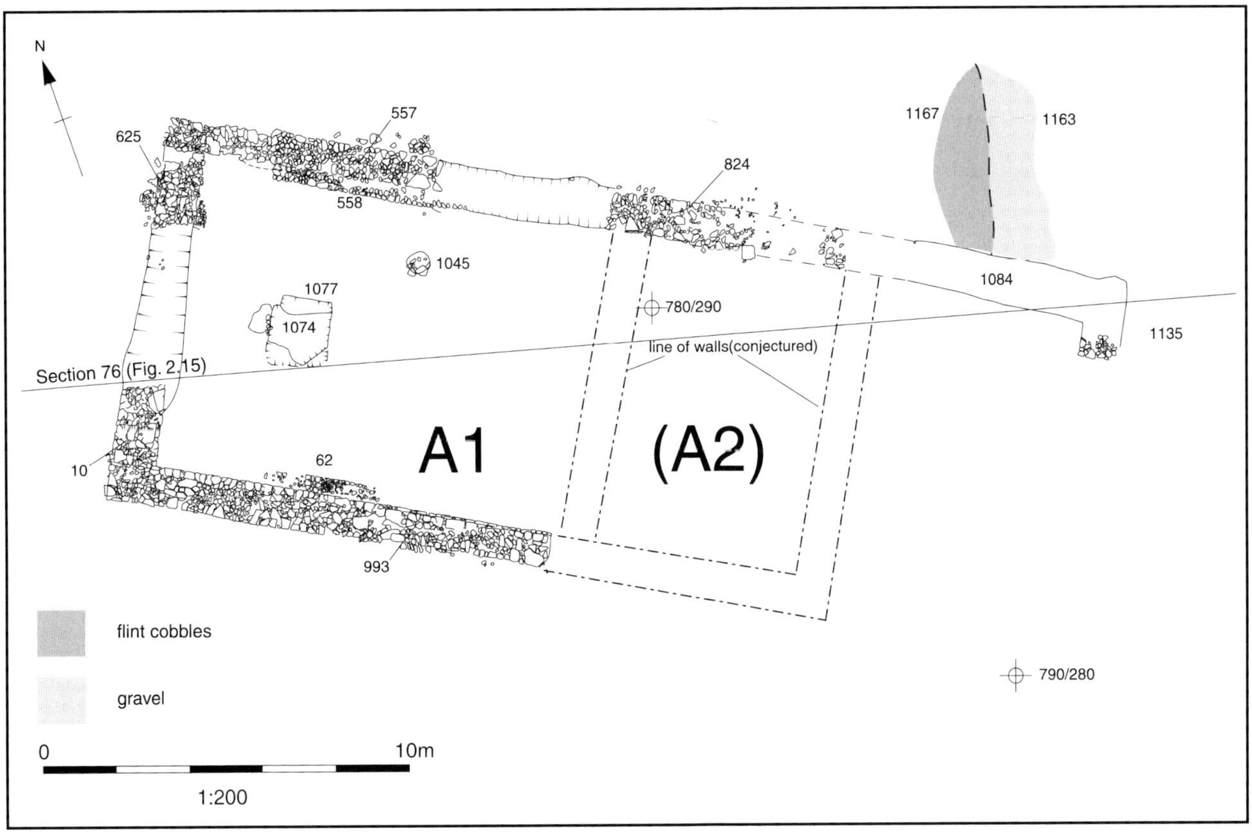

Figure 2.8 Detailed plan of Building A1 – Phase 2.

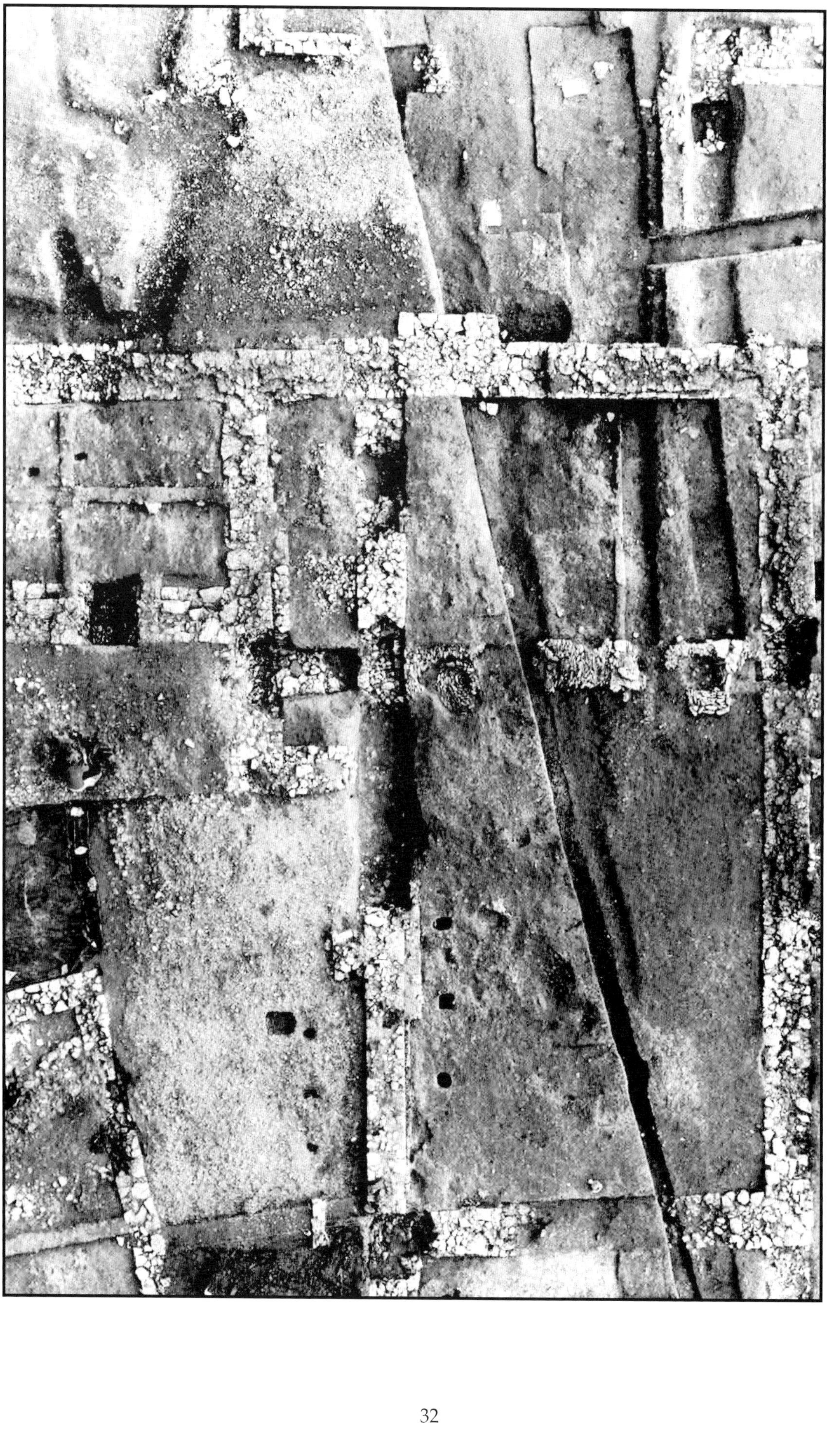

Plate 2.2 The main domestic range (looking north) during excavation, showing Building A1, rooms A10, A9, A8, and part of A4. Note southern edge of original Trench 1.

that it was of tile-on-edge construction, possibly with a limestone kerb, though it had been almost completely destroyed. The hearth was surrounded and, where not truncated, overlain by a spread of burnt silty clay (1074).

Two stone features (62, 558), each *c* 5 m long and projecting approximately 0.10 m above the surviving floor level, were set opposite each other against the walls at this end of the building. Incorporated in the construction of one of them (558) was a penny of Alexander III of Scotland datable to the period 1250–80 – see Archibald, Chapter 3, coin no. 20.

The eastern bay of the building was initially designated A2, although only a very patchy occupation layer (925) overlying layer 942 may possibly be associated with it. The layer may equally well be an early deposit associated with Room A10 (see below).

Only the northern wall (824) of the original east end of the building survived; however, a further 9.0 m length of robbed wall trench (1084) was identified. It was of similar width and depth to the walls described above and was traced to a convincing return to the south (1135). However no clear evidence of an east end wall to the building was found. Immediately to the north-east of robber trench 1084 was a flint cobbled surface (1167) and a gravel surface (1163), both heavily truncated by later activity. The fragmentary remains of a flint cobbled surface (973) were recorded immediately to the south-west of Building A1, within the area later occupied by the porch (Room A6 – see Fig. 2.10). The layer was not excavated, so its association with the Phase 2 Building A1 remains likely, but unconfirmed.

Building D (*Figs 2.2, 2.9*)

Building D was only partially revealed, and was also subject to some disturbance during the topsoil stripping. The structure was situated between Building A1 and the northern arm of the moat, and was defined by trench-built rubble foundations (712, 1090, 693, 720), generally 0.65 m wide × 0.30 m deep, set into the moat upcast (924). These defined a rectangular building measuring *c* 12.0 m long × 6.5 m wide, with the west end extended to form a 5.0 m × 4.0 m annex. The western wall of the extension appeared to be more substantial, possibly suggesting either an entrance or a fireplace. An isolated footing (774) coupled with the possible gap in the southern wall adjacent, may indicate a more plausible access, at least to the east end of the building. The remains of two small buttress bases were located against the exterior of the north wall of

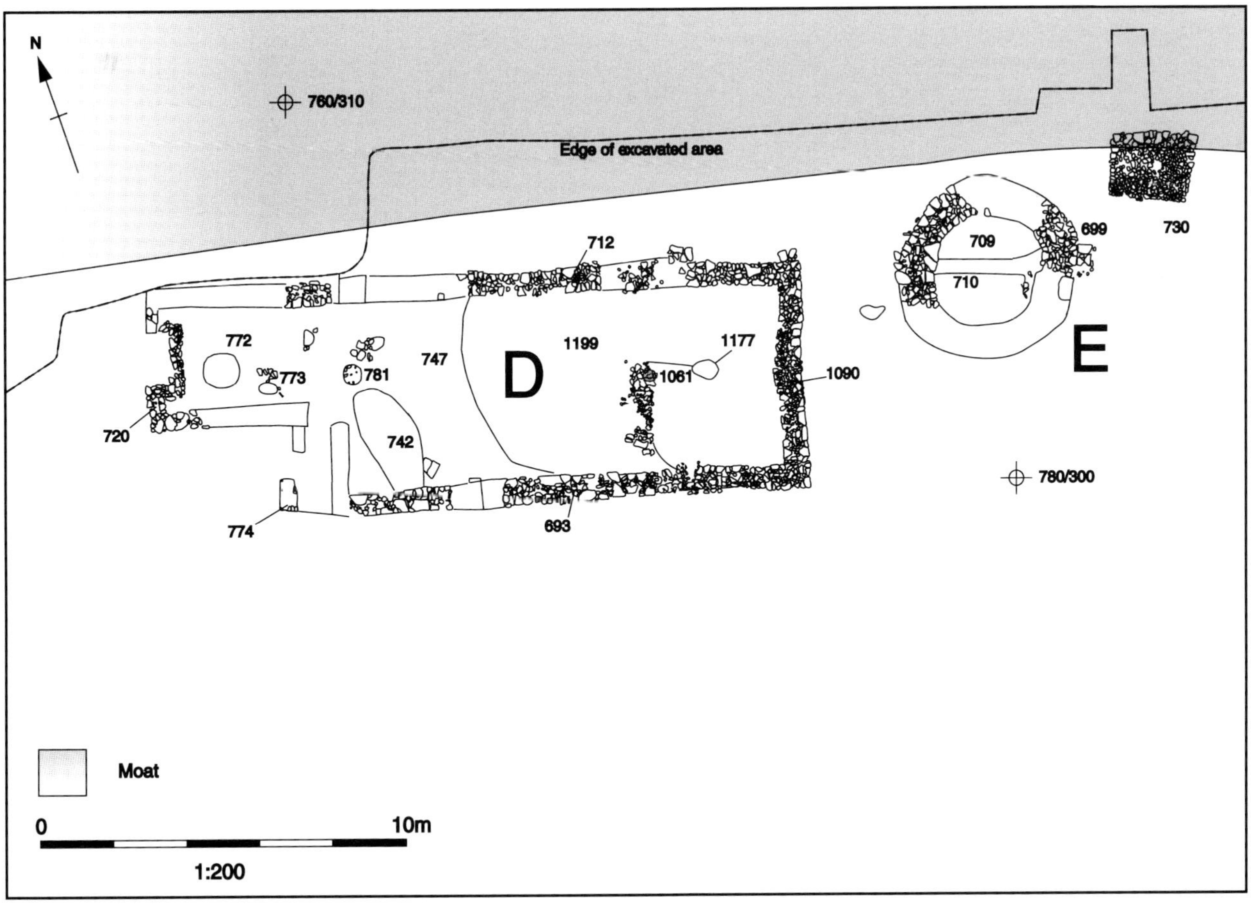

Figure 2.9 Detailed plan of Buildings D, E and the bridge abutment 730.

the building, and apparently incorporated into the wall footing, rather than butted against it. Given the proximity of the north wall to the edge of the moat, their presence is not surprising.

Within the building deposit 1199, a silty clay with a high proportion of charcoal, may represent remains from an occupation layer. At the west end of the building, this layer was identified as context 747. Two possible internal post-settings (1061 and 1177) were identified on the longitudinal axis of the east end of the building, and posthole 781 was similarly aligned at the west end. The stone packing of 1061 contained a mortar rim with an ornate pouring lug (Fig. 3.28.4). Evidence for two, or possibly three, ovens or hearths (742, 772, 773) was found at the west end of the building, contemporary with the occupation floor surface 747. The few pottery sherds recovered from Building D contexts were mostly mid to late 13th-century in date.

Building E (Figs 2.2, 2.9, Pl. 2.1)

This structure was partly revealed to the east of Building D, and immediately west of the possible abutment 730 (see above). The remains appeared to define a circular structure with an internal diameter of 3.1 m and a maximum external diameter of 5.0 m. The width of the surviving rubble foundation (699) approached 1 m in places. Within the structure, a possible make up layer (709) was identified, cut by a very ephemeral and shallow linear feature (710) running across the centre, and possibly representing a beam slot. No dating material was recovered from the building contexts; as its footings were cut directly into the upcast (924), and overlain or truncated by Phase 4 structures, its construction is tentatively assigned to Phase 2 on stratigraphic grounds, although some support may come from its possible functional association with Building D (see Chapter 6).

Other features (Figs 2.12, 2.15)

The possible base of a hearth or oven (Fig. 2.15 Section 73: cxts 778 and 849) was identified to the north-east of Building A (Trench XIV). The features appear to be burnt areas of the platform material, edged (in the case of 778) with limestone rubble. Two concentrations of charcoal (Fig. 2.12 and Fig. 2.15 Section 73: 778/2, 849/1) overlay the remnants of a possible surface of redeposited chalk head mixed with clay (cxts 778/3, 849/2). The hearth base was partly overlain by a sub-rectangular spread of ash (534) (Fig. 2.12, and Fig. 2.15 Section 73), measuring *c* 7.0 m by 3.5 m, which could define the interior footprint of a building within which the hearth base was situated. Fragments of tile and mortar were found in the demolition debris and a clay floor tile was recovered from the ash spread. Some ironworking slags were also found in the ash layer, which may indicate the purpose of the hearth. A considerable quantity of 12th- to 13th-century pottery, including two cooking pots, was also found within the hearth contexts.

Buildings N, O, Q and U (Fig. 2.2)

To the south-west of the domestic buildings were the fragmentary remains of four probably contemporary structures. They were defined by insubstantial robber trenches or rubble footings and associated cobble surfaces. Structure Q was defined by partially robbed footings (360), and robber trenches (460, 467), which represented the west, south and east walls of the building. The building had a floor surface (415) of medium-sized and large flint cobbles, which was overlain by wall 273 of Phase 4 Building H (see Fig. 2.18). Some artefactual material was recovered from a slight depression in this floor, including late 13th- to 14th-century pottery, a whetstone (SF 212) and a Jew's harp (SF 310, Fig. 3.24.135). Evidence in the demolition debris (468, 441, 447) indicated that Building Q may have been roofed with clay peg tiles. The insubstantial remains of another robber trench (463) were observed to the south and parallel to 461. A narrow strip of cobbling surface (459) separated the two trenches. It is likely that these features relate to the Phase 2 buildings but the possibility exists that they are associated with Building H of Phase 4 (see below).

Structure N was located immediately to the south of structure Q and approximately on the same alignment. The remains of three wall footings and foundations (296, 297 and 298) survived. Structure O was located to the south-east of Structure N and also survived only as the fragmentary footings of two walls (299, 300). The remains of a pitched stone hardstanding (301) were set against the southern corner. Neither structure produced any artefactual evidence.

Structure U, situated to the south-west of Structure N, and close to the south-west moat, was defined by the remains of a wall (303) and extension (302), which appeared to represent a boundary wall extending northwestwards to the moat edge. While the footing 303 appeared to be the only surviving element of a precursor to the Phase 3 Building K, it is possible that the robber trenches 307, 308 and the north-west part of 305 (see Fig. 2.18) define walls that were originally parts of Building U, incorporated into the later Building K.

Phase 3 (early 14th century) (Figs 2.3, 2.10–20)

Summary

The phase is represented by a major programme of building, which entailed the development of a cross wing containing a series of rooms to the east end of Building A1 (A4, A5, A8, A9, A10, A7), an extension to the west end of the building (A3), and to the south side (A6). Further buildings and structures were added to the area between the main complex and the eastern arm of the moat (Buildings A7, W and B, Area F), and two further buildings (I and J) were

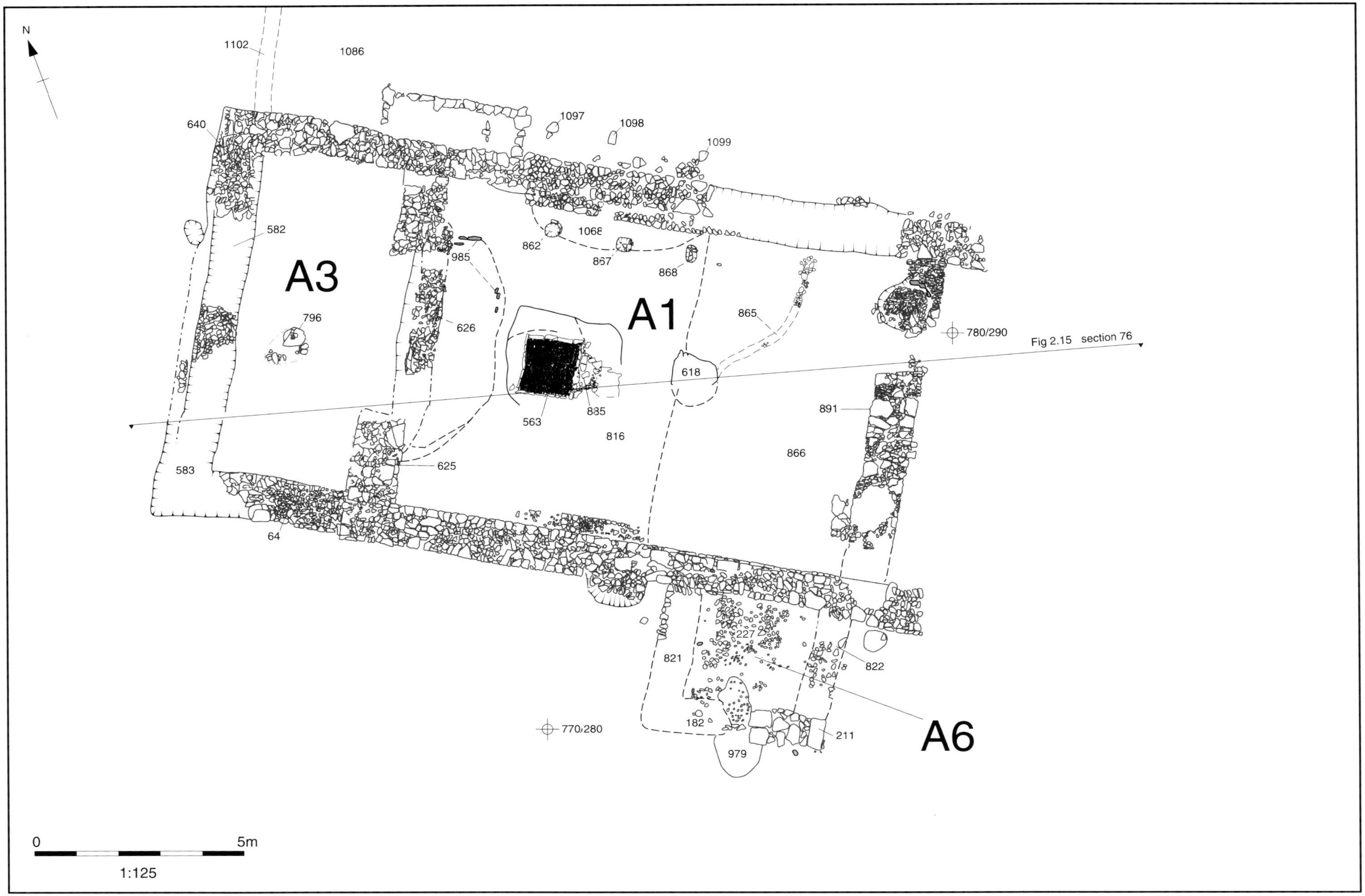

Figure 2.10 Detailed plan of Building A1 and later hearth development.

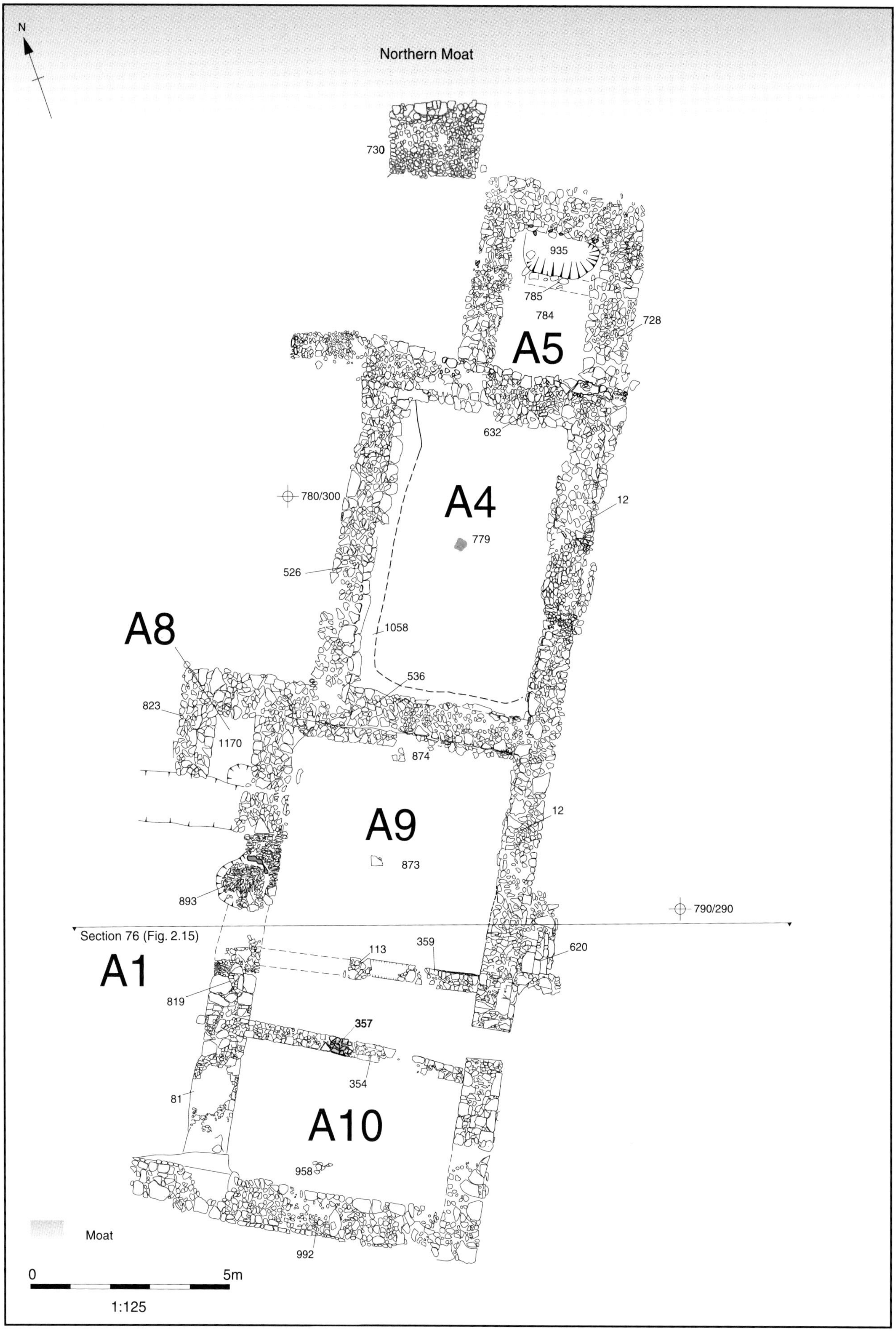

Figure 2.11 Detailed plan of the cross wing – Rooms A10, A9, A8, A4, and A5.

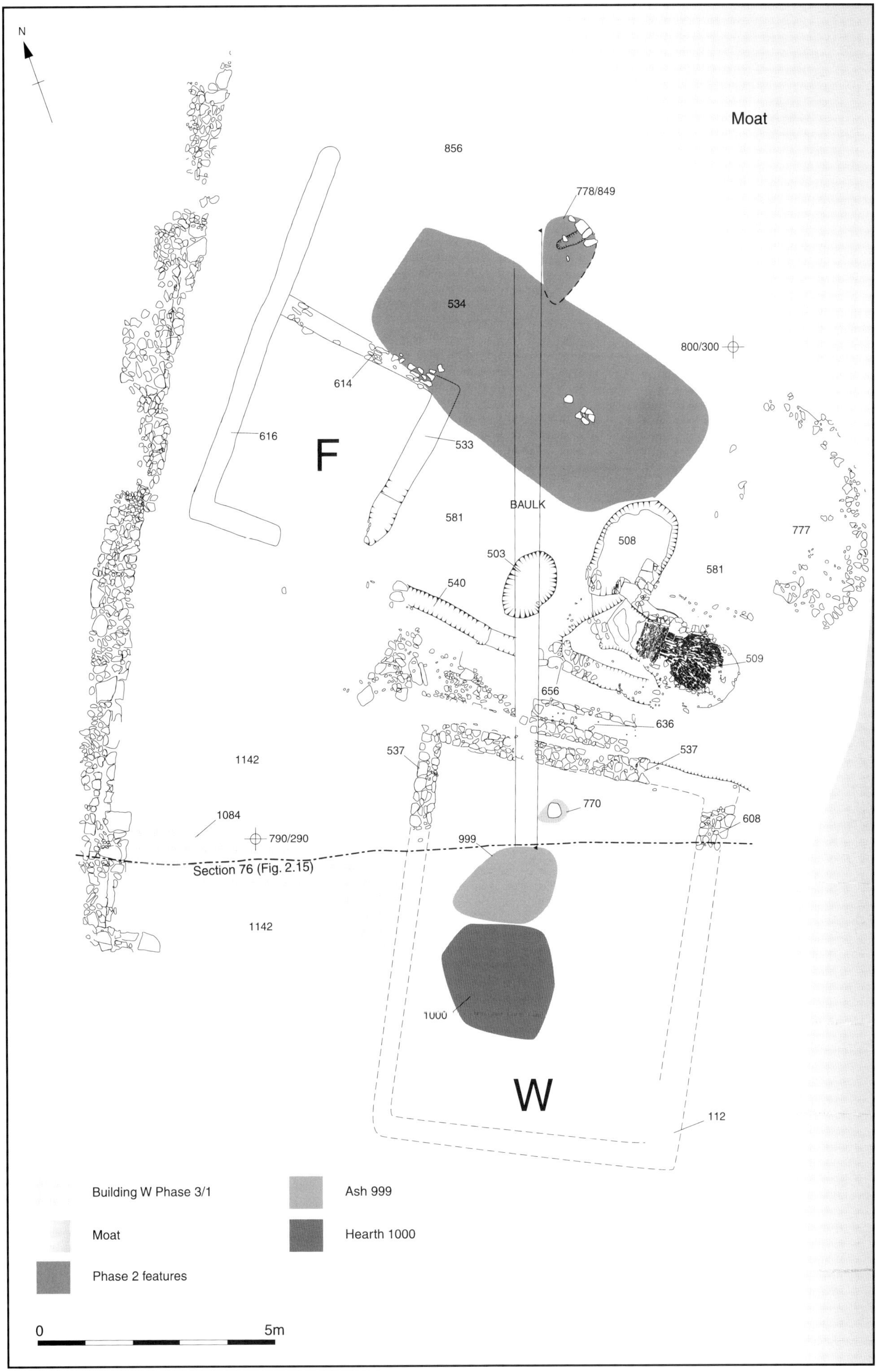

Figure 2.12 Detailed plan of Area F and Building W Phase 3.

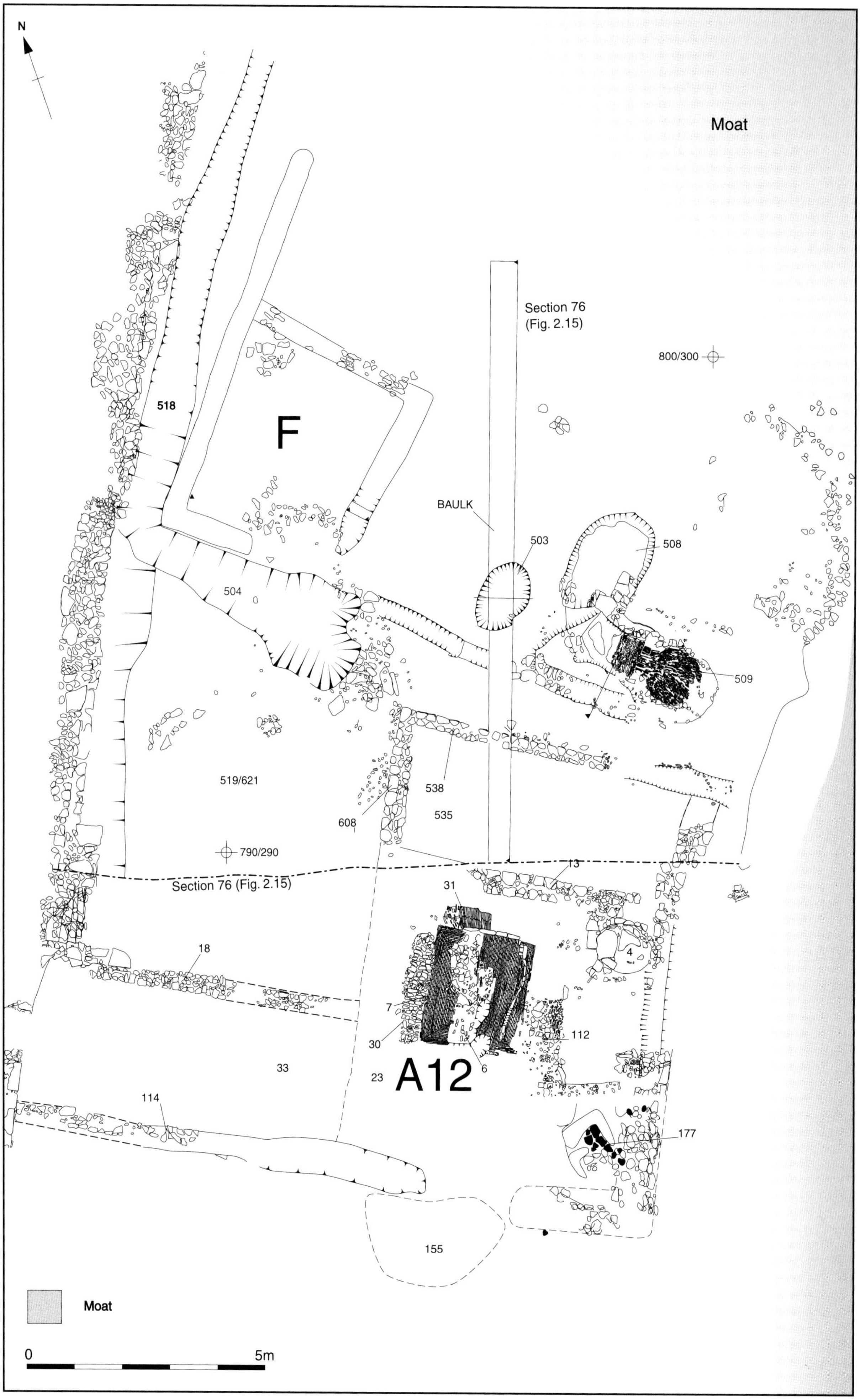

Figure 2.13 Detailed plan of Area F and Building A12 Phase 4.

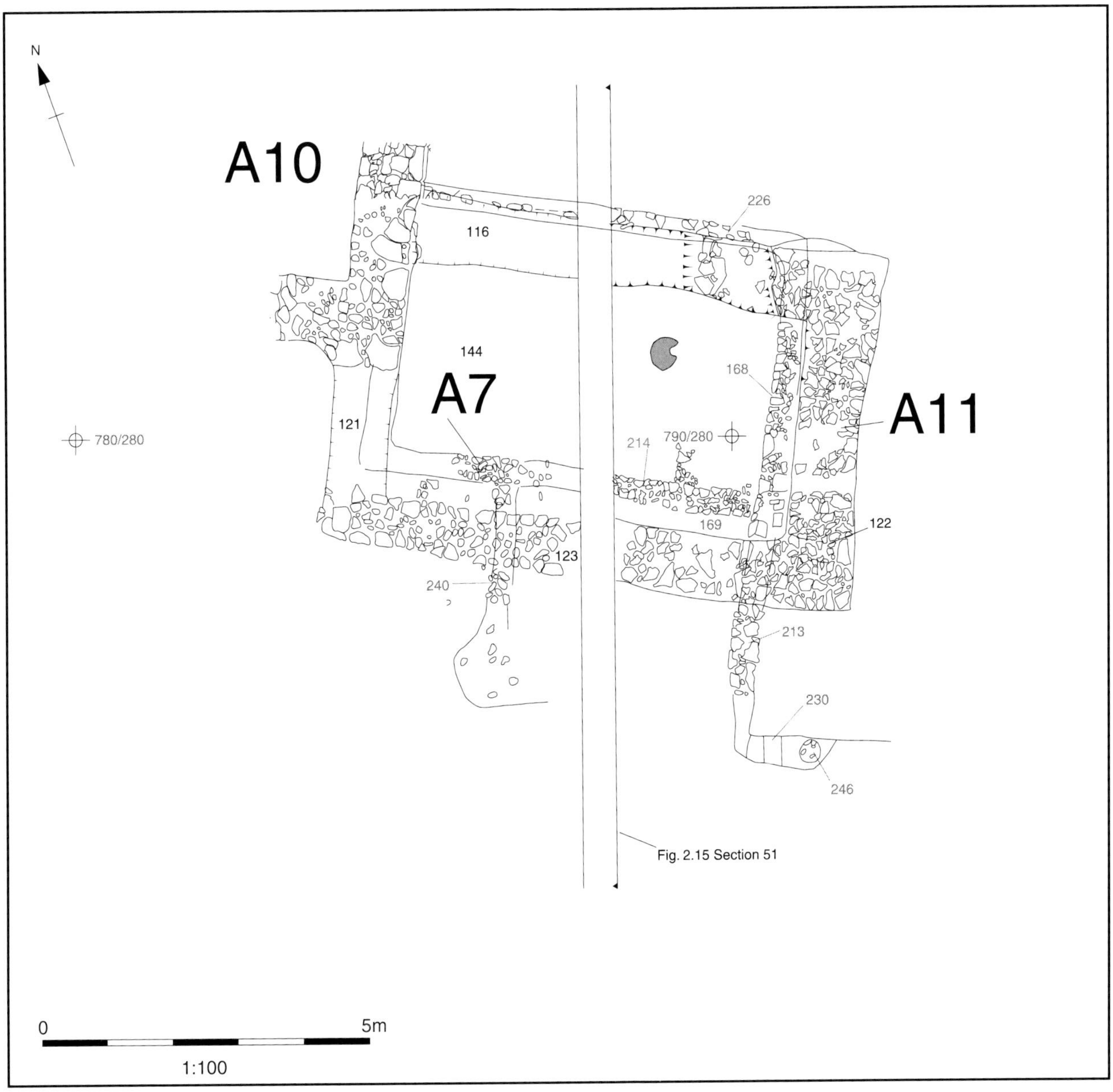

Figure 2.14 Detailed plan of Buildings A7 and A11.

constructed to the south west of the main block. Definitive dating of this redevelopment is hampered by general lack of closely datable artifacts within the relevant deposits.

While the hall remained intact, the development of the cross wing implies a much greater sophistication and elaboration of manorial life. The old service end of the hall was replaced by Rooms A9 and A10, bisected by a passage leading to a separate kitchen. Further north, Rooms A4 and A5 are suggested to be a wardrobe and garderobe, both serving the upstairs private chambers, which themselves were accessed by the stairs in Room A8. Room A3 is suggested to be a private annex at the west end of the main hall. To the east of the cross wing, Building A7, W, B, and Area F are interpreted as a storehouse, kitchen, dairy and oven area respectively. More substantial agricultural buildings (J, I and K) now border the west and south sides of the main island.

The moat bridge (*Figs 2.3, 2.9, Pl. 2.1*)

The excavation revealed the possible remains of a bridge (730). This lay just to the east of Building E and consisted of an abutment of rubble limestone measuring 2.3 m by 1.8 m and situated on the edge of the moat. Unfortunately, it was not possible to establish if an opposing abutment survived on the north bank of the moat ditch. As the stratigraphy associated with the abutment had been removed by topsoil stripping, it was not possible to archaeologically confirm the dating of this structure.

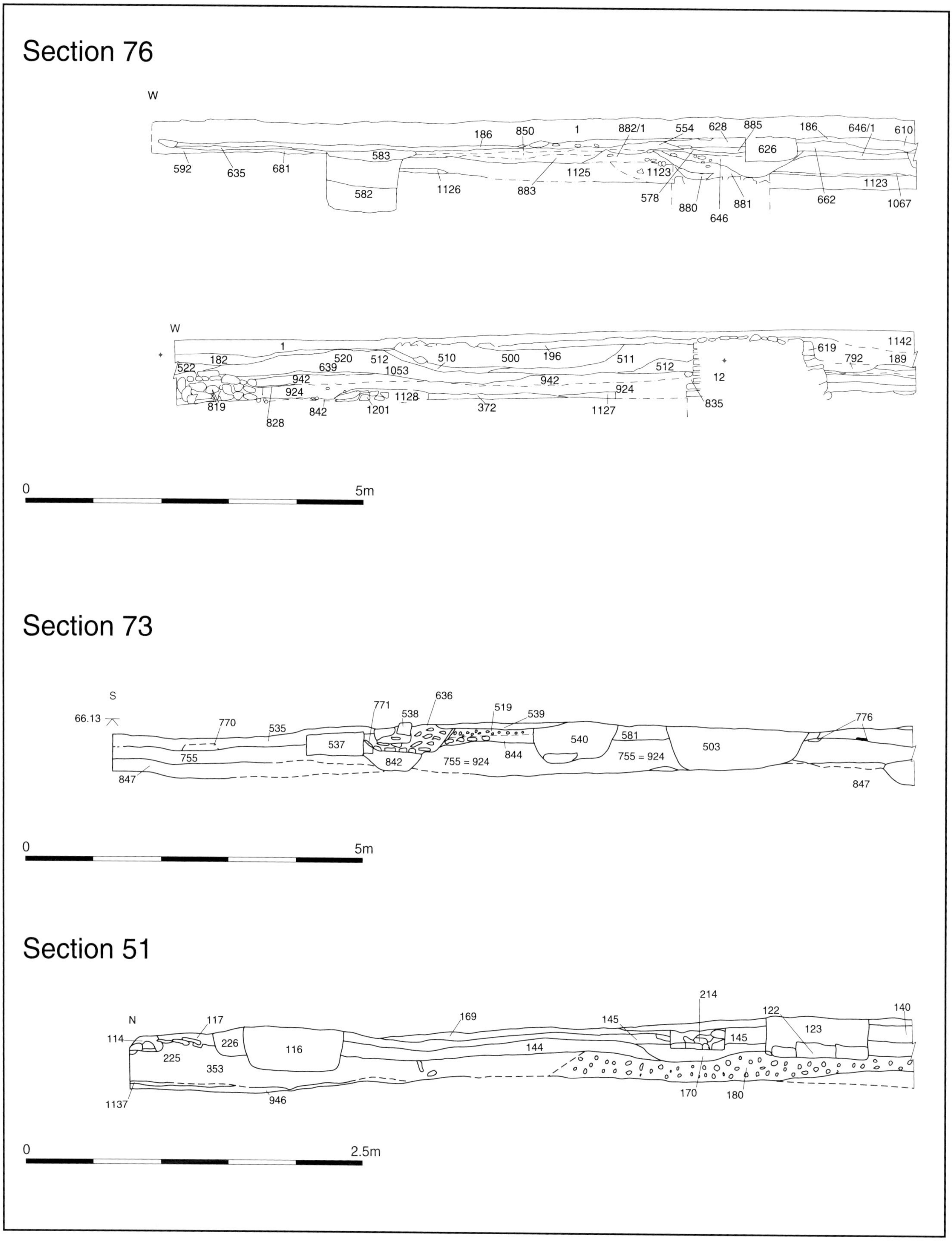

Figure 2.15 Sections 76, 73 and 51 through the domestic building complex.

Section 76 continued

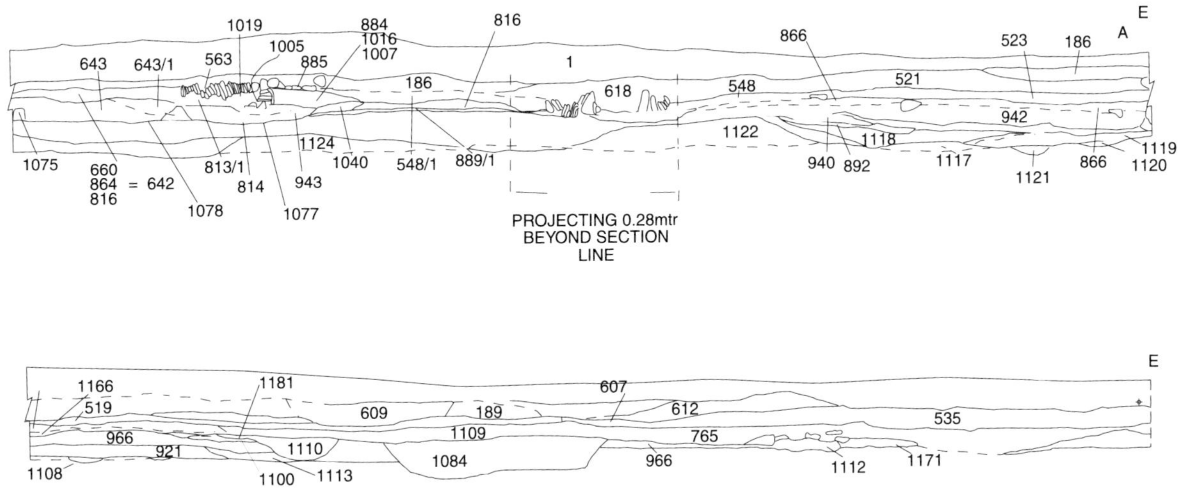

Section 73 continued

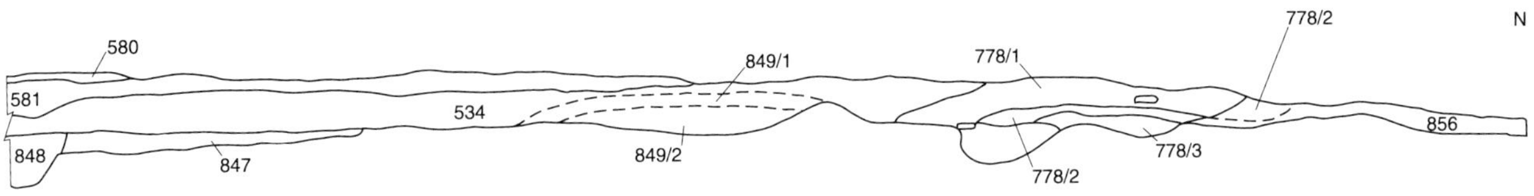

Section 51 continued

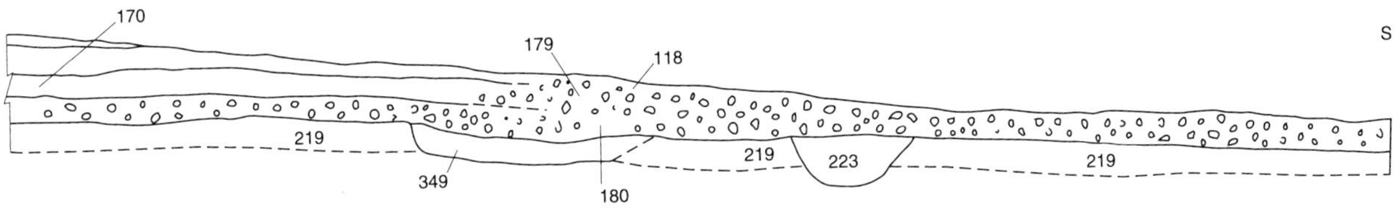

igure 2.15 Continued.

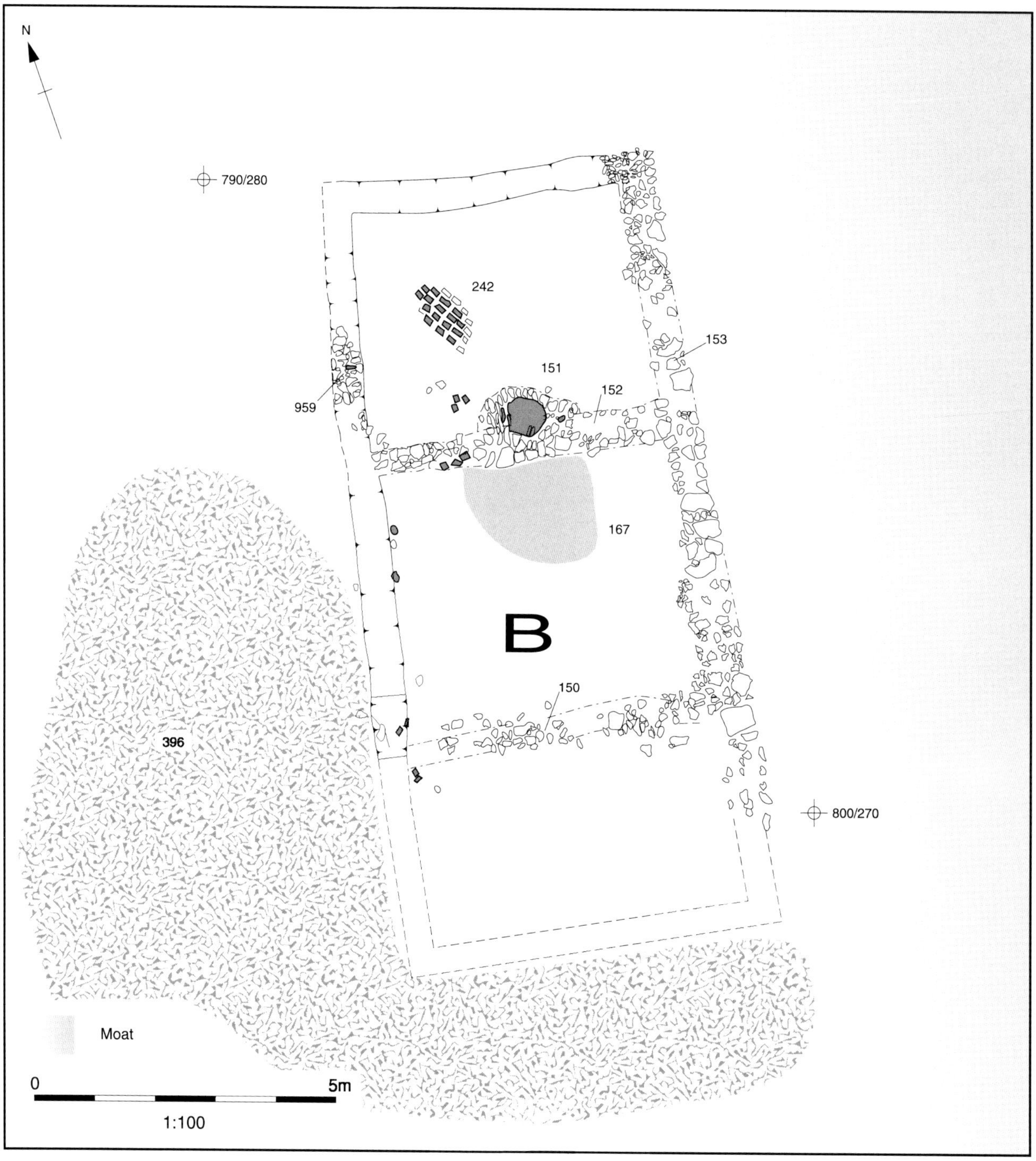

Figure 2.16 Detailed plan of Building B.

Rooms A10 and A9 *(Fig. 2.3, 2.11, Plate 2.2)*

Rooms A10 and A9 were defined by the south wall of Building A1 (992), an east wall (12), a north wall (536) and a west wall (819).

These two rooms were evidently designed as a single construction bisected by an east-west passage defined by the truncated remains of two partition walls (354 and 359) providing access from Building A1 to the yard area to the east. The base of the door jambs from the passage to the yard survived in situ, indicating a door width of approximately 1.1 m. A probable doorway from the passage into the northern room A9 was indicated by a stone-free gap immediately east of post-setting 113. An opposite doorway into A10 was suggested by flat slabs in the footings. At the west end of the passage, the large flat slabs at this point in the run of wall footing 819 appear to define the access way into the hall A1.

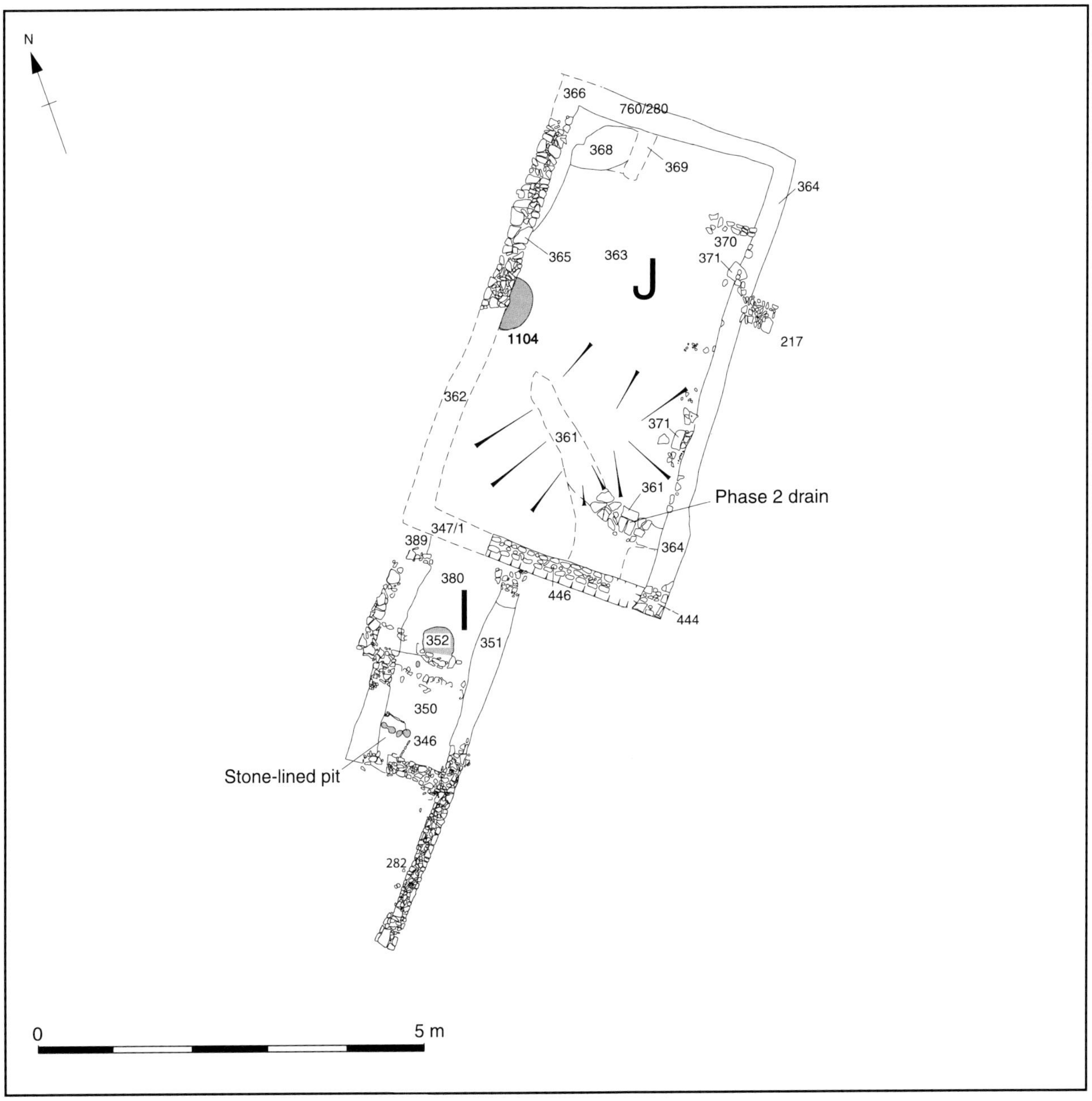

Figure 2.17 Detailed plan of Buildings J and I.

In both rooms the upper levels of the platform material were contaminated with construction debris (Fig. 2.15: Section 76: cxt 942/2). A make up layer (734) was then spread through both rooms, and it was noted that this predated the construction of the passage walls. Five postholes or stone-reinforced settings (874, 873, 113, 357 and 958) were identified along the north-south centre line of the Rooms A10/A9. Two of them (113 and 357) were incorporated into the walls of the passage.

The traces of a plain lime plaster surviving on the footings of Rooms A9 and A10 indicate that both were finished with a plaster rendering, in contrast to the passage walls, which appeared to have been left unrendered.

A stone footing (620), was built against the exterior eastern wall (12) of Room A9; the two features were bonded together in the upper surviving courses, but not at their base. Feature 620 could represent the base of an exterior chimney stack; the absence of any sign of a suitably situated interior fireplace in Room A9 would suggest that the stack would have served a first-floor fireplace.

Some indications of the details of the superstructure of this wing derive from the fragments of stone moulding recovered from the demolition layers overlying this part of the building; at least one appears to have been part of a window. In addition lead cames were also recovered (see Chapter 4).

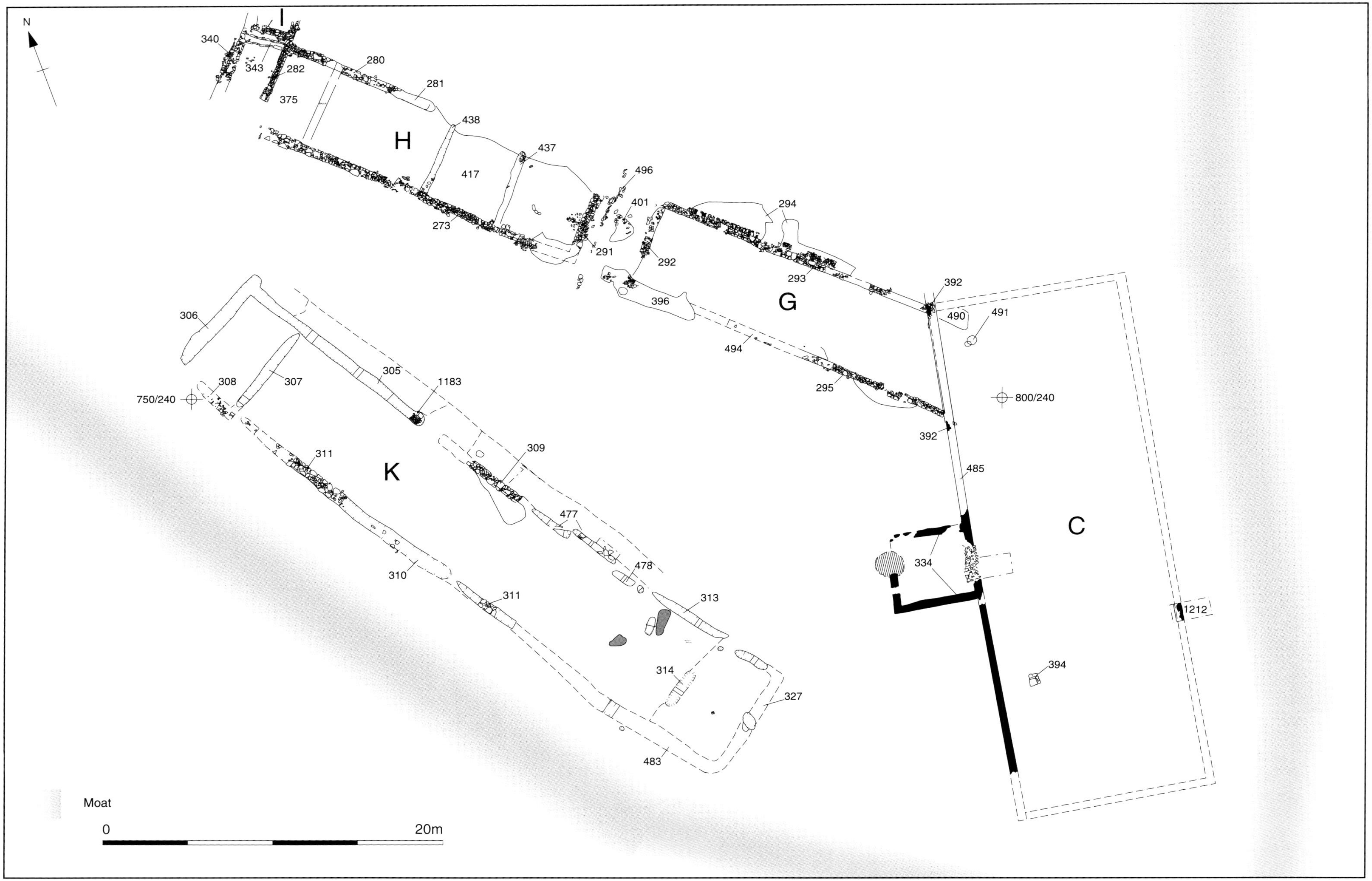

Figure 2.18 Agricultural buildings H, G, C and K, 14th–15th century.

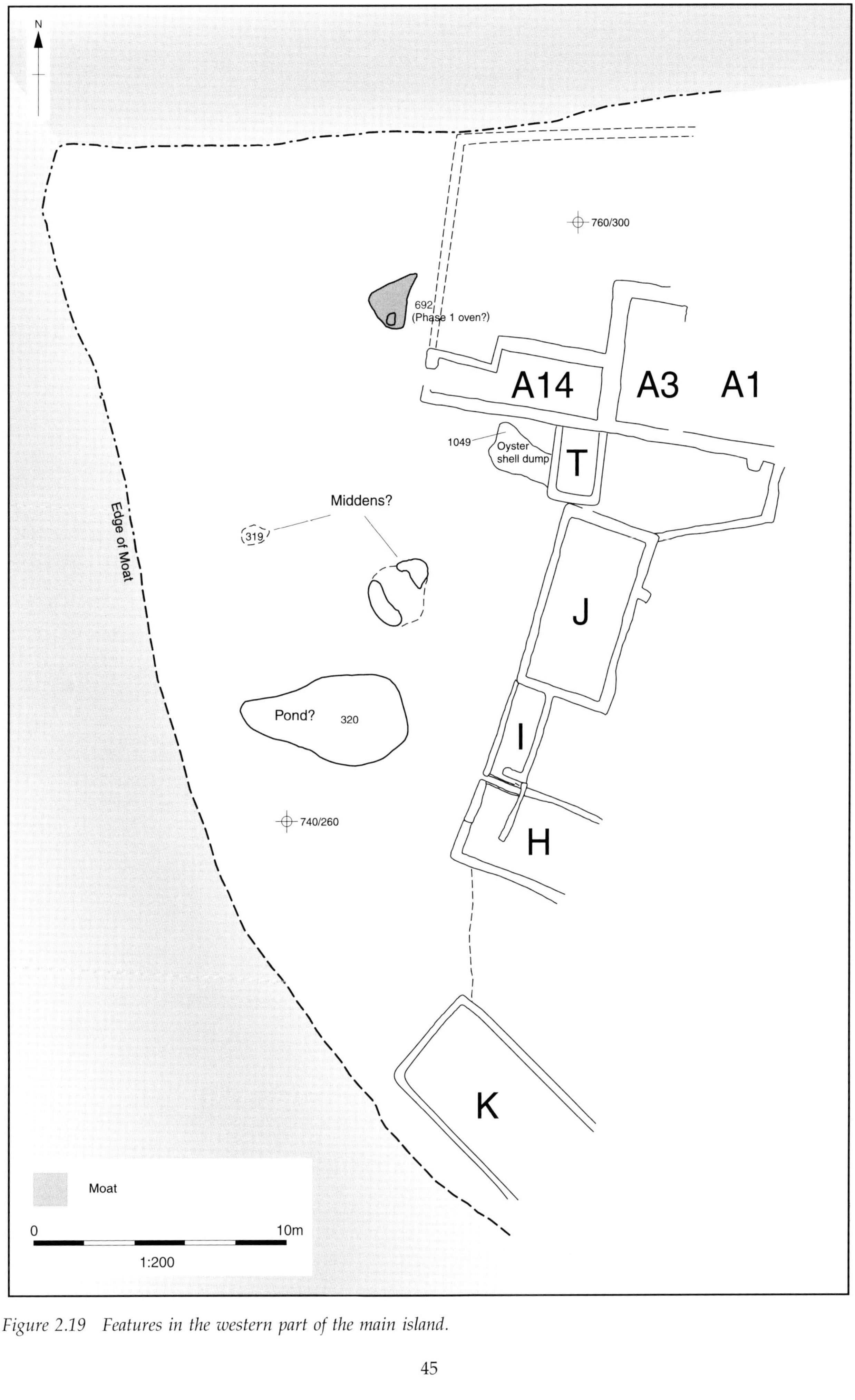

Figure 2.19 Features in the western part of the main island.

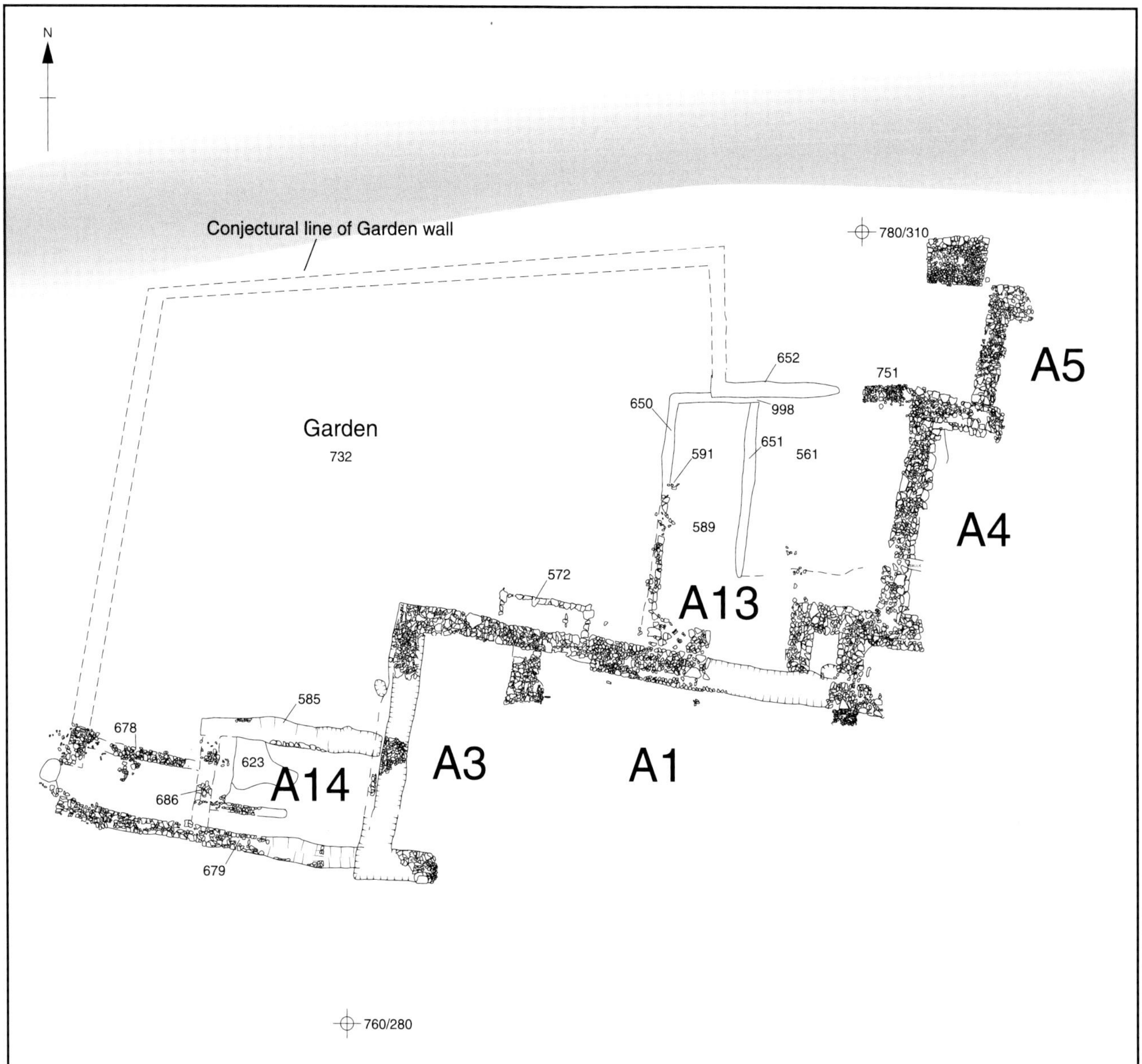

Figure 2.20 Buildings A13 and A14 and the garden – Phase 4.

Room A8 (*Fig 2.11*)

A small chamber with external dimensions of 3.2 m by 2.75 m was located in the re-entrant angle provided between the north wall of room A1 and the west wall of the new wing (819). The footings (823) butted against those of both A1 and A9 and their size – up to 0.80 m wide – suggests that the structure could have carried up to the first floor. The room contained a relatively thick layer of clay and flint material (1170), which levelled up the interior surface. Only a very small amount of pottery was recovered from associated contexts.

Room A4 (*Fig.2.3, 2.11*)

Room A4 (footings 526, 536, 12, 632) adjoined the north end of room A9 and appeared to be a contemporary construction. A door threshold was identified in the common wall; there was no evidence of an external access. In the middle of the room was a single roughly squared stone block (779) measuring 0.40 m square and with a flat surface which appeared to be an upstanding post pad. It is possible that the column fragments found in Room A9 had been dumped from this room. Evidence of construction debris (1058) comprising mortar fragments and sand abutted the walls, as in the other rooms. This material was sealed by a composite layer (600) up to 0.30 m deep, consisting of lenses of mortar, silty clay and spreads of charcoal-rich sandy loam, interspersed with at least one small patch of flint cobbling. A small quantity of 14th-century pottery was recovered from this material, along with a number of small finds, including a key (SF 127; Fig. 3.22.97) and a gaming die (SF 299).

***Room A5** (Fig. 2.3, 2.11)*

The footings (728) of a small structure, measuring 4.0 m W–E × 4.2 m N–S were revealed abutting the northern end of Room A4, and extending to within 3 m of the edge of the north arm of the moat. The substantial nature of the footings suggests that the structure could have carried up to a first floor. The footings (785) of a narrow stone wall were identified within this chamber, dividing its ground plan into two parts. The deposits within the southern part comprised a greyish brown silty clay (784), which overlay what appeared to be moat upcast material (786). A small depression or pit in the surface of 784 contained a quantity of pottery, generally of a 13th- to 14th-century date, and a number of small finds, including part of a pair of scissors (SF447, Fig. 3.18.29), a strap (SF 448, Fig. 3.20.59), a key (SF186, Fig. 3.22.94), a cramp (SF 449, Fig. 3.18.31) and a pottery sherd displaying a human face (Fig. 3.3.8). A shallow depression (935) in the northern part of Room A5 contained a green/grey cess-like material.

***Room A6** (Fig. 2.3, 2.10)*

The structure was situated against the southern side of Building A1, and stratigraphically appears to belong to Phase 3/1 although there was no material dating evidence for its construction. The structure was defined by two parallel footings, mostly robbed but identified from shallow robber trenches (821, 822) 2.4 m apart, extending approximately 4.0 m from the south wall of A1. The eastern footing (822) stopped against a small area of limestone slabs (211). To the west this had been robbed, leaving a shallow trench (182) in front of the wall footing/robber trench (821). The nature of 211 and 182 suggests that the facade of the structure may have been of timber, resting on a stone plinth. The interior of the structure revealed a cobbled surface (227), overlying the probable Phase 2 layer 973 (not illustrated). A spread of flint and gravel (979) extended south from Room A6 and probably represents a path surface.

***Building A7** (Figs 2.3, 2.14, 2.15, Plate 2.3)*

The partially robbed stone footings were found of a building abutting the south-east corner of the cross-wing. The footings (168, 214, 226) were lightly founded and up to 0.42 m wide, defining a building footprint of 6.8 m × 4.5 m. (see Fig. 2.15 Section 51). Two further very insubstantial footings (213 and 240) extended from the south wall, possibly representing a small additional structure. The line of footing 213 appeared to be extended south and east by robber trench 230, terminating in a posthole (246) close by the west wall of Building B. No dating material or other artefacts securely associated with the structure were recovered. A layer of mortar (169) containing fragments of tile was noted, in places respecting the north side of wall 214 (see Section 51). However, the excavator considered that this deposit was almost certainly associated with the floor make-up for the Phase 4 successor to this building, A11 (see below).

***Building W** (Figs 2.3, 2.12, 2.15)*

A detached rectangular building measuring up to 9.5 m long × 6.5 m wide was identified to the east of the main cross-wing, close to the edge of the eastern arm of the moat. It was defined by partially surviving rubble footings of the north-east and north-west walls (537), mortar-bonded and measuring 0.43 m wide × up to 0.19 m deep (Fig. 2.15; section 73). Two short lengths of wall surviving along the eastern side of the building (112 and 608) may represent the eastern wall of the building, although their phasing was uncertain, and they could equally well be elements of Phase 4 Building A12 (see below). In any case, while the building's maximum width can be deduced by the proximity of the moat, its length is only cautiously inferred by the proximity of probably contemporary buildings to the south (Room A7 and Building B; see Fig. 2.3). Within Building W was evidence of a large hearth (1000), with an area of ash immediately to the north (999). The only other internal feature was a single posthole (770) located 1.0 m in from the north wall. No evidence was found of a doorway in the surviving footings. A few sherds of 13th- to 16th-century pottery were recovered from within the building fabric, and a fragment of vessel glass (SF 302, not illustrated) was recovered from the ashy layer 999. The fact that the line of the west wall of this building lies directly alongside the eastern end of the north wall (1135) of Phase 2 Building A1 could suggest that Building W was constructed in Phase 2, before the construction of the north-south range.

***Area F** (Figs 2.3, 2.12)*

Area F was situated in the north-eastern corner of the large island, and was defined by two robber trenches (540, 616), bordering an area in the north-east corner of the main island of approximately 130 sq m.; some surviving footings were noted (656). No evidence of an east or north wall was found, suggesting that this was an enclosed area, rather than a roofed building. There was a break in the south-west robber trench approximately 1.2 m wide,

Plate 2.3 The eastern edge of the main island, showing Buildings A7, A11, B, and edge of eastern moat. Note evaluation trenches.

which appears to define an entrance or gateway from the courtyard to the south. A cobbled area (777) was revealed alongside the moat edge, and the disturbed remains of a silty clay surface (581), up to 0.12 m deep, which produced a large quantity of sherds of mainly 13th- to 15th-century pottery. Other objects recovered from this deposit included a pin (SF 172; Fig. 3.13.96), a brooch (SF 142, Fig. 3.7.5), a chain link (SF 130, Fig. 3.22.106), and a buckle (SF 229, Fig. 3.23.130). In the angle formed by the robber trenches 616 and 656 an insubstantial and partly robbed footing (614), and a shallow linear feature (533) possibly defined a small covered building or subsidiary enclosure within Area F. It was noted that the surface 581 did not extend into this area.

Three ovens (508, 509, 503) were located within the structure, placed on, or cut into surface 581. Two of these (508, 509) were placed at right-angles to each other in the southern corner of the Area. They were both covered by a substantial layer of wood ash. Oven 509 had a well-preserved floor and a rake-back of pitched tiles, set into the floor surface. Oven 508, though largely robbed out, had traces of a stone floor set *c* 0.25 m below the ground surface. The third oven (503) survived only as a sub-oval pit, 0.30 m deep with steep sides (Fig. 2.15, Section 73). There was evidence that these sides had been lined with wattle-and-daub, pieces of daub being found within the demolition debris of the oven. All three ovens contained charcoal fragments.

The north-east courtyard (*Fig. 2.12*)

A yard surface of flint and gravel was identified between the cross-wing and Building W (1142). A drain (636), stone-lined and tile floored, was set into the yard surface alongside the north wall of Building W, draining into the eastern arm of the moat (Fig. 2.15: Section 73).

Building B (*Figs 2.3, 2.16, Plate 2.3*)

The footprint of a rectangular building was identified to the south-east of Building A7, and aligned alongside the eastern arm of the moat. It was represented by very fragmentary stone footings (153, 959) averaging 0.60 m wide, set into shallow trenches. Most of the southern part of the building was completely truncated, possibly by the topsoil stripping, but an approximation of the original footprint was detectable from the edge of the courtyard surface (396) which had apparently respected the building's walls. The inferred size of the building was *c* 12 m × 6 m, with two interior partitions represented by rubble footings 150 and 152. Incorporated within the partition wall 152 was a small tile-on-edge oven (151) with a heavily burnt surface. There was no evidence of burning in the northern bay, although a spread of burning (167) ran back from the south side of the same partition. Two sherds of 13th- to 16th-century pottery were recovered from the occupation deposits of the building, and a horseshoe was retrieved from the matrix of wall 150 (SF 363, Fig. 3.24.140).

The central courtyard (*Figs 2.3 & 2.16*)

A spread of coarse flinty gravel in a silty clay matrix (396) was identified over the central area of the large island. It sealed the remains of Phase 2 Buildings O, N and Q, and respected Phase 3 Buildings J, I and K to the west and Building B to the east. It extended north to a line between the north-east corner of Building J and the western wall of Building A6. To the north of this line was a contemporary layer of silty loam (237). Similarly, the surface ran to an edge between the east wall of A6 and Building B; north of this was a silty clay layer (170). The surface was also traced to within 3 m of the edge of the eastern arm of the moat (279) to the south of Building B, but no definite edge or border survived.

The western area (*Fig. 2.19*)

The area of the island to the west of the building complex appears to have been devoid of structures or a metalled surface. A substantial cut feature (320), interpreted as a possible pond, *c* 5.0 m across, was identified during the initial investigation of the site and a small trench was machine-excavated through the silty clay fill. No structural evidence was found, nor were any finds recovered. During the topsoil stripping, possible midden dumps were identified to the north of feature 320.

Buildings J and I (*Figs 2.3, 2.17. Pl. 2.4*)

Building J was situated approximately 5.0 m south of the west end of Building A1. It was defined by partially robbed rubble footings (365, 444) averaging 0.60 m wide, and associated robber trenches (362, 347, 364 and 366). The footing (446) of the south wall (444) was seen to be slightly narrower than the overlying wall. The excavator considered this a possible indication of a rebuild of the south end of the building. Evidence of external structural details was confined to a single buttress footing (217) against the east wall.

Internally, the division of space was suggested by the presence of two short partitions, represented by footing 370 and robber trench 369. A thin spread of mortar (368) was revealed in the north-west corner of the building, confined by robber trench 369. Otherwise a levelling layer (363) of pale brown clay silt was identified over the interior, although the absence of finds on or within this layer support the likelihood that this layer represented a bedding layer for a flagged or tiled floor. The apparent subsidence in the southern part of the building may have been the result of the underlying Phase 2 drain (361).

A small tile-on-edge hearth (1104) was identified, set against the mid-point of the western wall, although there was no evidence for an associated fireplace.

The finds from this building were almost exclusively associated with Phase 5 demolition deposits, and are described below.

Building I abutted the south-west side of Building J, and was defined by stone footings one course deep (283, 341 and 389), averaging 0.60 m wide. In the south-west corner was a stone-lined pit *c* 0.40 m deep (346; Pl. 2.4). Its two internal sides were lined with slabs of limestone, while on the north-west side the inside facing of the wall of the building (341) was carried down to form the side of the pit. Interestingly, the south-west side of the pit was not lined by a corresponding deepening of the south-west wall (283 (robber trench 344). A small tile-on-edge hearth (352) was identified in the centre of the building footprint. Two broadly similar sandy loam surfaces were identified, 380 to the north of the hearth, 350 to the south. It seems likely that these represent bedding layers for a flagged or tiled floor.

Building K (Figs 2.3, 2.18)

The south-west side of the courtyard was bordered by Building K which backed onto the edge of the moat, and measured 42 m × 8.0 m. The building's walls had been heavily robbed, but could be identified from stretches of 0.65 m wide limestone rubble foundations (309, 311, 1183) and shallow robber trenches (305–8, 310, 313–4, 327, 477–8, 483). There was very little debris associated with the demolition of this building, which may be related to its construction, but could be the result of the inevitable damage caused by topsoil stripping, for at its southern end the robber trenches had all but disappeared. An absence of clay roof tile in the demolition debris may indicate that the building was thatched or possibly roofed with wooden shingles. There was one identified entrance, off-centre on the north-east wall, its west side defined by a post-setting incorporated into footing 1183. Two rooms or bays of *c* 4.0 m in length were identified at either end, delimited by partitions 307 and 314. The floor throughout Building K was (where it survived) a mix of gravel and flint cobbles (398) set in a silt loam that contained some small fragments of floor tile (388).

A short length of wall (282, Fig, 2.17) abutted the south-west side of Building I and ran for just over 4 m towards the north-west corner of Building K. This may have represented part of a boundary wall of the courtyard, enclosing the area between the two buildings. The wall ended in a slight pier which may indicate the position of a gatepost. The wall appeared to be incorporated into Building H in Phase 4.

Phase 3/2 (early to mid 14th century)

This sub-phase involved the construction of new hearths within Room A1 and the addition of a small bay (A3) to the north-west end of the room. A new courtyard was laid to the north of Building A1.

Building A1 and Room A3 (Figs 2.3, 2.10, 2.15)

Room A3 had an external length of 4.8 m with walls (64, 640, 861) that had the same construction and dimensions as those of the Phase 2 Building A1. Wall 640 was partly removed by robber trench 582 (Fig. 2.15, Section 76). The rubble foundations were not pitched, as those of the cross-wing extension were, which could suggest that this extension represented a separate building episode. The walls were bonded into those of the main Building A1 and presumably were carried to the same height.

To link Room A3 and Building A1, the internal surface was raised by a succession of dumped layers (Fig. 2.15, Section 76: cxts 578, 850, 851, 881, 883, 1031), probably the material excavated from the construction trenches for the walls. The process of levelling up seems to have taken place during the construction of the bay, for sandwiched between the layers of dump was a layer of construction debris (Section 76: 882). A worked boar's tusk (SF 321) was also recovered from this deposit. A small central hearth (796) with associated burning was found in room A3, possibly used during the construction process. Once the floor level in Room A3 was up to that of Building A1, a 4.0 m gap was knocked through the original west wall (625) of A1 to link the two spaces. A step (626) was inserted slightly to the east of the original wall line, and further material (554) was dumped into Room A3. No evidence of a finished floor surface was found *in situ*. The disturbed remnant of a tiled surface (985) up to 1.0 m wide was revealed immediately east of step 626 and west of the central hearth of Building A1.

Subsequent to the structural alterations the old hearth (1077) in Building A1 was robbed out and a new hearth (context 1078 – Fig. 2.15, Section 76) constructed immediately to the south. What form the hearth took is conjectural owing to the later robbing of the feature. However, since the two later surviving hearths in the hall were of tile-on-edge construction set in a shallow pit, flush with the floor, it is reasonable to suggest that 1078 was of similar construction. A coin of Edward I (SF13) was recovered from the fill (22) at the bottom of the hearth's construction pit.

The remains of a very patchy occupation layer (1070) were identified against the north-west wall of Building A1, overlain by an equally patchy layer of pinkish mortar (1068), possibly the slight remains of a floor layer. Contained within this was an iron trefoil finial (Fig. 3.20.74: SF 311), possibly from an interior fitting.

The Phase 3/2 hearth (1078) was in due course replaced by another hearth just to its north, of tile-on-edge construction, with a kerb of roof tiles (1005) set into a mottled layer (1007). The floor area of the high end of the hall, particularly around the hearth, had shown signs of wear immediately prior to this phase and, apparently to level up the surface, a layer of grey clay loam (816) (Fig. 2.15, Section 76) was deposited, which abutted the comparatively unworn

Plate 2.4 The storage pit in Building 1. (Phase 3 – early 14th century.)

surface at the east end of the hall (866). After this a floor of hard lime mortar was laid (1017), which survived in patches. There was no evidence that the floor in Building A1 was ever tiled or flagged, and the wear around the hearth in Phase 4 (see below) would seem to support this contention.

External features (*Fig. 2.10*)

A substantial gravel and flint layer (1086) was laid to the north of the main building, respecting the added Room A3 and the Phase 2 Building D. The remains of a slight wall (1102) were identified bordering the western limit of the courtyard, between the north-west corner of A3 and Building D.

Three small, evenly spaced postholes (1097–9) were recorded, cut through the yard surface just to the north of Building A1. They were located 1.30 m out from the wall of the hall and may have been part of a scaffold used to repair or effect an alteration to that stretch of wall.

Phase 4 (late 14th to early 15th century) (Fig. 2.4)

Summary of development

The apogee of the development of the manor was reached, reflecting the changing aspirations of the family. The expanded kitchen (A12) was linked to the cross wing, and the storehouse A7 was replaced with what is interpreted as a private chapel (A11), which it is suggested would have been accessed from the cross-wing first floor. The north part of the island was cleared of the old buildings D and E; in their place was built an enclosed garden with a pentice (A13). A possible store room (A14) relating to the new garden was built against the west end of the main hall. To the south, the agricultural complex was expanded with barns and stables (principally G, H and C) that now ringed the island and divided the large central courtyard in two.

Building A1 (*Figs 2.4, 2.10, 2.15, Pl. 2.5*)

Within the main building the central hearth was again rebuilt. Its construction trench cut through the old hearth slightly to its south-west, such that some of the tiles-on-edge of the previous hearth survived *in situ*. The new hearth (563, Plate 2.5), set in bedding layer 1019 within cut 813, measured *c* 1.35 m by 1.25 m and was of the same construction as the old hearth, that is of roof tiles set on edge. These were set at right-angles to the tiles of the earlier hearth and edged with a limestone kerb. Layer 814 (Fig. 2.15, Section 76), consisting of clay and white silts, may either represent the demolition from an earlier hearth, now completely reused, or bedding for hearth 563. Against the south-east side of the hearth 563 was a base of limestone flags some 0.50 m wide (885) set into a silty clay deposit (884). Adjacent to the north side of the hearth and still *in situ* was the remains of an iron upright *c* 6 mm square in section and set *c* 0.09 m into the ground. There was no direct evidence of an upright on the other side of the hearth.

At the lower end of the main building, approximately 4.3 m from the east end wall, was a substantial limestone-packed post setting (618), measuring 1.0 m in diameter × 0.10 m deep, set to accommodate a post approximately 0.35 m thick (Fig. 2.15: Section 76). The post setting was further strengthened by a packing of broken roof tiles pitched in towards the stones. Three further stone- and tile-packed postholes (862, 867, 868), averaging 0.14 m in diameter and 0.25 m deep were located on the north-east side of the room and each cut through the mortar floor at that point (866). There was no evidence of corresponding posts on the south side of the room.

One other feature of significance was identified. This consisted of a vestigial gully containing a line of roof tiles laid flat (865), extending from the east side of the central posthole (618) in an arc to the north wall of the hall. Although badly disturbed, the tiles appeared originally to have been set into a mortar bed. In places this feature had a depth of 0.07 m with a slight V-shaped profile. No evidence of a corresponding feature was recorded on the opposite (south side) of the room.

Evidence of wear around the main hearth was indicated by an accumulation of ashy silt (548) around its north, south and east sides. An assemblage of material was recovered from this layer, including three pins (SF 90, Fig. 3.13.95), pottery and bone, along with an early 15th-century groat (SF 94) and a fragment of post-medieval glass (intrusive). This layer merged with a general spread of dark grey silty clay (593 = 1002) which was seen to respect the three postholes 862, 867, and 868. The layer produced a large number of objects, including two jettons (SFs 295 and 297) and one coin (SF 298) dated to the late 13th or early 14th century.

To the north-west of the hearth a silty clay layer (622), with some evidence of a tile-on-edge revetment (799), overlay the Phase 3/2 tiled surface 985.

Although a comparatively large number of small finds were associated with this phase in the hall, only 23 sherds of pottery were recovered, none of which was diagnostic.

Rooms A9 and A10 (*Figs 2.4, 2.15*)

A sequence of floor make up layers, floors layers and occupation debris was found inside rooms A9 and A10. The fragmentary nature of these layers indicated extensive wear and frequent patching. Therefore the chronological dating of these layers is uncertain, beyond defining apparent end dates for the sequence as a whole.

Overlying fragmentary patches of floor make-up (not illustrated) was a floor of redeposited chalk head (733, 923, 44, 41 – not illustrated) that could be traced throughout both rooms and the intervening passage. In the larger of the two rooms (A9) there

Plate 2.5 Central hearth 563 in Building A1. (Phase 4 – late 14th century.)

was evidence that this floor had been repaired by patches of flinty gravel (739, 746 – not illustrated) and it was overlain by a patchy accumulation of occupation debris (639 – Fig.2.15, Section 76), which was rich in small fishbones and eggshell fragments.

***Building A11** (Figs 2.4, 2.14, 2.15, Plate 2.3)*

The building overlay the footprint of Phase 3 Building A7, attached to the south-east corner of Room A10.

The surviving wall foundations (122) were of large rubble limestone, 0.85 m wide, set in shallow foundation trenches 0.15–0.20 m deep, bonded with a yellowish silty clay. The southern wall had been partly removed by robber trench 123 (Fig. 2.15, Section 73), and the northern wall was also truncated (robber trench 116). The western wall was represented by robber trench 121.

Up to three courses of stone survived *in situ*, but unlike with Room A10, no wall superstructure was evident, possibly implying that the internal floor surface was set higher than the adjacent building (A10). This could explain why no evidence of a doorway was found. The debris (144) from the destruction of the earlier building (A7) was contained within the new building and appears to have been used to seal the earlier structure's footings. An iron buckle (SF 74 Fig. 3.23.116) was found within this material, along with some floor tile fragments (see Chapter 4).

***Building A12** (Figs 2.4, 2.13 & 2.15)*

Building W was demolished and replaced by a rectangular building (A12). The building was defined by shallow limestone footings (608, 538), which were extended (18, 114) in the south-west to form a passage linking the building to the passage between Rooms A9 and A10. Within the main body of A12, an earth floor was identified, (23); this respected an internal wall (13), which divided the building into two unequal bays. The floor layer contained a large quantity of bone, oyster shell and fragments of floor and roof tile, and evidence showed that the surface of the floor rose by approximately 0.10 m during the building's lifetime. Where the floor extended into the corridor it changed to a sandy grey loam (33) and this difference was sufficiently abrupt to suggest that there was a doorway or screen separating the passage from the southern bay.

The larger southern bay was dominated by a tile-on-edge hearth (7) measuring 2.0 m by 2.3 m, situated off-centre to the west but on the same alignment as the building. The surface of the hearth was approximately 0.05 m above the original level of the floor (23). On the west side of this hearth was a heavily burnt limestone base (30), similar to that associated with the central hearth in A1. Set into the eastern corners of this bay were two ovens (4 and 177). Oven 177 had been badly disturbed but seems to have had a diameter of *c* 0.80 m with a floor of tiles laid flat. The ground surface associated with it was burnt orange and red. Oven 4 was fairly well preserved and had an internal diameter of 1.1 m, with a floor of limestone slabs with rubble limestone walls. The partially robbed footings of a 0.75 m wide wall (112) were identified immediately to the east of the hearth base 7, and west of the ovens. How it related to the hearth or ovens is unclear.

Within the northern bay, the floor layer (535, overlain by rubble 612) was a sandy loam with small fragments of limestone embedded in it, which represent the demolition debris from the earlier building (W). It also contained a socketed iron axe head (SF95, Fig. 3.16.1). No other features were identified in the bay.

The remains of the walls of Building A12 were too fragmentary to determine the position of any doorway other than that into the corridor leading to the domestic range. However, immediately outside the southern side of the building there was a spread of occupation material (155), similar to the material inside, which could suggest an entrance at this point.

During the use of this building the original hearth (7) was replaced by another, cut directly into the old one. This new hearth (6) was 2.4 m long and its width, indeterminate owing to later disturbance, was a minimum of 1.5 m. It was constructed of pitched tiles bordered by a kerb of limestone blocks. An apron of tiles-on-edge (31) abutted its north side.

A substantial quantity of pottery was recovered from the building, much of which comprised cooking and domestic wares (see Chapter 3). Six cooking pots, six kitchenware vessels, a bowl, four jugs, two bottles and a cup were found.

***The north-east courtyard** (Figs 2.13, 2.15)*

A new yard (519, 621) in bedding layer 844, 972 was laid out, enclosed by the cross-wing and Building A12 and Area F. The yard sealed the robber trench (1084) and its fill 1109) of the earlier wall 1135 (Fig. 2.15, Section 76). The northern wall of the new Building A12 was constructed partly over the drain associated with the earlier detached Building W. A shallow depression (504) was identified against the south of Area F, which appeared to link to a drainage or eavesdrip gully (518), draining into the moat to the north. This may have been an alternative method to remove excess water from the enclosed yard area.

***Structure A14** (Figs 2.4, 2.15, 2.19, 2.20)*

A rectangular structure A14, defined by partially robbed limestone rubble footings (585, 686) defining an internal area of 6.5 m × 3.5 m, was added to the west end of the domestic range (A3), built against the perimeter wall 679. The floor (673) consisted of a layer of brown silt loam, heavily mottled with white clay. Two lead cames were recovered from this material (SF 198), although, given their provenance, they are likely to be residual. No other internal features were identified, and no evidence was found of an access from this building to room A3.

A further slight wall foundation (678, Fig. 2.20), *c* 0.40 m wide, oriented north-west to south-east, was revealed to the west of A14. This may represent an additional outbuilding, enclosing an area 2.10 m by 4.50 m, inserted into the south-west corner of the perimeter.

An extensive area of gravel and flint (732) survived around the northern side of the main domestic range. A small rectangular structure (572, Fig. 2.20), which was rather crudely constructed of a single width of limestone rubble, was identified, situated against the north-east wall of the domestic range. Whether this represented the footings of a small structure against the north wall of the hall, or a garden feature, was not clear.

The garden (Figs 2.19, 2.20)

Although there was considerable disturbance to this area from the topsoil stripping, the surviving evidence suggests that this entire area north and west of the domestic range and the cross wing was redesigned as an enclosed area. Buildings D and E were demolished and the area immediately south of the north edge of the moat was levelled up with a dump of sandy loam (573 – not illustrated). The area was bounded on the north side by a limestone wall, which only survived as footing 751 and a possible robber trench 652, extending from the northern corner of cross-wing Room A4. The footing was interrupted by a gap, possibly representing access to the bridge to the north.

The west end of the garden wall was represented by a footing of similar proportions (679) extending the line from the west end of the Phase 4 hall extension A14 by approximately 4.5 m, before turning to the north (697). It is suggested that this wall continued north to the moat edge and turned east to link with footing 751, although as the north-west corner of the island was not systematically investigated, this contention remains conjectural.

Structure A13 (Figs 2.4, 2.20)

The structure was defined by a pair of insubstantial stone walls (591), 0.20–30 m in width, extending north from the north wall of room A1. The full extent of both walls was traced by the footings or robber trenches (650, 651) to a point just before the line of the perimeter wall (751/652); the intervening gap was filled with a drain (998), consisting of a line of upturned ridge tiles, immediately to the south of robber trench 652.

The partly surviving floor of Structure A13 consisted of a layer of sand (980), overlaid by a spread of lime mortar (589), a bedding for floor tiles. Two complete examples were found *in situ* (SF 181 and 182 – Type CLXXXI – see Chapter 4), set square to the western walls of the structure, and impressions of approximately 12 others were revealed in the surface of the mortar.

The structure enclosed a small cloister-like courtyard of gravel and flint (561), alongside the west wall of Room A4.

The central courtyard (Fig. 2.4)

On the south-west side of the house, on either side of Room A6, the division between the central courtyard surface and the two unsurfaced areas of silty clay loam, possibly gardens (120, 140) first laid out in Phase 3/1, were maintained. In Phase 4, their boundaries were more formally defined by partially robbed stone walls (127 to the west of Room A6, 187 to the east). Both walls were noted as overlying the latest courtyard surface of flinty gravel (118). A posthole (1054) was noted, cutting the edge of 118 along the line of wall 127, 0.75 m from wall 821 of Room A6. This may represent a gate giving access from the courtyard into area 120.

Building T (Figs 2.4, 2.19)

Insubstantial remains of a small building or enclosure were identified between (and respecting both) Building J and the wall of A14 to the north. It was defined by insubstantial and partly robbed rubble footings (271, 1047, 1048), which defined an area of approximately 7 m × 3 m. Two postholes (264, 408 – not illustrated), possibly defining a gateway or doorway *c* 1.0 m wide, were identified just outside the line of the east wall. No internal floor surface or other features were identified; however immediately beyond the west wall was a dumped layer containing a high concentration of oyster and cockle shells (1049).

Buildings H and G (Figs 2.4, 2.18)

Buildings H and G were constructed, apparently as a pair, effectively dividing the central courtyard into two. Building H abutted the south end of Building I while Building G abutted the north-west side of Building C. Access from the outer to the inner area was evidently through the gap between H and G, approximately 3.4 m wide. This was surfaced with crushed limestone and flint chippings (401), and incorporated a limestone block kerb and gutter on its western side (496).

From the surviving deposits, the two buildings differed in their construction and internal disposition. Building G was defined by partially robbed insubstantial 0.50 m wide limestone footings (292, 293, 295) laid directly onto the Phase 3 courtyard surface (396), which also formed the internal floor surface. The wall lines were completed by robber trenches 292, 396 and 494. No internal partitions or other structural elements were identified, although a pitched stone hardstanding (294) was set along the exterior of the north wall.

Building H, in contrast, was more substantial, as indicated by wall foundations 273, 280, 291, 340, averaging 0.70 m wide, set in shallow foundation trenches, surmounted by walls which stepped in to

0.50 m wide, and robber trench 280. The Phase 3/1 wall 282, which abutted Building I, was possibly retained as an internal partition, creating a small bay or room at the north-west end of the building. A stone-edged, stone-lined drain (343) was revealed, running the width of the bay and extending beyond the end wall (340). Two other slight partitions (437, 438) divided the rest of the building into three unequal bays, of lengths 10.8 m, 4.1 m and 4.8 m. The floor surface within the building consisted of a layer that varied from a light yellowish brown silt loam (375) at the western end to an orange sandy loam, with natural iron staining (417), throughout the rest of the building. The floor surface overlay the Phase 3/1 yard surface (396).

Alterations to Building I (*Figs 2.4, 2.17*)

The stone-lined pit in Building I (Fig. 2.17) probably went out of use with the construction of Building H and its opening was now blocked. The backfill of the pit appears to have been sealed by a layer of grey silty clay (350, 380) within Building I. The small, central tile-on-edge hearth (352) was possibly constructed at the same time. Only a single piece of 14th- to 15th-century pottery was found within the interior deposits of the building.

Building C (*Figs 2.4, 2.18*)

A large rectangular structure with a porch on its western side was identified in the south-eastern corner of the large island. It was built on top of the courtyard surface (396) and therefore could represent the latest in the complex of buildings in the southern half of the island in this phase, although no finds were recovered from the building contexts to support this contention. The building was represented by fragmentary rubble footings (334, 392, 1212) and a very shallow robber trench (485) up 0.40 m wide. Since no evidence survived for gable end walls the length of this building is inferred from the scatter of roof tile debris (393) which appeared to respect the west wall and a hypothetical north wall line. If the location of the porch, represented by a stone footing (334), is assumed to mark the centre of the building, then the southern wall can be correspondingly inferred, which places it just to the north of the approximate edge of the southern corner of the moat. This gives an overall, albeit conjectural length for the building of 33.0 m, and a width of 12.0 m. Internally one substantial postpad (394) and another disturbed postpad (491) were found, suggesting that the building was probably aisled.

Phase 5 (mid to late 15th century) (Fig. 2.5)

Summary of development

The phase principally concerns the demolition of the manor complex. The archaeological evidence for the speed of this process is very limited, although there is some evidence for the short-term alternative use of part of the complex, especially Room A4. Elsewhere, a single new building (M) was identified, which (from documentary inferences) is suggested could have been a culver house or dovecote. Similarly, there is some documentary evidence to show that Building C may have survived as late as the end of the 16th century.

Final activity in the domestic range

Archaeological evidence of the process of abandonment and demolition of the buildings was inevitably compromised, particularly in areas away from the main domestic range and cross-wing, by modern disturbance and the machine stripping of the topsoil. However, within the limited areas excavated, some stratigraphic sequences post-dating the buildings' occupation were identified.

Within rooms A1 and A3, the latest Phase 4 floor layers were sealed by a general layer of rubble (186) containing plaster and tile fragments and numerous artefacts (see Chapters 3 and 4). This layer extended to the north of the range footprint (south of room A1 the same material was recorded as 119). Within Rooms A9 and A10 to the east, layers of silty clay and rubble (511, 520) contained high proportions of plaster, presumably collapsed from the wall faces. In the north of Room A9 a similar layer (590 – not illustrated) produced plaster, nails and evident signs of burning.

Further burnt material was evident in room A4 to the north, overlying the accumulated floor deposits of layer 600 (see above), although this material appeared to be beech and oak charcoal derived from young trees, not structural timbers (see Chapter 5). The charcoal-rich spread was observed to extend over the footprint of Room A5, sealing the robber trenches of the wall.

Subsequently a layer of sand (510) was deposited, overlain by a thick layer of demolition rubble (500). This layer, although somewhat disturbed by later activity, appeared to extend to a point close to the possible north bridge.

The agricultural buildings

While evidence of demolition was evident over the footprint of the domestic range, a spread of roof tile (242) was found in the northern bay of Building B (see Figure 2.15), lying in a way that suggests the roof had collapsed through dereliction rather than demolition. Spreads of roof tiles were also noted around the footprint of Building C.

Building M (*Fig. 2.5*)

Building M was situated within the footprint of the west end of Building H. The slight stone footings appeared to be set into the demolition material of Building H. No internal features or surfaces were identified in association with this building.

Chapter 3: Finds

POTTERY

by P Page and C Tremolet

Editor's note

A total of 2915 sherds are recorded in the pottery assemblage. The analysis was carried out shortly after the excavation, using an adapted version of the system devised for 1968–76 Oxford sites (Mellor 1980, fiche EO6). Sherd counts were used to record the fabrics from each provenance within each phase, and the fabric type series is set out in Table 3.1. Fabrics were divided into four main groups:

Group IA	shelly limestone
Group IB	oolitic and other limestone
Group II	flint
Group III	sand

Modern fabrics and residual sherds were grouped together (fabric number 99); this category contained several sherds of St Neot's type ware, and some probable Iron Age and Romano-British pottery. Table 3.2 and Table 3.3 show fabric quantities by phase, and by building, room or area. Tables 3.1–3.3 were not part of the authors' original version of the report, and have been compiled subsequently by Kate Atherton from the records in archive. During the final stages of preparation of this volume in the spring of 2004, Table 3.1 was checked and revised by Carole Wheeler and Maureen Mellor to reflect the current fabric codes and names within the Oxfordshire medieval pottery series (Mellor 1994) and the Museum of London type series. Classification of forms followed the systems developed at OAU at the time the analysis was carried out (Haldon 1977; Mellor 1980), with the addition of fine tablewares which include thin walled sherds, richly glazed both internally and externally, known as Tudor types. Full pottery records are available in the project archive.

Funding for post-excavation at the time was limited, and the pottery report was therefore based on a simplified catalogue, which summarised the pottery from each phase and building/context group, and described a selection of key sherds. The entries are organised in order of fabrics, with the fabric identified by fabric group and number (for example, FIII.46 is Fabric 46, which falls within fabric group III).

The pottery illustrations (Figs 3.1–3.6) were arranged by phase, building and fabric type in order to show the forms and decoration associated with different production centres. Figure 3.1 covers pottery from Phases 1 and 2; Figure 3.2 illustrates pottery from the Phase 3 construction and early occupation of the remodelled manor of the early 14th century, and sub-phase 3/2, contexts associated with the construction of Room A3 (western extension to the main hall, Building A1). Figure 3.3 illustrates a selection of pottery from the Phase 3 and 4 occupation of the manor, arranged by building, room or area; some pottery from demolition levels is also included. Figure 3.4 is a selection from the large assemblage of pottery from Building A12 (Phase 4), the latest kitchen. Figure 3.5 illustrates pottery associated with Phase 4 works and Phase 5 demolition in the garden area north of the main range of buildings, the construction and demolition of Structure A13 (pentice), the latest use of Rooms A9 and A10 (the service rooms), and agricultural Building H. Figure 3.6 is pottery from stratified and unstratified demolition layers.

Catalogue

Phase 1 (late 12th–early 13th century) *(Fig. 3.1)*

Building P

The pottery from this building in the pre-moat settlement included four cooking pots, one dated to the Iron Age and therefore presumably residual; also found were decorated sherds almost certainly from pitchers.

FII.20	Cooking pot rim (Fig. 3.1.3); Kitchen ware base.
FIII.41	Cooking pot rim with applied strips (Fig. 3.1.1–2); Base; Body sherds, 1 grooved deco, dk green glaze; 1 white slip deco, lt green glaze.
FIII.99	Cooking pot rim, probably Iron Age.

Building R

Only one recognisable form was recovered from this building in the pre-moat settlement.

FIII.62	Shoulder.

External surfaces and dump layers

The other contexts in this phase associated with the pre-moat settlement yielded a cooking pot, a deep-sided bowl, a shallow dish, a jug and a number of Brill-type decorated sherds from jugs and pitchers. A residual sherd of St. Neot's-type was also recovered.

FII.20	Cooking pot rim (Fig. 3.1.6); Kitchen ware rim, possibly a deep-sided bowl (Fig. 3.1.7); Bases × 2.
FIII.41	Shallow dish with pinched lip and combed deco, glazed lt green (Fig. 3.1.4); Jug base (Fig. 3.1.5); Body sherd, orange glaze.
FIII.46	Body sherds, 1 applied strips and mot green glaze; 1 reg and horiz. grooves, mot green glaze; 1 mot green glaze
FIII.60	Base.
FIII.63	Cooking pot base.
99	Incl. body sherd, St. Neot's type.

Oven (Phase 1? or later)

Few sherds were associated with the oven.

FII.20	Kitchen ware rim; Base.
FII.21	Body sherd.
FIII.41	Kitchen ware rim; Body sherds, 1 white slip 'trellis' deco; 1 mot orange glaze; Base.
FIII.69	Body sherd.

Phase 2 (mid to late 13th century) *(Fig. 3.1)*

The moat upcast

[Editor's note. The construction of the moat defines the start of Phase 2, and the pottery from the upcast was catalogued with

Table 3.1 Pottery fabric descriptions and parallels

Fabric	Comparisons	Dates	Frequency	Inclusions	Potting techniques	Forms	Decoration	Munsell Code	Other parallels
Group II Flint fabrics									
20	OXAQ	Late 12–early 15C	Mod	Coarse to v coarse angular grey flint, irreg limestone, occ voids	Coil-made Th 8–10	Cp; Bowl; KW	Combed, incised, thumbed	Ext reddish yellow (5YR/6/6); Core: lt grey (7.5YR/7/0); Int: v dark grey (2.5YR/3/0)	Abingdon type C; Newbury type; Tetsworth; Wallingford
21	OXAQ	Late 12–early 15C	Mod	Coarse to v coarse angular grey flint, irreg limestone, quartz, occ voids		Kw	Combed	Ext pinkish grey (7.5YR/6/2); Core & int: lt grey (10YR/7/1)	Lewknor
22	?	?type 12–13C	Mod	Coarse grey limestone, angular grey flint		Colander		Pink (7.5YR/7/4)	
23	?prehistoric		Mod	Coarse					
Group III Sand or no grains visible									
40	?	glaze 14–15C	Mod	Fine grey/white grains. Occ red brown pellet. Sparse mica	Wheel thrown Th. 5	Jug; bottle	Incised; glazed	Core: grey (7.5YR/6/0)	
41	OX162	12–early 14C	Abundant	White rounded quartz, grey, white, sub rounded quartz	Wheel thrown; Th 5	Cp; jugs; shallow dish; bowl; Kw; bottle	White slip; incised; stamped; combed; glaze	Core: reddish yellow (5YR/3/3)	Tetsworth
42	Misc	?							
43	Cheam white ware or N French fabric	?1350–1500	Sparse	Angular white grey quartz, sub-rounded quartz	Wheel thrown. Th 5		Glaze, incised	Core: white (2.5YR/8/2)	?Surrey border ware
44	OXAG	Late 11–early 15 C			Coil-made; Th: 4–9	Kw, Cp; fine cistern	Grooves; thumbed; thin strips; white slip; wide strips		
45	?	?12–13C	Abundant	Fine, sub-rounded voids and quartz				Grey (2.5YR/5/0)	?possibly continental
46	?OXAM	Mid 13–15 C	Sparse-abundant	Fine red-brown and colourless grains, occ red-brown mineral	Wheel thrown. Occ knife trimmed; Th 4	Jugs; Cp; Kw; skillet; bottle; bung-hole; jar	Plain & rouletted strips; slip; incised; glaze	Very pale brown (10YR/8/4)	?Banbury types; ?Abingdon type D; ?Wallingford
47	OXBG	Late 13–15/16 C	Mod	Red-brown, white sub-rounded quartz; occ coarse grain	Wheel thrown; Th 3–7		Glaze, incised	Very pale brown (10YR/7.5/3)	A Farnborough Hill; Surrey type; Abingdon type N; Newbury; Reading
48	Misc	?							
49	OXCC	*c* 1300	Sparse	Fine-coarse red-brown iron ore, occ Colourless quartz.	Wheel thrown; Th 4	Jug	Slip; glaze	White (2.5YR/8/2)	Saintonge

50	?	12–14C	Mod	Sub-rounded white glassy quartz	Wheel thrown; Th 4		Glaze, incised	Dk grey (10YR/4/1); Core: light grey (10YR/7/1); Int: v pale brown (10YR/7/3)	
51	CH51	Late 13–mid 16 C	Mod	Fine quartz, occ black iron ore	Wheel thrown; Th 4–8	Jug; bottle; storage jar; fine, table ware	Slip; applied strips; incised; glaze	Reddish yellow (7.5YR/7/6)	
53	?		Abundant	Fine white grey quartz, red-brown iron ore				Brown (7.5YR/5/4)	
54	OXBN	14–16 C	Abundant	Fine white, grey quartz	Wheel thrown; Th 4	Lobed dishes; fine table ware	Rouletted strips; glaze	Very pale brown (10YR/8/3)	Tudor Green
55	?	Late medieval	Abundant	Fine, white, grey quartz	Wheel thrown; Th 8		Glaze	Pink (7.5YR/8/4)	Surrey borderware
57	?	13–15C	Mod	Sub-rounded & angular quartz, red-brown ore	Wheel thrown; Th 7		Glaze	Reddish yellow (7.5YR/7/6)	
58	CBW – Coarse Surrey/Hants border ware	1270–1500	Mod	Sub-rounded grey, white & colourless quartz, occ. Sub rounded red & black grains	Wheel thrown; Th 7	Cp	Incised; glazed	White (7.5YR/80)	
59	Surrey border ware	15 C	Sparse – mod	Sub-rounded grey, white grains	Wheel thrown; Th 4–7	Fine table ware; lobed cup; lobed sih; jug	Incised; glazed	Core: pink (7.5YR/8/4)	Tudor type
60	NE3	Mid 13–16 C	Abundant	Fine-coarse sub-rounded grey, colourless quartz & quartzite	Wheel thrown; Th 5–6	Bottle; bowl	Slip; incised; applied strips; glaze	Very pale brown (10YR/8/3)	Like Soundess kiln, Nettlebed 1982. At Hamel
61	OXAM	14–16 C			Wheel thrown; coil-made; Th 3–6	Bottles; jugs	Grooves; finger tipped; thumbed; white slip; slim white strips		
62	?		Abundant	Sub-rounded grey, white quartz, occ limestone	Wheel thrown; Th 6	Kw		Ext: very pale brown (10YR/7/3); Int: very dark grey (7.5YR/3/0)	
63	?	Mid 13–16 C	Abundant	Fine-mod grey, white quartz	Wheel thrown; Th 5–6	Jug; Cp; Kw; dripping pan	Incised; applied thumbed strips; slip; glaze	Ext & int: reddish yellow (7.5YR/7/6); Core: Lt red (2.5YR/6/8)	SE Oxon type
64	?OXBX	14–15 C	Mod	Coarse grog, red-brown and white grains	Wheel thrown; Th 6–12		Glaze	Reddish yellow (5YR/7/8)	?Brill type. At Hamel

Table 3.1 (Continued)

Fabric	Comparisons	Dates	Frequency	Inclusions	Potting techniques	Forms	Decoration	Munsell Code	Other parallels
65	?		Mod	Red, brown, white grains	Wheel thrown; Th 5–6		Incised; glaze	Ext: Reddish yellow (5YR/7/6); Core: grey (2.5YR/6/0); Int: (7.5YR/5/2)	
66	Rouen type	13–14 C	Abundant	Fine red brown grains	Wheel thrown; Th 2–Jug 4		Slip; glaze	Pink (7.5YR/8/4)	
67	KING – Surrey whiteware, Kingston type	1230–1400	Abundant	Sub-rounded grey, white and colourless grains	Wheel thrown; Th 6–Bottle 8			Pinkish white (7.5YR/8/2)	?Surrey type
68	BORDY – Surrey/Hants border white ware	1550–1700	Mod	Fine to coarse grey-white and red-brown grains and red iron ore			Slip; glaze	Very pale brown (10YR/7/3)	? Surrey type
69	KING – as 67 above		Abundant well-sorted	Sub-round grey, white and colourless grains, occasional red iron ore	Wheel thrown; Th 5– Jug; bowls 6		Applied rouletted strips; slip glaze	White (10 YR/8/2)	
70	SW Oxon type		Abundant	Sub-rounded grey, white and colourless quartz; occ. coarse limestone				Light grey (10Y/7/1)	
71	Oxford redware	late 15–16 C	Abundant	Fine colourless grains			Glaze	External: dark grey (10YR/4/1) Core: lt red (2.5YR/6/8)	
72	KING – as 67 above		Moderate	Sub-rounded angular red-brown and glassy quartz; occasional red iron ore			Glaze	Int: pink (5YR/8/3)	? Surrey ware

Fabrics 43, 58, 67, 68, 69, 72 identified using the Museum of London type series and with advice from Lucy Whittingham and Jacqui Pearce. Other fabrics identified by Carole Wheeler with advice from Maureen Mellor.

Table 3.2 Pottery fabric traditions by phase

Fabric	Phase 1	Phase 2	Phase 3	Phases 3–4	Phases 3–5	Phase 4	Phase 5	Unphased	Total
Residual/Modern	11	4	10	1	2	13	33	13	87
Group II									
20	57	90	42	2	10	85	45	5	336
21		3	5		2				10
22						1			1
23		4				1			5
Group III									
South-East Oxford									
41	25	109	120	27	37	207	158	25	708
59			10	5	10	29	67	12	133
Brill									
44	6	44	9	2	3	21	12	1	98
46	5	65	174	10	16	296	164	29	759
53	4	1			1			6	
55		1	1				5	1	8
57		1	1		1	4	13	1	21
58					2	1	4		7
62	2	19	1			1	1		24
64							1		1
65						3			3
69		10	21	1	1	6	30	4	73
Surrey									
43			2			4	3	4	13
47		6	2			13	5		26
54			1		1	8	15	1	26
67		1	1				5		7
68						1	3	3	7
Henley/Nettlebed									
51		6	11		3	18	84	7	129
60	1	1	2			16	37	1	58
61		4	46			43	16	1	110
63	2	19	34	14	30	45	34	10	188
Other									
40		1	1			2	6		10
70	1	3	3				3		10
71						1			1
42					1	3			4
45		3	3				8		14
48							1		1
50			2			1	4		7
72					1				1
Foreign									
49		1	12			1		2	16
66		1				1			2
Frechen							2	1	3
Spain								1	1
Total	110	400	515	62	120	826	759	123	2915

other pottery contemporary with the construction and occupation of the Phase 2 manor. It is likely that a considerable, although unquantifiable, proportion of this assemblage is in fact redeposited in this phase, and derives from earlier occupation of the site.] Some 376 sherds were recovered from the dump levels. Vessels included two cooking pots, nine kitchen ware vessels, seven jugs and the base of a bottle with 'wire' marks. The highly decorated sherds suggest the apogee of the jug industry, with regional imports from Surrey and a continental import from Rouen present. Residual Romano-British and Saxon sherds were also recovered.

FII.20 Large cooking pot rim (Fig. 3.1.9); Kitchen ware rim; Kitchen ware rim or base; Bases × 4; Handle with thumbed edges (for a parallel handle pot without

Table 3.3 Pottery fabrics by building

Fabric	Domestic range													Auxiliary buildings						Agricultural buildings										U/S	Grand total
	A1	A2	A3	A4	A5	A6	A8	A9	A10	A11	A12	A13	A14	B	D	P	R	W	Total	F	H	I	J	K	Q	T	Moat upcast	Yards	Total		
99*	1		2	4			1	1	2		4			2	1	2			20	8	2		2				4	1	17	50	87
Grp II																															
20	7	1	1	9	7			35		1	2	2	5	1	2	45	2		120	10	2		2				41	5	60	156	336
21	1		1	1	2			1											6	1							2		3	1	10
22																														1	1
23															1				1											4	5
Grp III																															
40				1				1											2									1	1	7	10
41	27	1	17	27	28	1		93	13		27	2	16	6	5	19	2	3	287	14	11			1	2		49	27	104	317	708
42					1						3								4												4
43									2										2	1	2								3	8	13
44		2	1	3	3			7			4		3			2			25								32	4	36	37	98
45					1			1			1								3	1							2	1	4	7	14
46	34	4	2	25	10		2	116	9	6	46	3	6	1	44	1	3	6	318	27	1		8	2	1		46	33	118	323	759
47					1						5			1					7	1							3		4	15	26
48																														1	1
50	1										2								3											4	7
51	5			10	1			1	1	7	33		1						59	3	6					2	1	5	17	53	129
53								1						1					2											4	6
54				1	2			3	3				6						15									1	1	10	26

55				1				1			1								3	1			1				1		3	2	8
57				1					1		6			3					11								1	1	2	8	21
58					2														2											5	7
59	4		5	14	3			9	21		4								60		1	1	5					2	9	64	133
60				3					3		1	1		2					10	1			12						13	35	58
61	31							10			9	1	1						52	1							3	3	7	51	110
62																	1	1	2	1							19		20	2	24
63	1		16	21	20	10	1	3	1	1	10		1	1					86	3	1						17	3	24	78	188
64											1								1												1
65											1		1						2											1	3
67	1				1						2								4	2							1		3		7
68	1												1						2											5	7
69	6		6		5			9			7			2					35	1							5	3	9	29	73
70			2										1						3								2		2	5	10
71																										1			1		1
72				1															1												1
Tin																														1	1
Foreign																															
49								11											11	2									2	3	16
66																											1		1	1	2
Frechen																														3	3
Spain																														1	1
Total	101	8	53	122	87	11	4	303	56	15	169	9	42	20	53	69	8	10	1159	78	26	1	30	3	3	3	230	90	464	1292	2915

* Modern and residual fabrics

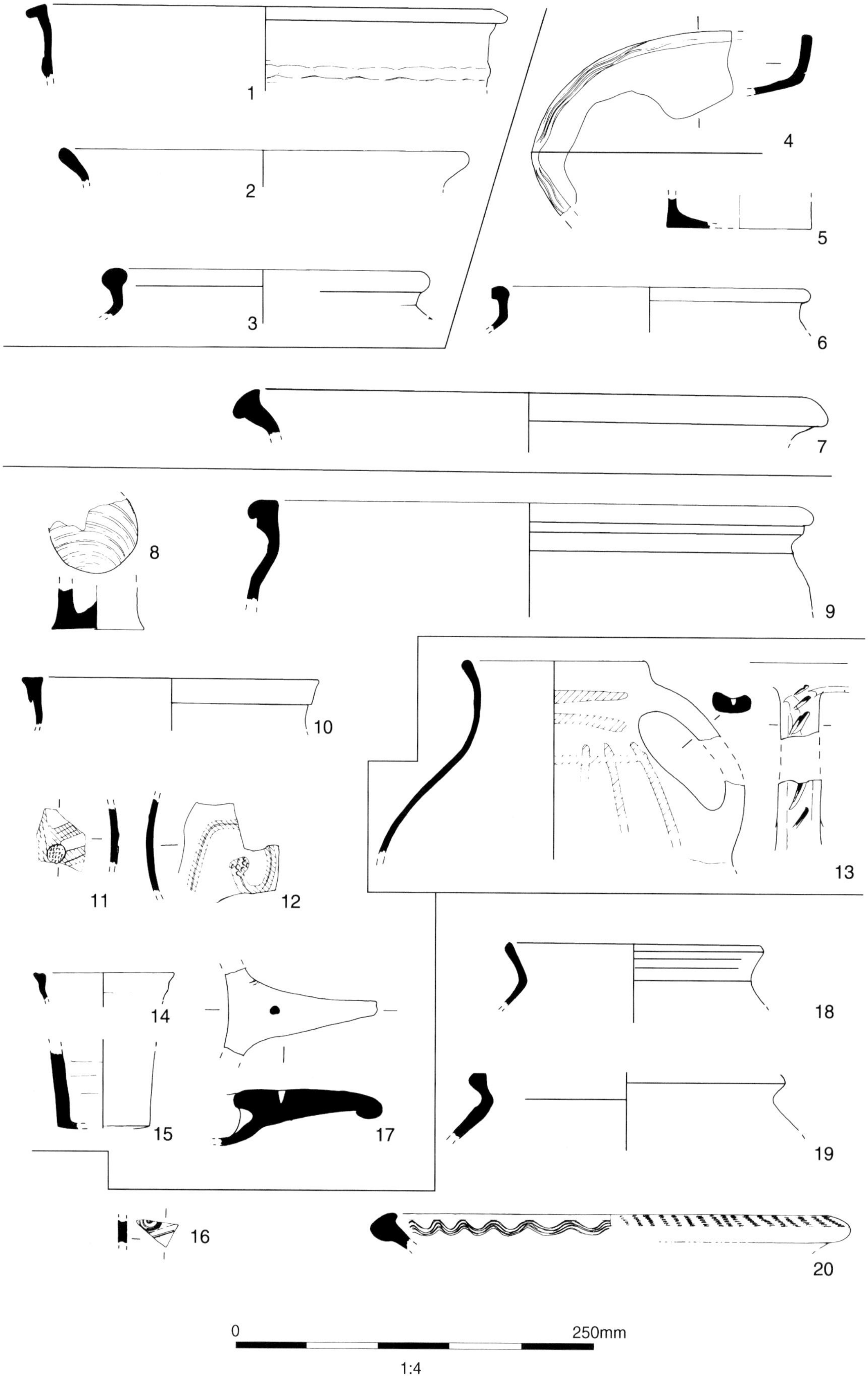

Figure 3.1 Pottery from Phases 1 and 2.

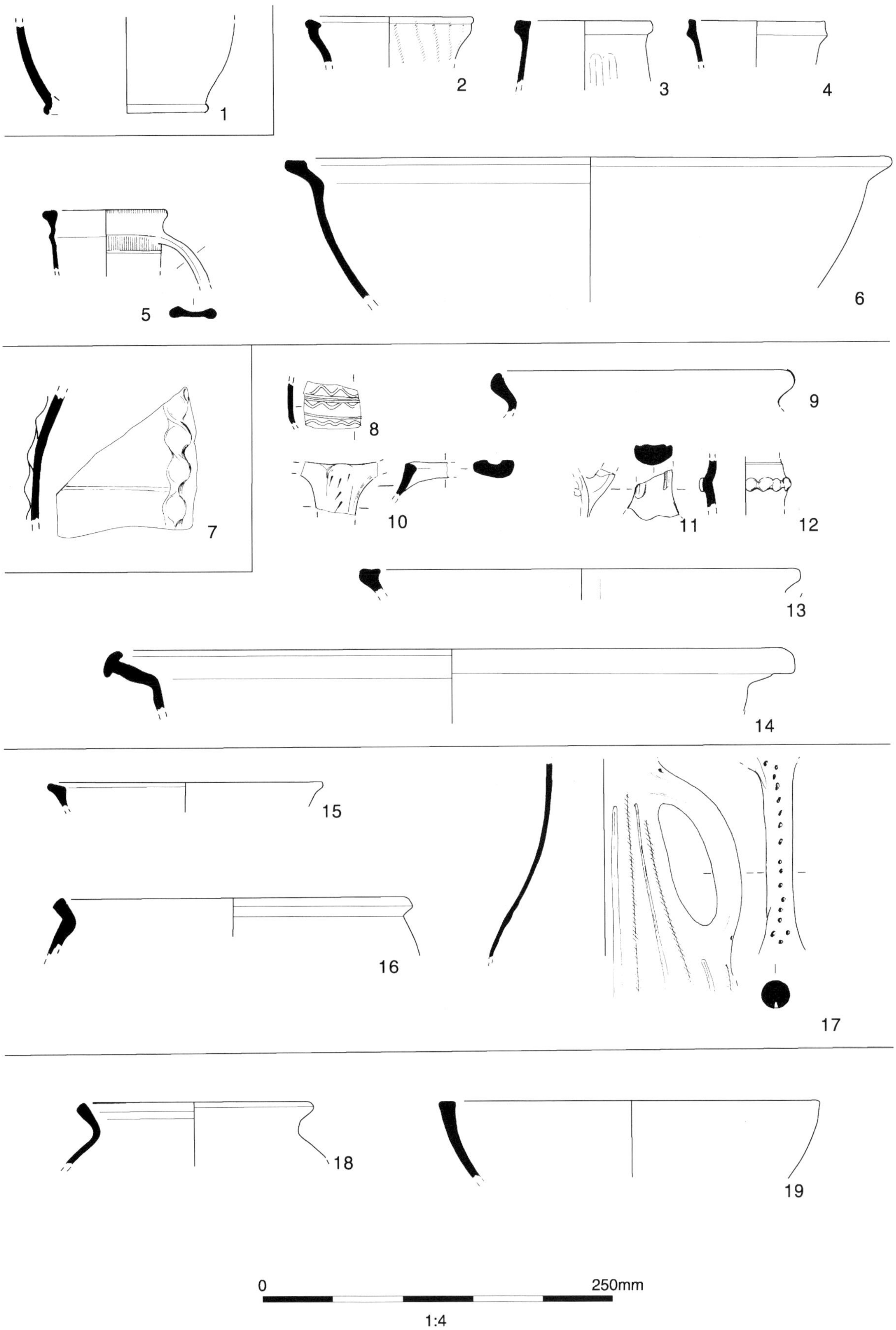

Figure 3.2 Pottery from Phase 3 construction and occupation.

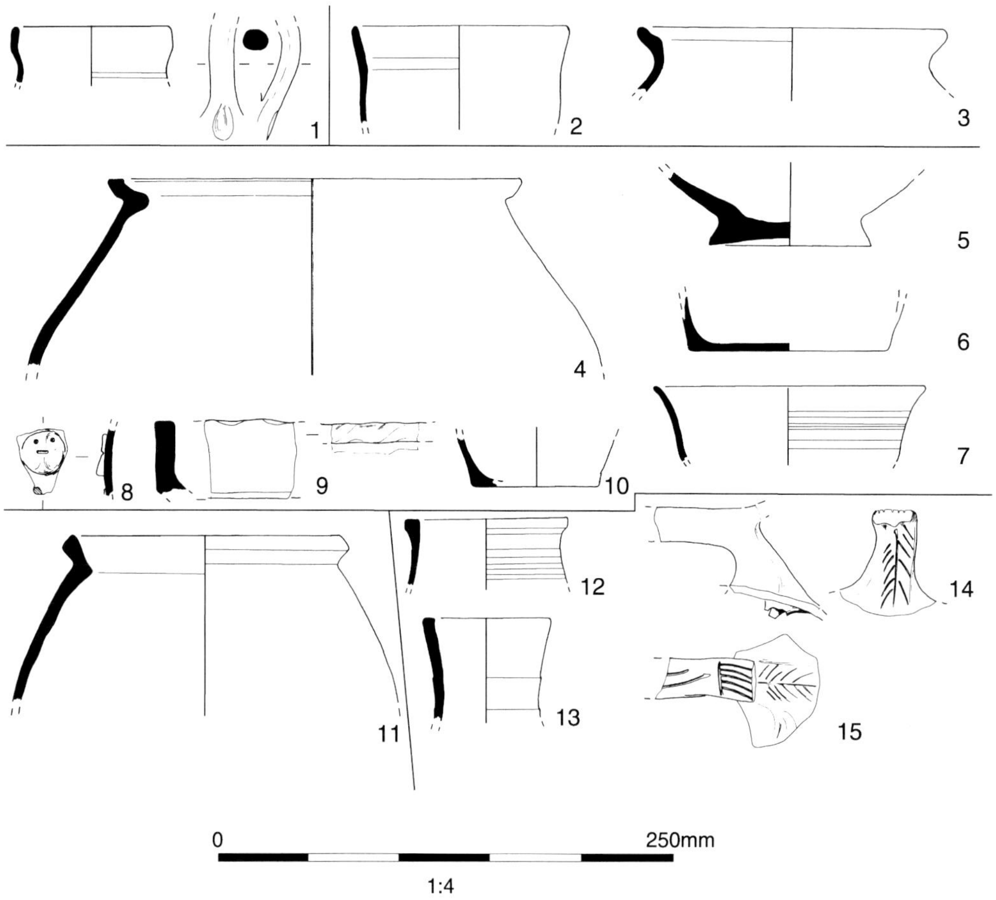

Figure 3.3 Pottery from Phases 3 to 5, occupation and demolition.

thumbed edges see Durham 1977, 131 fig. 24 no. 2); Body sherd, thumbed deco.

FII.21 Body sherd.

FIII.41 Jug, white slip deco, partially glazed green (Fig. 3.1.13); Cooking pot rim; Kitchen ware rims × 6; Bases × 5, incl. 1 green glazed int; Body sherds, × 2 grooved deco; 1 lt green glaze.

FIII.45 Body sherd.

FIII.46 Bottle base with 'wire' marks (Fig. 3.1.8); Cooking pot with undercut rim (Fig. 3.1.10); Skillet handle, possibly intrusive (Fig. 3.1.17); Kitchen ware rim; Bases × 3, mot orange glaze; Handles × 2; Jug, belly with applied rouletted strips and mot green glaze (see Palmer 1980 fig. 14 no. 14 for style of rouletting); Body sherds, 1 with stamped grid deco, mot green glaze (Fig. 3.1.11); 2 mot green glaze, probably from a start baluster type jug (Fig. 3.1.12); 2 applied plain white strips; 1 dk green glaze; 1 mot green glaze; 1 applied alternating red and white strips, mot green glaze; 2 red slip deco, incl 1 with dk green, 1 mot green glaze; 1 rouletted deco, mot green glaze; 3 applied red stripes; 1 lt green glaze; 1 shoulder of jug with red slip, dk green glaze; 2 mot green glaze; 6 dk green glaze; 1 lt green glaze int and ext; 1 mot yellow glaze.

FIII.47 Jug rim, partially glazed ext; Body sherd, partially glazed.

FIII.51 Body sherds, 1 red slip deco, dk green glaze int; 1 applied red strips, lt green glaze.

FIII.53 Body sherd.

FIII.55 Body sherd.

FIII.57 Body sherd.

FIII.60 Bottle base (Fig. 3.1.15).

FIII.62 Kitchen ware rim.

FIII.63 Jug rim, partially glazed orange; Base.

FIII.64 Base.

FIII.66 Jug rim, red slip dots, lt yellow glaze, from Rouen (Fig. 3.1.14).

FIII.69 Handle with applied strip, lt yellow glaze; Jug shoulder, red slip and applied rouletted strip; Body sherd, grooved deco, lt green glaze.

99 Incl. Romano-British and Saxon sherds.

Dump layers and demolition of Phase 1 structures

The other areas yielded a wider range of fabric types and included two cooking pots, six kitchen ware vessels, a bottle, two jugs and a number of highly decorated Brill-type sherds and a sherd from a Saintonge-type jug from south-west France.

FII.20 Cooking pot rim (Fig. 3.1.19; see Palmer 1980 fig. 15 no. 9); Kitchen ware rims × 3, incl. 1 with combed deco (Fig. 3.1.20); Bases × 3.

FIII.40 Bottle neck, lt green glaze.

FIII.41 Body sherds, 1 impressed concentric circles, mot green glaze (Fig. 3.1.16; the fabric and style of decoration are paralleled in Newbury, Alan Vince pers. comm.); 1 white slip, orange glaze; 2 grooved deco, incl 1 glazed dk green; Cooking pot rim (Fig. 3.1.18); Kitchen ware rims × 3; Base, partially glazed lt green

FIII.46 Jug rim, glazed orange int. and ext. (P981/1/1 is a parallel); Body sherds, 1 red slip, applied strips of alternating colour; 1 stabbed deco, mot green glaze; 2 grooves reg and horiz, incl 1 mot green, 1 lt green glaze; 2 red slip deco, incl 1 mot green, 1 orange glaze.

FIII.49 Body sherd, mot green glaze, a Saintonge type.

FIII.51 Jug rim, partially glazed lt green.

FIII.60 Body sherd, red slip, mot green glaze.

FIII.62 Body sherd.

FIII.69 Body sherd, applied horiz strips, mot green glaze.

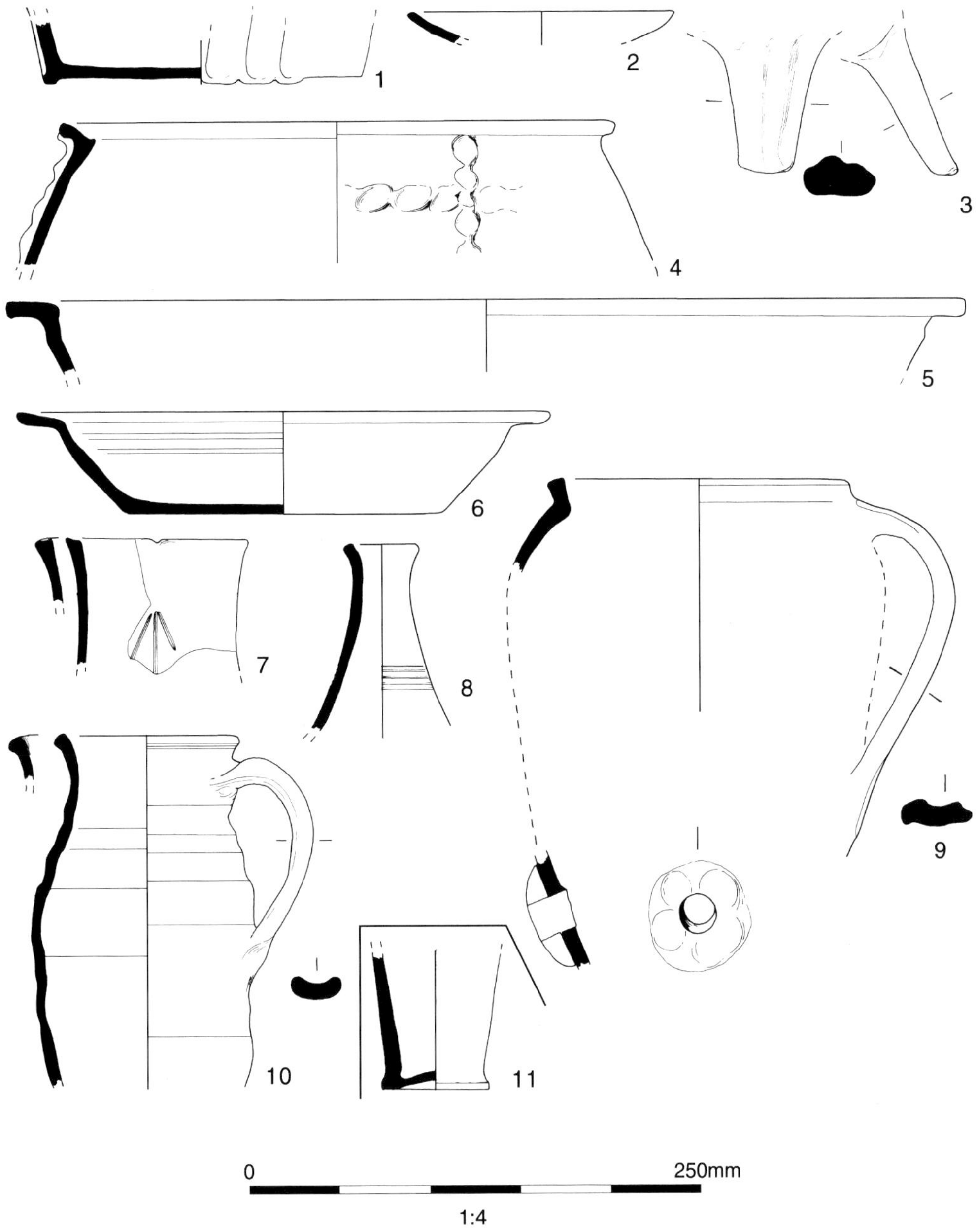

Figure 3.4 Pottery from Building A12, the latest kitchen, Phases 4 and 5.

Building A1

Only two kitchen ware vessels were found.

FII.20 Kitchen ware rims.

Building Q

Only one sherd was recovered.

FIII.41 Body sherd.

The moat upcast in the south of the moated island, in the vicinity of Buildings N, O, Q and U

The upcast yielded yet another residual sherd of St Neot's type, which dates to the 10th and 11th centuries in Oxford.

FIA.99 Body sherd, St Neot's type.

FII.99 Body sherd, probably Iron Age.
FIII.46 Body sherd.

Building D

This building also yielded very little pottery.

FII.20 Base.

Phase 3 (construction and early occupation of the remodelled manor: early 14th century) *(Fig. 3.2)*

Building A1

No vessel rims were recovered from the robber trench of a wall of Building A.

FIII.41 Jug shoulder, white slip deco, lt green glaze; Body sherd, white slip dots, partially glazed.

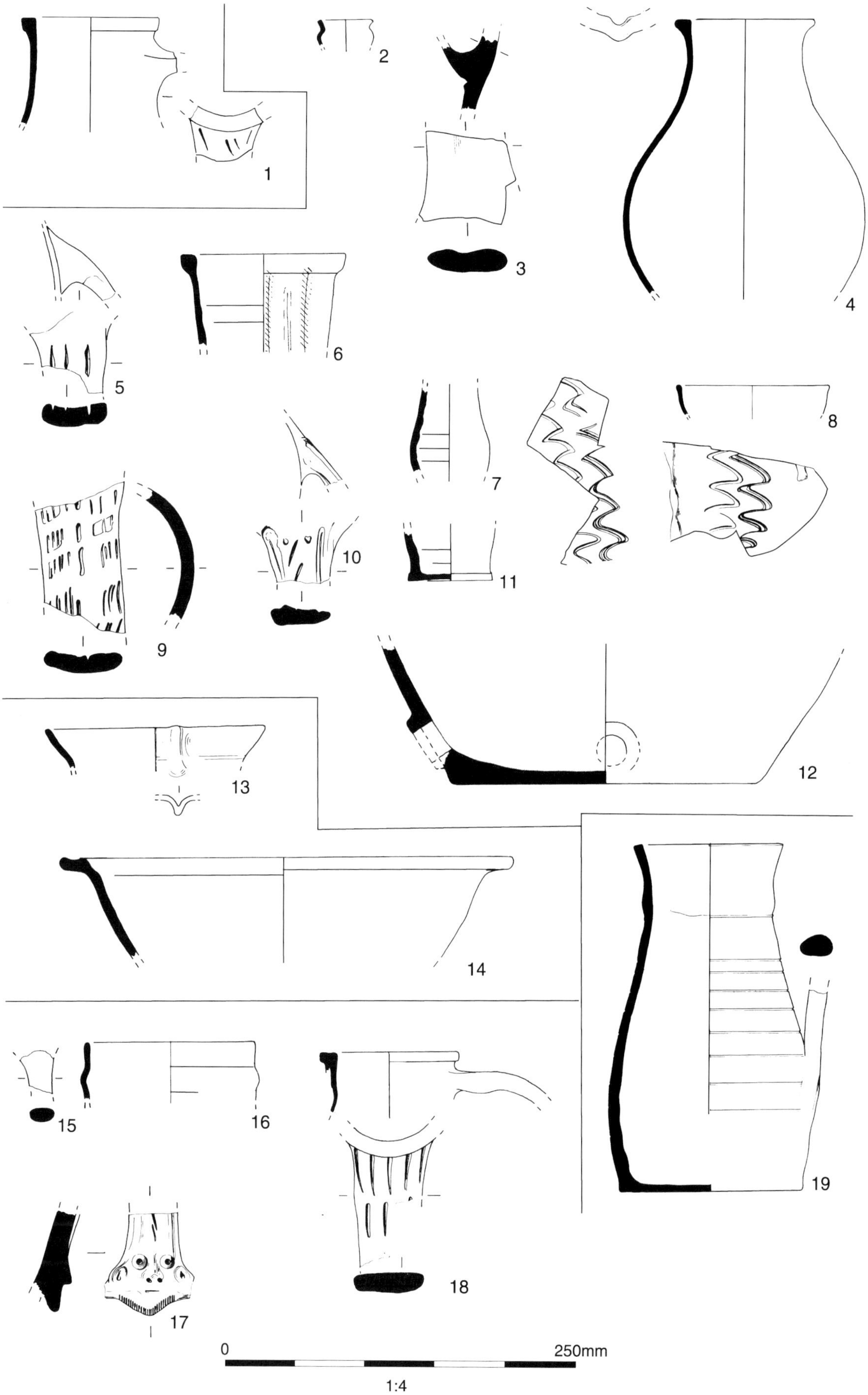

Figure 3.5 Pottery from Phases 4 and 5.

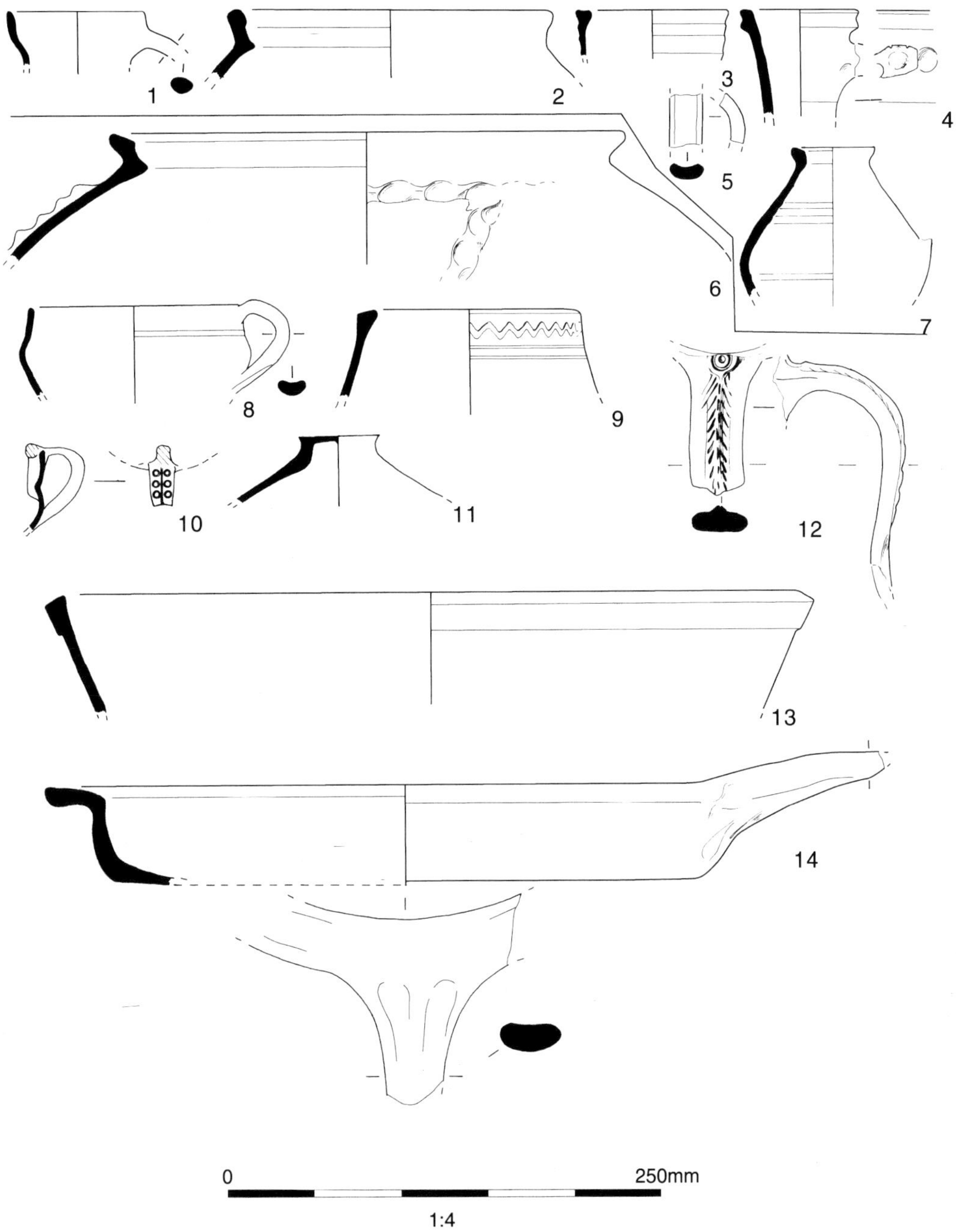

Figure 3.6 Pottery from stratified and unstratified demolition.

FIII.46 Jug base, mot green glaze (Fig. 3.2.1); Body sherds, 8 applied red strips, mot green glaze; 1 applied alternating red and white strips, lt green glaze.
FIII.69 Jug shoulder, reg and horiz grooves, mot green glaze.

Building A1 east bay [Editor's note: originally designated A2, but probably the east bay of Phase 2 Building A1, or possibly even an early layer of Phase 3 Room A10: see Chapter 2]

FIII.46 Jug rim, lt yellow glaze ext; Body sherd, applied red strips, mot green glaze.

Room A4

Very few sherds were recovered related to the construction and early occupation of Room A4.

FII.20 Body sherd.
FII.21 Body sherd, combed deco.
FIII.41 Rim of unknown vessel type.
FIII.46 Body sherd, lt yellow glaze.

Room A8

Only two sherds were recovered from the probable staircase.

FIII.46 Jug rim.

Room A9

This sequence of floor layers in Room A9 yielded one kitchen ware vessel, three bowls, six jugs including a globular Saintonge type and a bottle.

FII.20 Kitchen-ware rim; Base.
FII.21 Kitchen-ware, carbon deposits int, cross-joins between F866 and F1053.
FIII.41 Jug, white slip, partially glazed (Fig. 3.2.2); Bowl; Body sherds, 1 partially glazed (Fig. 3.2.3); 1 white slip, partially glazed; 1 lt green glaze, red mottles.
FIII.46 Jug rims (Fig. 3.2.4), incl 1 applied alternating red and white strips, partially glazed mot green, 1 with red slip, lt green glaze; Jug Bases × 2, incl 1 lt green glaze, kiln scar, deep mark where pot levered off wheel; Handle, notched grooves, mot green glaze; Jug shoulders, reg and horiz grooves, lt green glaze; Jug bellies × 2, applied rouletted red strips, lt green glaze; Bottle; Body sherds, 11 red slip, 7 mot green, 1 lt yellow; 4 applied red rouletted strips, lt green glaze; 2 applied white strips, incl 1 dk green, 1 lt green glaze; 13 applied red strips, incl 3 dk green, 4 lt green, 3 lt yellow, 1 orange, 1 mot green glaze; 2 grooved deco, lt green glaze; 5 lt green, 14 mot green, 8 also glazed mot green int; 1 mot orange, 2 dk yellow glaze; 1 cross-joins F766 with F971 and F981.
FIII.49 Jug rim with kiln scar on rim and handle, cross-joins between F975, F1052 and F1053 (Fig. 3.2.5); Body sherd with shield design, part of globular Saintonge jug (information from Bob Thomson), cross-joins F962 and F1053; another cross-joins F975 with F745.
FIII.53 Body sherd.
FIII.63 Body sherd, white slip, partially glazed.
FIII.69 Bowls × 2 (Fig. 3.2.6), incl 1 with applied strips, mot red glaze; Body sherds, 12 red slip, 1 mot green, 1 lt green; 2 applied white strips, 1 mot red, 1 mot green glaze; 1 mot red glaze.

Room A10

Few sherds were recovered from the small area excavated.

FIII.41 Body sherds, 2 partially glazed orange.
FIII.46 Body sherds, 1 applied white strips, yellow mottled glaze; 1 grooved deco, mot green glaze.

Area F

The pottery assemblage included two bottles, and fragments of jugs.

FIB.99 Body sherd, probably Iron Age.
FII.20 Kitchen ware base.
FIII.41 Kitchen ware base; Body sherds, 1 red slip deco, lt green glaze; 1 partially glazed orange
FIII.43 Body sherd, mot red glaze.
FIII.46 Bottle rim; Body sherds × 2, red slip, lt yellow glaze; Bases × 2, incl 1 partially glazed, 1 mot green glaze; Body sherds, 1 applied white strips and red slip, mot green glaze; 1 applied red strips, lt yellow glaze; 3 red slip, dk green glaze.
FIII.51 Bottle rim.
FIII. ? Body sherd, red slip, dk green glaze.
FIII.63 Body sherd, grooves reg and horiz, mot green glaze
99 Body sherd, mot green glaze.

Building W

Very few sherds were recovered from the probable detached kitchen.

FIII.41 Body sherds, 1 applied thumbed strip (Fig. 3.2.7); 1 partially glazed.
FIII.46 Jug shoulder with reg and horiz grooved deco, mot green glaze; Body sherd, applied red strips, lt green glaze.
FIII.62 Kitchen ware rim.

Courtyard and dump layers between the cross-wing (Rooms A9, A10, A4) and Building W

Two cooking pots, 4 kitchen vessels, 1 jug, a bottle and a rim of a fine table ware vessel were recovered and the belly of a cruet. The Tudor-type fragment may be intrusive in this phase.

FII.20 Kitchen ware rim (Fig. 3.2.14); Kitchen ware base.
FIII.40 Body sherd, wavy and horizontal grooves, dk green glaze (Fig. 3.2.8).
FIII.41 Cooking pot rim (Fig. 3.2.9); Kitchen ware rims × 3 (Fig. 3.2.13); Body sherds, 1 white slip, partially glazed; 1 grooved deco, lt green glaze; 1 reg and horiz grooves, lt green glaze; Base.
FIII.43 Body sherd, mot red glaze.
FIII.46 Skillet handle, incised deco (Fig. 3.2.10); Handles × 2, stabbed deco, mot green glaze, 1 with grooves (Fig. 3.2.11); Belly of cruet, with applied horiz thumbed strip (Fig. 3.2.12; see Hinton 1973 no. 16); Base of ?jug, mot orange glaze; Body sherds, 1 with applied red strips, mot orange glaze; 2 applied strips in alternating colour, green glaze; applied red rouletted strips, lt green glaze; 1 lt green glaze int and dk green ext; 1 applied white strip, lt green glaze; 1 grooved deco, mot green glaze; 3 applied red strips, 1 lt green, 1 mot green, 1 dark yellow glaze; 1 applied alternating red and white strips, mot orange glaze; 2 mot green, 1 with mortar; 1 mot orange; Jug rim, partially glazed, lt yellow; Belly of jug, glazed mot green, cross-join between F1001 and F1072, mortar present.
FIII.50 Body sherd.
FIII.51 Bottle rim, grooves reg and horiz; Body sherd, red slip, lt green glaze.
FIII.57 Body sherds, 6 mot orange glaze.
FIII.59 Fine table ware rim, dk green glaze int and mot green ext.
FIII.63 Base, dk green glaze int.
FIII.69 Body sherd, applied white rouletted strip.

The central courtyard (gravel surface 396) (group 9)

A cooking pot, 2 bowls, a storage jar of a type generally believed to date to the second half of the 15th century and a jug were recovered. One bowl from the West Surrey kilns had a T-shaped rim; similar rims found in the Trig Lane sequence, London were dated to 1340–1440 (T-shaped rims date to 1340–1440, Alan Vince pers. comm.).

FII.20 Body sherd.
FIII.41 Bowl rim (Fig. 3.2.15); Body sherds, 3 partially glazed int; Rim.
FIII.46 Jug rim, applied red strips, orange glaze; Rod handle with stabbed deco, yellow glaze (Fig. 3.2.17); Shoulder of jug, applied alternating red and white strips, yellow glaze; Body sherd, red slip deco, lt yellow glaze.
FIII.47 Body sherd, lt green glaze.
FIII.51 Storage jar rim, lt yellow glaze, possibly intrusive (Fig. 3.2.16).
FIII.53 Body sherd.
FIII.60 Bowl rim, mot green glaze, cross-joins between F161 and F790/275.
FIII.63 Body sherds × 3, 1 with misc grooves; Cooking pot rim P211/2/1 (F228 group 7 cross-joins).
FIII.69 Body sherds, 1 reg and horiz grooves, dk green glaze; 1 yellow glaze int.

Sub-phase 3/2 (early to mid 14th century: addition of Room A3 to the west end of Building A1) *(Fig. 3.2) (group 5)*

Much of the pottery was recovered from the dump levels associated with levelling up the interior of the extension (A3) to the hall (Building A1). The pottery included two kitchen ware vessels, a bowl and decorated sherds from jugs or pitchers including a Brill type.

FII.20 Base.
FII.21 Body sherd.
FIII.41 Cooking pot rim (Fig. 3.2.18); Bowl rim (Fig. 3.2.19); Bases × 2; Kitchen ware shoulder
FIII.46 Body sherd, applied red strips, lt yellow glaze.
FIII.62 Kitchen ware base.
FIII.63 Bases × 2.
FIII.69 Shoulder with reg and horiz grooves.

Area west of Room A3 (group 6)

FII.20	Body sherd.
FIII.41	Jug rim, orange glaze.
FIII.46	Body sherd, applied red rouletted strips, orange glaze.
FIII.51	Body sherd, glazed lt green int and dk green ext.
FIII.62	Body sherd.

Phase 3 occupation (early to mid 14th century)

Building A1 and Room A3 (group 8)

All the sherds with the exception of one (fabric 62) were recovered from floor layers within Building A1. No rims of vessels were recovered, but the assemblage was dominated by jug fragments.

FIA.99	Body sherd, St. Neot's type.
FIII.41	Kitchen ware base; Body sherds, 1 mortar adhering to both sides; 1 lt green glaze int.
FIII.46	Shoulders of jug × 2, incl 1 applied white strips and red slip, 1 with applied alternating strips, green glaze; Bellies of jugs × 3, 1 with applied strips in alternating colour, green glaze, 1 with applied white strip, green glaze, 1 with applied red strips, green glaze; Body sherds, 1 red slip; 4 applied white strips, 3 with lt green glaze, 1 with red mottled glaze and applied wide strip; 1 applied white strips, lt green glaze; 3 applied strips of alternating colour, 1 mot green glaze, 1 red mottled glaze; 4 applied red strips, 1 lt yellow glaze, 2 dk green glaze; 2 lt green glaze.
FIII.51	Body sherds × 2, applied strips of alternating colour, mot green glaze; 4 applied red strips, lt green glaze.
FIII.60	Body sherd, mot green glaze.
FIII.62	Body sherd.
FIII.69	Body sherds, 1 applied strips, lt green glaze; 1 applied red rouletted strips, mot green glaze; 1 reg and horiz grooves, dk green glaze.

Other surfaces (group 8)

Four sherds came from the external surfaces associated with this group. They included 1 jug and a kitchen vessel, plus a sherd of fine tableware, the latter probably intrusive to this phase.

FII.20	Kitchen ware rim.
FIII.41	Rim; Body sherd, mot green glaze
FIII.46	Jug rim, partially glazed; Body sherds, 1 applied alternate red and white strips, dk green; 1 applied strips, dk yellow glaze.
FIII.59	Body sherd of fine tableware, lt green int and ext.
FIII.69	Body sherds × 2, applied alternating red and white rouletted strips, mot green.

Phase 3–5 occupation and demolition (14th to late 15th century) *(Fig. 3.3)*

Room A3 later occupation and demolition (group 11)

These fragmentary sherds included a higher proportion of Tudor-type tablewares and the demolition area above Room A4 yielded a local Tudor-type jug, with streaky mottled green glaze (Fig. 3.3.1).

FIII.41	Body sherd, glazed orange int.
FIII.54	Body sherd, glazed lt green int and dk green ext.
FIII.59	Handle of fine table ware, dk green int and mot green ext; Body sherds, 2 dk green int and mot green ext; 1 grooved deco, mot green int and dk green ext; 1 mot green int and lt green ext.
FIII.63	Body sherd.
FIII.69	Body sherd, red slip and partially glazed.
99	Body sherd.

Room A4 later occupation and demolition (group 12)

The pottery assemblage from Room A4 yielded a cooking pot, a storage jar, two jugs and some Tudor-type tablewares. The demolition levels above also included Tudor green type wares including a ?bowl or possible cup (Fig. 3.3.2), glazed mot green int and ext.

FII.20	Body sherd.
FIII.41	Storage jar rim (Fig. 3.3.3); Kitchen ware base; Body sherds, 1 applied thumbed strips yellow mot glaze; 1 mortar adhering to both sides
FIII.46	Jug with pinched spout; Jug rim, applied strips of alternating colour; Body sherds, 1 applied red rouletted strips, dk green glaze; 1 mot green glaze; 1 applied red stripe, dk green glaze; 1 mot green glaze; Belly of jug, mot green glaze.
FIII.51	Body sherd, partially glazed.
FIII.57	Body sherd.
FIII.59	Rim, glazed dk green int and ext; Body sherds, 1 dk yellow int and dk green ext; 1 dk green ext; 1 lt yellow int and mot green ext; 1 lt yellow int and ext.
FIII.63	Cooking pot rim; Body sherds × 2, partially glazed int
FIII.72	Body sherd, mot green glaze.

Room A5 later occupation and demolition (group 13)

The pottery from Room A5 (garderobe) includes material which may be contemporary with Phase 2 as well as fine tablewares, typical of Phase 4. Two cooking pots, a shallow dish and a face mask, typical of types found in Oxford, but very abraded, were recovered. The demolition levels above included two storage jars with bifid rims (Fig. 3.3.4, fabric 41); 1 with applied thumbed strip (see Palmer 1980, 174 fig. 20 no. 4, early to mid 16th century, for a parallel); a footring of a shallow dish (Fig. 3.3.5, fabric 46); a fine Tudor-type bowl, with rilling externally and mottled green glaze internally and externally (Fig. 3.3.7, Fabric 54), and the base of a Tudor-type jug, glazed mottled green internally and externally (Fig. 3.3.6, fabric 54).

FII.20	Cooking pot rim.
FII.21	Kitchen ware base.
FIII.41	Cooking pot rim; Base, mot green glaze; Kitchen ware base; Body sherds × 7, partially glazed ext; 1 applied red strips and white slip, lt green glaze
FIII.46	Face mask, applied red strip below pad, mot green glaze (Fig. 3.3.8), very abraded; Body sherds, 1 mot green glaze; 2 applied red strips, mot green glaze; 2 reg and horiz. grooves, dk green glaze; 1 mot green glaze.
FIII.58	Base of ?cup, dk green glaze int, mot green glaze ext (Fig. 3.3.10); Body sherd, reg and horz grooves, dk green glaze int and ext.
FIII.63	'Dripping pan', finger tipped, orange glaze int, carbon ext (Fig. 3.3.9).

Possible middens, western part of moated island (group 14)

Surprisingly few sherds were recovered from the possible midden dumps; a cooking pot, two kitchen ware vessels and a bottle.

FIII.41	Cooking pot; Kitchen ware rim; Kitchen ware base; Base, orange glaze int; Body sherds, 1 partially glazed; 1 applied horiz. thumbed strips; 1 orange glaze int.
FIII.46	Bottle; Body sherd, partially glazed mot green
FIII.63	Kitchen ware rim; Kitchen ware bases × 2.

Phase 4 (late 14th to early 15th century) *(Fig. 3.3)*

Building A11 (group 26)

Only five sherds were recovered from the probable chapel, Building A11. The robber trench in the destruction phase yielded a hard fired storage jar (Fig. 3.3.11), a type that can be paralleled in Oxford (also v. group 18; Sturdy 1959, 31 fig. 14 no. 9 for fabric and rim form; Palmer 1980, 173 fig. 19 for general fabrics and forms).

FIII.46	Body sherds × 3, mot green glaze, 1 with red slip; 1 slim applied strips alternately red and white colour, khaki glaze
FIII.51	Body sherd.

Enclosed gardens south of Building A1, to either side of Room A6 (probable porch) (group 18)

The pottery from this group was recovered from the gardens on either side of the Porch. Two kitchen ware vessels and three jugs were recovered.

FII.20 Kitchen ware rim.
FIII.40 Body sherd.
FIII.41 Kitchen ware rim; Jug handles × 2, stabbed deco, orange glaze; Body sherds × 2, white slip, 1 lt green, 1 orange glaze.
FIII.43 Body sherd, grooved deco, mot green glaze.
FIII.46 Jugs × 2, 1 with reg and horiz grooved deco and mot green glaze (Fig. 3.3.13), 1 with dk green glaze (Fig. 3.3.12); Handle of probable aquamanile, stabbed deco, dk green glaze, dk green int. and ext (Fig. 3.3.14); Splayed base of jug; Jug handle, stabbed deco, lt green glaze.
FIII.47 Body sherd.
FIII.51 Jug, applied white strips, mot green glaze; Base.
FIII.54 Body sherd, applied white rouletted strips, mot green glaze int and dk green glaze ext.
FIII.59 Body sherds, 1 applied white rouletted strips, lt green glaze; 1 mot green glaze int and ext.
FIII.69 Body sherd.
FIII.71 Body sherd, glazed green int.
99 Body sherd, of tinglazed earthenware, blue deco and white glaze.

Destruction of Building W (group 19)

Very few sherds were associated with the destruction levels of Building W.

FIII.41 Kitchen ware rim.
FIII.46 Body sherds, 1 applied red strips, mot green glaze; 1grooved deco, dk yellow glaze; 1 dk yellow; 1 dk green; 1 mot yellow glaze.

Building A12 (latest kitchen) (Fig 3.4).

A substantial amount of pottery was recovered from Building A12, including 6 cooking pots, 6 kitchen ware vessels, a bowl, 4 jugs, 2 bottles and a cup. Fragments of Tudor-type tablewares although present did not dominate the assemblage. One jug was decorated with an incised arrow sign; similar marks have been noted on late medieval jugs in Oxford (see Durham and Mellor 1977, 265).

The demolition levels included a partially thumbed base of a jug (Fig. 3.4.1, fabric 46) which cross-joins F798 with F5; a rim of a ?shallow dish (Fig. 3.4.2, fabric 64) which can be paralleled at the Hamel (Palmer 1980, fig. 18 no. 4); a leg of a tripod cooking pot (Fig. 3.4.3, fabric 60; see Moorhouse 1971–2, 119 fig. 1 no. 1); a storage jar with applied thumbed strips (Fig. 3.4.4, fabric 60) which also parallels one at the Hamel (Palmer 1980, 174 fig. 20 no. 4); a deep-sided flanged dish (Fig. 3.4.5, fabric 60), and a near-complete bowl, with flanged rim, glazed yellow internally, with flecks of mottled green glaze externally (Fig. 3.4.6), cross-joins between F12, F14 and F19; and a large bunghole jar (Fig. 3.4.9, fabric 51) with splashes of green glaze and thumbed spigot (see Sturdy 1959, 31 fig. 14 no. 3 for general form).

FII.20 Cooking pot with thumbed rim Bowl rim Kitchen ware rims × 2; Bases × 5; Body sherds × 2, 1 with stabbed deco, 1 with grooved deco.
FII.22 Base of colander.
FIII.41 Cooking pot rims × 5; Kitchen ware rims × 4, 1 partially glazed, 1 glazed green int, 1 partially glazed orange int, 1 with yellow residue int; Bases × 5, 1 glazed orange int, 2 glazed lt green int, 1 glazed mot orange int; Body sherds × 3, grooved deco, 2 with dk green glaze; 1 white slip deco, glazed mot green; 1 reg and horiz. grooves, partially glazed; 5 glazed orange int; 1 mot green glaze; 1 glazed mot green int; 1 glazed green int and ext.
FIII.46 Jugs × 4, 1 with pinched spout, dk green glaze (Fig. 3.4.10), 1 with rod handle, mot green glaze, 1 with strap handle, pinched lip and mot green glaze int. and ext., 1 with pinched lip and incised 'arrow' sign, partially glazed dk green (Fig. 3.4.7); Shoulders of jugs, 1 mot green glaze and consignment mark; 1 with applied scales and mot green glaze; 1 with applied pad with 'grid' stamp and applied red strips and mot orange glaze; 1 with applied red rouletted strips and plain white strips, mot orange glaze; Belly of jug with rod handle, applied strips of alternating colour, lt green glaze; Handles with stabbed deco × 2, 1 with lt green glaze and 1 with mot green glaze; Bases × 2, partially glazed on the underside; Bottle, glazed lt green; Body sherds × 2, reg. and horiz grooves, 1 partially glazed int., 1 glazed dk green int and mot green ext.; 1 applied rouletted strips, lt green glaze; 1 applied red rouletted strips, dk green glaze; 31 applied red strips, 1 with mot green glaze, 1 with lt green glaze, 1 with orange glaze; 1 applied strips, dk green glaze; 1 applied rouletted strips, dk green glaze; 1 red slip deco, dk green glaze; 1 glazed dk green int, mot green ext; 10 mot green; 2 mot yellow; 2 lt green glaze.
FIII.47 Base, partially glazed; Body sherds × 2, mot green glaze
FIII.50 Body sherd, glazed mot green int. and ext.
FIII.51 Cup, glazed dk green int. and ext.; Body sherds, 1 reg and horiz. grooves, glazed lt green int. and dk green ext.; 1 glazed dk green int. and ext.
FIII.57 Body sherd.
FIII.59 Bottle (Fig. 3.4.8) with reg and horiz. grooves, mot green glaze; Handle, glazed dk green; Body sherd, glazed mot green.
FIII.60 Strap handle, stabbed deco, lt green glaze; Body sherd, reg. and horiz. grooves, glazed mot green.
FIII.63 Base, thumbed, carbon deposits int. and ext.
FIII.65 Body sherd, reg and horiz. grooves, red mottled glaze.
FIII.66 Base, glazed lt green.
99 Incl. body sherd, Romano-British.

Courtyard outside Building A12 (group 19) (Fig 3.4)

The area associated with the final phase of the Kitchen included 2 kitchen ware vessels and jug fragments.

FII.20 Body sherd.
FIII.41 Kitchen ware rims × 2; Body sherds, 1 applied red rouletted strips, mot green glaze; 1 mot green glaze int and ext; 1 applied white rouletted strips, mot green glaze.
FIII.46 Base of probable bottle (Fig. 3.4.11); Body sherds, 1 applied strips in alternating colour, lt green glaze; 2 applied strips, 1 lt green, 1 mot yellow glaze; 3 applied white strips, 1 mot yellow, 1 mot green glaze; 1 glazed orange int; 1 glazed orange; 1 glazed mot orange; Base, glazed orange int
FIII.51 Body sherd, applied white strips, mot green glaze.
FIII.54 Body sherd, glazed dk green int. and ext.
FIII.59 Body sherd, lt green int and partially glazed dk green ext.
FIII.63 Body sherds × 2, 1 orange, 1 lt green glaze.

Building A1 (group 20)

Few sherds were associated with the final phase of Building A1.

FII.20 Body sherd.
FIII.46 Body sherds × 4, applied red strips, 1 lt green, 1 mot yellow glaze; 3 applied white strips, lt green glaze; 2 lt green glaze; 1 mot red glaze.
FIII.51 Rim.
FIII.59 Body sherds, 1 dk green glaze int. and ext.; 1 dk green ext and lt green int.
FIII.68 Body sherd, mot green glaze.

Demolition of Building D (group 21) (Fig. 3.5)

Fragmentary jug sherds only were associated with the demolition of this building.

FIII.46 Jug rims × 4 (Fig. 3.5.1), 1 with lt green glaze (see Palmer 1980, 168 fig. 14 no. 5, dated mid 13th century); 1 mot green glaze, 1 dk green glaze; Body sherds × 2, applied red strips, 1 partially glazed, 1 mot green glaze; 5 applied white strips, 1 mot green, 4 dk green glaze; 1 applied red rouletted strips, dk green glaze; 1 dk green glaze int. and ext.; 1 mot green; 2 dk green glaze.

Gardens north of Building A1; levelling layers following demolition of Buildings D and E (group 21)

As in the kitchen area, a substantial amount of pottery was recovered. It included only 1 kitchen ware vessel, but 6 jugs, a bottle and 5 Tudor-type tablewares: a lobed dish, a cup, a dish and a small jug.

FIB.99 Body sherd.
FII.20 Kitchen ware base; Body sherd, combed deco.
FIII.41 Kitchen ware thumbed rim; Bases × 7, 1 glazed lt green int; Jugs × 2, 1 with pinched spout (Fig. 3.5.4); Belly of jug, lt green glaze; Jug handle, stabbed deco, brown glaze (Fig. 3.5.5); Body sherds, 1 applied red strips, mot green glaze; 1 grooved deco, lt green glaze; 8, 1 lt green glaze, 1 lt yellow; 1 partially glazed lt yellow; 3 partially glazed int; cross-joins between F673 and F682.
FIII.46 Jug rims × 3, 1 with applied strips of alternating colour (Fig. 3.5.6), 1 with pinched spout, dk green glaze; Jug bases × 2; Bellies of jugs × 2, 1 with applied strips in alternating colour, dk green glaze and with lt green glaze; Strap handles × 2, with stabbed deco, 1 with mot green (Fig. 3.5.9), 1 with mot yellow glaze (Fig. 3.5.10); Body sherd of bottle, lt green glaze (Fig. 3.5.7); Base of probable bottle (Fig. 3.5.11); Base of bunghole jar, mot green glaze int. and ext. (Fig. 3.5.12) cross-joins F725 with F186/1; Body sherds, 1 applied thumbed strips, dk green glaze int. and ext.; 6 grooves reg. and horiz., 2 mot yellow, 3 lt green glaze; 4 grooved deco, 1 dk green glaze, 2 mot orange glaze; 1 grooves wavy and horiz, dk green glaze; 1 grooved deco; 11 applied red strips, 1 dk yellow, 2 dk green, 4 mot green, 3 lt green, 2 mot orange, 1 yellow glazed; 3 applied rouletted strips, 1 mot green, 1 orange, 1 dk green; 11 applied white strips; 5 dk green, 2 dk yellow, 1 lt green, 1 orange, 1 mot green glaze; 1 applied 'grid' stamp, lt green glaze; 4 applied strips in alternating colour, mot green glaze; 6 red slip, lt green glaze; 1 int glazed orange; 1 partially glazed orange; 1 with orange mottles; 1 partially glazed dk green; 2 mot green glaze; 2 mot yellow glaze, kiln scar evident; 3 lt green glaze; 1 mot orange glaze; 1 lt green int, mot green glaze ext; 1 cross-joins between F700 and Fll34.
FIII.51 Fine table-ware rim of jug with strap handle, stabbed deco, mot green glaze.
FIII.54 Body sherd, dk green glaze int and mot green glaze ext.
FIII.58 Body sherd, dk green int and ext.
FIII.59 Lobed cup; Body sherds × 2, dk green int and ext; 2 lt green int and ext; Cup rim, lt green int and ext (Fig. 3.5.8).
FIII.60 Body sherds, 1 applied red strips, lt green glaze; 1 dk yellow glaze; 2 partially glazed green int.
FIII.63 Body sherds, 1 orange int; 1 mot brown int; 2 applied white strips, lt green glaze; 2 lt green glaze; 1 grooved deco, lt green glaze.
FIII.65 Body sherd, orange glaze int.
FIII.69 Body sherd, lt green glaze int and ext.
99 Jug, partially glazed lt green; Kitchen ware body sherd, possibly dated to the Iron Age.

Structure A13 (pentice) (group 21)

As in Building D only fragmentary jug sherds were associated with this structure. The demolition levels above yielded a broad strap handle, partially glazed green (Fig. 3.5.3, Fabric 46); a small ointment pot (Fig. 3.5.2, Fabric 54) glazed lt yellow internally and externally, this parallels one from Abingdon (see Parrington 1975, 74 fig. 53 no. 53, found in association with Cistercian types).

FIII.46 Body sherds, 1 applied white strips, mot green glaze; 1 dk green glaze.
FIII.60 Body sherd, lt green glaze.

Room A9 (group 21)

The final phase included a cooking pot, 3 kitchen ware vessels, a bowl, a jug and a lobed dish.

FII.20 Cooking pot rim; Kitchen ware rims × 2.
FIII.41 Bowl, partially glazed dk green int (Fig. 3.5.14), mortar adhering; Body sherds, 1 partially glazed internally; 1 lt green glaze, 1 other.
FIII.46 Base of cooking pot; Kitchen ware jug rim, applied white strips, dk green glaze; Body sherds, 1 dk green glaze; 2 red slip, 1 mot green glaze; 1 dk yellow glaze; Fine wares incl: body sherds, 1 dk yellow int and dk green ext; mot green glaze; 2 lt green int, mot green ext; 1 red slip, mot green glaze; 1 applied white strips; 3 applied strips of alternating colour, dk green glaze; 2 applied red strips, dk green glaze, cross-joins between F737 and F520; 1 combed deco, glazed yellow ext; 1 white rouletted strips, mot green glaze.
FIII.54 Body sherds × 2, lt green int and ext.
FIII.59 Lobed dish, dk green glaze int and ext (Fig. 3.5.13); Body sherds × 2, lt green int and ext; 1 dk green int and ext.
FIII.63 Body sherd.

Room A10

The final phase of Room A10 yielded mainly fine tablewares, and a bearded face mask, reminiscent of Hendon types, a bottle and a jug. The broad, well glazed strap handles from jars or pitchers are unparalleled earlier. The demolition levels above yielded a ?jug, glazed internally and externally mottled green (Fig. 3.5.16).

FIA.99 Body sherd, St. Neot's type.
FIII.40 Body sherd.
FIII.41 Bottle.
FIII.43 Body sherds, 1 mot green ext; 1 dk green int and mot green ext.
FIII.46 Body sherd, applied strips of alternating colour, mot green glaze; applied strips, dk green glaze.
FIII.51 Body sherd, lt green glaze.
FIII.54 Rim of fine table-ware, glazed mot green int and ext; Body sherds × 3, 1 glazed dk green int, 1 dk green int and lt green ext, 1 glazed lt green int and ext.
FIII.59 Rims of fine table-ware × 2, 1 lt green int and mot green ext, 1 dk green int and lt green ext; Handle, mot green glaze (Fig. 3.5.15); Jug rim, dk green glaze int and ext; Body sherds × 6, incl dk green glaze int and ext; 2 lt green int and ext; 2 dk green glaze ext; 1 lt green int and mot green ext.
FIII.60 Strap handle with face mask, dk green glaze (Fig. 3.5.17); Base, partially glazed ext.
FIII.63 Broad strap handle and rim, incised deco, partial yellow glaze (Fig. 3.5.18, cross-joins F44 and F186/1); Body sherd, grooved deco, green glaze int and ext.
99 Body sherd, grooved deco.

Construction of agricultural buildings H and G (group 17)

Very few sherds were associated with Building H and none with G.

FIII.41 Kitchen ware base.

FIII.51	Jug profile (Fig. 3.5.19), with irreg and horiz. grooves, partially glazed lt green, the handle was luted to the lower part of the vessel with a thumb impression, cross-joins occurred between F417 and F186 (see Cornmarket 1935.537 in the Ashmolean Museum Reserve Collection).

Phase 5 (mid to late 15th century) *(Fig. 3.6)*

Destruction of Buildings H and G; construction of Building M

Few sherds were associated with the destruction of Buildings H and G and construction of Building M.

FII.20	Base.
FIII.41	Body sherds, 1 dk green glaze; 1 mot green glaze int.
FIII.43	Body sherds × 2, lt green glaze.
FIII.46	Jug with pinched spout, partially glazed ext.
FIII.59	Body sherd, dk green glaze int and lt green glaze ext.
FIII.63	Body sherd, grooved deco, mot green glaze.
99	Body sherds, 1 Romano-British; 1 19th-century white earthen-ware (intrusive).

Stratified Destruction

This phase included some ceramic vessels unparalleled amongst the earlier stratified material. Where these vessels occurred above individual rooms/buildings, they are illustrated with pottery from that room/building, but some vessels could not be attributed to specific buildings with any certainty. These included a Tudor-type mug or jug with mottled green glaze, which had been overfired (Fig. 3.6.1, Fabric 51), and a handle of another Tudor-type jug, glazed dark green externally (Fig. 3.6.5, Fabric 59).

The destruction level above Structure A14 included a cooking pot with a bifid rim (Fig. 3.6.2), a style of rim not found before the 15th century in Oxford along with a very narrow necked jug, with thumb-impression at the top of the handle, despite the fact that the handle had not been luted out of the jug but rather pushed through into the body of the vessel (Fig. 3.6.4, Fabric 40). It was glazed dark green externally and light green internally. A Rouen-type jug rim with applied red slip 'dots' and rich yellow glaze externally (Fig. 3.6.3, Fabric 60) was also found and may well be part of the same vessel found in the dump levels of Phase 2/1 (Group 3). A small bulbous jug, partially glazed mottled green (Fig. 3.6.7, Fabric 46) may parallel the belly of the jug illustrated from the Hamel (Palmer 1980, 172 fig. 18 no. 6, 15th century).

Unstratified

In the initial cleaning-up above Structure T a large storage jar with applied thumbed strips (Fig. 3.6.6, Fabric 46) was recovered along with a Tudor-type biconical dish with handle (Fig. 3.6.8) glazed dark green internally and partially glazed dark green externally. In the area above Building G the initial clean-off yielded a ?jar with incised decoration and blistered mottled green glaze externally (Fig. 3.6.9, Fabric 51) and glazed orange internally, and a handled ?jar (Fig. 3.6.12, Fabric 46), the handle of which was decorated in a manner unparalleled elsewhere in Oxfordshire. An applied central strip had been added to the handle, with incised 'feather' decoration and stamped with a concentric circle at the top of the handle. Other vessels included a deep-sided bowl with undercut rim (Fig. 3.6.13, Fabric 61; see Biddle 1961–2, 164 fig. 27 no. 2 for parallel); a lobed dish, with impressed stamps on the handle (Fig. 3.6.14) and a decorative 'fural' of red clay, glazed internally and externally mottled green (Fig. 3.6.10, Fabric 59); a lid or shallow dish (Fig. 3.6.11) can be paralleled with one from the Hamel, Oxford, and Grove, near Wantage (see Palmer 1980, 172 fig. 18 no. 20, but without drilled holes, dated 15th century, and Moorhouse 1971–2, 119 fig. 1 no. 4).

Discussion

Some chronological trends could be observed within the ceramic assemblage. The pottery from the pre-moat settlement, dating from the late 12th to early 13th century, indicates that two major coarse industries were supplying the site at this period, represented by Group II fabric 20 and Group III fabric 41. The repertoire of both industries included cooking pots, bowls and shallow dishes, but the coil-made flint and chalk tempered vessels of fabric 20 occurred in larger forms than the wheel-thrown sandy vessels of fabric 41. This may account for the small but steady demand throughout the history of the site for the flint and chalk-tempered wares. Pitchers were also made in fabric 41 and were often decorated with white slip and a thin lead glaze. These pitchers were gradually superseded in Phase 2 by finer sandy jugs (Group III, fabric 46), often highly decorated. This finer sandy ware occurred in a wider range of products such as bottles and the occasional kitchen ware including skillets. The sandy ware used for cooking pots and other domestic vessels (Group III, fabric 41) continued in use until the demolition of the site, as did the finer sandy ware specialising in jugs (Group III, fabric 46).

There was little evidence of the poorly executed jugs found from this period on tenement sites in Oxford (Haldon 1977, Mellor 1980). Certainly the quality of workmanship of the decoration had deteriorated but the jugs were still well-executed. Plain or partially glazed jugs, pitchers and bunghole jars were found amongst the demolition at Chalgrove; these jars and pitchers appear to have superseded the traditional medieval jars in Oxford and their occurrence at Chalgrove suggests that the traditional jug industry may have declined from *c* 1450–1485.

Tudor-type tablewares (Group III, fabrics 54 and 59), including cups, small jugs and lobed dishes, occurred fairly consistently from Phases 3–4 until the demolition of the site. No other sites in Oxfordshire have yielded such a quantity of fine tablewares. The majority of these tablewares were Tudor green probably from the West Surrey kilns, but local types were also present. Other regional imports from West Surrey also occurred (Group III, fabrics 43 and 47). These regional imports accounted for the slightly wider variety of fabrics and forms in the final phase of occupation of the site (Phase 4).

Continental imports from Rouen and Saintonge in France occurred in Phases 2 and 3. Although parallels are known in Oxford, vessels from France are rare and their presence on the site must imply that the inhabitants had some standing in the community. It has been suggested that the Saintonge jugs imported to this country were 'seconds' and were used as a gimmick to sell wine from the Bordeaux region (Bob Thomson pers. comm.). Certainly the Chalgrove examples bear kiln scars and might be regarded as 'seconds'.

Although the majority of the products were from local kiln sites, the occurrence of continental imports and the fine tablewares suggests a succession of well-to-do and well-connected inhabitants at the site.

Several kiln sites are known in the region, one at Brill/Boarstall in Buckinghamshire (Farley 1979, 127) and another at Henley (W. O. Hassall pers. comm.; Henley Borough Ancient Deeds 5 held in County Record Office). Both were known to have been operating by the mid 13th and late 13th century respectively. Another documentary record refers to kilns within the Manor of Bensington (Midgley 1942, 98). This could possibly refer to the Henley kilns but it may point to yet another production centre. By the mid 15th century a potter was also working in Nettlebed, some six miles to the north-west of Henley (Minister's Accounts 1442, PROSC 6/961, 21–6, 21–8, Henry VI).

The moated site at Chalgrove is almost equidistant from Brill and Henley. However, there is little evidence to suggest that much pottery was coming from either Henley or Nettlebed. The major sandy ware (Group III fabric 41) belongs to the same tradition that supplied Abingdon, Wallingford and Reading, which differs from the tradition that supplied Oxford.

The kilns for this sandy ware were probably to the west of Reading and it may have been transported up river to markets at Wallingford and Abingdon. The flint and chalk tempered wares (Group II fabric 20) were marketed over a much wider area and probably originate beyond Newbury. These wares were also found at Tetsworth to the north-west of Chalgrove but the site was abandoned in the mid 13th century. The fine sandy ware as typified by jugs originates from the Brill/Boarstall kilns directly to the north of Chalgrove. The local Tudor types, in a fabric very similar to the Brill/Boarstall fabrics, may also originate from there. The regional imports from Surrey may have been marketed along the same route as the sandy wares via Reading and then up river. Alternatively they may have come overland from Henley. Two other fabric types and their products may originate to the south-east of Chalgrove (Group III fabrics 60 and 63), but the percentage of these fabrics on the site was relatively insignificant (their combined number of sherds at 246 represents approximately 8.5% of the total number of sherds from the excavation).

Sherds associated with the buildings were very fragmentary and only the demolition layers yielded much information concerning the vessel forms. The buildings were obviously cleaned regularly and even the garderobe produced little material. No rubbish pits and no wells were uncovered in the trenches.

The comparison of vessel forms between individual rooms was hindered by the small number of vessels recovered from many of the buildings. The dump levels associated with Phase 2 showed the expected range of domestic wares and jugs for the second half of the 13th century, suggesting that the site had been occupied for some time. The dump level associated with the pentice area (A13) also produced a substantial quantity, with a preference for jugs and tablewares.

Comparison between the rural site of Chalgrove and urban sites in Oxford was difficult, since few of the farm buildings yielded much pottery. However, it would appear that in general more domestic vessels associated with cooking were evident during the 14th and 15th centuries than in Oxford. Bottles were also more common at Chalgrove. The demolition levels did produce a number of bowls with flanged or undercut rims from the Brill/Boarstall kilns which can be paralleled with the deserted medieval village at Seacourt and the Hamel, Oxford. However, the Brill/Boarstall domestic wares were generally less popular in Oxford than in the later levels at Chalgrove and Seacourt, suggesting perhaps that they were better suited to activities concerned with small holdings and farms.

Note:

Following the analysis of the pottery, a kiln site was discovered at Soundess Field, Nettlebed (Mellor 1982).

Illustrated pottery

Figure 3.1

Phase 1

Building P:

3.1.1 Cooking pot rim with applied strips (Ctx 43, FIII.41)
3.1.2 Cooking pot rim with applied strips (Ctx 88, FIII.41)
3.1.3 Cooking pot rim (Ctx 88, FII.20)

External surfaces and dump layers:

3.1.4 Shallow dish, glazed light green, pinched lip and combed decoration. (Ctx 1171, FIII.41)
3.1.5 Jug base (Ctx 966, FIII.41)
3.1.6 Cooking pot rim (Ctx 804, FII.20)
3.1.7 Kitchen-ware rim, possibly a deep-sided bowl (Ctx 1171, FII.20)

Phase 2

The moat upcast, dump layers and demolition of Phase 1 structures

3.1.8 Bottle base with 'wire' marks (Ctx 532, FIII.46)
3.1.9 Large cooking pot rim (Ctx 691, FII.20)
3.1.10 Cooking pot with undercut rim (Ctx 530, FIII.46)
3.1.11 Body sherd with stamped grid decoration, mottled green glaze (Ctx 75, FIII.46)
3.1.12 Body sherd, mottled green glaze, possibly a start baluster jug (Ctx 353, FIII.46)
3.1.13 Jug, white slip decoration, partially glazed green (Ctx 1095, FIII.41)
3.1.14 Jug rim, red slip dots, light yellow glaze, from Rouen (Ctx 786, FIII.66)
3.1.15 Bottle base (Ctx 898, FIII.60)
3.1.16 Body sherd, impressed concentric circles, mottled green glaze (Ctx 534, FIII.41)
3.1.17 Skillet handle, possibly intrusive (Ctx 237, FIII.46)
3.1.18 Cooking pot rim (Ctx 534, FIII.41)
3.1.19 Cooking pot rim (Ctx 534, FII.20)
3.1.20 Kitchen ware rim with combed decoration (Ctx 534, FIII.46)

Figure 3.2

Phase 3 construction and early occupation, and sub-phase 3/2

Building A1

3.2.1 Jug base, mottled green glaze (Ctx 1084, FIII.46)

Room A9

3.3.2 Jug, white slip, partially glazed (Ctx 1053, FIII.41)
3.3.3 Partially glazed jug rim (Ctx 975, FIII.41)
3.3.4 Jug rim (Ctx 766, FIII.46)
3.3.5 Jug rim, kiln scar on rim and handle (Ctx 962 + cross-joins 975, 1052, 1053, FIII.49)
3.3.6 Bowl, mottled red glaze (Ctx 971, FIII.49)

Building W

3.2.7 Body sherd, applied thumbed strip (Ctx 537, FIII.41) *Courtyard and dump layers between the cross-wing and Building W*
3.2.8 Body sherd, wavy and horizontal grooves, dark green glaze (Ctx 1142, FIII.40)
3.2.9 Cooking pot rim (Ctx 960, FIII.41)
3.2.10 Skillet handle with incised decoration (Ctx 1147, FIII.46)
3.2.11 Handle with grooved decoration, mottled green glaze (Ctx 1147, FIII.46)
3.2.12 Belly of cruet with applied horizontal thumbed strip (Ctx 170, FIII.46)
3.2.13 Kitchen ware rim (Ctx 960, FIII. 41)
3.2.14 Kitchen ware rim (Ctx 144, FII.20)

Central courtyard (gravel surface 396)

3.2.15 Bowl rim (Ctx 488, Fabric III.41)
3.2.16 Storage jar rim, light yellow glaze, possibly intrusive (Ctx 118, FIII.51)
3.2.17 Rod handle with stabbed decoration, yellow glaze (Ctx 179, FIII.46)

Room A3 added to Building A1(sub-phase 3/2)

3.2.18 Cooking pot rim (Ctx 1031, FIII.41)
3.2.19 Bowl rim (Ctx 1031, FIII.41)

Figure 3.3

Later occupation, Phases 3 and 4, and demolition, Phase 5

Room A3 demolition

3.3.1 Local Tudor-type jug, mottled green glaze (Ctx 186)

Room A4 occupation and demolition

3.3.2 Tudor green type, ?bowl or cup, mottled green glaze int. and ext. (Ctx 599)
3.3.3 Storage jar rim (Ctx 1015+cross-joins 161, 790/275, FIII.41)

Room A5 occupation and demolition

3.3.4 Storage jar with bifid rim (Ctx 726 demolition, FIII.41)
3.3.5 Shallow dish foot rim (Ctx 717 demolition, FIII.46)
3.3.6 Base of Tudor-type jug, mottled green int. and ext. (Ctx 717 demolition, FIII.54)
3.3.7 Fine Tudor-type bowl, rilling ext., mottled green glaze int. and ext. (Ctx 717 demolition, FIII.54)
3.3.8 Abraded face mask, applied red strip below pad, mottled green glaze (Ctx 633 occupation, FIII.46)
3.3.9 'Dripping pan', finger tipped, orange glaze int., carbon ext. (Ctx 633 occupation, FIII.63)
3.3.10 Base of ?cup, dark green glaze int., mottled green glaze ext. (Ctx 633 occupation, FIII. 58)

Room A11 demolition

3.3.11 Hard fired storage jar (Ctx 116)

Gardens south of Building A1, and Structure T

3.3.12 Jug with dark green glaze (Ctx 269, FIII.46)
3.3.13 Jug with reg. and horiz. grooved decoration, mottled green glaze (Ctx 267, FIII.46)
3.3.14 Handle of probable aquamanile, stabbed decoration, dark green glaze. Vessel dark green glaze int. and ext. (Ctx 120, FIII.46)

Figure 3.4

Pottery from Building A12 the latest kitchen, Phase 4 construction and occupation and Phase 5 demolition

3.4.1 Partially thumbed jug base (Ctx 5 and cross-joins 798, FIII.46)
3.4.2 Rim of shallow ?dish (Ctx 14, FIII.64)
3.4.3 Leg of tripod cooking pot (Ctx 14, FIII.60)
3.4.4 Storage jar with applied thumbed strips (parallel with Hamel) (Ctx 5, FIII.60)
3.4.5 Deep-sided flanged dish (Ctx 5, FIII.60)
3.4.6 Near-complete bowl, flanged rim, glazed yellow int., flecks of mottled green glaze ext. (Ctx 14+cross-joins 12 and 19)
3.4.7 Jug, pinched lip, incised 'arrow' sign, partially glazed dark green (Ctx 23, FIII.46)
3.4.8 Bottle with reg. and horiz. grooves, mottled green glaze (Ctx 20, FIII.59)
3.4.9 Large bung-hole jar, splashes of green glaze, thumbed spigot (Ctx 5, FIII.51)
3.4.10 Jug with pinched spout and dark green glaze (Ctx 23, FIII.46)

Courtyard outside Building A12

3.4.11 Base of probable bottle (Ctx 621, FIII.46)

Figure 3.5

Pottery from Phase 4 occupation and Phase 5 demolition

Building D demolition

3.5.1 Jug rim (Ctx 1144, FIII.46)

Buildings A14 and A3 demolition

3.5.2 Small ointment pot, glazed light yellow int. and ext. Abingdon parallel (Ctx 186, FIII.54)
3.5.3 Broad strap handle, partially glazed green (Ctx 186, FIII.46)

Levelling layers in the garden and pentice area north of Building A1

3.5.4 Jug with pinched spout (Ctx 573, FIII.41)
3.5.5 Jug handle, stabbed decoration, glazed brown (Ctx 700, FIII.41)
3.5.6 Jug rim with applied strips of alternating colour (Ctx 573, FIII.46)
3.5.7 Bottle body sherd, light green glaze (Ctx 573, FIII.46)
3.5.8 Cup rim, light green int. and ext. (Ctx 573, FIII.59)
3.5.9 Strap handle, stabbed decoration, mottled green glaze (Ctx 1013, FIII.46)
3.5.10 Strap handle, stabbed decoration, mottled yellow glaze (Ctx 700, FIII.46)
3.5.11 Base of probable bottle (Ctx 1013, FIII.46)
3.5.12 Bung-hole jar base, mottled green glaze int. and ext. (Ctx 725+cross-joins 186, FIII.46)

Rooms A9 and A10 Phase 4 occupation and Phase 5 demolition

3.5.13 Lobed dish, dark green glaze int. and ext. (Ctx 639, FIII.59)
3.5.14 Bowl, partially glazed dark int., mortar adhering (Ctx 639, FIII.41)
3.5.15 Handle, mottled green glaze (Ctx 923, FIII.59)
3.5.16 Possible jug, mottled green glaze int. and ext. (Ctx 132 Ph5)

3.5.17 Strap handle with face mask, dark green glaze (Ctx 41, FIII.60)
3.5.18 Broad strap handle and rim, incised decoration, partial yellow glaze (Ctx 44 + cross-joins 186, FIII. 63)

Construction of Building H

3.5.19 Jug profile with irreg. and horiz. grooves, partially glazed light green. Handle luted to lower part of vessel with a thumb impression (Ctx 417 + cross-joins 186, FIII.51)

Figure 3.6

Phase 5 demolition

Stratified demolition

3.6.1 Tudor-type mug or jug, mottled green-glaze, overfired (Ctx 100, FIII.51)
3.6.2 Cooking pot with a bifid rim (Ctx 186)
3.6.3 Rouen-type jug with applied red slip dots, rich yellow glaze ext. (Ctx 186, FIII.60)
3.6.4 Narrow necked jug, thumb impression at top of handle (Ctx 518, FIII.40)
3.6.5 Tudor-type jug handle, glazed dark green ext. (Ctx 337, FIII.59)

Unstratified demolition

3.6.6 Large storage jar with applied thumb strips (Ctx 584, FIII.46)
3.6.7 Small bulbous jug, partially glazed mottled green (Ctx 1044, FIII.46)
3.6.8 Tudor-type biconical dish with handle, glazed dark green int., partially glazed ext. (Ctx 1044)
3.6.9 Possible jar, incised decoration, blistered mottled green ext. and orange glaze int. (Ctx 1129, FIII.51)
3.6.10 Decorative 'fural' of red clay, mottled green glaze int. and ext. (Ctx 413, FIII.59)
3.6.11 Lid or shallow dish (Ctx 911)
3.6.12 Handled ?jar, decorated applied central strip for handle (Ctx 1129, FIII.46)
3.6.13 Deep-sided bowl with undercut rim (Unstratified, FIII.61)
3.6.14 Lobed dish with impressed stamps on the handle (Ctx 279)

THE COINS AND JETTONS
by Marion Archibald

Introduction

A total of 10 coins and 11 jettons were recovered from the excavation. These ranged in date from the mid 13th century to the mid 15th century. The coins included one find unusual from an English excavation, a double mite (7) of Philip the Bold, Duke of Burgundy (1384–1405). There was also a penny (20) of Alexander III, King of Scots (1249–86). The jettons included both English and French examples. The catalogue is in order of Small Find number (SF) with a note of the original context in which the coin or jetton was found (C; U/S denotes unstratified finds), and the phase to which the context has been assigned.

Catalogue

1. Henry III, 1216–72
Cut halfpenny, Long-cross type Class Vb or c, struck *c* 1255. Mint: Canterbury.
Wt. 0.68 g. (10.5 gr.). SF4, C20, Phase 4.
This coin is not much worn but such coins could remain in circulation for long periods without showing appreciable wear. The Long-cross issue went rapidly out of circulation after the introduction of the sterling type in 1279, so the *terminus ante quem* for the deposition of this coin is *c* 1280.

2. **French jetton**, early 15th century (Barnard 1916, pl VI, 47 for general type)
Obv: +PIEIBAR*DV*A AnEI; shield of France modern. Rev: Cross fleur-de-lisee with A in each angle within a quatrefoil with a mullet between two pollets in each angle, all within outer circle.Wt. 3.96 g. Diam. 22 mm. SF10, C186, Phase 5.

3. Edward I, 1272–1307
Penny, Class IXb star on breast, struck *c* 1300. Mint: London Wt. 0.88 g. (13.6 gr.). Diam. 22 mm. SF13, C22, Phase 3 Building A1
This coin is somewhat worn and was probably deposited *c* 1320–30.

4. **French jetton** of Dauphin, mid-15th century (Barnard 1916, pl. VII, 62)
Obv: +AVE MARIA GRACIA P–A; dolphin to left. Rev: Cross fleur-de-lisee with A in each angle within quatrefoil, A,V,E and M each between two annulets in the angles, all within outer circle. Wt. 4.31 g. Diam. 21 mm. SF14, U/S.

5. **English jetton**, *c* 1300 (Berry 1974, pl. 4, 6A)
Obv: Crowned leopard's head; border of pellets in place of legend. Rev: Cross moline with a pellet in each angle; border of pellets in place of legend. Wt. 1.92 g. Diam. 20 mm. SF17, C156, Phase 3.

6. **English jetton** of French type, early 15th century(?) (Barnard 1916, pl. VI, 38, rev. only for French prototype, and pl. III, 59 for English copy)
Obv: Uncertain shield with five irregular lines above ?cross border of strokes in place of legend.
Rev: Bowed cross fleur-de-lisee with fleur-de-lis in centre; border of strokes in place of legend. Incomplete piercing from reverse. This jetton is in very crude style. Wt. 4.81 g. Diam. 22 mm. SF35, C143, Phase 5, Building A6.
This jetton is very difficult to date. It looks later than the group of coins of French type produced in the 14th century.

7. Philip the Bold, Duke of Burgundy, 1384–1405 (Duby 1790, 151, pl. lii, 1)
Double mite struck for Flanders.
Obv:+PHILLIP DVX BVRG. Pellet stops, shield of Burgundy within inner c.
Rev:+MONETA FLANDRES. Pellet stop, short cross pattee within inner circle. Wt. 1.22 g. (18.8 gr.). SF38, C157, Phase 5.
All foreign coins were officially proscribed from circulation in England and it is rare to find them, even as site finds, except in coastal places. In 1464, however, a convention was signed between Edward IV and his brother-in-law, Charles the Bold of Burgundy, to allow the silver groats of England and the silver double patards of the Burgundian territories to circulate freely in the lands governed by both rulers. The convention did not include the base-metal coinages of the Netherlands and so officially this coin should have been taken to the exchange with its fellows on entry and converted into English money.
I have no record of any coin of this particular group having been excavated on a site in England, although various base-metal coins from the Netherlands have been shown to me (e.g. a mite of Louis de Nevers, Count of Flanders, 1322–46, from Dover in 1970). The close trade relations between England and the Low Countries would account for the arrival of such pieces and the escape of a few into unauthorized circulation. The present coin is in relatively unworn condition and is most likely to have been deposited in the reign of Philip the Bold or shortly afterwards. It is so different in design from the English issues that it is unlikely to have survived long in circulation here.

8. Edward III, 1327–77
Penny, Pre-Treaty Coinage, Series C, 1351–2. Mint: London Wt. 1.06 g. (16.3 gr.) SF41, C142, Phase 4.
This coin is fairly worn and was probably lost at the end of the 14th century but almost certainly before 1413, when the weight of the penny was reduced.

9. Henry VI, 1st Reign, 1422–61
Groat, Annulet type, 1422–7. Mint: Calais
Wt. 3.63 g. (56.0 gr.) SF94, C548, Phase 4.
This coin is unclipped and scarcely worn. It was probably deposited by *c* 1440 and almost certainly before 1464 when the weight of the silver coinage was reduced.

10. **French jetton**, mid 15th century
Obv: xAVE MARIA GRACIA, annulet stops; shield of France modern with one pellet above and three at each side. Rev: Cross fleur-de-lisee with four annulets at the centre, with two 'A's and two 'M's in opposing angles, all within a quatrefoil with an annulet between two pellets in each outer angle, all within inner circle. Wt. 5.02 g. Diam. 29 mm. SF97, C551, Phase 5, Building A1.
This jetton is in very rough style, and its date would accord with its discovery in the destruction-level of the Hall. It is not possible to say whether it is of 1460 or 1470. Nothing of this style is illustrated in by Barnard (1916), but it is not an uncommon group.

11. **French jetton**, mid-later 14th century (Barnard 1916, pl, v, 28, where the castle is topped by a fleur-de-lis, not a crown)
Obv:+AVE MARIA GRACIA PLENA, double pellet stops; stylised 'castle of Tours', crowned. Rev: Cross fleur-de-lisee within quatrefoil with a fleur-de-lis on each cusp, a crown between two annulets in each outer angle, all within outer circle. Wt. 1.63 g. Diam. 26 mm. SF113, U/S.
This jetton is in fine style. The crowned castle was introduced onto the coinage by Philip IV in 1337.

12. Edward III, 1327–77
Penny, Florin Issue, 1344–51. Mint: London
Wt. 0.55 g. (8.5 gr.). SF128, C599, Phase 5, Room A4.
This coin is very worn and clipped. It is in much worse condition than those of comparable issue-date in the Attenborough hoard buried in *c* 1422. It is therefore most likely to have been deposited in the mid-15th century.

13. Richard II, 1377–99
Penny. Mint: York
Wt. 0.67 g. (10.3 gr.) chipped. SF143, C609, Phase 5
This coin is very worn and clipped. It is at least as poor in condition as comparable coins in the Attenborough hoard and so was probably deposited in *c* 1425–50.

14. **French jetton**, mid-14th century (Barnard 1916, pl. iv, 16)
Obv:+ISPART.IISPLTRARTIS; Agnus Dei. Rev: Cross fleury with quatrefoil in centre and fleur-de-lis in each angle, all within cartouche, AVE., OVE. in alternate outer angles. Wt. 2.30 g. Diam. 28 mm. SF259, C119, Phase 5.
Despite the illiterate legends, this piece is of fine style.

15. **French-type jetton**, *c* 1400 (Barnard 1916, pl. vi, 45, obv., and pl. xxiii, 1, rev., for jettons of this rough heavy style)
Obv: XAVE MARIA GRACIA, double annulet stop between last two words only; shield of France modern with an annulet between two pellets at top and at each side. Rev: Cross fleury with four annulets around a central pellet in centre, 'A' and 'M' in alternating quarters, all within a quatrefoil, an annulet between two pellets in each angle. Wt. 7.61 g. Diam. 30 mm. SF289, C424, Phase 4, Building H.
The style of this piece is very rough, on a very thick flan.

16. **French jetton**, *c* 1400 (Barnard 1916, pl. vi, 43)
Obv:+AVE MARIA GRACIA PLN ('lombardic' N), double cross stops; shield of France modern (but with the base of a lis just visible at the top of the field) with crown above. Rev: Cross fleury with quatrefoil in centre all within a quatrefoil in centre, all within quatrefoil at each angle; in the outer angles, +E+, +V+, +A+, (and probably, although illegible here, +G+). Wt. 1.60 g. Diam. 24 mm. SF295, C593, Phase 4, Building A1.
The obverse type is based on the ecu a la couronne introduced by Charles VI of France in 1385. This jetton was found in the same level as coin No. 18 below, whose deposition is dated to the early 15th century, so its date fits this chronology satisfactorily.

17. **English jetton**, early 14th century
Obv: Eagle with head turned back within inner circle; border of pellets within continuous branched border in place of legend. Rev: Cross moline with a pellet in each angle within inner circle; border of pellets in place of legend (double struck). Wt. 0.47 g. (corroded). Diam. 19 mm. SF297, C593, Phase 4, Building A1.
Jettons of this type with reverse with a cross moline with pellets in the angles are very securely datable to the later 13th and early 14th centuries and it is therefore curious to find an example in the same level as jetton No. 16 and coin No. 18, both of which are datable to *c* 1400 or early 15th century. Jettons would not normally be expected to survive for so long but if the stratigraphy is secure, then this is a useful demonstration that they occasionally could and this possibility must be borne in mind when considering the date of deposition of jettons.

18. Edward III, 1327–77
Penny, Pre-Treaty Coinage, Series D, 1352–3. Mint: Durham
Wt. 0.80 g. (12.3 gr.). SF298, C593, Phase 4, Building A1.
This coin is considerably worn and clipped and is comparable in condition to coins of the same issue-period in the Attenborough hoard buried *c* 1420. This coin was therefore most probably deposited in the early 15th century. This would tally with the date of the jetton No. 16 found in the same layer but is considerably later than the date of the other jetton found there, No. 17. While coins could become worn and clipped abnormally early, there is virtually no likelihood that this coin was deposited in the mid 14th century.

19. **English jetton**, *c* 1310–30 (Berry 1974, Type 5, pl. 3, 10)
Obv: Three leopards of England passant gardant within an inner circle; border of pellets in place of legend. Rev: Cross moline within smaller than usual inner circle; border of pellets in place of legend. Wt. 1.47 g. Diam. 22 mm. SF307, C646, Phase 3, Building A1.

20. Alexander III King of Scots, 1249–86
Penny, 1st coinage, Long-cross type, 1250–80, Stewart class III. Mint: Berwick
Moneyer: Walter
Wt. 1.23 g. (19.0 gr.). SF336, C558, Phase 2.
This coin is folded almost double but the edges of the letters which remain visible enable it to be identified. The Scottish coins of this period were of as good metal as their English contemporaries and of comparable weight; they therefore circulated freely south of the border and are found in English hoards, comprising up to 2–5%. They were demonetised in both Scotland and England after the introduction of the solid-cross sterling coinage in 1279, so that this item was almost certainly deposited before *c* 1280. It was therefore neither false nor unacceptable in England and even after the type was demonetised, it was unlikely to have been thrown away as it had a bullion value. I have seen other coins bent double this way.

21. Edward II, 1307–27
Penny, class XIb *c* 1310–14. Mint: London
Wt. 1.01 g. (15.6 gr.). SF337, C726, Phase 5.
This coin is unclipped and hardly worn. It was certainly deposited before *c* 1350, most probably before *c* 1330.

OBJECTS OF COPPER ALLOY (FIGS 3.7–3.13)
by Alison Goodall with additional contributions by Kate Atherton

Introduction

A total of 233 copper alloy objects were found during the excavations. These were identified and catalogued by Alison Goodall shortly after the end of the fieldwork, with extended notes on objects of particular interest. The catalogue has subsequently been revised for publication by Kate Atherton, with the addition of measurements, and further information about the contexts and buildings in which objects were found. The catalogue has been divided into broad functional categories, comprising devotional

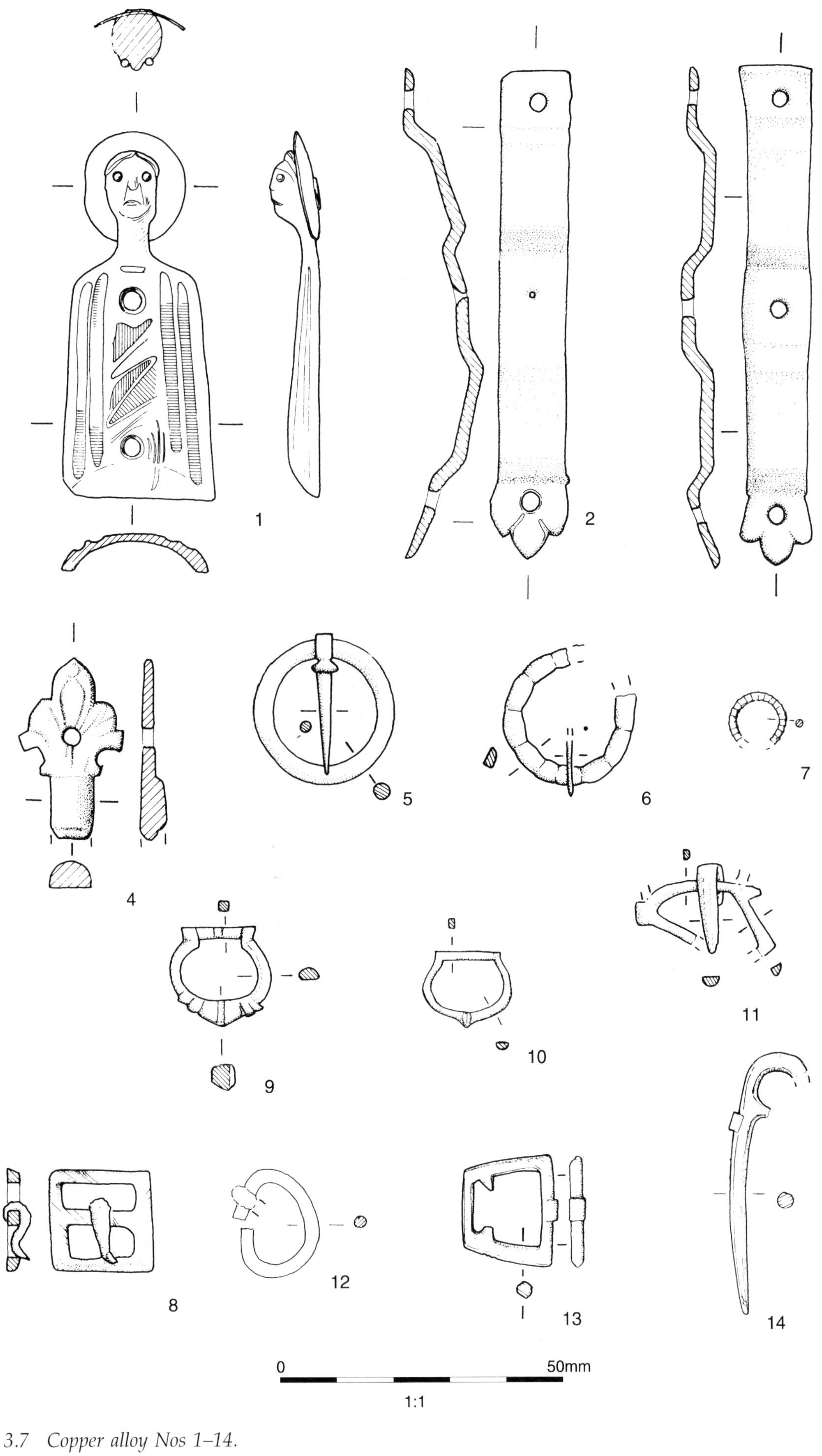

Figure 3.7 Copper alloy Nos 1–14.

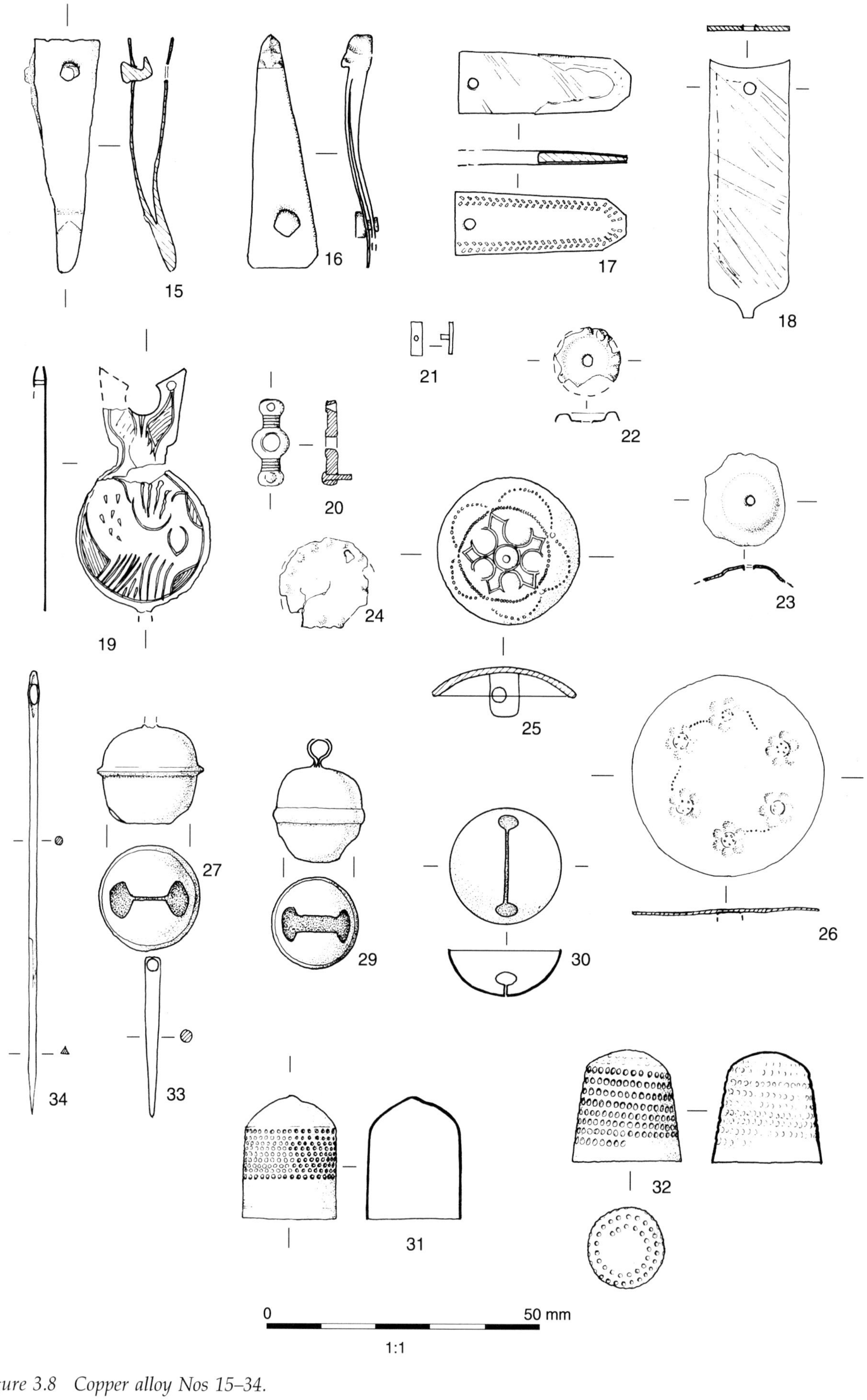

Figure 3.8 Copper alloy Nos 15–34.

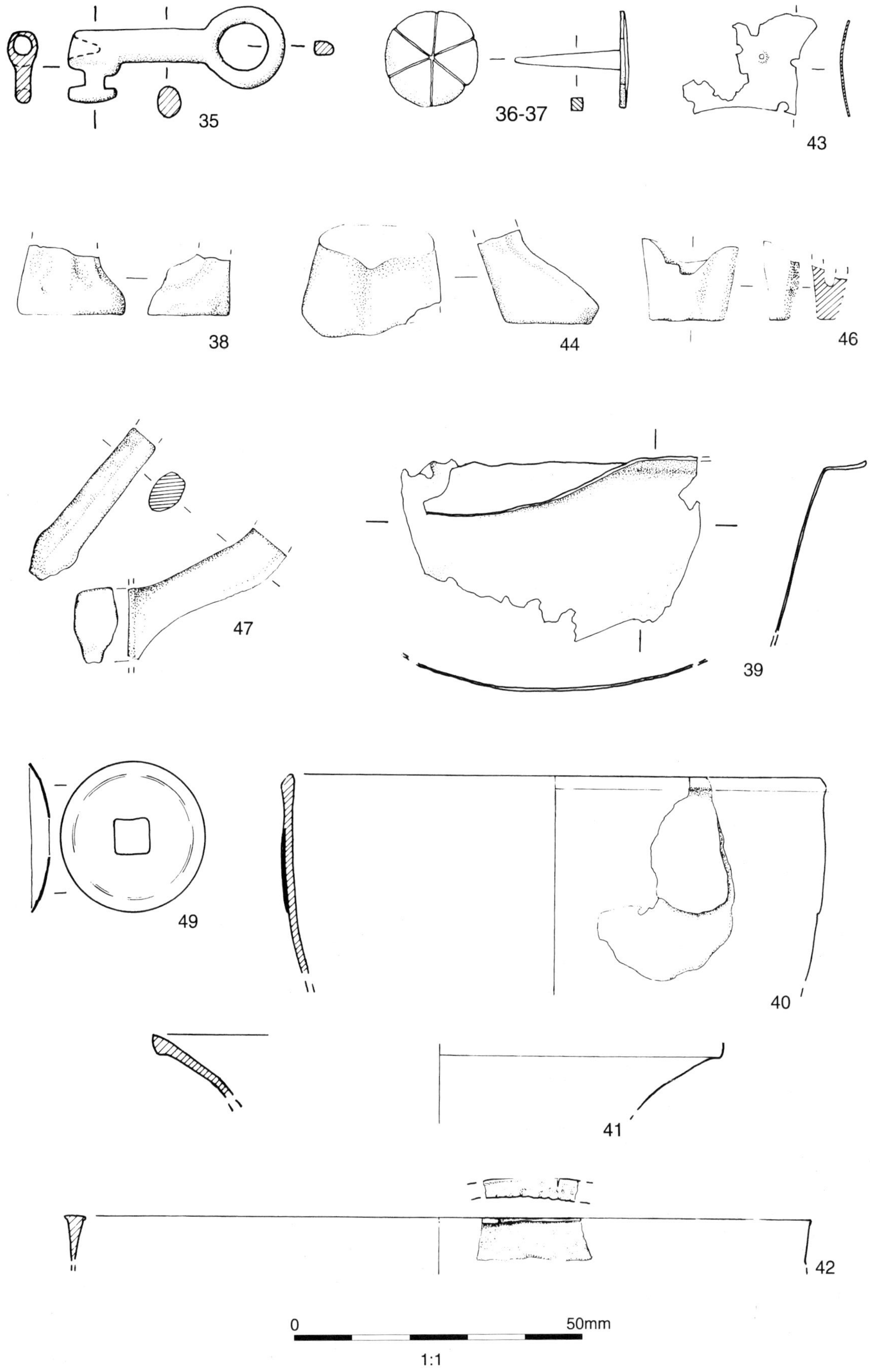

Figure 3.9 Copper alloy Nos 35–49.

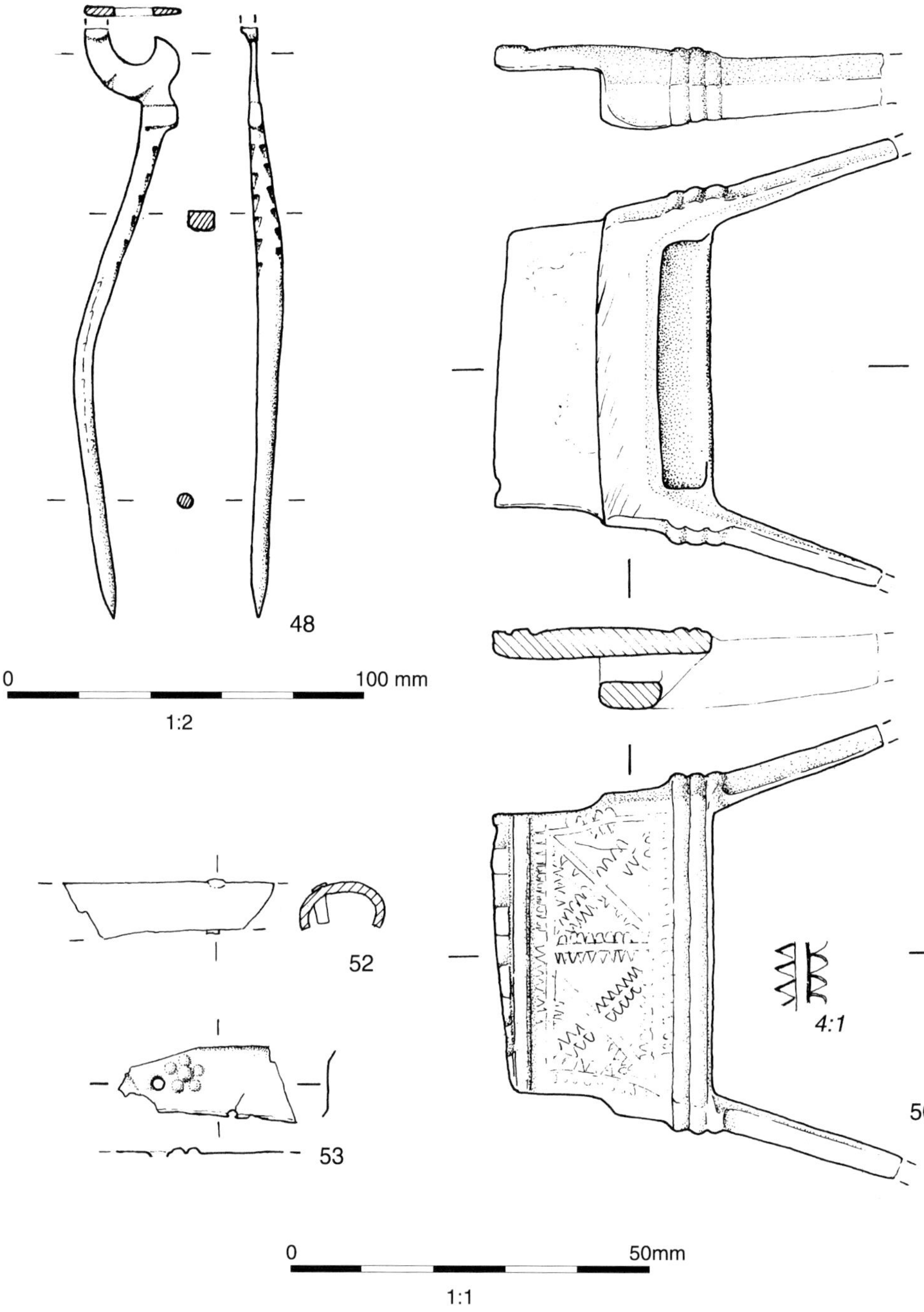

Figure 3.10 Copper alloy Nos 48, 50, 52 and 53.

objects (1 item), decorative fittings (3 objects), personal objects (23 objects), bells (4 objects), domestic items (25 objects), fixtures and fittings (39 objects) and lace tags and pins (29 and 107 items respectively). Two miscellaneous items were unidentifiable.

The most interesting of the copper alloy objects is a Limoges enamelled figure of a saint (No. 3.7.1), probably from a shrine or reliquary. It is closely comparable with one from St. Augustine's Abbey, Canterbury, and probably dates from the 12th or 13th centuries. Two gilt strips (Nos 3.7.2 and 3) may be the base fittings from ornamental harness mounts. There are two annular brooches (Nos 3.7.5 and 6) and the buckles (Nos 3.7.8–11) are of medieval type. Two strap-ends (Nos 3.8.15 and 16) date from the Anglo-Saxon period and have poorly defined zoomorphic terminals. No. 3.8.19 is a broken strap-end hook with an engraved animal's head on its plate. The decorated handle from a Roman spoon (No. 3.10.48) is a residual find. No. 3.10.50 is probably a distorted scabbard mount.

Devotional object (Fig. 3.7.1)

The most interesting of the copper alloy objects is an enamelled figure of a saint that probably derived

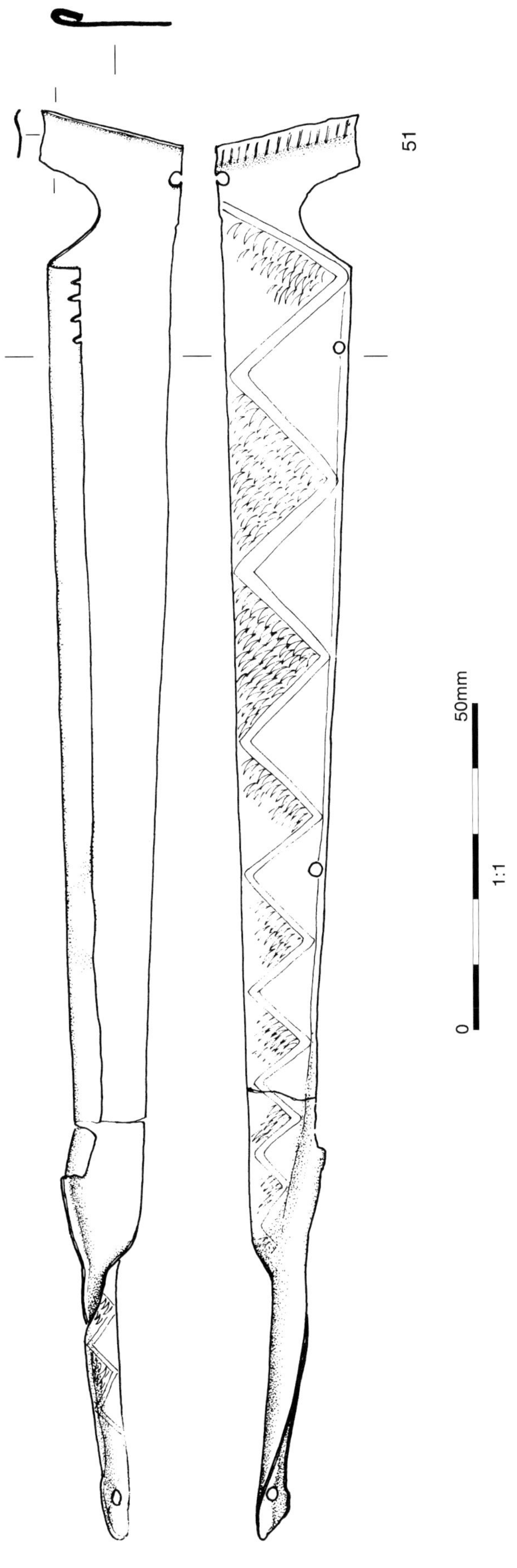

Figure 3.11 Copper alloy No. 51.

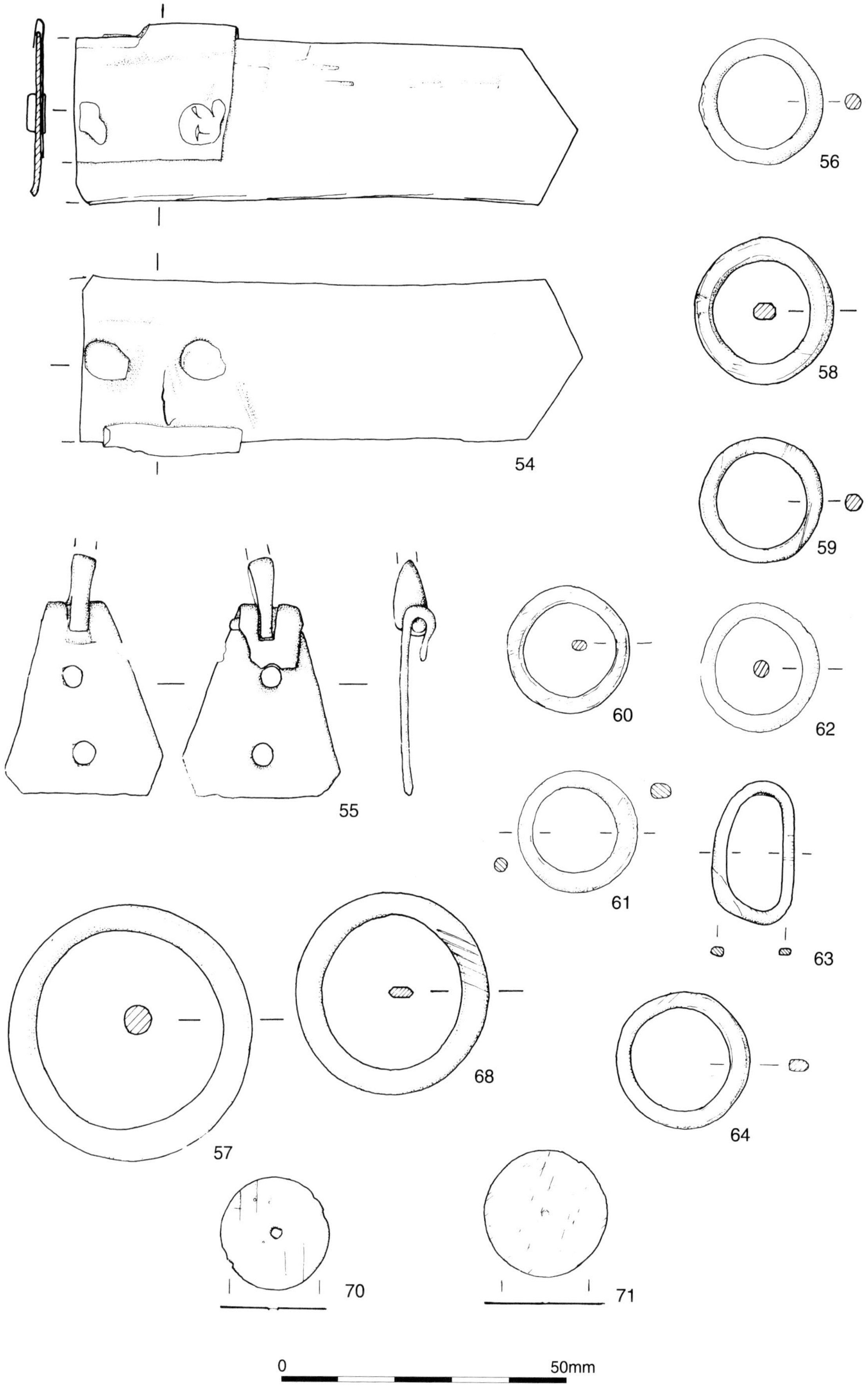

Figure 3.12 Copper alloy Nos 54–71.

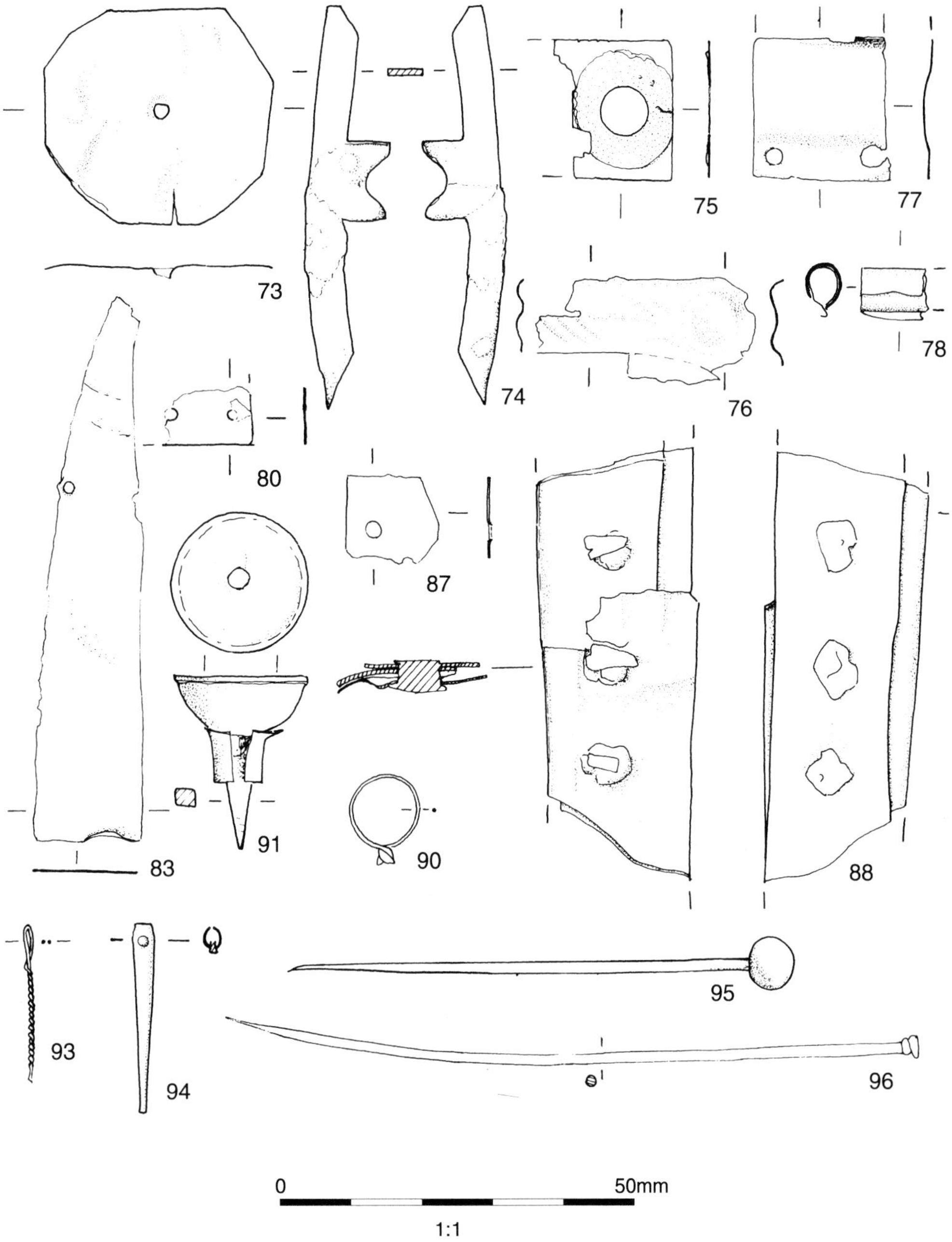

Figure 3.13 Copper alloy Nos 73–96.

from a shrine or reliquary. Traces of red, blue and possibly white enamel survive on the body and the eyes are inlaid with opaque blue glass beads. The halo is made from thick sheet which has been riveted onto the back of the head. Fragments of gilding survive on the halo, hair and face. The figure is approximately 60 mm tall and there are two rivet holes in the body. The object is closely comparable with one from St Augustine's Abbey, Canterbury and is almost certainly a product of the same workshop (Rigold 1970, 345–47). The figures were probably made in Limoges in the 12th or 13th century. Unfortunately the figure was found in a Phase 5 demolition context that cannot be related to a particular building.

Catalogue

3.7.1. **Figure of a saint**, enamelled and traces of gilding, Ht: 60 mm (SF 148, Ctx 629, Ph5).

Decorative fittings (Fig. 3.7.2–4)

Two similar gilt strips (Nos 3.7.2 and 3.7.3) were found, one from a Phase 2 context and the other from a finds reference context relating to Building A10.

Both strips have a decorated trefoil-shaped terminal at one end and three rivet holes with raised sections of strip between the holes. The strips are similar to the base fitting of a complex harness mount in the British Museum (Ward-Perkins 1949, 1–7). A fragment from a similar base fitting was also found at Netherton, Hampshire, in association with a suspension arm from a harness mount and several pendants (A R Goodall 1990, no. 157). The third decorative fitting (No. 3.7.4) is an ornamental terminal, trefoil shaped, from a belt with a rivet hole and traces of gilding.

Catalogue

3.7.2. **Decorative fitting**, L: 85 mm, W: 12 mm (SF 248, Ctx 355, Ph2).
3.7.3. **Decorative fitting**, L: 85 mm, W: 13 mm (SF 3, Ctx 72, unstratified above Building A10).
3.7.4. **Decorative fitting**, L: 31 mm, W: 18 mm (SF 2, Ctx 76, unstratified).

Personal objects (Figs 3.7.5–3.8.26)

Twenty-three objects have been classified as personal ornaments and dress accessories. Two annular brooches were found, one from Area F (No. 3.7.5) and another from Room A9 (No. 3.7.6). The former has an undecorated ring and a moulded pin; the latter has a lobed ring, and the point of the pin is corroded onto it. A small gilt, beaded ring was found in a Phase 5 context (No. 3.7.7). This ornate object may either be a small brooch or part of an ornamental boss from which the centre has entirely corroded away.

Seven copper alloy buckles were found from different parts of the manor. One each was found associated with Buildings J, G, B and Room A9 and the remaining three were from Phase 2 and 4 dump layers and from a Phase 5 demolition layer. No. 3.7.8 is a plain rectangular buckle with a pin that is probably iron. Nos 3.7.9 and 10 are single-looped buckle frames of 13th- to 14th-century type. No. 3.7.11 is a fragment from a rectangular double-looped buckle and No. 3.7.12 is possibly a simple buckle with a wire frame and part of the pin adhering to it. No. 3.7.13 is a belt-loop with internal projecting lugs and a knop on the front. A possible miniature buckle or stirrup fitting (SF 594, not illustrated) was recovered from a soil sample after the excavation. No. 3.7.14 is a pin from a brooch or buckle with ornamental moulding.

Five strap ends were found, two of which can be typologically dated to the 9th century (Nos 3.8.15–16). Both are triangular and have poorly defined zoomorphic terminals, and dome-headed rivets located at the split end. The former was found in Phase 2 platform material in the footprint of Building A1; the latter was unstratified. No. 3.8.17 is a tongue-shaped strap end that was made from two plates, one decorated, enclosing a forked spacer but lacking the terminal knop. No. 3.8.18 is a single plate, which may originally have had a spacer or may have been soldered directly onto another plate. The fifth strap end, No. 3.8.19, was probably originally hooked and has a rounded plate engraved with an animal's head. Similar strap hooks are discussed by Fingerlin (1971, 121–48) and dates in the late 14th and 15th centuries may be suggested for the type.

There are five strap ornaments, two of which were found in Phase 2 dump and levelling contexts (Nos 3.8.20 and 21). The first of these is a bar with a central perforated boss and a rivet hole at each end; the second is a simple small rectangular mount. Of the three remaining strap ornaments, two have a repoussé pelleted border and a central perforation (Nos 3.8.22 and 23). The fifth example is similar but the perforation is not central and is instead placed close to the edge (No. 3.8.24). Two buttons, Nos 3.8.25–26, are both from late or post-medieval contexts. Both have stamped decoration and the former is gilded.

Catalogue

3.7.5. **Brooch**, D: 24 mm (SF 142, Ctx 581, Ph3 Area F).
3.7.6. **Brooch**, D: *c* 25 mm (SF 226. Ctx 639, Ph4 Room A9).
3.7.7. **Gilt ring**, D: 10 mm (SF 135, Ctx 512, Ph5 Room A9).
3.7.8. **Buckle**, L: 18 mm, W: 18 mm (SF 59, Ctx 242, Ph2).
3.7.9. **Buckle**, L: 17 mm, W: 16 mm (SF 322, Ctx 573, Ph4).
3.7.10. **Buckle**, L: 15 mm, W: 12 mm (SF 204, Ctx 317, Ph5 Building J).
3.7.11. **Buckle**, L: *c* 26 mm (SF 480, Ctx 186, Ph5).
3.7.12. **Buckle**, L: 17 mm, W: 14 mm (SF 333, Ctx 1129, Ph3 Building G).
3.7.13. **Buckle**, L: 15–20 mm (SF 16, Ctx 138, Ph5 Building B).
(NI). **Buckle?** (SF 594, Ctx 639, Ph4 Room A9, soil sample).
3.7.14. **Brooch/buckle pin**, L: 45 mm (SF 291, Ctx 170, Ph3).
3.8.15. **Strap end**, Saxon, L: 42 mm (SF 313, Ctx 842, Ph2 platform of Building A1).
3.8.16. **Strap end**, Saxon, L: 42 mm (SF 486, unstratified).
3.8.17. **Strap end**, L: 31 mm, W: 11 mm (SF 15, Ctx 120, Ph4).
3.8.18. **Strap end**, L: 44 mm, W: 15 mm (SF 190, Ctx 115, Ph4).
3.8.19. **Strap end**, L: 38+mm, W: 24 mm (SF 80, Ctx 512, Ph5 Room A9)
3.8.20. **Strap ornament**, L: 15 mm (SF319, Ctx 386, Ph2).
3.8.21. **Strap ornament**, L: 7 mm, W: 3 mm (SF134, Ctx 534, Ph2).
3.8.22. **Strap ornament**, D: *c* 12 mm (SF48, Ctx 501, Ph5 Room A9).
3.8.23. **Strap ornament**, D: *c* 15 mm (SF495, Ctx 56, Ph3 Room A10).
3.8.24. **Strap ornament**, D: *c* 16 mm (SF274, unstratified).
3.8.25. **Button**, D: 26 mm (SF239, Ctx 186, Ph5).
3.8.26. **Button**, D: 35 mm (SF477, Ctx 74, post-medieval).

Bells (Fig. 3.8.27–30)

Four small plain bells made from sheet metal were recovered, two of which were complete (Fig. 3.8.27 and 29). Bells of this type are shown in contemporary monuments and illustrations attached to the collars of pet dogs, or to clothing.

Catalogue

3.8.27. **Bell**, D: 17 mm (SF50, Ctx 170, Ph3).
28 (NI). **Bell**, L: 34 mm, W: 11 mm (SF277, Ctx 926, Ph3 Room A10).
3.8.29. **Bell**, Ht: 23 mm, D: 17 mm (SF26, unstratified).
3.8.30. **Bell**, D: 17 mm (SF109, unstratified).

Domestic objects (Figs 3.8.31–3.12.55)

This category contains objects that were associated with the household and domestic activities and items include needlework tools, elaborate furniture fittings and copper alloy vessels.

The two thimbles have the pits arranged spirally, with plain areas at the top and the bottom (Nos 3.8.31–2). The first also has a rim around the base. There were two needles (Nos 3.8.33–34), one associated with Room A4 and the other with Building A1. The first is short with a round section and a round eye; the other is long with the triangular-sectioned point associated with leatherworking, and an elongated eye set in a groove.

A casket key (No. 3.9.35) was found in a Phase 2 platform context. It has an annular bow and a solid stem that is bored at one end. Two studs (Nos 3.9.36–7) were found in a demolition layer associated with Room A5. They form a pair, with gilded heads decorated with incised lines. One has an iron nail attached to its shank by corrosion.

Four fragments from copper alloy vessels (Nos 3.9.44, 46 and 47, and No. 45 not illustrated) were found associated with the occupation and demolition of Building A12, the Phase 4 kitchen. Nos 3.9.44 and 46 were found in floor layer 23. Two other fragments were associated with the Phase 4 occupation of Rooms A9 and A10 (Nos 4.9.43 and 40 respectively), and another (No. 3.9.42) with the possible dairy, building B. No. 3.9.47 is a cauldron handle, and Nos 3.9.44 and 38 are feet from cauldrons. Copper alloy tripod cauldrons first appeared in England in the 13th century and were increasingly used in the 14th and 15th centuries (Biddle 1990b, 947). Nos 3.9.40–42 are rims from cast vessels and No. 3.9.43 consists entirely of body fragments. No. 3.9.39 is part of the rim of a sheet metal basin; similar examples were dated from the late 11th to the late 12th century at Netherton (A R Goodall 1990, no. 157) and to the late 13th to 14th century at Newbury (A R Goodall 1980, no. 18).

No. 3.10.48 is a handle from a spoon of Roman type, with notched decoration on its upper surface. A handle plate (No. 3.9.49) from a knife or dagger came from a context associated with Room A5. No. 3.10.50 may be from a late 14th-century lyre-shaped strap end, or a mount from the mouth of a scabbard. Four binding strips (Nos 3.10.52–3, 3.11.51 and 3.12.54) were found in Phase 5 demolition layers associated with Rooms A4, A5 and A9. No. 3.11.51 has incised and traced decoration on one side. A Phase 1 context associated with Building P produced a triangular shaped fragment of plate (No. 3.12.55) with two rivet holes, which has been bent round an iron pivot.

Catalogue

3.8.31. **Thimble**, Ht: 22 mm, D: 17 mm (SF 8, Ctx 5, Ph5 building 12).
3.8.32. **Thimble**, Ht: 20 mm, D: 18–20 mm (SF 24, unstratified).
3.8.33. **Needle**, L: 28 mm (SF 301, Ctx 1015, Ph3–5 Room A4).
3.8.34. **Needle**, L: 79 mm (SF 141, Ctx 995, Ph4 Building A1).
3.9.35. **Casket key**. L: 38 mm (SF 303, Ctx 386, Ph2).
3.9.36–7. **Gilded studs**, L: 19 mm, Head D: 17 mm (SF 216, Ctx 726, Ph5 Room 5).
3.9.38. **Vessel, cauldron foot**, W: 19 mm (SF 476, Ctx 49, Ph2).
3.9.39. **Vessel rim**, L: 52 mm (SF 236, Ctx 784, Ph3–5 Room A5).
3.9.40. **Vessel rim**, Th: 2–4 mm (SF 6, Ctx 44, Ph4 Room A10).
3.9.41. **Vessel rim**, L: 16 mm (SF 475, Ctx 1, unstratified).
3.9.42. **Vessel rim**, L: 34 mm (SF 44, Ctx 161, Ph4 Building B).
3.9.43. **Vessel fragments** (SF 191, Ctx 639, Ph4 Room A9).
3.9.44. **Vessel, cauldron foot**, W: *c* 17 mm (SF 472, Ctx 23, Ph4 Building A12).
45 (NI). **Vessel** (SF 478, Ctx 177, Ph4 Building A12).
3.9.46. **Vessel**, W: 13 mm (SF 474, Ctx 23, Ph4 Building A12).
3.9.47. **Vessel, cauldron handle**, L: 64 mm (SF 7, Ctx 5, Ph5 Building A12).
3.9.49. **Handle plate**, D: 25 mm (SF 175, Ctx 633, Ph3–5 Room A5).
3.10.48. **Spoon handle**, Roman, L: 160 mm (SF 153, unstratified).
3.10.50. **Strap end or scabbard mount?** L: 58 mm, W: 38–62 mm (SF 167, Ctx 186, Ph5).
3.10.52. **Binding strip**, L: *c* 29 mm, W: 7 mm (SF 217, Ctx 726, Ph5 Room A5).
3.10.53. **Binding strip**, L: 22 mm (SF 68, Ctx 507, Ph5 Room A4).
3.11.51. **Binding strip**, L: *c* 215 mm (SF 139, Ctx 520, Ph5 Room A9).
3.12.54. **Binding strip**, L: 87 mm, W: 29 mm (SF 77, Ctx 512, Ph5 Room A9).
3.12.55. **Plate**, L: 37 mm (SF 5, Ctx 73, Ph1 Building P).

Fixtures and fittings (Figs 3.12.56–3.13.91)

This group of 38 items consists of 13 rings, 5 discs or washers, 17 sheet fragments and three fragmentary objects. The majority of the rings have round or irregular cross-sections and may have functioned as belt-links or textile hangers, such as curtain rings (Hinton 1990d, 1095). Most were unstratified or from Phase 5 demolition layers.

Seventeen fragments of sheet were found, three of which were of particular interest. No. 3.13.74 is an object cut from sheet metal with a pair of projections on one long side. No. 3.13.75 is a fragment of perforated strip with a disc soldered to it. No. 3.13.76 is a small piece of thin sheet with repoussé decoration. The remaining fourteen pieces are fragments of sheet including perforated fragments and offcuts. One fragment (No. 3.13.78) consists of two pieces rolled one inside the other and a third piece formed into a cylinder. Another perforated fragment (No. 3.13.88) has been patched.

No. 3.13.91 is a stud-like object with a pointed rectangular-sectioned shank and a cup-shaped head that is closed at the top by a disc. There is a penannular collar around the top of the shank.

Catalogue

3.12.56. **Ring**, D: 21 mm (SF180, Ctx 600, Ph3–5).
3.12.57. **Ring**, D: 43 mm (SF37, Ctx 161, Ph4).
3.12.58. **Ring**, D: 24 mm (SF42, Ctx 142, Ph4).
3.12.59. **Ring**, D: 21 mm (SF121, Ctx 588, Ph5 Building A1).

3.12.60. **Ring**, D: 21 mm (SF317, Ctx 732, Ph4 courtyard).
3.12.61. **Ring**, D: 21 mm (SF169, Ctx 186, Ph5).
3.12.62. **Ring**, D: 21 mm (SF219, Ctx 717, Ph5 Room A5).
3.12.63. **Ring**, squashed? L: 24 mm, W: 14 mm (SF484, Ctx 186, Ph5).
3.12.64. **Ring**, D: 23 mm (SF242, unstratified).
65 NI. **Ring**, (SF490, unstratified).
66 NI. **Ring**, (SF491, unstratified).
67 NI. **Ring**, (SF492, unstratified).
3.12.68. **Ring**, D: 34 mm (SF477, Ctx 74, post-medieval).
69 (NI). **Perforated disc or washer**, D: 20 mm (SF 45, Ctx 163, Ph5 Room A6).
3.12.70. **Perforated disc or washer**, D: 19 mm (SF 62, Ctx 507, Ph5 Room A4).
3.12.71. **Disc**, with central impressed dot, D: 22 mm (SF 69, Ctx 520, Ph5 Room A9).
72 (NI). **Disc**, thin and slightly crumpled, D: (SF 479, Ctx 186, Ph5).
3.13.73. **Disc**, D: 30–33 mm (SF 149, Ctx 189, Ph5).
3.13.74. **Object** cut from sheet metal L: 54 mm, W: 11 mm (SF 9, Ctx 23, Ph4 Building A12).
3.13.75. **Perforated strip**, W: 19 mm, hole D: 5 mm (SF 100, Ctx 565, Ph4 Building 1).
3.13.76. **Decorated sheet**, L: *c* 31 mm, W: 13 mm (SF 218, Ctx 186, Ph5).
3.13.77. **Sheet**, perforated, W: 20 mm (SF 99, Ctx 554, Ph3–4 Building A3).
3.13.78. **Sheet**, L: 9 mm (SF179, Ctx 600, Ph3–5 Room A4).
79 (NI). **Sheet** (SF496, Ctx 1081, Ph4).
3.13.80. **Sheet**, L: 11 mm (SF12, Ctx 23, Ph4 Building A12).
81 (NI). **Sheet**, L: 26 mm, W: 9 mm (SF104, Ctx 550, Ph5).
82 (NI). **Sheet** (SF 481, Ctx 186, Ph5).
3.13.83. **Sheet**, L: 76 mm (SF482, Ctx 186, Ph5).
84 (NI). **Sheet** (SF 483, Ctx 186, Ph5).
85 (NI). **Sheet** (SF 485, Ctx 506, Ph5).
86 (NI). **Sheet** (SF 487, unstratified).
3.13.87. **Sheet**, L: *c* 12 mm(SF 268, unstratified).
3.13.88. **Sheet**, L: 59 mm, W: 23 mm (SF 488, unstratified).
89 (NI). **Sheet** (SF 489, unstratified).
3.13.90. Wire twist **loop**, D: 10 mm (SF 213, Ctx 284, Ph5).
3.13.91. **Stud** object, L: 24 mm, D: 19 mm (SF 170, Ctx 186, Ph5).
92 (NI). **Cast fragment** (SF493, unstratified).
93 (NI) **Sheet**, L: 39 mm, W: 14 mm (SF 315, unstratified).

Lace tags (Fig. 3.13.93–94 and Table 3.4)

The excavations produced 29 lace tags, the majority from Phase 5 contexts. No. 3.13.93 is made from wire that has been folded and slightly twisted. No. 3.13.94 is made from rolled sheet metal secured by a single rivet at the top. Thirteen other lace tags are riveted and eight contain remains of leather or textile laces. Table 3.4 catalogues the lace tags by context and phase.

Catalogue

3.13.93. **Lace tag**, L: 20 mm (SF 34, Ctx 139, Ph3).
3.13.94. **Lace tag**, L: 25 mm (SF 43, Ctx 142, Ph4).

Pins (Fig. 3.13.95–96 and Table 3.5)

The excavations produced a total of 107 pins, full details of which are presented in Table 3.5. Two examples have been illustrated; the first (No. 3.13.95) is a long pin with a globular head, and the second (No. 3.13.96) is a long pin with a head of coiled wire. The remaining pins mostly have heads of coiled wire, with the exception of SF 241 which has a domed head. Most are between 30 and 50 mm in length.

Table 3.4 Copper alloy lace tags

SF no	Ctx no	Phase	Building/ Room	No	Type	Length (mm)
61	245	3	A1	1	Rivet	30
34 (ill.)	139	3	S yard	1	Twisted	20
574	554	3–4	A3	1	?	
573	554	3–4	A3	2	?	
162	554	3–4	A3	1	Tapered, rivet missing	35
43 (ill.)	142	4	A6	1	Rivet	25
328	573	4	NW yard	1	Rivet	31
571	238	4	A1	1	?	
572	535	4	A12	2	?	
584	186	5	demolition	1	?	
575	584	5	A3	1	?	
577	663	5	A14	2	?	
65	520	5	A9	1	Rivet	30+
122	588	5	A1	1	Rivet	28
578	665	5	demolition	1	?	
580	186	5	demolition	1	?	
576	588	5	A1	1	?	
581	186	5	demolition	1	?	
583	186	5	demolition	1	?	
570	222	5	demolition	2	?	
579	119	5	demolition	1	?	
119A	590	5	A1	1	Rivet missing	26
582	186	5	demolition	2	?	
585	1	modern	topsoil	1	?	
Total				27		

ill.: illustrated

Catalogue

3.13.95. **Pin**, L: 72 mm (SF 90, Ctx 548, Ph4).
3.13.96. **Pin**, L: 101 mm (SF 172, Ctx 581, Ph3 Area F).

Miscellaneous

Catalogue (Not illustrated)

Fragments (SF 305, Ctx 816, Ph3 Building A1).
Lump, Wt: 13 g (SF 318, unstratified).

OBJECTS OF LEAD AND PEWTER (FIGS 3.14–3.15) *by Alison Goodall, with additional contributions by Kate Atherton*

Introduction

A total of 44 objects made from lead and pewter were recovered, excluding window came. These were identified and catalogued by Alison Goodall shortly after the end of the fieldwork, with extended notes on objects of particular interest. The catalogue has subsequently been revised for publication by Kate Atherton, with the addition of measurements

Table 3.5 Copper alloy pins

SF no	Ctx no	Phase	Building/Room	No	Length (mm)
550	530	2	moat upcast	2	?
36	139	3	S yard	1	36
73	526	3	A4	2	2 × 37
172 (ill.)	581	3	F	1	101
559	1017	3	A1	1	41
124	554	3–4	A3	1	38
165	554	3–4	A3	1	36
151	554	3–4	A3	1	37
163	554	3–4	A3	1	38
155	554	3–4	A3	1	35
158	554	3–4	A3	1	95
159	554	3–4	A3	1	30
177	554	3–4	A3	3	31; 34; 54
166	554	3–4	A3	1	33
178	600	3–5	A4	1	34
553	600	3–5	A4	1	?
89	543	4	A10	1	36
90 (ill.)	548	4	A1	1	72
126	548	4	A1	1	36
110	548	4	A1	2	2 × 37
551	561	4	NE Yard	1	?
140	573	4	NW yard	1	*c* 48
116	589	4	A13	1	35
241	593	4	A1	2	2 × 40
136	622	4	A1	1	*c* 37
554	639	4	A9	2	
223	639	4	A9	1	*c* 28
224	741	4	A9	1	39
558	1002	4	A1	1	41
30	119	5	demolition	1	32
28	119	5	demolition	2	38; 42
569	119	5	demolition	1	?
27	119	5	demolition	1	*c* 53
31	121	5	A11	1	47
168	186	5	demolition	1	47
562	186	5	demolition	1	?
561	186	5	demolition	1	?
563	186	5	demolition	2	?
131	186	5	demolition	1	39
173	186	5	demolition	1	38
568	186	5	demolition	2	?
564	186	5	demolition	1	?
161	500	5	A9	1	37
54	510	5	A9	1	39
56	512	5	A9	1	34
78	512	5	A9	1	35
60	512	5	A9	1	32
137	512	5	A9	1	35
58	515	5	A9	1	Fragment
152	518	5	F	1	*c* 26
63	518	5	F	1	39
70	520	5	A9	1	35
85	527	5	demolition	1	35
71	529	5	F	1	*c* 41
91	542	5	A1	1	41
93	542	5	A1	1	44
101	542	5	A1	1	35
111	559	5	A1	1	34
108	570	5	demolition	1	Fragment
133	588	5	A1	1	38
125	588	5	A1	1	39
123	588	5	A1	1	26
114	588	5	A1	1	43
117	590	5	A1	2	40; 33
119B	590	5	A1	1	30
552	599	5	A4	1	?
147	629	5	demolition	1	49
154	629	5	demolition	1	40
201	665	5	demolition	1	48
197	666	5	A14	4	32; *c* 35; 38; 38
555	717	5	A5	1	?
556	726	5	A5	2	?
560	1080	5	demolition	1	45
249	278	modern		1	27
106	566	modern	A3	1	34
107	566	modern	A3	4	26; 35; 38; 43
193	659	modern		1	32
557	991	modern	A9	2	40; ?
250	1213	modern	A1	4	*c* 28; 36; 38; 39
145	0	modern		1	*c* 59
146	0	modern		1	27
29	0	modern		1	34
567	0	modern		1	?
566	0	modern		1	?
565	0	modern		1	?
Total				107	

ill.: illustrated

and further information about the contexts and buildings in which objects were found. The catalogue has been divided into broad functional categories, comprising 16 personal and domestic items, 10 structural objects and 18 miscellaneous items, including plain strips, off cuts and rods. A report on window came, by Barry Knight, can be found in Chapter 4, below.

Personal and domestic objects (Figs 3.14–3.15)

Two buckles (Nos 3.14.1–2), one circular and one rectangular, have beaded outer edges and remains of iron pins. No. 3.14.3 is a pewter ring, possibly from a brooch or buckle. Four pewter spoons were retrieved from demolition contexts. All have hexagonal-sectioned stems that terminate in acorn knops which, on No. 3.14.6 and No. 7 (not illustrated), are finely made. Only No. 3.14.4 is complete, and has a fig-shaped bowl with a short rat's tail on the back. Nos 3.14.6 and 7 are almost identical. This is the most common form of spoon from the early 14th to the early 16th centuries. A rim fragment from a pewter dish or plate (No. 3.15.8) was also found in a demolition context. Eight lead objects were probably used as weights, one of which (No. 3.14.9) is a disc with a faintly incised cross on one side.

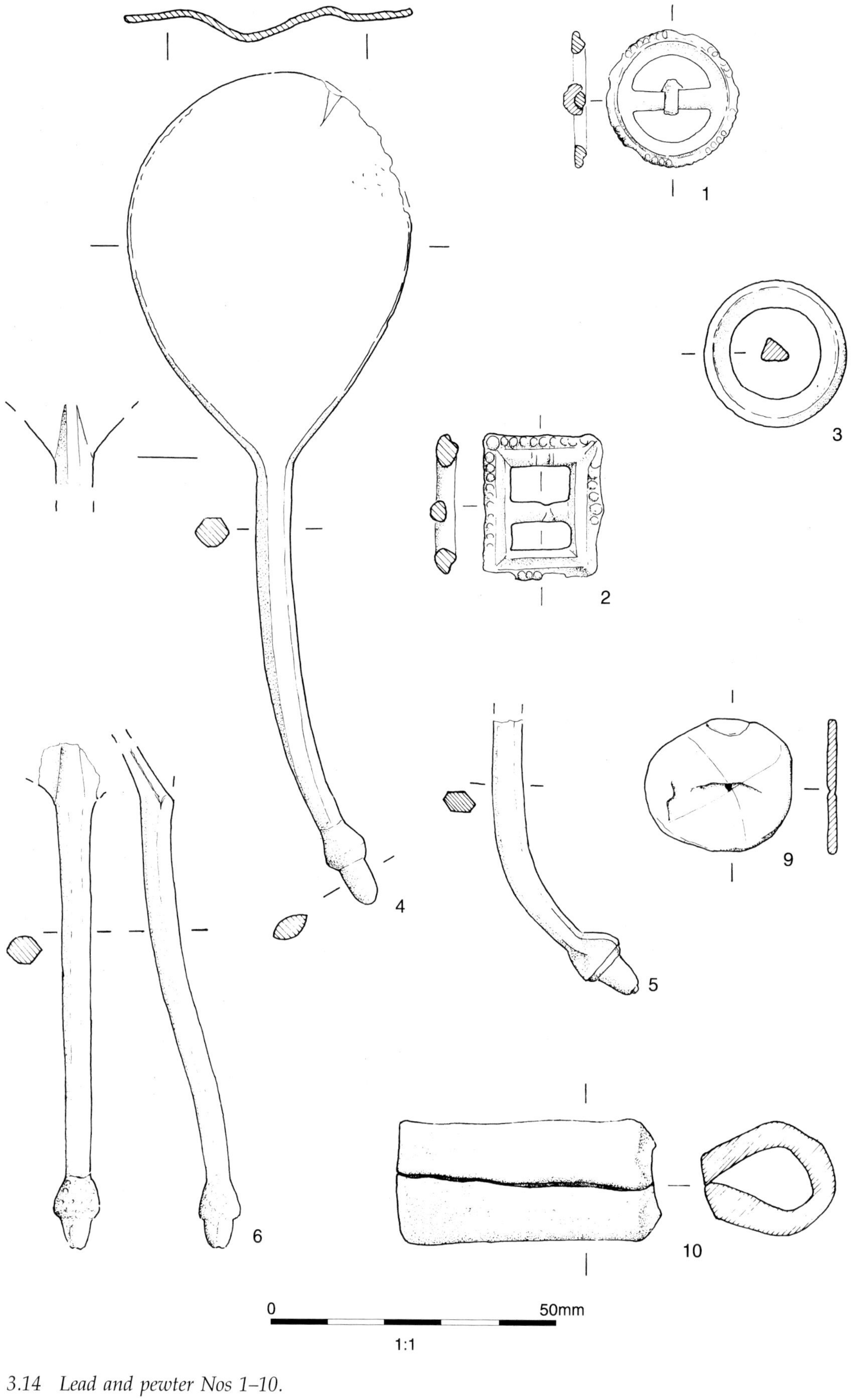

Figure 3.14 Lead and pewter Nos 1–10.

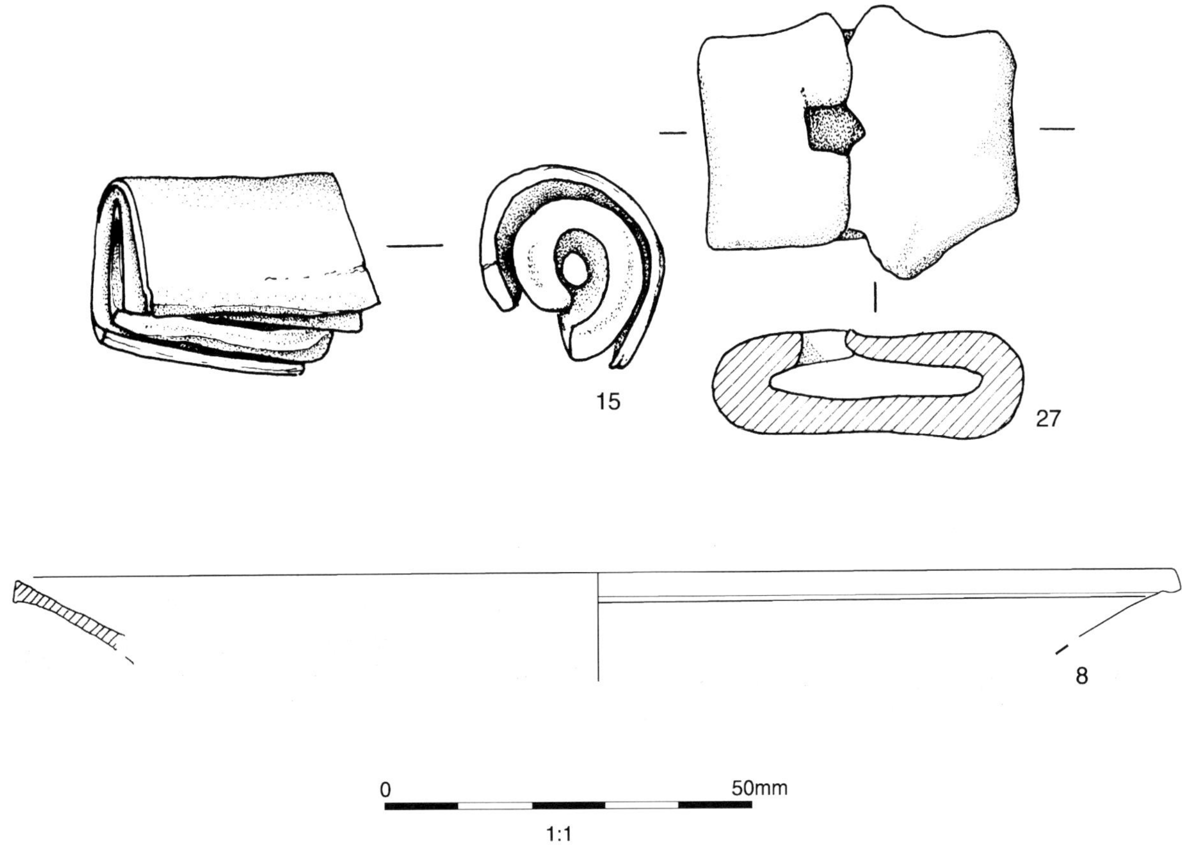

Figure 3.15 Lead and pewter Nos 8, 15 and 27.

Catalogue

3.14.1. **Buckle**, D: 23 mm (SF 286, Ctx 420, Ph5 Building H).
3.14.2. **Buckle**, L: 24, W: 20 mm (SF 280, unstratified).
3.14.3. **Brooch/Buckle ring**, D: 25 mm (SF 498, Ctx 186, Ph5).
3.14.4. **Spoon**, complete, L: *c* 140 mm (SF 211, Ctx 338, Ph5 Building J).
3.14.5. **Spoon**, L: *c* 49 mm (SF 267, Ctx 186, Ph5).
3.14.6. **Spoon handle**, L: *c* 87 mm (SF 55, Ctx 504, Ph5).
7 (NI). **Spoon handle**, L: 83 mm (SF 82, Ctx 527, Ph5).
3.15.8. **Vessel**, D: 156 mm (SF 79, Ctx 541, Ph5 Room A4)
3.14.9. **Disc**, L: 25, W: 22 mm (SF 497, SF 23, Ph4 Building A12).
3.14.10. **Weight**? L: 42, W: 17 mm (SF 157, Ctx 186, Ph5).
11 (NI). **Weight**? L: 44, W: 19, D: 20 mm (SF 171, Ctx 186, Ph5).
12 (NI). **Weight**? L: 44, W: 19 mm (SF 176, Ctx 186, Ph5).
13 (NI). **Weight**? L: 50 mm, Wt 97 g (SF 256, Ctx 368, Ph3 Building J).
14 (NI). **Weight**? L: 36 mm, Wt: 53 g (SF 308, Ctx 1044, finds ref. Building T).
3.15.15. **Weight**? L: 41 mm, Wt: 87 mm (SF 300, Ctx 1015, Ph3–5 Room A4).
16 (NI). **Cylinder**, L: 55, D: 30 mm, Wt: 234 g (SF 329, Ctx 477, Ph5 Building K).

Structural lead (Fig. 3.15.27)

The structural lead includes five fragments of caulking, three of which came from demolition layers associate with Room A10. Fragments of lead came (No. 22) are discussed in Chapter 4 (Knight, below).

Catalogue

17 (NI). **Caulking**, containing part of an iron bar (SF 501, Ctx 37, Ph5 Room A10).
18 (NI). **Caulking** (SF 500, Ctx 37, Ph5 Room A10).
19 (NI). **Caulking** (SF 502, unstratified).
20 (NI). **Caulking** (SF 505, Ctx 26, Ph5 Building A12).
21 (NI). **Caulking** (SF 504, Ctx 19, Ph5 Room A10).
23 (NI). Lead **strip** with nail holes and rounded impressions of nail heads, L: *c* 126 mm (SF 312, Ctx 1073, unstratified).
24 (NI). Lead **strip** with nail holes, L: *c* 58 mm (SF 331, Ctx 519, Ph4 courtyard).
25 (NI). Lead **strip** with nail holes, L: 120 mm, W: 35–38 mm, Th: 4 mm (SF 230, Ctx 737, Ph4 Room A9).
26 (NI). Lead **strip** with nail holes (SF 503, unstratified).
3.15.27. Lead **strip**, folded, with ?nail hole through the junction of the ends, L: 42mm, Wt: 98 g (SF 283, Ctx 421, Ph4 Building H).

Miscellaneous

Strips and off cuts were found all over the manor and in all phases, although 8 out of 14 came from demolition layers.

Catalogue (Not illustrated)

28. **Bar** (SF 499, Ctx 535, Ph4 Building A12).
30. **Strip**, L: *c* 145 mm (SF 225, Ctx 639, Ph4 Room A9).
31. **Strip**, L: 86 mm (SF 320, Ctx 118, Ph3 courtyard).
32. **Offcut** (SF 531, Ctx 604, Ph3 Area F).
33. **Sheet** (SF 530, Ctx 139, Ph3).
34. **Droplet/off cut** (SF 506, Ctx 74, post-medieval).
35. **Strip/off cut** (SF 507, Ctx 123, Ph5 Building A11).
36. **Strip/off cut** (SF 508, Ctx 186, Ph5).

37. **Strip/off cut** (SF 509, Ctx 186, Ph5)
38. **Strip** (SF 510, Ctx 507, Ph5 Room A4).
39. **Sheet** (SF 511, Ctx 512, Ph5 Room A9).
40. **Strip/off cut** (SF 512, Ctx 514, Ph5).
41. **Strip/off cut** (SF 513, Ctx 541, Ph5 Room A4).
43. **Strip/off cut** (SF 515, unstratified).
44. **Strip**, L: 26 mm (SF 238, Ctx 186, Ph5).
45. **Object**, L: 68 mm (SF 39, Ctx 116, Ph5 Building A11).
46. **Fragment** (SF 326, Ctx 1109, Ph4).
47. **Fragment** (SF 516, unstratified).

IRON OBJECTS (FIGS 3.16–3.25)

by Ian Goodall with additional contributions by Kate Atherton and Blanche Ellis

Introduction

A total of 234 iron objects were found during the excavations. Most identifiable objects (Nos 1–168) were catalogued by Ian Goodall shortly after the end of the fieldwork, with extended notes on objects of particular interest. The catalogue was recently revised by Kate Atherton, adding notes on the miscellaneous uncatalogued material (unnumbered items), overall quantifications and the contexts in which objects were found. A note on two spurs and a spur buckle has been contributed by Blanche Ellis. The ironwork assemblage comprises tools (11 objects), knives, shears and scissors (21, 1 and 2 respectively), building ironwork and furniture fittings (77 objects), locks and keys (16 objects), household ironwork (12 objects), buckles and personal fittings (21 objects), horse equipment (29 objects) and weapons (7 objects). Objects and fragments that were too fragmentary or in too poor a condition to identify were classified as miscellaneous items (37 objects).

Significant objects include tools 1–8, most of which are associated with woodworking and leatherworking. Knives 11 and 12 have inlaid decoration on their blades; several others have cutlers' marks, and 22–23 have simply-decorated handle ends. Nos. 43–46 are the most complete of the hinges, and 47 and 50 are types of strap terminal. Nos. 74–78 are pieces of casket binding, and hasps 82–84 may be from chests or doors. Lock furniture includes padlock keys 88–89, locks 90–91, and several keys of which only 93, 97 and 101 are stratified. Nos. 103–105 are socketed candleholders. Buckles from dress and harness include 115, 117, 123–4 and 127–33, the latter a spur buckle. No. 135 is a Jew's harp. Horseshoes comprise the bulk of the horse equipment; most are late medieval and 141 and 143 are typical. No. 157 is from a bridle bit, 160–61 are spurs, and 163–4, 166–7 are representative arrowheads.

Tools (Fig. 3.16.1–8)

Notable tools include an axe head (No. 3.16.1) with lugs below the triangular eye, made by wrapping the iron round the eye and welding it against the side of the blade. The butt has been damaged, probably by excessive use as a hammer. No. 3.16.2 is a possible bench knife, and No. 3.16.3 is a reamer, which would have been used to enlarge holes drilled in wood. The tang was perforated close to the tip to enable the handle to be firmly secured.

No. 3.16.4 is a broken arm from a pair of dividers, and No. 3.16.5 is a long and slender pick. It tapers equally to both ends and could have been a slater's tool, used to make holes in slates, or alternatively it could have been a mill-pick used to dress millstones. Either way it would have fitted into a wooden handle when in use. Arkell (1947, 133–5) illustrates modern slaters' tools; see Freese (1957, 102–7) for tools associated with milling. A blade from a sickle (No. 3.16.8) was found in a Phase 2 levelling context.

An iron awl (No. 3.16.6, which has a flattened bolster between the blade and tang) and a needle (No. 3.16.7) are leather-working tools. The needle has a circular section that becomes triangular towards the tip. The tip itself is missing. A similar needle (No. 3.8.34), although made from copper alloy, was found in a Phase 4 context (see above). The remaining three tools consisted of a possible spade blade, a possible wedge and an unidentified object from demolition layers.

Catalogue

3.16.1. **Axe**, L: 150 mm (SF 95, Ctx 535, Ph4 Building A12).
3.16.2. **Bench knife**? L: 84 mm (SF 279B, Ctx 926, Ph3 Room A10).
3.16.3. **Reamer**, L: 202 mm (SF 392, Ctx 186, Ph5).
3.16.4. **Dividers**, L: 83 mm (SF 40, Ctx 139, Ph3).
3.16.5. **Pick**, L: 314 mm (SF 64, Ctx 518, Ph5).
3.16.6. **Awl**, L 74 mm (SF 468, Ctx 1026, Ph4).
3.16.7. **Needle**, L: 60+mm (SF 374, Ctx 186, Ph5).
3.16.8. **Sickle**, L: *c* 230 mm (SF 49, Ctx 207, Ph2).
(NI). **Spade**? L: *c* 127 mm, W: *c* 97 mm (SF 335, unstratified).
(NI). Unidentified **tool** (SF 355, Ctx 119, Ph5).
(NI). **Wedge**? (SF 408, Ctx 235, Ph5 Building A1).

Knives, shears and scissors (Fig. 3.17.9–3.18.30)

Whittle tang knives

Two examples (Nos 3.17.9–10) have cutler's marks, that on No. 10 inlaid. Two others have inlaid decoration on the blades; the first (No. 3.17.11) is decorated with an enriched running scroll, and the second (No. 3.17.12) with a series of crosses, some now without inlay. The inlay is probably the result of a pressure weld rather than one using a solder and, therefore, the loss of individual pieces is not surprising. Decorative inlay, particularly as ornate as that on the first example, is rare on knives and the closest parallel is probably a knife found in a 13th- to 14th-century context at King's Lynn, Norfolk (I H Goodall 1977, 293, fig. 133, 29, pl. V, D). No. 3.17.12 also has a decorative bevel known as a swage along its back and it retains a decorated bone handle (see below).

Scale tang knives

Nos 3.17.23, 24 and 25 are only tang and handle fragments. Three examples (Nos. 3.17.15–16, 18)

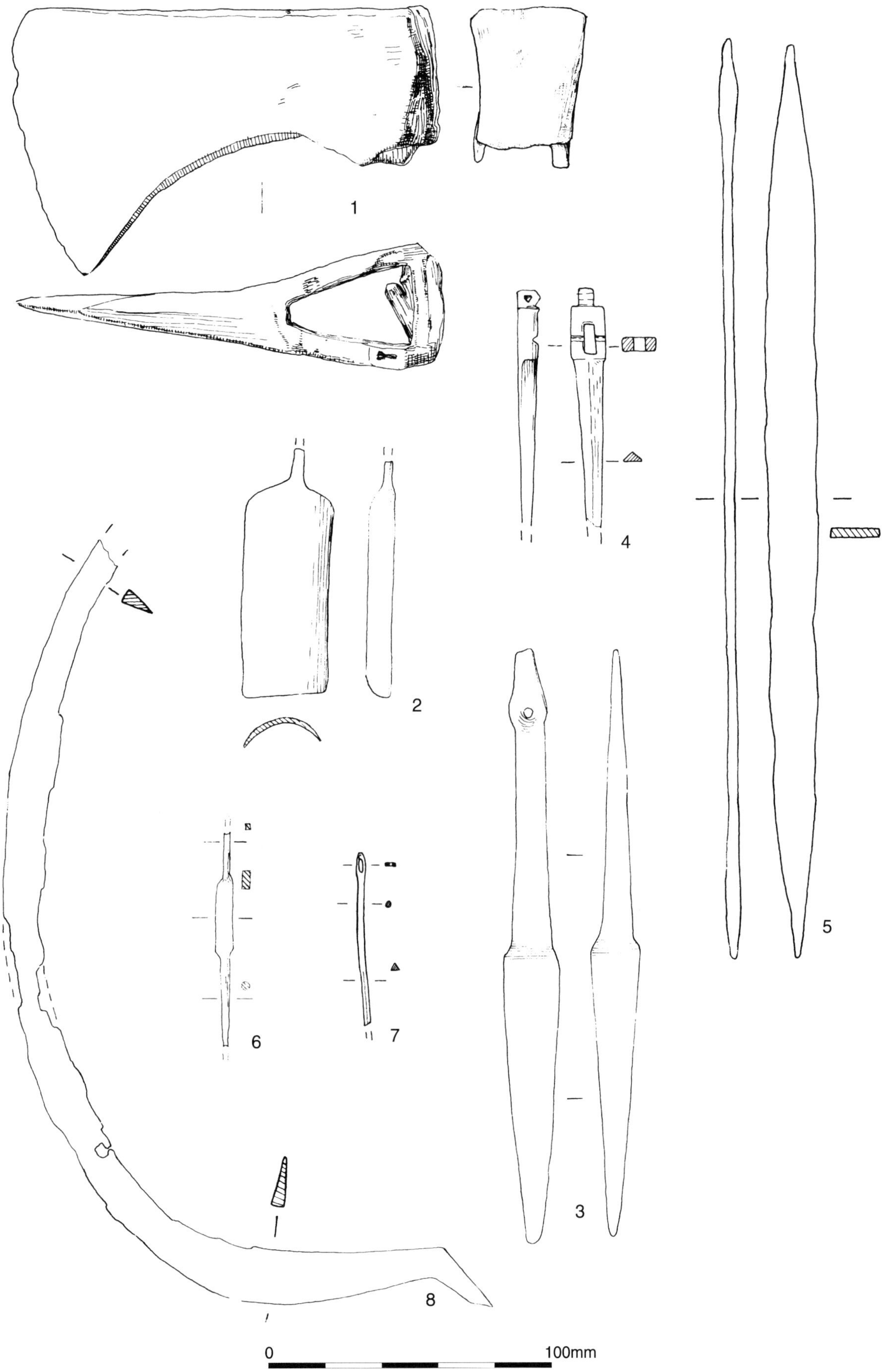

Figure 3.16 Iron Nos 1–8.

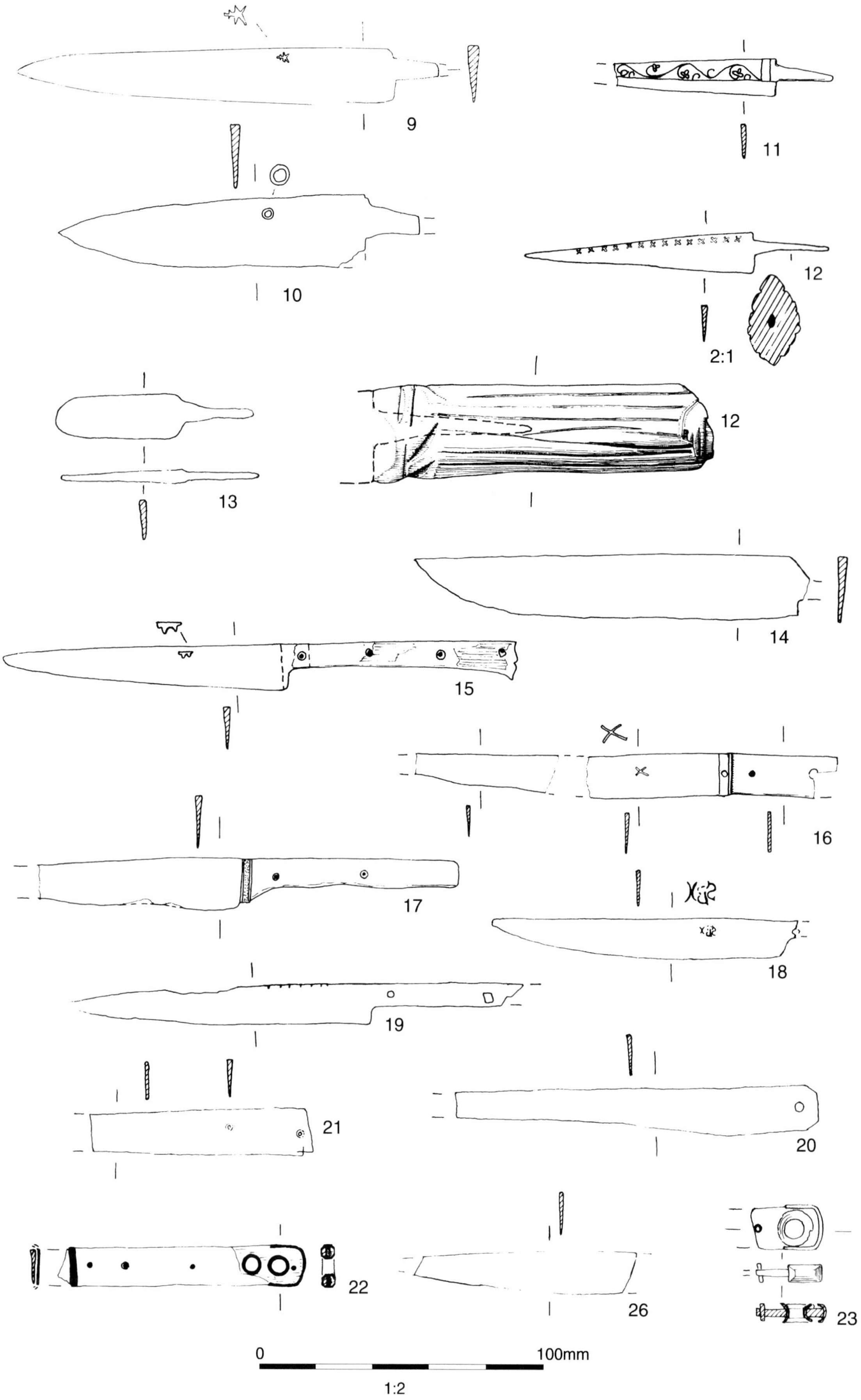

Figure 3.17 Iron Nos 9–26.

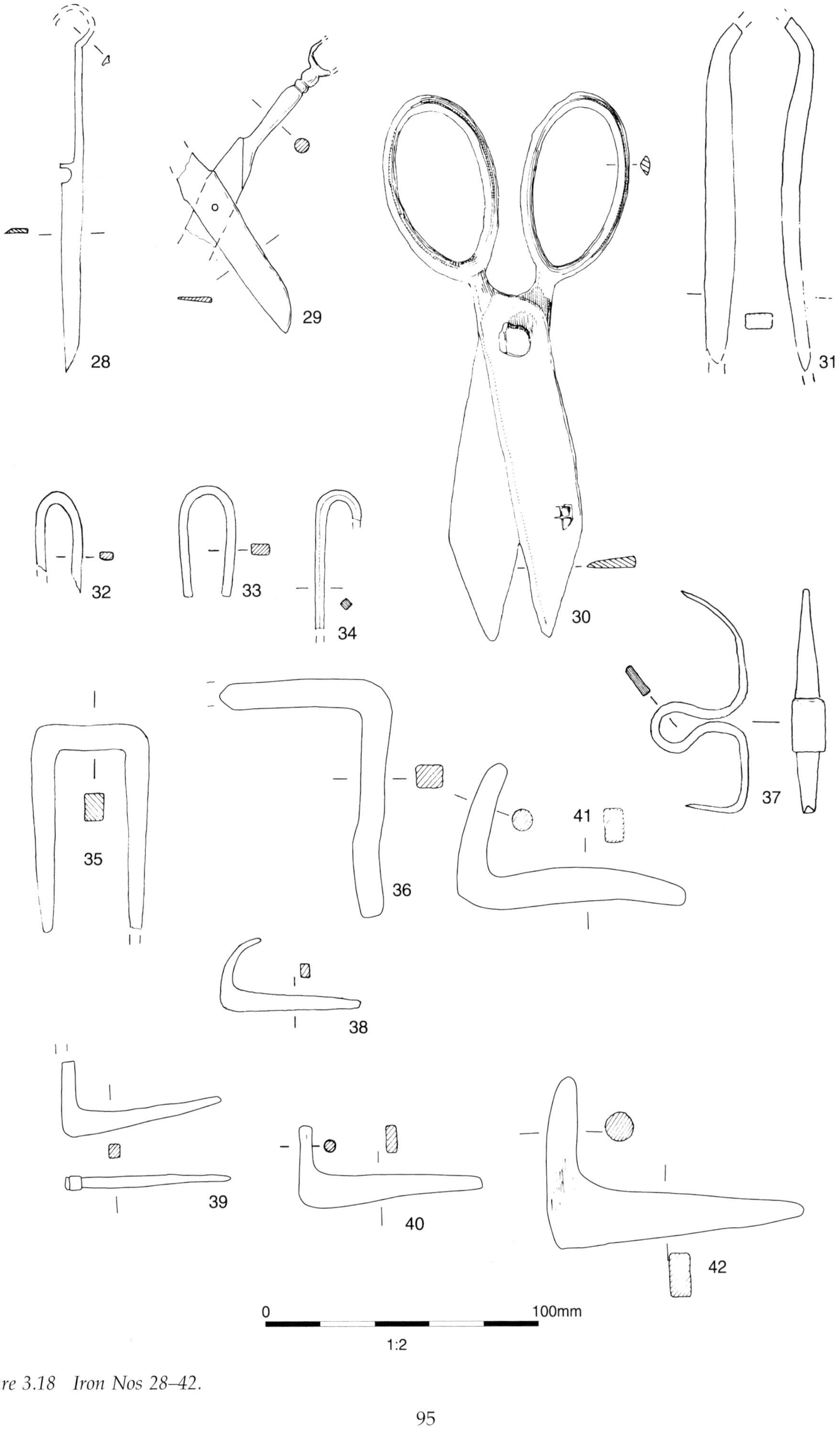

Figure 3.18 Iron Nos 28–42.

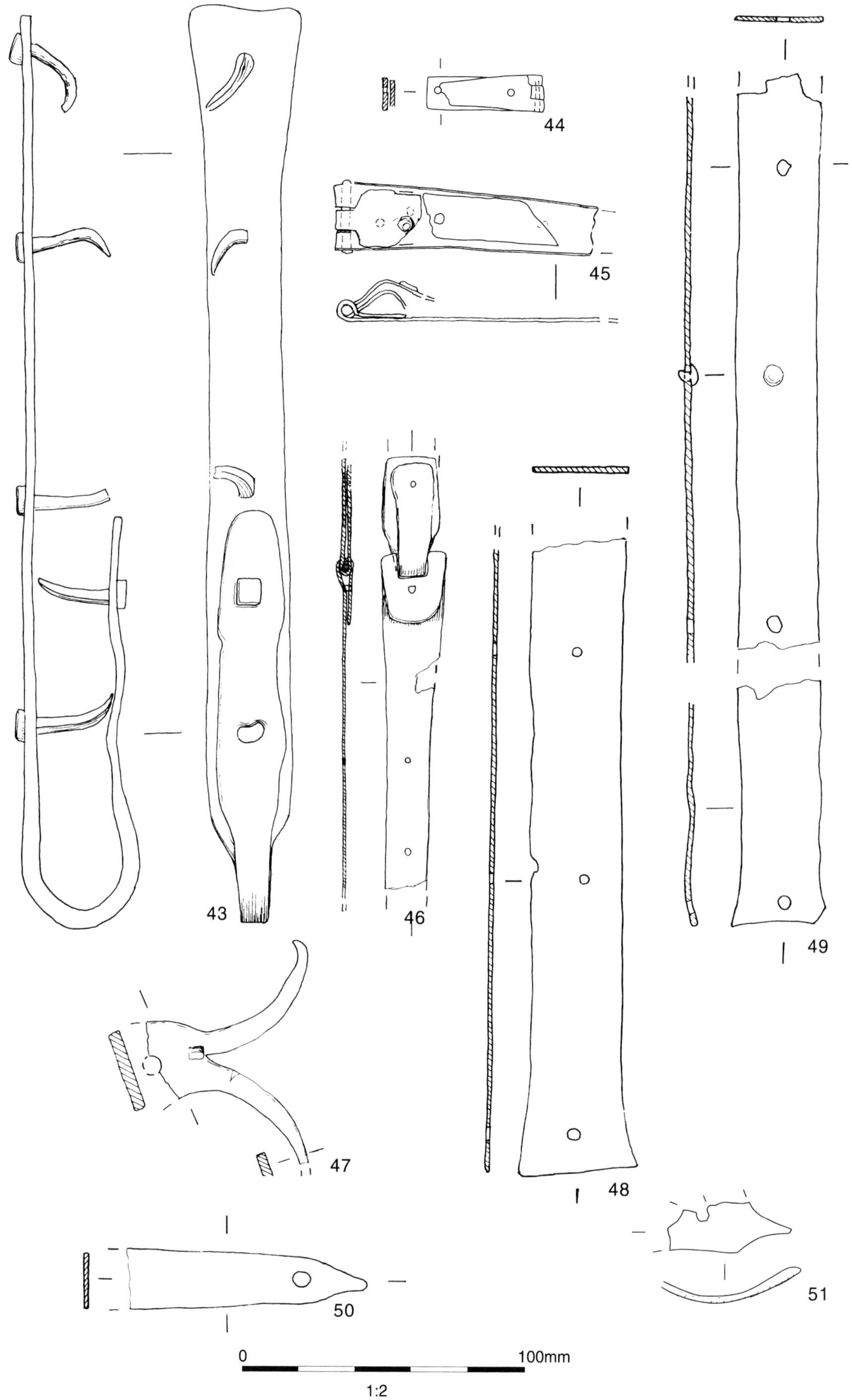

Figure 3.19 Iron Nos 43–51.

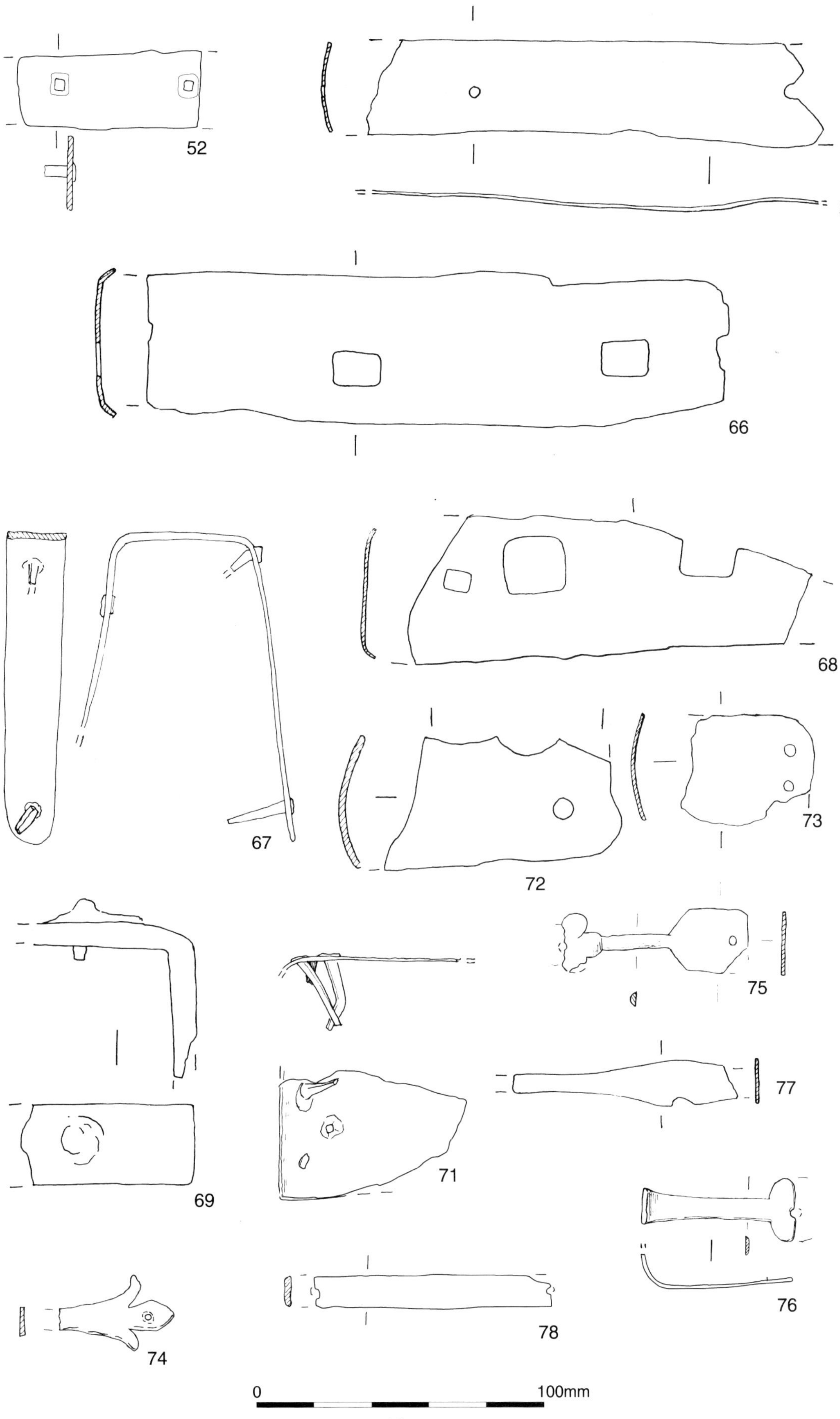

Figure 3.20 Iron Nos 52–78.

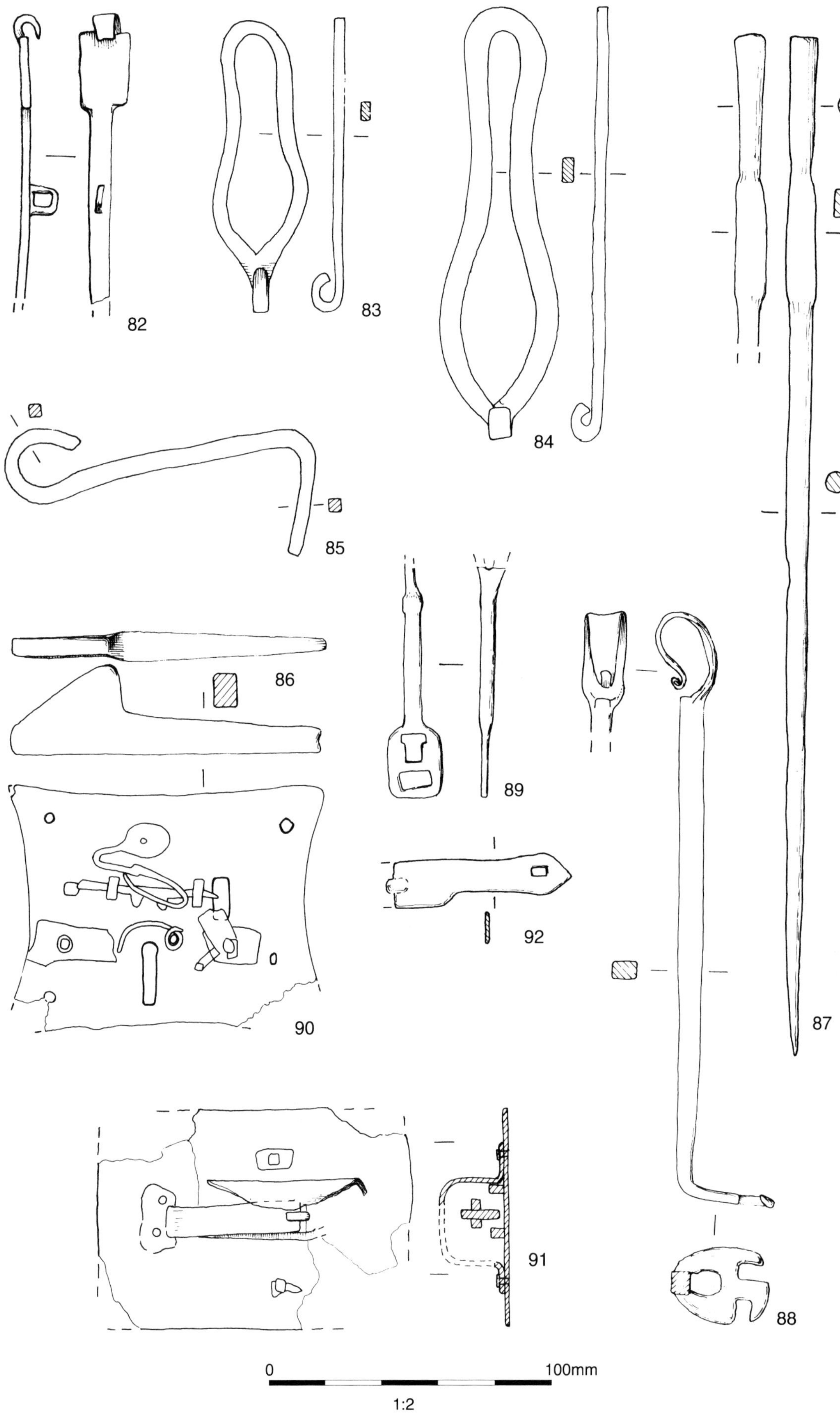

Figure 3.21 Iron Nos 82–92.

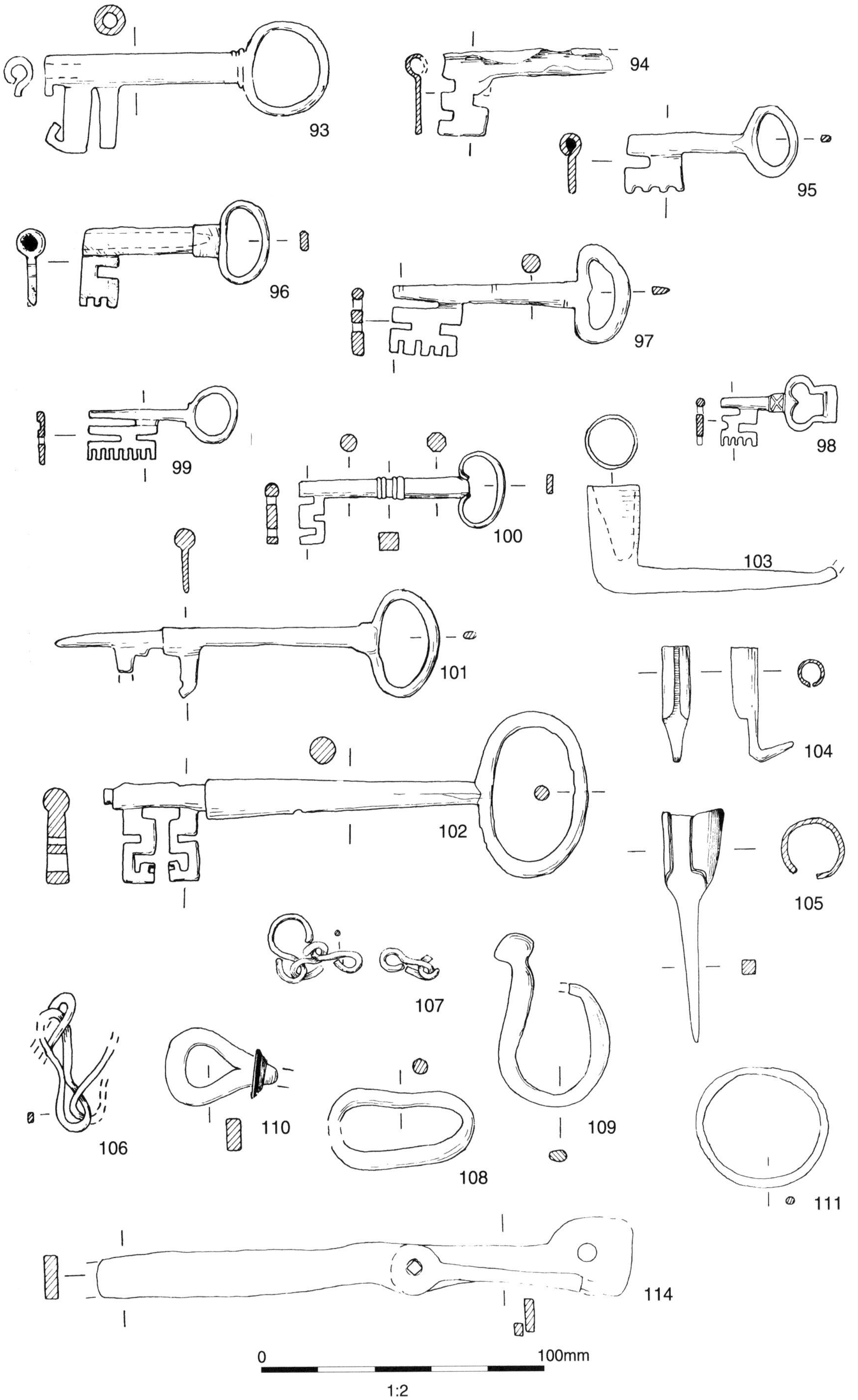

Figure 3.22 Iron Nos 93–114.

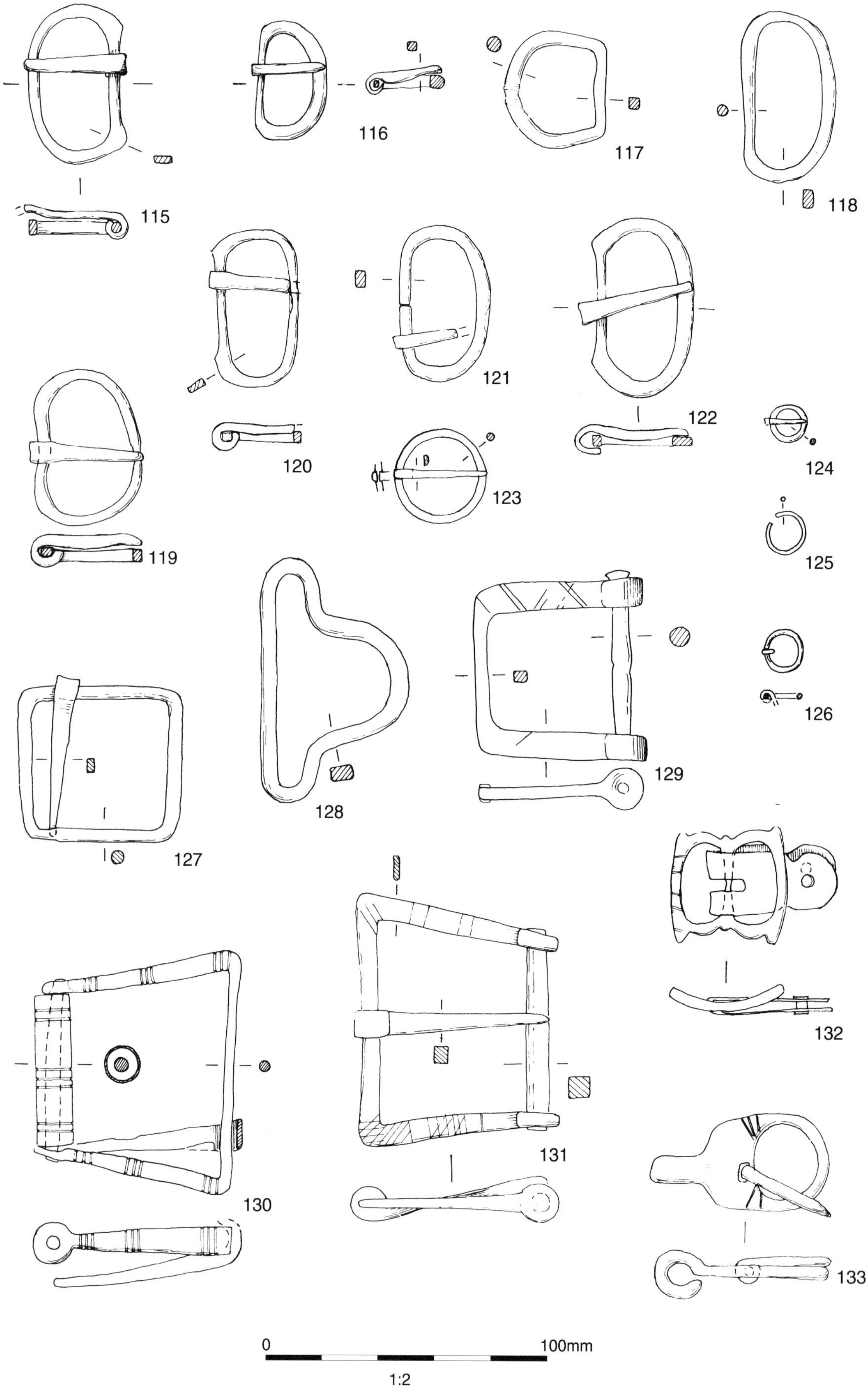

Figure 3.23 Iron Nos 115–133.

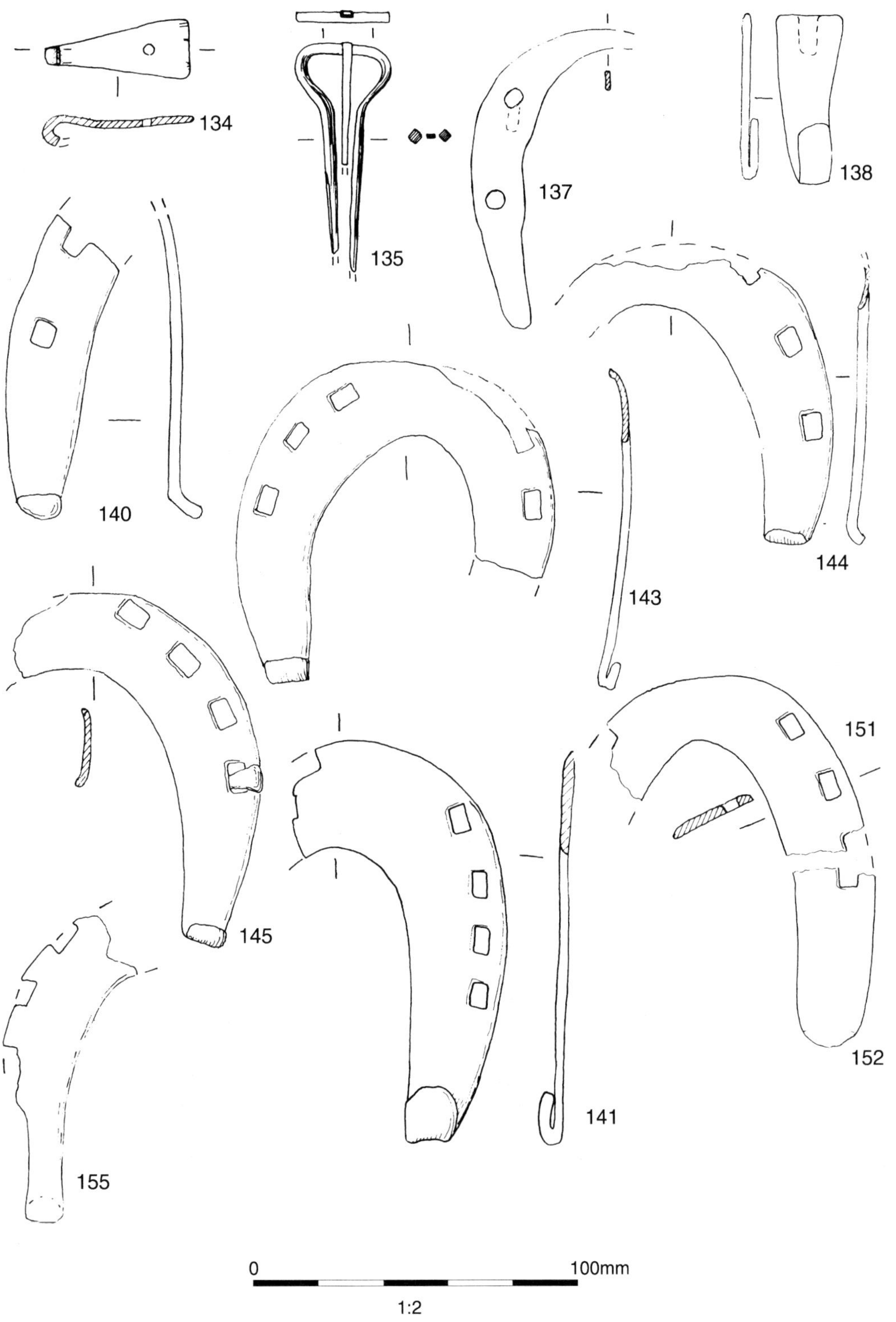

Figure 3.24 Iron Nos 134–155.

have cutler's marks on the blade, that on No. 18 inlaid. No. 3.17.19 has decorative nicks across the back of the blade. Nos 3.17.15–16 have riveted shoulder plates, although one is missing on No. 15. No. 3.17.22 retains one soldered shoulder plate and another (No. 3.17.17) retains the solder alone. The handles of Nos 3.17.15, 17 and 21 were held together with iron rivets; on Nos. 3.17.16, 3.17.22–3 and 25 they are of copper alloy. Nos 3.17.22–3 also have decorative copper alloy end caps and collars. The remains of wooden handles impregnated with iron remain on Nos 3.17.15 and 3.17.22.

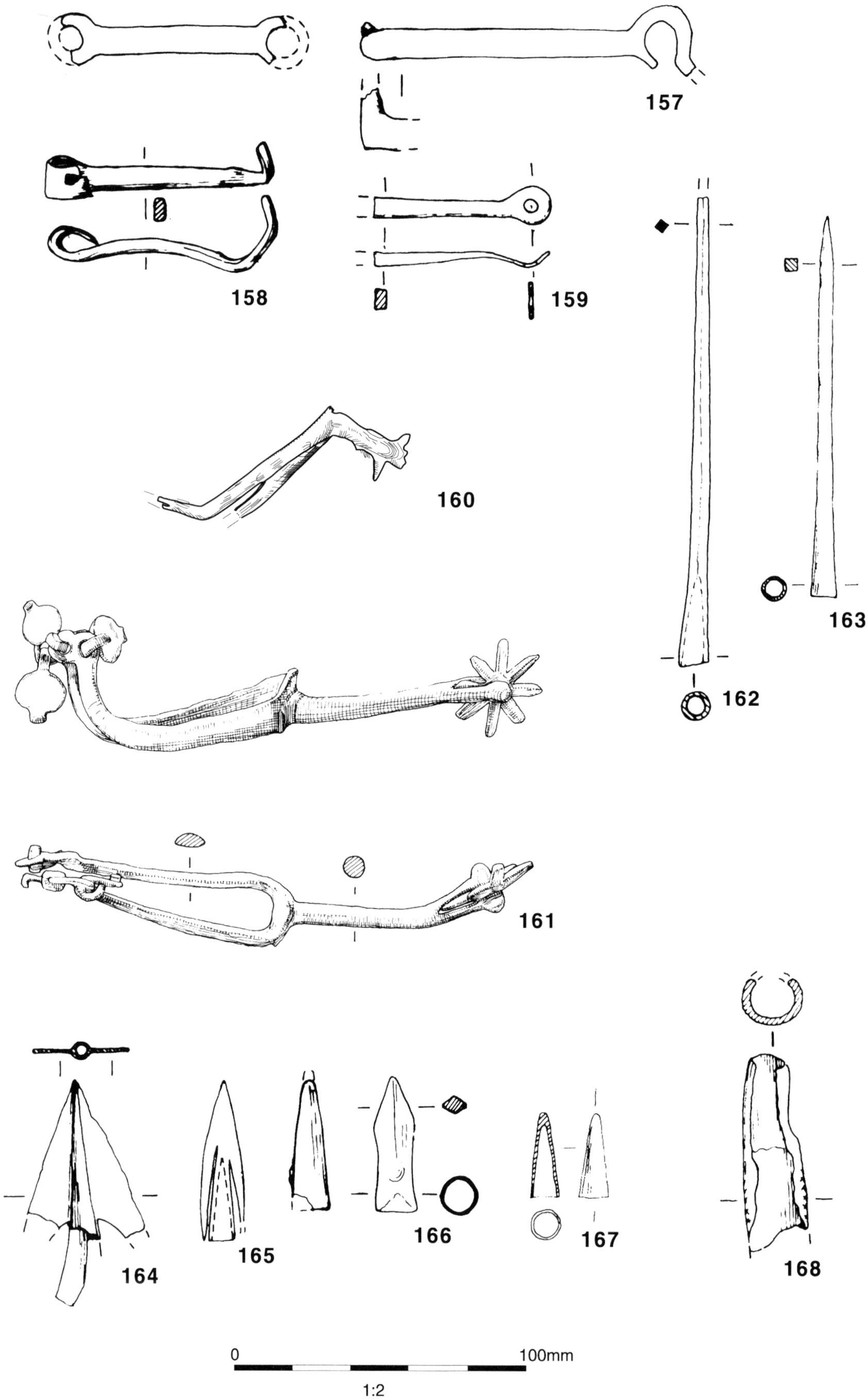

Figure 3.25 Iron Nos 158–168.

Scissors and shears

No. 3.18.28 is one arm from a pair of shears; the blade has a cusped top and the bow is moulded. Two pairs of scissors were found (Nos 3.18.29–30), both typologically post-medieval. No. 3.18.30 are complete; these scissors would have been used for cutting cloth and have the same cutler's mark on each blade, neither inlaid.

Catalogue

3.17.9. **Whittle tang knife**, Blade L: 134 mm (SF 595, unstratified).
3.17.10. **Whittle tang knife**, Blade L: 112 mm (SF 359, Ctx 120, Ph4).
3.17.11. **Whittle tang knife**, Fragment L: 76 mm (SF 263, Ctx 518, Ph5).
3.17.12. **Whittle tang knife**, L: 80 mm (complete length: 98 mm) (SF 262, Ctx 518, Ph5).
3.17.13. **Whittle tang knife**, complete L: 72 mm (SF 381, Ctx 186, Ph5).
3.17.14. **Whittle tang knife**, Blade L: 140 mm (SF 98, Ctx 553, Ph5).
3.17.15. **Scale tang knife**, L: 184 mm, Blade L: 102 mm (SF 352, Ctx 56, Ph3 Room A10).
3.17.16. **Scale tang knife**, Blade L: 106+mm (SF 379, Ctx 186, Ph5).
3.17.17. **Scale tang knife**, L: 150 mm, Handle L: 78 mm (SF 373, Ctx 186, Ph5).
3.17.18. **Scale tang knife**, Blade L: 104 mm (SF 132, Ctx 605, Ph3).
3.17.19. **Scale tang knife**, Blade L: 112 mm (SF 412, Ctx 284, Ph5).
3.17.20. **Scale tang knife**, L: 128+mm (SF 382, Ctx 186, Ph5).
3.17.21. **Scale tang knife**, L: 80+mm (SF 349, Ctx 90, Ph4).
3.17.22. **Scale tang knife**, L: 90+mm (SF 372, Ctx 186, Ph5).
3.17.23. **Scale tang handle**, L: 34 mm, W: 17 mm (SF 32, Ctx 115, Ph4).
24 (NI). **Scale tang fragment** (SF 445, Ctx 600 Ph3–5 Room A4).
25 (NI). **Scale tang handle**, W: 16 mm, rivet D: 13 mm (SF 285, Ctx 421, Ph4 Building H).
3.17.26. **Blade**, L: 78+mm (SF 342, Ctx 14, Ph5 Building A12).
27 (NI). **Knife fragment** (SF 465, Ctx 915, unstratified).
NI. **Possible knife fragment** (SF 345, Ctx 23, Ph4 Building A12).
NI. **Possible knife fragment** (SF 451, Ctx 639, Ph4 Room A9).
3.18.28. **Shears arm**, L: *c* 127 mm (SF 138, unstratified).
3.18.29. **Scissors**, incomplete (SF 447, Ctx 633, Ph3–5 Room A5).
3.18.30. **Scissors**, L: *c* 195 mm (SF 112, unstratified).

Building ironwork and furniture fittings
(Figs 3.18.31–3.21.87)

Catalogue

3.18.31. **Cramp**, L: 126 mm (SF 449, Ctx 633, Ph3–5 Room A5).

U-shaped, rectangular and looped staples:

3.18.32. **Staple**, L: 34+mm (SF 453, Ctx 639, Ph4 Room A9).
3.18.33. **Staple**, L: 40 mm (SF 384, Ctx 186, Ph5).
3.18.34. **Staple**, L: 50+mm (SF 436, Ctx 573, Ph4).
3.18.35. **Staple**, L: 74 mm (SF 469, Ctx 1107, Ph7 Building K).
3.18.36. **Staple**, L: 82, W: 56+mm (SF 457, Ctx 700, Ph4).
3.18.37. **Staple**, L: 82 mm (SF 393, Ctx 186, Ph5).
3.18.38. **Wallhook**, L: 52 mm (SF 156, Ctx 629, Ph5).

Hinge pivots with tapering shanks:

3.18.39. **Hinge pivot**, L: 62 mm (SF 439, Ctx 588, Ph5 Building A1).
3.18.40. **Hinge pivot**, L: 69 mm (SF 421, Ctx 507, Ph5 Room A4).
3.18.41. **Hinge pivot**, L: 84 mm (SF 444, Ctx 599, Ph5 Room A4).
3.18.42. **Hinge pivot**, L: 95 mm (SF 460, Ctx 847, Ph1 Building R).

Hinges:

3.19.43. **Hinge** with nailed U-shaped eye and simply shaped strap, L: 324 mm (SF 353, Ctx 14, Ph5 Building A12).
3.19.44. **Pinned hinge** with non-ferrous plating, L: 42 mm (SF 233, Ctx 784, Ph3–5 Room A5).
3.19.45. **Pinned hinge** with non-ferrous plating, L: 94 mm (SF 67, Ctx 520, Ph5 Room A9).
3.19.46. **Pinned hinge**, L: 151 mm (SF 406, Ctx 186, Ph5).

Hinge straps retaining shaped terminals:

No. 3.19.47 is part of a serpent head terminal found on such 12th-century doors as the south door at Stillingfleet, North Yorkshire (Addyman and Goodall 1979). The other terminals are simpler; Nos 48 and 49 resemble strap hinge No. 44.

3.19.47. **Hinge strap**, L: *c* 68 mm (SF 272, Ctx 174, Ph2).
3.19.48. **Hinge strap**, L: 43 mm (SF 414, Ctx 284, Ph5).
3.19.49. **Hinge strap**, L: *c* 275 mm, W: 28–30 mm (SF 276, Ctx 434, Ph1).
3.19.50. **Hinge strap**, L: 87 mm (SF 390, Ctx 186, Ph5).
3.19.51. **Hinge strap**, L:42 mm (SF 423, Ctx 512, Ph5 Room A9).

Broken lengths of strap, all plain:

Most are probably from doors or chests, but some, including the broader and heavier pieces, might be from carts.

3.20.52. **Strap**, L: 69, W: 23 mm (SF 246A, Ctx 825, Ph4 Room A9).
53 (NI). **Strap**, L: 115, W: 25 mm (SF 354, Ctx 14, Ph5 Building A12).
54 (NI). **Strap**, L: 58, W: 26 mm (SF 258, Ctx 921, Ph1).
55 (NI). **Strap**, L: 148, W: 26 mm (SF 399, Ctx 186, Ph5).
56 (NI) **Strap**, W: 28 mm (SF 228, Ctx 763, Ph3 Room A9).
57 (NI). **Strap**, joins no. 64, L: 55, W: 29 mm (SF 244A, Ctx 825, Ph4 Room A9).
58 (NI). **Strap**, slightly curved in cross-section, L: 71, W: 29 mm (SF 428, Ctx 527, Ph5).
3.20.59. **Strap**, L: 159, W: 32 mm (SF 448, Ctx 633, Ph3–5 Room A5).
60 (NI). **Strap**, L: 72, W: 33 mm (SF 425, Ctx 518, Ph5).
61 (NI). **Strap**, L: 108, W: 35 mm (SF 346, unstratified).
62 (NI). **Strap**, L: 197, W: 38 mm (SF 419, Ctx 354, Ph3).
63 (NI). **Strap**, L: 58, W: 40 mm (SF 383, Ctx 186, Ph5).
64 (NI). **Strap**, joins no. 57, edges down turned, L: 84, W: 40 mm (SF 244, Ctx 825, Ph4 Room A9).
65 (NI). **Strap**, perforated square hole, L: 141, W: 50 mm (SF 288, Ctx 418, Ph5 Building H)
3.20.66. **Strap**, two separate pieces forged together, edges downturned, L: 205, W: 51 mm (SF 294, Ctx 593, Ph4 Building 1).
NI. **Studs**, found with strap SF 246A, L: 36 and 44 mm, Head D: 26 and 29 mm (SF 246B, Ctx 825, Ph4 Room A9).

Binding straps and sheet fragments:

Four fragments of binding strap were recovered. Two are U-shaped, the other two are angle binding. Three fragments of sheet (Nos 3.20.71–73) had nails or the holes for them. Five fragments of casket binding were recovered (Nos 3.20.74–8), all of which are incomplete and variously moulded and shaped. All have non-ferrous plating. Surviving caskets of this period frequently have bindings of gilt bronze or silver and the plating on these fragments was intended to simulate this (Pinder-Wilson and Brooke 1973; Cherry 1982).

3.20.67. U-shaped **binding strap**, L: *c* 125 mm (SF 234A, Ctx 347, Ph5 Building J).
3.20.68. U-shaped **binding strap**, L: *c* 135 mm (SF 234B, Ctx 347, Ph5 Building J).
3.20.69. Angle **binding strap**, L: 62 mm (SF422, Ctx 522, Ph5 Room A9).
70 (NI). Angle **binding strap** (SF 350, Ctx 101, finds reference Building A12)
3.20.71. Perforated **sheet**, W: 18–23 mm (SF 234, Ctx 347, Ph5 Building J).
3.20.72. Perforated **sheet**, L: 68 mm (SF 287, Ctx 421, Ph4 Building H).
3.20.73. Perforated **sheet**, L: 42 mm (SF 160, Ctx 629, Ph5).
3.20.74. **Casket binding** (SF 311, Ctx 1068, Ph3 Building A1).
3.20.75. **Casket binding** (SF 195, Ctx 186, Ph5).
3.20.76. **Casket binding**, L: *c* 57 mm (SF 237, Ctx 518, Ph5).
3.20.77. **Casket binding** (SF 431, Ctx 541, Ph5 Room A4).
3.20.78. **Casket binding** (SF 375, Ctx 186, Ph5).
79 (NI). **Strip**, L: 121, W: 12 mm (SF 417, Ctx 342, unstratified).
80 (NI). **Strip**, L: 124, W: 14 mm (SF 270, Ctx 923, Ph4 Room A10)
81 (NI). **Strip**, L: 111, W: 17 mm (SF 388, Ctx 186, Ph5).

A total of 17 further fragments of **strip** (not illustrated) were recovered from the following contexts:
Ph1–4, SF 456, Ctx 692; Ph2, SF 407, Ctx 207; Ph3, SF 347, Ctx 56, Room A10; SF 466, Ctx 975, Room A9; Ph4, SF 427, Ctx 519, courtyard; SF 440, Ctx 589 Structure A13; SF 441, Ctx 593, Building 1; SF 452, Ctx 639 Room A9; Ph5, SF 360, Ctx 124; SF 362, Ctx 149, Building B; SF 394, Ctx 186; SF 415, Ctx 310, Building K; SF 420, Ctx 505; SF 430, Ctx 531, Room A4; SF 438, Ctx 582, Room A3; SF 442, Ctx 599, Room A4; Finds reference Building G, SF 471, Ctx 1129

Other structural ironwork:

3.21.82. Pinned stapled **hasp**, L: 97+mm (SF 357, Ctx 119, Ph5).
3.21.83. Figure-of-eight **hasp**, L: 102 mm (SF 324, Ctx 353, Ph2).
3.21.84. Figure-of-eight **hasp**, L: 147 mm (SF 325, Ctx 353, Ph2).
3.21.85. Looped **hook**, L: *c* 110 mm (SF 115, Ctx 586, Ph5 Structure A14).
3.21.86. **Latch rest**, L: 112 mm (SF 255, Ctx 700, Ph4).
NI. Possible **latch**. SF 387, Ctx 186, Ph5.
3.21.87. **Spike**, L: 350, Th: 9, D: 11 mm (SF 57, Ctx 515, Ph5 Room A9).

Locks and keys (Figs 3.21.88–3.22.102)

No. 3.21.90 is a flat, hollow-sided lockplate and near-complete mechanism that consists of an S-shaped tumbler, a toothed bolt, a semicircular collar, a single ward and the ends of the mount in which the key tip was formerly located. The mechanism compares closely with that in a lock from Oxford castle (Goodall 1976, 300, fig. 28.59). The same context produced a fragment of latch with a rectangular plate, No. 3.21.91. The remaining lock item (No.3.21.92) may be part of a broken lock tumbler. All the keys are medieval with the exception of Nos 3.22.100 and 102, which are typologically post-medieval and were found in unstratified contexts.

Catalogue

3.21.88. **Padlock key** with hooked terminal, L: 197 mm (SF 196, Ctx 284, Ph5).
3.21.89. **Padlock key** originally with looped terminal, L: 68+mm (SF 343, unstratified).
3.21.90. **Lock** fragments (2) (SF 401A, Ctx 186, Ph5).
3.21.91. **Latch** with rectangular back plate, L: *c* 114 mm (SF 401B, Ctx 186, Ph5).
3.21.92. Part of broken **lock tumbler**?, L: 65 mm (SF 356, Ctx 110, Ph5).
3.22.93. **Key** with the bit rolled in one with the hollow stem, and non-ferrous plating or brazing metal, L: 103 mm (SF 314, Ctx 983, Ph2).
3.22.94. **Key** with the bit rolled in one with the hollow stem, L: 60+mm (SF 186, Ctx 633, Ph3–5 Room A5).
3.22.95. **Key** with the bit rolled in one with the hollow stem, L: 64 mm (SF 23, unstratified).
3.22.96. **Key** with separately applied bit, and non-ferrous plating or brazing metal, L: 67 mm (SF 18, unstratified).
3.22.97. **Key** with solid stem, and non-ferrous plating or brazing metal, L: 84 mm (SF 127, Ctx 600, Ph3–5 Room A4).
3.22.98. **Key** with solid stem, L: 43 mm (SF 129, unstratified).
3.22.99. **Key** with solid stem, L: 53 mm (SF 19, unstratified).
3.22.100. **Key** with solid stem, L: 74 mm (SF 189, unstratified).
3.22.101. **Key** with solid stem, L: 137 mm (SF 92, Ctx 518, Ph5).
3.22.102. **Key** with solid stem, L: 172 mm (SF 251, unstratified).

Household ironwork (Fig. 3.22.103–114)

Catalogue

3.22.103. Socketed **candleholder**, Ht: 37, L: 90+mm, (SF 279A, Ctx 926, Ph3 Room A10).
3.22.104. Socketed **candleholder**, Ht: *c* 39 mm (SF 378, Ctx 186, Ph5).
3.22.105. Socketed **candleholder**, Ht: 80 mm (SF 370, Ctx 189, Ph5).
3.22.106. **Chain**, L: *c* 50 mm (SF 130, Ctx 581, Ph3 Area F).
3.22.107. **Chain and hook**, L: *c* 32 mm (SF 380, Ctx 186, Ph5).
3.22.108. **Chain link**, L: 52 mm (SF 467, Ctx 1007, Ph3 Building A1).
3.22.109. **Swivel hook**. L: *c* 58 mm (SF 398, Ctx 186, Ph5).
3.22.110. **Loop**. L: *c* 41 mm (SF 368, Ctx 176, Ph3).
3.22.111. **Ring**, D: 40–46 mm (SF 222, Ctx 639, Ph4 Room A9).
112 (NI). **Ring**, D: 24 mm (SF 376, Ctx 186, Ph5).
113 (NI). **Ring**, D: 30 mm (SF 377, Ctx186, Ph5).
3.22.114. **Fitting**, L: *c* 190 mm (SF 304, Ctx 1026, Ph4).

Buckles and personal fittings (Figs 3.23.115–24.135)

This assemblage of personal items includes 18 iron buckles, a strap loop and heel iron, and a Jew's harp. A number of the buckles are moulded or decorated with incised lines which retain traces of non-ferrous plating. Non-ferrous plating is evident on eleven of the buckles (Nos 3.23.115–6, 119–20, 122, 124, 128–32). The probable strap loop (No. 3.24.134) also has traces of non-ferrous plating; it resembles Saxon hooked fasteners, which are occasionally made of iron, but would be larger than most. The shoe heel iron is post-medieval in date.

Catalogue

3.23.115. **D-shaped buckle**, L: 53, W: 34 mm (SF 174, Ctx 633, Ph3–5 Room A5).
3.23.116. **D-shaped buckle**, L: 40, W: 25 mm (SF 74, Ctx 145, Ph4 Building A11).

3.23.117. **D-shaped buckle**, L: *c* 43, W: 34 mm (SF 245, Ctx 825, Ph4 Room A9).
3.23.118. **D-shaped buckle**, L: 58 mm (SF 309, Ctx 423, Ph4 Building H).
3.23.119. **D-shaped buckle**, L: *c* 53, W: 42 mm (SF 194, Ctx 186, Ph5.).
3.23.120. **D-shaped buckle**, L: 54, W: 34 mm (SF 188, Ctx 186, Ph5).
3.23.121. **D-shaped buckle**, L: 54, W: 34 mm (SF 371, unstratified).
3.23.122. **D-shaped buckle**, L: 62, W: 34 mm (SF 340, unstratified).
3.23.123. **Circular buckle**, D: 32 mm (SF 205, Ctx 319, Ph3–4).
3.23.124. **Circular buckle**, D: 16 mm (SF 271, Ctx 923, Ph4 Room A10).
3.23.125. **Circular buckle**, D: *c* 17 mm (SF 150, Ctx 621, Ph4 courtyard).
3.23.126. **Circular buckle**, D: *c* 16 mm (SF 120, Ctx 584, Ph5 Room A3).
3.23.127. **Rectangular buckle**, L: 62, W: 57 mm (SF 273, Ctx 118, Ph3 courtyard).
3.23.128. **T-shaped buckle**, L: 84, W: 53 mm (SF 46, Ctx 174, Ph2).
3.23.129. **Buckle** with revolving pin arm in rectangular frame, L: 60, W: 56 mm (SF 391, Ctx 186, Ph5).
3.23.130. **Buckle** with revolving pin arm in trapezoidal frame, L: 78, W: 74 mm (SF 229, Ctx 581, Ph3 Area F).
3.23.131. **Buckle** with revolving pin arm in trapezoidal frame, L: 91, W: 72 mm (SF 252, Ctx 3, Ph4 Building A12).
3.23.132. Double-looped **buckle** with **buckle plate**, complete L: 60, buckle: 40 × 40 mm (SF 316, Ctx 561, Ph4 courtyard).
3.24.134. **Strap loop**, L: 47 mm (SF 208, Ctx 700, Ph4).
3.24.135. **Jew's harp**, L: 69 mm (SF 310, Ctx 432, Ph2 Building Q).
136 (NI). **Heel iron** (SF 397, Ctx 186, Ph5).

Horse equipment (Figs 3.23.133, 3.24.137–3.25.161)

No. 3.24.137 is an arm, and Nos 138 and 139 tips, from horseshoes with countersunk nailholes. Nos 3.24.140–153 have rectangular nail holes and are of the type that succeeded Nos 137–139 during the 13th century. No. 3.24.155 is probably an ox shoe. Two fragments are likely to be from the same shoe (Nos 3.24.151–152).

Catalogue

3.24.137. **Horseshoe**, L: *c* 95+mm, W: 16 mm (SF 264, Ctx 911, unstratified).
3.24.138. **Horseshoe** fragment (SF 247, Ctx 355, Ph2).
139 (NI). **Horseshoe** (SF 366, Ctx 119, Ph5).
3.24.140. **Horseshoe**, L: 92+, W: 24 mm (SF 363, Ctx 150, Ph3 Building B).
3.24.141. **Horseshoe**, L: 120, W: *c* 34 mm (SF 410, Ctx 267, Ph4 Building T).
142 (NI). **Horseshoe** (SF 455, Ctx 639, Ph4 Room A9).
3.24.143. **Horseshoe**, L: 98, W: *c* 26 mm (SF 402, Ctx 186, Ph5).
3.24.144. **Horseshoe**, L: 96, W: *c* 26 mm (SF 403, Ctx 186, Ph5).
3.24.145. **Horseshoe**, L: 105 mm (SF 404, Ctx 186, Ph5).
146 (NI). **Horseshoe** (SF 405, Ctx 186, Ph5).
147 (NI). **Horseshoe** fragment (SF 396, Ctx 186, Ph5).
148 (NI). **Horseshoe** (SF 369, Ctx 189, Ph5).
149 (NI). **Horseshoe** (SF 418, Ctx 347, Ph5 Building J).
150 (NI). **Horseshoe** fragment (SF 389, Ctx 186, Ph5).
3.24.151. **Horseshoe**, L: *c* 96, web *c* 26 mm (SF 76, Ctx 512, Ph5 Room A9).
3.24.152. **Horseshoe**, L: *c* 60 mm (SF 75, Ctx 512, Ph5 Room A9).
153 (NI). **Horseshoe** (SF 437, Ctx 582, Ph5 Room A3).
154 (NI). **Horseshoe** (SF 470, Ctx 1129, finds reference for Building G).
3.24.155. **Horseshoe/oxshoe** fragment (SF 334, Ctx 118, Ph3 courtyard).
NI. **Horseshoe** (SF 339, Ctx 1, unstratified).
NI. **Horseshoe** (SF 411, Ctx 272, unstratified).
NI. **Horseshoe** (SF 586, Ctx 1044, finds reference for Building T).
156 (NI). **Fiddle key nail**, L: 36 mm (SF 209, Ctx 702, Ph5).
3.25.157. **Bridle bit**, in 2 pieces, including a mouthpiece link. Non-ferrous plating. L: *c* 114 mm (SF 257, Ctx 207, Ph2).
3.25.158. **Mouthpiece link from bridle bit**, L: *c* 77 mm (SF 278, unstratified).
3.25.159. **Currycomb** fragment, L: 60+mm (SF 400, Ctx 186, Ph5).

The spur buckle and spurs (*Figs 3.23.133 and 3.25.160–161*)
by Blanche Ellis

Two iron rowel spurs were recovered; one from a demolition context associated with Area F (No. 3.25.160) and one from an unstratified layer (No. 3.25.161). The slender sides of No. 160 are broken and their terminals are gone. The sides plunge downwards from their junction with the neck and the more complete one bends at approximately 140 degrees under the wearer's ankle. An X-ray shows thin double diagonal lines and a vertical line, perhaps mouldings, flanking this bend. The sides appear to have been of round section but their surfaces, and those of the short straight neck, are badly pitted with rust. The rowel originally had about seven separated points, all but one of which are now damaged. The spur is dated typologically to the mid 13th to early 14th century. The earliest rowel spurs were slender with deeply curved or bent sides, features which continued throughout this period, and it is not possible to date this incomplete spur more closely, although what remains is of similar form and proportions to early rowel spurs Nos 322 and 324 from London (Ellis 1995, 133–5, fig. 95 nos 322 and 324).

The second spur (No. 3.25.161) is a long spur (terminology ibid., 126). Its rowel-box is now bent to one side and the sides have become compressed together. The D-sectioned sides lay horizontally around the wearer's heel with their front ends curving upwards to become vertical, supporting small horizontal figure-8 terminals. A flange above the junction of sides and neck may have originally been the base of a pointed crest. The low-set neck, round and slender, projects below the flange. The rowel-bosses are conical and quite prominent and the rowel has eight separated points. The terminals retain three hook attachments for the spur leathers. Their centres are formed by oval discs but their hooks are now broken. The terminal ring left empty by the missing buckle reveals that the spur was worn on the right foot, because the buckles were worn on the outside. Surface traces of non-ferrous plating are most likely to have been tin (Jope 1956). This type of spur can be dated typologically from the mid to second half of the 15th century.

The spur buckle (No. 3.23.133) was recovered from a demolition context associated with Room A9.

It is flat with its top edge curved to form the frame, and the buckle pin is looped into a central hole. The lower part of the buckle is elongated and terminates in an open ring loop which would have attached it to the terminal of a spur side. The pin is flanked by some incised line decoration, and the whole object has non-ferrous plating which may be tin or silver; medieval iron spurs were often plated with tin (Jope 1956, 35–8). This buckle is typical of spur buckles of the late medieval period, such as that on a cabled iron rowel spur of about 1400 in the Museum of London (*Catalogue of the Collection of London antiquities in the Guildhall Museum* 2nd edition, 1908, 266, no. 40, pl. lxxxii,6; the spur is now renumbered 7373).

Catalogue

3.23.133. **Spur buckle**, L: 70, W: 35 mm (SF 81, Ctx 512, Ph5 Room A9).

3.25.160 **Spur** fragment, L: *c* 80 mm, neck L: 22 mm. rowel D: originally *c* 22 mm (SF 53, Ctx 503, Ph5 Area F).

3.25.161. **Spur**, L: 172 mm, neck L: 74 mm, rowel D: 35 mm (SF 214, unstratified).

Weapons (Fig. 3.25.162–168)

The arrowheads are of various types but all are socketed. The remaining object is a broken socket with decorative grooves, perhaps from a spearhead.

Catalogue

3.25.162. **Arrowhead**, L: 154 mm (SF 344, Ctx 23, Ph4 Building A12).

3.25.163. **Arrowhead**, L: 127 mm (SF 462, Ctx 862, Ph4 Building A1).

3.25.164. **Arrowhead**, tip L: 54, W: 35 mm (SF 207, Ctx 267, Ph4 Building T).

3.25.165. **Arrowhead**, L: 52 (SF 338, Ctx 1, unstratified).

3.25.166. **Arrowhead**, L: 43, W: 14, D: 14 mm (SF 52, Ctx 224, Ph5).

3.25.167. **Arrowhead**, L: 31, D: 11 mm (SF 11, Ctx 19, Ph5 Room A10).

3.25.168. Broken **socket**, perhaps from a spearhead, L: 65+mm (SF 361, Ctx 135, Ph5).

Miscellaneous

The remaining 37 iron objects consist of fragmentary or poorly preserved objects that have been classified as miscellaneous items. This group consists of 6 plate fragments, 5 bars, 16 small unidentified objects and lumps, 9 small pieces of sheet and 1 small fragment of iron. These items were found in all parts of the building complex and from Phases 2 to 5.

SLAGS
by Chris Salter

Introduction

The collection of material examined consisted of samples from 23 different locations on the site (Table 3.6). The chemical analysis of a glassy substance in sample 9 is shown in Table 3.7. The material was classified into five general groups (A to E) and the approximate total weight for each group (excluding group E) is presented in Table 3.8. The five groups are characterised by the following:

Table 3.6 Slag samples with site provenance and phasing

Slag sample no.	Phase	Context	Building/ Room	Comment
1	4	700	NW yard	Ironworking slag
2	5	546	demolition	Ironworking slag
3	5	119	demolition	Ironworking slag
4	modern	911	finds ref	Ironworking slag
5A	4	23	A12	Corroded iron artefacts
5B	modern	6	A12	Corroded iron artefacts
6	2	49	moat upcast	Ironworking slag
7	5	8	A12	Copper based alloy
8	4	23	A12	Mixed iron and copper corrosion products
9	4	23	A12	Copper based alloy and glass
10	4	23	A12	Mixed iron, copper, burnt clay corrosion products
11	5	186	demolition	Ironworking slag
12	2	534	NE yard	Ironworking slag
13	5	500	A9	Natural iron cemented sand
14	5	19	A10	Furnace lining material
15	modern	0	U/S	Ironworking slag
16	3	1088	A1	Ironworking slag
17	modern	0	U/S	Slag driplet
18	3	756	NW yard	Ironworking slag
19	5	504	demolition?	Natural
20	5	186	demolition	Furnace lining
21	3–5	600	A4	Furnace lining material
22	5	547	demolition	Furnace lining material
23	modern	0		Ironworking slag

A. Ironworking slags.

B. Reaction products due to the interaction of heat, charcoal and ironworking slag on the furnace lining material.

C. Various copper based alloys.

D. Natural materials.

E. Other items, such as corroded iron objects and some glassy material (not weighed).

Group A (ironworking slags)

It is difficult to distinguish definitely between the various different types of slags produced at each stage of the ironmaking process, either by chemical means or on the basis of the visual appearance of the

Table 3.7 Analysis of glassy substance in sample 9 (context 23) in weight % of oxide

Substance	Weight % of oxide
Na-O	0.4
MgO	0.6
Al-O-	3.4
SiO	71.4
P-O-	0.4
K-O	16.2
CaO	6.9
FeO	1

slags. However, there are a number of features in this case which would indicate that the slags were blacksmithing slags. The largest single piece of slag weighed only 305 g, which must have represented at least 80% of the original mass of the slag. The plano-convex shape seen on some of the samples also indicates that these slags probably cooled where they formed, at the base of a bowl-shaped furnace. There were no signs of any of the slag having been tapped from the furnace. Chemically the slags were often heterogeneous, containing globules of metallic iron. Similar structures have been produced by the author during experimental welding operations, when the metal became overheated. Therefore, all of the evidence points to these slags being the results of a small amount of blacksmithing.

Group B (furnace-lining material)

The samples assigned to this group varied considerably, ranging from clays baked to a brick red colour to highly-fired high silica sands and clays. The compositions and firing states of these materials show that the temperatures used ranged from as low as 500°C to at least 1450°C. In a number of samples virtually pure silica had been fused.

Other samples contained partially dissolved flints, and other material which had either fallen into the hearth or had been pulled away from the lining of the hearth. One sample (20) consisted of globules of iron oxide held together by thin films of material rich in silicon and calcium. This would also support the idea that these slags were the result of blacksmithing operations. It is interesting to note that some of the lining materials are ideally suited to resist prolonged exposure to high temperatures, but this could have been accidental or deliberate depending on the nature of the local supplies of sands and clays.

Table 3.8 Slag groups by weight (g)

Slag group	Lab. slag no.	Weight (g)
A	1–4, 6, 11–12, 15–18, 23	1480
B	10 (part of), 14, 21–22	50
C	7–10 (part of)	390
D	13, 19	40
E	5, 9 (part of)	-
Total		1960

Group C (copper-based alloys)

This group of materials appeared as green-stained sandstone from the exterior, where the corrosion products had cemented the surrounding sand to the surface of the object. Internally they were badly corroded and although some retained some metallic copper it was usually badly penetrated by corrosion. Therefore, although chemical analysis was carried out on the samples, it is unlikely that the results bear much relationship to the original composition. The analyses that were obtained showed a very mixed set of alloys containing copper, lead, antimony and sometimes tin, zinc and traces of iron. The shape of the samples did not suggest any object but instead they appeared to be the results of drips from casting or melting operations. However, the corroded state of the objects makes any interpretation of them impossible.

Group D (natural objects)

The natural objects consist of cemented quartz sands which could either belong to the local geology or have been formed since the burial of the site. The sample (13) was an iron oxide cemented sandstone which could have been formed by the leaching of iron from corroding iron objects or from iron naturally present in the ground waters. The other natural object (19) was iron-sulphide cemented sandstone.

Group E (other objects)

One sample (5) consisted of completely corroded iron objects, probably nails. Amongst the material in another sample (sample 9 from context 23) there was a fragment from a possible crucible. On one edge of this there was a clear transparent blue glassy substance. A small sample was analysed and the results are presented in Table 3.7.

Discussion

The material provides good evidence of a blacksmith working in the vicinity of Chalgrove. However, the amount of slag recovered would not result from a long period of working but perhaps a few weeks of continuous working or a longer period of non-continuous work. In addition, the slag was found in fairly scattered pockets, making it difficult to estimate accurately the amount of working. The percentage recovery is therefore likely to have been low, especially as such slag is likely to have been mixed up with domestic rubbish that was removed off the excavated site. The copper working was probably confined to the melting-down of scrap metal, indicated by the copper alloys being of a rather odd and heterogeneous composition, although all of them had fairly high lead contents. There was also evidence for possible glass working in the form of a crucible which would probably have been used to melt glass.

OBJECTS OF ANTLER, BONE AND IVORY
(FIG. 3.17.12 AND FIG. 3.26)
by Robert White

Introduction

A total of eight objects of antler, bone and ivory were recovered. These included an ivory doublesided comb, two gaming pieces (one of ivory, the other of antler), a bone die and the broken carved bone handle of an iron knife.

Discussion

These objects are mainly luxury or recreational items; only the toggle and probably the boar's tusk are utilitarian in nature. The size and shape of pig metapodials makes them ideal for use as toggles, but an alternative use as bobbins has been suggested for some pierced metapodials found in Saxon contexts at Northampton (Oakley and Harman 1979, 313–314, fig. 139, WB65–71). The function of the boar's tusk is not known. The partial removal of one side would not be necessary if the tusk was to be used as a pendant. The perforation and the natural curvature of the tusk suggest that it may have been used in weaving.

Double-edged combs similar to No. 3.26.1 were in use from the late Roman period until the 17th to 18th century. They suffered a decline in popularity when single-edged combs were introduced by the

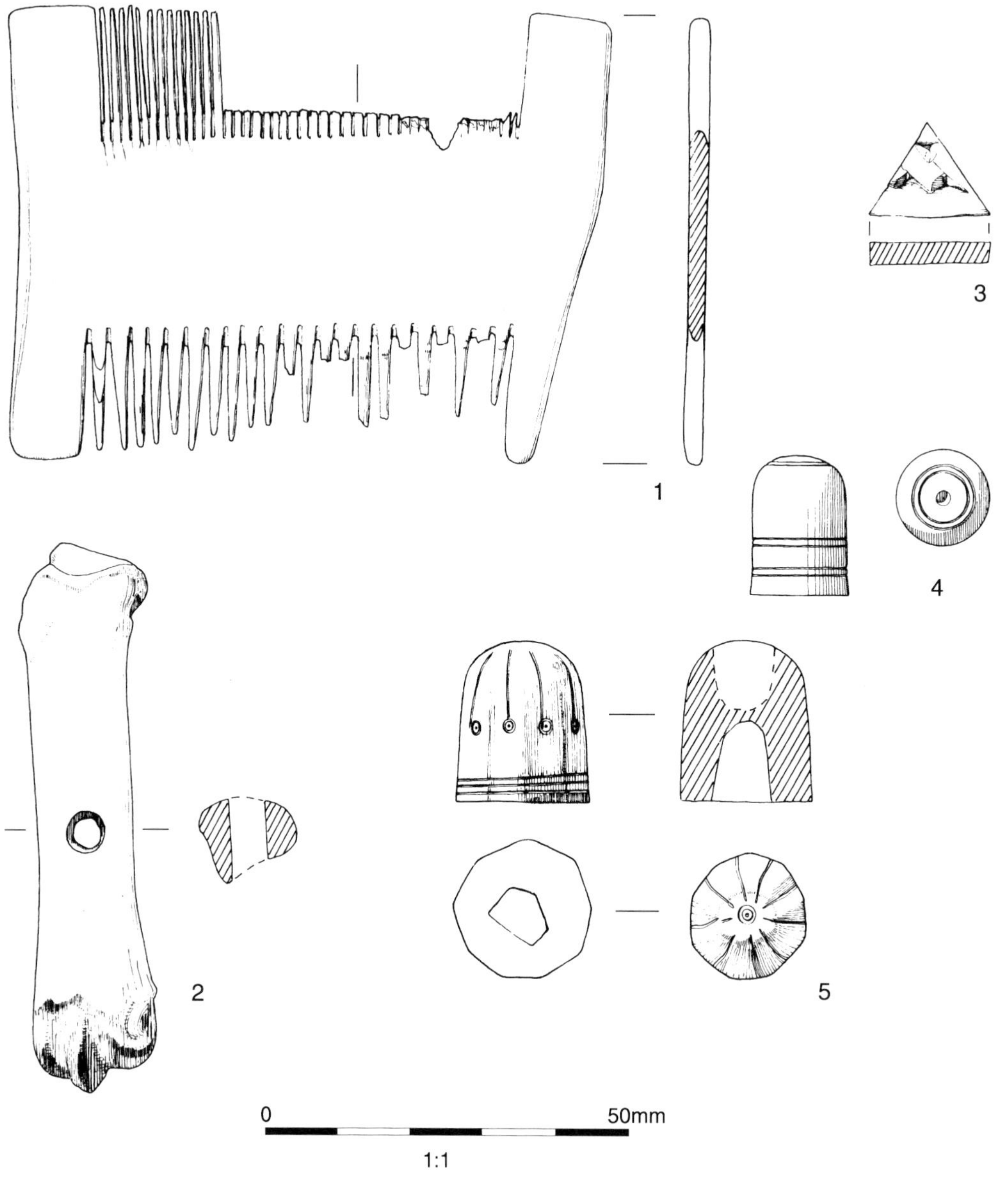

Figure 3.26 Objects of antler, bone and ivory.

Vikings, but regained popularity by the 12th century (Moorhouse 1977, 61). Imported ivory was in use throughout the medieval period (Oakley and Harman 1979, 310).

Chess was an important game, particularly amongst the higher levels of society, during the medieval period and two objects (Nos 3.26.4 and 5) are probably chess pieces. The comparative simplicity of decoration and the lack of protuberances suggest that these pieces may be pawns. The present pawn shape was in use by the 15th century (Murray 1913, 770) but medieval pawns varied considerably in shape and size. Eleven of the nineteen pawns found in the Isle of Lewis had octagonal bases. Close parallels have not been found for No. 3.26.5, but No. 3.26.4 is well matched by the pawns in an Italian set of *c* 1500.

Catalogue

3.26.1. Double-sided one-piece **comb** with broad central reservation. Ivory. Slightly rounded ends, one tapering. Fine teeth (23 per 30 mm) and coarse teeth (12 per 30 mm) on opposing sides. Some teeth missing. Two pieces, L: 82, W: 59, Th: 3.5–2 mm at tapering end (SFs 84 and 185, Ctx 535, Ph4 Building A12). *cf* Oakley and Harman 1979, 308–11, fig. 137, WB 44, 45.

3.26.2. Probable **Toggle**. Pig metapodial. Perforation in centre of shaft. Slight polish on shaft. L: 70, perforation D: 6.5 mm (SF184, Ctx 518, Ph5). *cf* Oakley and Harman 1979, 313–15, fig. 139, WB 65–9.

3.26.3. Triangular fragment of **inlay**. Bone. The base of the triangle and the upper and lower surfaces are sheared, the two sides are sawn. Decorated with 3 excised triangles on upper surface. Possibly from a casket. L (at base): 16.5 mm, sides: 14 mm, W: 2 mm (SF 254, Ctx 903 unstratified).

3.26.4. **Gaming piece**. Ivory. Cylinder with rounded top. Lathe-turned, and decorated with incised bands. Ht: 19, D: 13.5 mm (SF 260, Ctx 907, unstratified). *cf* Ashmolean Museum, Dept Western Art.

3.26.5. **Gaming piece**. Antler. Octagonal cylinder with rounded top. Irregular facets with smoothed corners. Plugs have been inserted into the cancellous cells at both ends. Incised bands near base. Roundels, comprising a dot and 2 concentric rings, on each facet, with irregularly positioned incised lines leading towards a central roundel on top. A similar plug has been inserted into the base of an undecorated bone heptagonal pawn from Oxford (Egan 1989). Ht: 21 mm, D: 16.5 mm (SF 293, Ctx 989, Ph3 Building A1).

6 (NI). **Die**. Bone. Sides slightly dished. Each unit is represented by a roundel comprising a dot and 2 concentric rings; the roundels are of uniform size and fairly even spacing. 8.5 mm cube (SF 299, Ctx 600, Ph3–5 Room A4). *cf* Harvey 1975, 274, fig. 249, 1945; Armstrong 1977, fig. 29, 150.

7 (NI). **Boar tusk**. Implement of unknown function, possibly for weaving. Sheared edges where one side has been removed. Both ends broken, broad end across perforation. No visible signs of wear. L: 82 mm (SF 321, Ctx 882, Ph3 Room A3).

3.17.12. **Knife handle**. Bone. One-piece handle carved in shape of figure draped in long robes. Broken above a horizontally positioned hand. A similar, ivory knife handle from Shire Ditch, St Aldates, Oxford depicts a woman in long robes holding a hawk (Ashmolean Museum 1886 13a). Total L: 142 mm. Knife L: 83 (SF 262, 518, Ph5).

VESSEL GLASS (FIG. 3.27)
by Jeremy Haslam

The medieval assemblage contains examples of pale green glass vessels, probably of English manufacture,

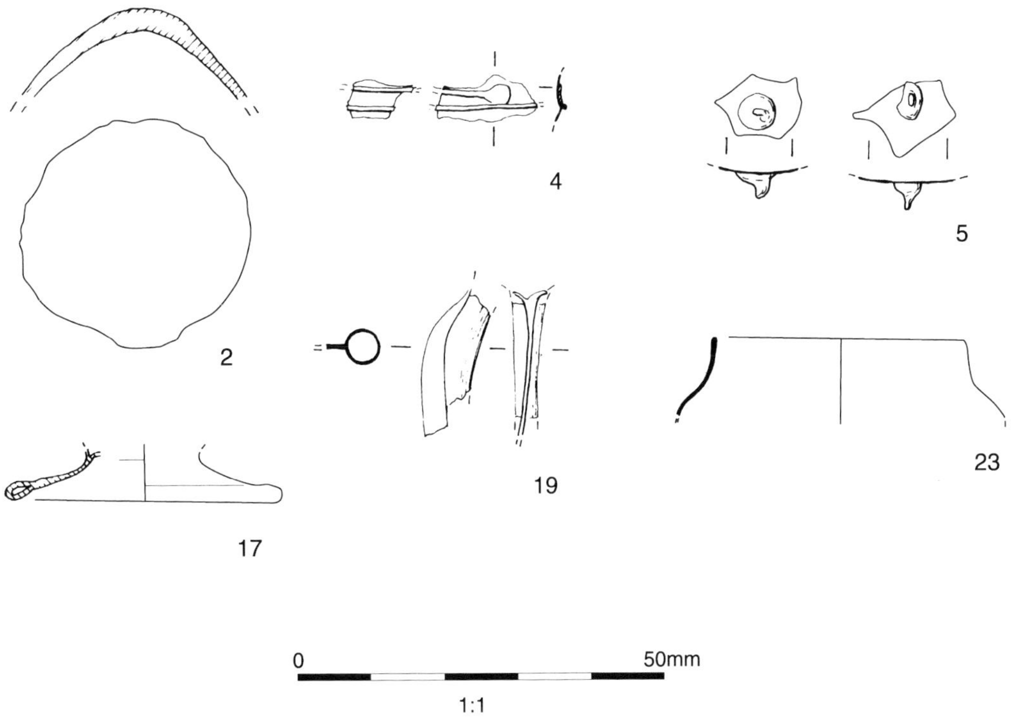

Figure 3.27 Vessel glass.

and imported vessels, with one exception of southern European (probably Italian) manufacture. There are a number of small fragments of glass bottles dating from the 18th and 19th centuries (Nos 8, 10–12, 14 and possibly 22). None of them is either large or significant.

English medieval glass

Fragments from seven individual vessels can be identified. These consist of two urine inspection flasks (Nos 6 and 15), a base of a large flask (No. 3.27.2), three vessels of indeterminate form (Nos 1, 21 and 22) and one possible vessel fragment (No. 16). The large flask and the urine inspection vessels are common finds in medieval contexts and both occur in later medieval groups in London (Haslam forthcoming).

Imported medieval glass

There are fragments of seven different medieval vessels, all from Phases 4 and 5. Two fragments from the same context (Fig. 3.27.4 and No.13), probably the same vessel, are of white glass, possibly originally colourless, with blue-green trails. No. 18 is from a vessel of pale yellowish-green glass. No. 3.27.5 is two fragments from a bulbous vessel of nearly colourless glass with a yellowish tinge and with applied prunts. Three fragments of clear glass vessels were found consisting of a base of a drinking vessel (Fig. 3.27.17), a rim (Fig. 3.27.23) and an unidentifiable fragment (No. 20). The seventh fragment was a piece from a kuttrolf of blue glass (No. 3.27.19).

These represent a group from the latest phase of occupation of the manor, and from layers resulting from its destruction. Glass is documented as being imported into London in 1399, implying that it was an established item of trade (Gasparetto 1968, 68), and the Barentins may have obtained imported vessels through personal connections there; in the late 14th century Drew Barentin (brother of Thomas Barentin II) was a wealthy goldsmith in the capital (see Blair, Chapter 1, above).

While most of the vessels are represented by fragments of too small a size to permit certain identification of vessel type, a number of broad identifications can be suggested. Nos 3.27.4 and 13, decorated with greenish-blue applied trails, belong to a class of Italian imports of the 14th century (Charleston 1968, 204; Charleston 1972, 45–8; Tait 1979, 11). These comprise cups, flasks, bowls and tall-stemmed wine glasses. Possibly also belonging to this group is the vessel with applied prunts (No. 3.27.5). The other fragments are possibly from undecorated vessels, the common 'cristallo' of southern European origin (Charleston 1975, 205–7).

The single exception is the fragment of the kuttrolf (No. 3.27.19) of blue glass. This is from a bottle with a neck constricted to form several narrow channels and used as a dropper for pouring small quantities of liquids such as scents (Thorpe 1935, 41–3; Rademacher 1933, 60–60). Finds of this type are rare from English contexts; three from unassociated contexts, of green glass, are known from London (Museum Of London accession numbers A12601 and A27738 and one nearly complete piece from the collection of Dove Brothers), which probably date from the 15th or 16th centuries (Haslam forthcoming). These appear to be of northern European manufacture, as well may be the find from Chalgrove.

Catalogue

1 (NI). Small fragments, originally probable green glass, much decayed, vessel of indeterminate form, pre 1255-*c* 1300 (SF 541, Ctx 69, Ph3 Room A10).

3.27.2. Base fragment, large flask of green glass, much decayed, late medieval (SF542 unstratified).

3 (NI). Small fragment, wine bottle, olive green glass, late 18th century (SF 25, unstratified).

3.27.4. Small fragment, possibly a lid, thin, opaque white glass, possibly originally colourless. Decoration of 2 horizontally applied trails of greenish-blue glass 1 mm thick; one ends in a thicker blob for beginning of trail. 14th century. Same vessel as No. 13 (SF 187, Ctx 639, Ph4 Room A9).

3.27.5. 2 fragments, thin, colourless glass with slight yellowish tinge, unweathered. From cylindrical or tall bulbous vessel of D: *c* 80 mm. Each fragment decorated with an applied prunt, 7–10 mm wide, in same coloured glass with slightly pinched top. Probably Italian, 14th or 15th century. (SF 221, Ctx 726, Ph5 Room A5).

6 (NI). Fragmentary remains of thin-walled vessel, probably green glass, possible urine inspection vessel; late medieval (SF 227, Ctx 561, Ph4 courtyard).

7 (NI). See Window glass, Chapter 4, below.

8 (NI). Small fragment, wine bottle, olive green glass, probably late 18th century (SF 543, Ctx 548, Ph4 Building A1).

9 (NI). See Window glass, Chapter 4, below.

10 (NI). Wine bottle fragment, olive green glass, probably 18th century (SF 545, Ctx 621, Ph4 courtyard).

11 (NI). 9 fragments, late post-medieval vessel glass, dark green, light bluish-green and light brown glass. Probably all 18th–19th century (SF -, Ctx 186, Ph5).

12 (NI). 4 fragments. 3 of dark green wine bottle, late 18th century, and 1 light green phial fragment, 18th century (SF -, Ctx 284, Ph5).

13 (NI). Small fragment, thin, opaque, white (possibly originally colourless) glass. Remains of 2 applied trails of greenish-blue glass of 1 mm diameter, 8 mm apart. Probably Italian, 14th century. Same vessel as No. 3.27.4 (SF -, Ctx 639, Ph4 Room A9).

14 (NI). Small vessel fragments, dark or pale green glass. All late post-medieval (SF 275, unstratified).

15 (NI). Many small fragments of thin-walled vessel, possibly urine inspection vessel, much decayed, medieval (SF -, unstratified).

16 (NI). Small fragments, decayed vessel or window glass (SF 265, Ctx 234, P5 building 10).

3.27.17. Folded base of drinking vessel, clear glass with slight brownish tinge, weathered on surface, probably Italian, 15th to 16th century (SF 266, Ctx 186, Ph5).

18 (NI). Small fragment, pale yellowish-green glass without noticeable curvature, late medieval southern European import (SF 269, Ctx 923, Ph4 Room A10).

3.27.19. Fragment of curved tube attached to flat flange, from neck of kuttrolf, pale blue glass, probably northern European, late medieval or 16th century (SF 282, Ctx 523, Ph5 Building A1).

20 (NI). Small fragment, clear colourless glass, no decoration, possibly Italian, 15th to 16th century (SF 284, Ctx 935, Ph3–5 Room A5).

21 (NI). Small fragments, much decayed, pale green glass, Th: 2.5, from vessel of indeterminate form, medieval (SF 290, Ctx 971, Ph3 Room A9).

22 (NI). Small fragment, pale olive green glass from? wine bottle, date uncertain (SF 302, Ctx 999, Ph3 Building W).

3.27.23. Rim of vessel, in 2 joining pieces, colourless glass only slightly weathered, Italian, 15th to 16th century (SF 306, Ctx 119, Ph5).

STONE OBJECTS

The mortar fragments (Fig. 3.28)

by Philip Carstairs with stone identifications by Philip Powell

Five mortar fragments were found during the excavation, two of which (Fig. 3.28.4) were from a Phase 2 posthole from building D, a possible kitchen, one from a Phase 4 context and the remaining two from unstratified contexts. The five fragments represented a maximum of four mortars, all of which were made from local stones, either limestone or Forest Marble. Four of the fragments were from rims and the fifth (No. 3.28.1) was from a base, with the bottom part of a lug surviving.

Mortars were used for the preparation of food, which was either pounded or ground in the mortar with a pestle. The patterns of wear indicated that all of the mortar fragments had been used for grinding rather than pounding. The rim fragments were all worn on the inside surface with a horizontal pattern of wear and increased wear towards the bottom parts of the fragments. The base fragment was worn at the break of slope with the sides rather than in the centre where the mortar would have been worn had it been used for pounding (Dunning 1977, 320).

Mortar base No. 3.28.1 and fragments No. 2 and No. 3.28.3 were made from Forest Marble, a fairly local limestone whose nearest source was *c* 30 km away at Filkins, Oxfordshire. No. 3.28.4 was made of Corallian limestone, another local limestone whose nearest source, at Wheatley, Oxfordshire, was only a few miles from the site.

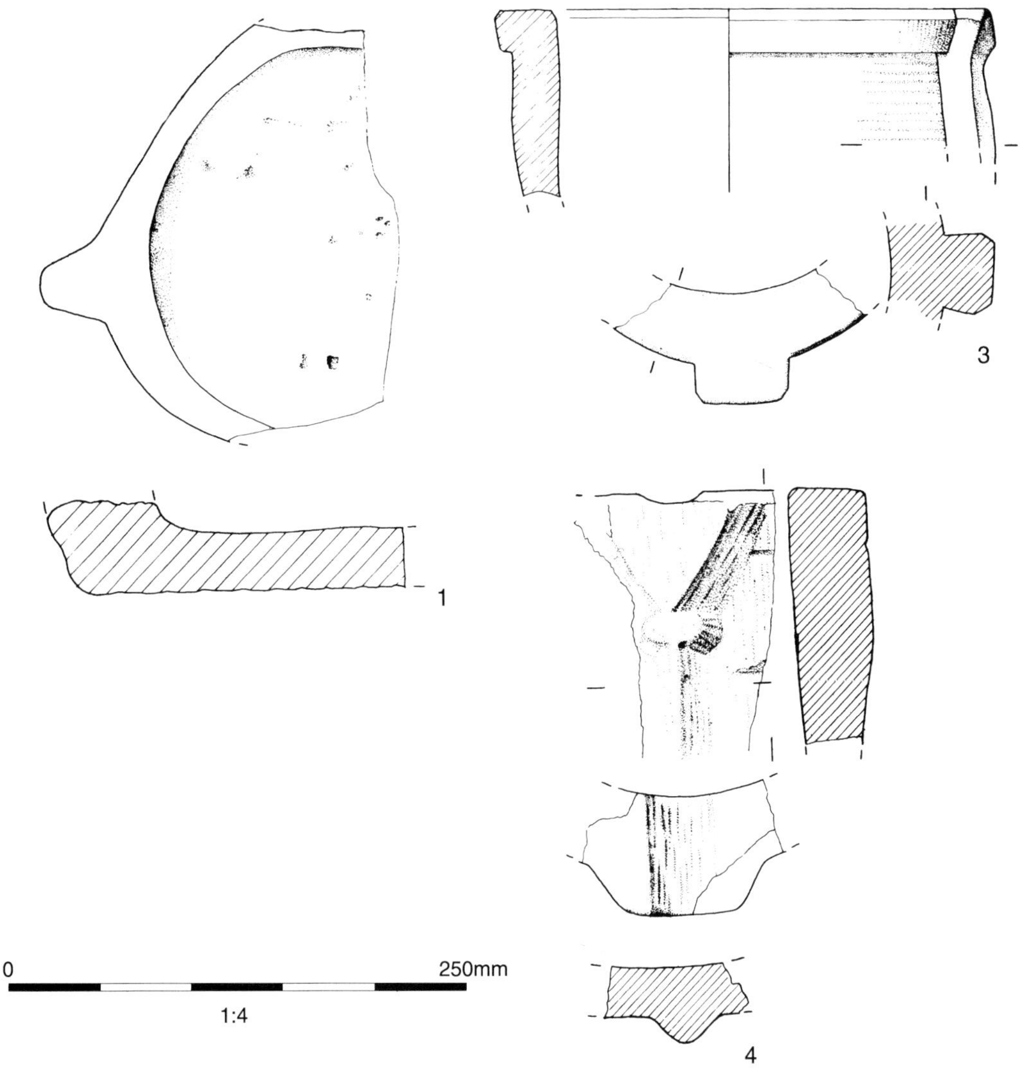

Figure 3.28 Stone mortar fragments.

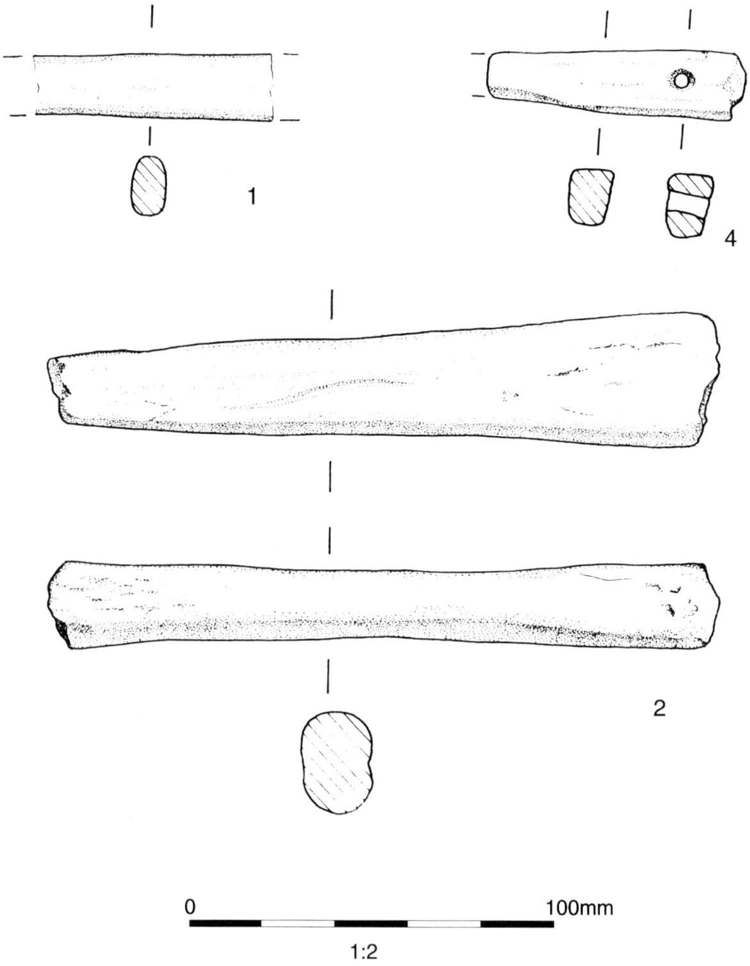

Figure 3.29 Stone hones and querns.

Catalogue

3.28.1. Mortar base, Forest Marble, vertical lug(s) (WS 11, unstratified).
2. (NI) Mortar rim, Forest Marble (WS 55, unstratified).
3.28.3. Mortar rim, 2 joining fragments, Forest Marble, square handle lug and flat rim (WS 48, Ctx 573, Ph4).
3.28.4. Mortar rim, Corallian limestone, ornate carved runnel (WS 46, Ctx 1061, Ph2 Building D).

The hones and querns (Fig. 3.29) *by Philip Page with stone identifications by Philip Powell*

Five hones were recovered, of which one was intact but worn (No. 3.29.2). They were all made from quartz mica schist with the exception of one quartzite hone (No. 5). All phases were represented except Phase 3. One was found associated with Building P in Phase 1 and three were found associated with various farm buildings, Q, G and H. The two quern fragments were made of Niedermendig lava (No. 6) and millstone grit (No. 7). The former was recovered from an occupation deposit associated with farm Building H and the other from a demolition layer associated with the main building A1.

Catalogue

3.29.1. **Hone**, L: 66 mm, W: 17 mm, Th: 10 mm (SF 21, Ctx 92, Ph1 Building P).
3.29.2. **Hone**, L; 182 mm (SF 210, Ctx 284, Ph5).
3 (NI). **Hone**, L: 89 mm, W: 39 mm, Th: 12–15 mm (SF 281, Ctx 417, Ph4 Building H).
3.29.4. **Hone**, L: 70 mm (SF 332, Ctx 1129, finds reference Building G).
5 (NI). **Hone**, L: *c* 69 mm (SF 212, Ctx 432, Ph2 Building Q).
6 (NI). **Quern fragment**, Niedermendig lava, L: *c* 40 mm, W: 20 mm, Th: 18 mm (SF 587, WS 54, Ctx 420, Ph5 Building H).
7 (NI). **Quern**, Millstone grit (SF -, WS 41, Ctx 618, Ph4 Building A1).

OTHER FINDS

A total of nine flints were recovered during the excavation, two of which proved to be unworked and natural. All were of indeterminate date and none identified any prehistoric features or deposits. A catalogue is available in archive. A total of 85 pieces of clay tobacco pipe were recovered and details are available in archive.

Chapter 4: Building Materials

SUMMARY

The assemblage of building materials recovered is modest, considering the number of buildings examined and the fact that the site was never redeveloped after the abandonment of the manor. Potential for understanding the architectural character of the manor is therefore limited without recourse to stylistic parallels. The documentary evidence strongly suggests that the site was methodically demolished and all usable materials recovered for use elsewhere.

TILE

by S Robinson

Floor tile (Fig. 4.1)

[Editor's note. The floor tile was recorded by Chris Storey and a report was prepared for publication by S Robinson shortly after the end of the fieldwork. The following account summarises the main elements and conclusions of Robinson's report, which is available in the project archive. Table 4.1 has been compiled by Kate Atherton from the records in archive.]

A total of 236 fragments of floor tile were found during the excavation, of which 55 were unstratified. Of the remaining 181 fragments, 107 had recognisable surface decoration, 31 had unidentifiable decoration and 43 were plain. The floor tiles were divided into groups according to their site provenance. Group 1 tile came from contexts located around and within the possible pentice, structure A13, and the main domestic buildings. Group 2 consists of the tile from building A11 (the probable chapel), and Group 3 contains tile from miscellaneous contexts, chiefly a general demolition layer. All contexts that produced only plain tile make up Group 4. Decorated tiles were classified according to Haberley (1937) and compared with published types from Penn (Hohler 1942). Three decorative designs were not identifiable amongst Haberley's types or the Penn material, and were classified as Types A, B and C. Table 4.1 presents the quantity of tile fragments, including unstratified tile, by group and decorative type. Types in Roman numerals are from Haberley. Two different fabric types were identified, which correspond to two fabrics recorded from the Hamel, Oxford (Mellor 1980, fiche 2: D10). The decorated floor tiles, and all but one of the plain tiles, are of the same fabric type (IIIC) with quartz and grog inclusions. The fabric of one plain tile (context 156) has pink and white quartz inclusions (IIIB), which is paralleled by a pottery fabric (AG) originating to the south of Oxford (Haldon 1977, 114–120).

Printed floor tiles were produced at Penn from the mid 14th century to the early 15th century and certainly no earlier (Eames 1968, 18). Several of the Chalgrove decorated tiles show similarities with the Penn designs suggesting that they were the products of a local workshop whose tilers possibly had some connection with Penn. Fabric type IIIC probably came from south-east Oxfordshire, centring on Nettlebed. Samples of decorated floor tile have been examined in detail by x-radiograph fluorescence and atomic absorption methods. The results show the Chalgrove tiles to be similar to decorated floor tiles from Stonor House (Bond *et al.* 1980), suggesting a similar area of production for both sets of tiles in south-east Oxfordshire.

Plain tiles

A total of 44 plain tiles were recovered and the majority (27 fragments) were retrieved from a single context (1005). These had been reused in a tile-on-edge hearth during the occupation of the main building (A1) during Phase 4. Other fragments came from various contexts including an ash deposit (context 534) that may represent the remains of a Phase 2 building or the demolition of an earlier structure (see above). Two plain tiles were found from a tile-on-edge oven (context 151) in Building B and other examples were found in a wall from Building H and from Area F's floor surface.

Decorated tiles

All of the decorated tiles are of the unkeyed, printed variety, such as were produced at Penn (Eames 1980, 221–6). Eleven different designs were identified but only three of the designs match the Penn types identified by Hohler (1942).

Group 1 (Main range and Structure A13, possible pentice)

The 60 tiles in this group all came from contexts located around and within the main group of domestic buildings (Building A1, Rooms A3, A4, A5 and A9, Structure A13 and Building A14). Of these, 48 are from Phase 5 demolition features and layers. One unidentifiable tile was found in a Phase 3 context in Room A5 and eleven tiles were found from four Phase 4 contexts, including two found *in situ* in the floor of the pentice, Structure A13. The four recognisable designs found in this group all correspond to types described by Haberley (1937) (see Table 4.1) and the complete tiles measure 115 mm square.

Group 2 (Building A11 and surrounding area)

The tiles in this group derive from occupation and demolition deposits associated with the possible chapel (building A11). Complete tiles measure

Figure 4.1 Decorated floor tiles.

Table 4.1 Quantification of decorated and plain floor tile by Haberley type (1937) and context classes

Type	Group 1	Group 2	Group 3	Group 4	Unstratified	Total
LXXIX	31		22		31	84
CIX	7		9			16
CLXXXI	9		4		5	18
A		9			6	15
B		4	1		2	7
C		4	1		4	9
CCLIV	1					1
LXXVII			1			1
CII			1			1
CVII			2		1	3
CXVI			1			1
Unrecog.	10	5	16		5	36
Plain	2	1	1	39	1	44
Total	60	23	59	39	55	236

c 115 mm square. A number of tiles were scored longitudinally before firing and were then broken in half as if to fit the edge of the floor. This implies that they were laid square to the walls of the building.

The three recognisable designs present do not occur among the types published by Haberley (1937) or Hohler (1942) and are illustrated in Figure 4.1 (Type A Fig. 4.1a; Type B Fig. 4.1b; Type C Fig. 4.1c). Type A has ornamental leaves and trefoils reminiscent of Penn types P88–89 (ibid.), while Type C has an unusual design featuring what appears to be the head of a monk within a central circle.

Group 3 (miscellaneous contexts)

This group contains tiles from miscellaneous contexts, of which the majority came from a general Phase 5 demolition layer (context 186). All but one of the tiles were decorated, although many were unidentifiable designs.

Roof tile

[Editor's note. A large quantity of roof tile was recovered from the excavations, of which only a sample was examined and recorded in detail. A subsequent cursory examination of the remainder suggested that the sample was representative of the site as a whole. The sample chosen comprised 204 fragments of tile from a single stratified sequence in the cross-wing (Rooms A9 and A10) and the immediately surrounding area. The analysis appears to have been undertaken with a view to identifying tile fabrics and any significant chronological or spatial patterns in fabric distribution. The data collected are set out in Table 4.2, and suggest that no useful results were obtained from this study since the great majority of fragments of all fabric types were recovered from demolition contexts. The report

Table 4.2 Fabric types from the stratified sequence of roof tiles (including miscellaneous)

Phase	Building	Context	IIIA	IIIB	IIIC	IV	Total
5	10	19	2	6	15		23
5	12	26		1	3		4
5	10	234			1		1
5	–	275		1			1
5	9	500	3	5	11	3	22
5	9	501		1	1		2
5	9	502	2	1			3
5	9	510			1		1
5	9	511		1	1		2
5	9	512	9	3	48	2	62
5	9	515		1	2		3
5	9	520	4	5	19	5	33
4	10	44			1		1
4	9	639		3	1		4
4	9	733		3			3
4	9	737	1		3		4
4	9	739	1				1
4	9	741	1				1
4	9	765	2		1		3
4	9	806			1		1
4	9	825			1		1
3	10	56	1	2	2		5
3	9	763		1			1
3	9	766	2		3		5
3	10	927	1				1
3	9	982	2	1	4		7
3	9	1053	1				1
2	Moat	356	1		4		5
2	Moat	924			2		2
1	–	839		1			1
Total			33	35	126	10	204

that follows here is a revised version of the original report by S Robinson, which is available in the project archive.]

The stratified sequence

Of the 204 tile fragments in the stratified sequence, 152 were positively identified as roof tiles. The remaining 52 were too small to identify and measure and have been classified as miscellaneous. All of the tile fragments recorded, with the exception of two, are flat roofing tiles with peg holes (hole diameter of 16 mm) for wooden pegs to hold the tiles onto the roof. Some tiles also have traces of mortar on their underside, suggesting they were mortared to prevent them moving. A few fragments are covered with mortar indicating that they were reused as building material. This interpretation is supported by a number of fragments found elsewhere on the site within a wall (context 992). Only one complete roof tile was recovered (context 19). It was 275 mm long and 170 mm wide. Several other half tiles were recovered, all with widths between 165 and 175 mm. No fragment is thicker than 18 mm and most are 13 or 14 mm thick. Two ridge tile fragments are present (contexts 44 and 520). Both are the same shape, with neither glaze nor any form of ridge decoration.

Four different fabric types were identified which have been described in detail elsewhere (Mellor 1980, fiche 2: D10). The fabric types present are characterised by pink quartz inclusions (IIIA), pink and white quartz and iron (IIIB), white quartz and grog (IIIC) and grey and white quartz and grog (IV). The variation in fabric types, especially the presence of the pink quartz fabric (IIIA), indicates that roof tiles were brought from different manufacturing centres to roof the buildings. No clear chronological patterning is evident in the use of the different fabric types.

The first fabric (IIIA) is paralleled by a pottery fabric type that derived from an area east of Oxford, centring on Brill and the second fabric (IIIB) is paralleled by one originating to the south of Oxford (Haldon 1977, 114–20, fabrics AM and AG respectively).

Three tile fragments are of particular interest. The first (context 19) is made from the white quartz and grog fabric (IIIC) and it contains a sizeable patch of white (pipe) clay within the body of the tile. White clay is found at Shotover, south of Oxford, in the Reading beds. A deposit of white clay also occurs in the parish of Henley (*Geol. Soc. Mem.* 1908). The presence of white clay suggests that tiles of this fabric may have been manufactured in south-east Oxfordshire, and there is documentary evidence to suggest that this white quartz and grog fabric is from this area of the county (Bond *et al.* 1980). It is likely that the grey and white quartz and grog fabrics (IV) were being produced in the same area. Documents of 1312–13 record the delivery of 15,000 flat peg and 150 crests and ridge tiles for the roofing of a new byre in Cuxham, the parish adjacent to Chalgrove. The place of manufacture of these tiles is not mentioned but it may well have been Nettlebed, which was a major production centre for roof tiles in the mid 14th century and probably was making tiles before this. The first reference to Nettlebed is in 1365, when 35,000 tiles were supplied for Wallingford Castle. References continue into the mid 15th century. There is also documentary evidence that ridge tiles were being manufactured at Penn in the late 13th century (Jope 1951, 86). This production centre is also a possible source for the Chalgrove roof tiles although Penn is twice the distance of Nettlebed from Chalgrove (*c* 15 km).

The other two fragments of interest (contexts 26 and 516) are made from the pink and white quartz and iron fabric (IIIB). Both tiles have been fired hard in reducing conditions and are vitrified. One also exhibits a grey 'glaze' on its unbroken edge, which is probably due to the presence of soda-sand during firing. The presence of this sand and the high degree of firing may be accidental but the introduction of soda-sand and the technique of hard firing were later used by brickmakers to produce decorative grey and blue headers.

The remaining tiles

The remaining roof tile fragments were cursorily examined and only three additional features were revealed which are worth noting.

In addition to the four fabric types already discussed, there were four tile fragments with limestone and white quartz inclusions and voids (VIIA). This fabric is dated to the later medieval period and this is supported by the contexts at Chalgrove from which the fragments were found.

Several tiles had impressions of animal feet. Dog paw prints and the hoof prints of goats or deer are represented. One fragment has a slightly curved line impression on its underside.

Examples were also found of corner or hip tiles, used for covering the corners on hipped roofs. These tiles have a square hole, measuring 8 mm in diameter, some showing signs of iron staining, which suggests that they were fixed by nails rather than wooden pegs.

BRICKS (FIG. 4.2)
by John Steane

Introduction

Samples submitted for identification and comment comprised two joining fragments from a single brick, and five other brick fragments. All were either unstratified or from Phase 5 demolition layers. At the time there was considerable doubt about the identification of these pieces as brick, since they were of a soft chalky/sandy fabric and a yellow-buff colour totally unlike other bricks from known medieval contexts in the area, such as Stonor Park, Ewelme and the Chantry House at Henley. The identification was confirmed following archaeomagnetic intensity investigation at the Research Laboratory for Archaeology and the History of Art at Oxford University, and consultation with the Brick Development Association. The bricks were made from an iron-depleted clay, probably Gault clay, which outcrops in the Chalgrove area. Further details are available in the project archive.

Catalogue

4.2.1. **Brick fragment**, soft, sandy fabric. Side: straw/grass impressions. Edge: mould impressions. Munsell 2.5Y 8/4. L: 190, W: 105, Th: 55 mm (WS 15, Ctx 26, Ph5 Building A12).

4.2.2. **Brick fragment**. Side: structures caused during moulding. Laminated clay has been pressed into a mould and the top layer of clay cleaned off with a strike or similar traditional brickmakers' tool. Other side: possible straw impressions. Munsell 10YR 8/3. L: 120, W: 105, Th: 55 mm (WS 52, Ctx 26, Ph5 Building A12).

4.2.3. **Brick fragment**. Mortar dab on underside. Top shows striations from smoothing the clay after it has been pressed in the mould. Underside pit-marked where the suction of the clay in the mould has caused some to be torn from base of brick. Munsell 2.5YR 8/4. L: 150, W: 90, Th: 60 mm (WS 32, Ctx 512, Ph5 Room A9).

4.2.4. **Brick fragment**, small, moulded. Smooth upper side, pitted lower side. Straw/grass impressions on one edge. Brick is bevelled with semi-circular section but bruising has removed the top surface and the original profile only survives on half the brick. Munsell 10YR 6/2. L: 110, W: 65, Th: 55 mm (WS 18, unstratified).

4.2.5. **Moulded brick**, sufficiently complete to make total reconstruction. 2 bevelled edges, one with rectangular piece cut out of one corner. The 2 bevelled edges and the top are smooth, the rest are pitted. Munsell SY 8/3. L: 230, W: 110, Th: 50 mm (WS 17, unstratified).

(NI). Small fragment (WS 53, Ctx 565, Ph5).

Discussion

These fragments illustrate some of the techniques of medieval brickmaking (Brooks 1939, 155–56; Firman and Firman 1967). They confirm that the brickmaker sanded or wetted his mould, then threw into it a lump of prepared clay. The surfaces of the bricks were distinctly sandy to the touch. Surplus clay was sliced from the top of the mould by a strike, a wooden stick, which has left striations on the surface. The wet moulded bricks were then taken to the drying ground and laid out to dry on straw or grass. Their weight and plasticity caused the stalk impressions noted in three of the fragments (1, 2 and 4). There are no stony inclusions, but an occasional void suggests the former presence of grass in the fabric which was burned out during firing. The fabric is uniform in colour throughout the brick and there is no core of material of a different colour suggesting overfiring. Perhaps the most interesting feature is the evidence for moulding and cutting the bricks into decorative shapes. Two fragments (4 and 5) were clearly specially moulded to fulfil particular functions in the overall design. The chamfered edges, on the other hand, may simply have been cut down from standard bricks. One fragment (6) has been cut as well as moulded.

The use of moulded brick is found in Belgium from as early as the 13th century (Sosson 1972, 129–53). Moulded brick was used on a limited scale at Stonor Park. In 1416–17 Thomas Stonor bought 200,000 bricks from Michael Warwick for £40 and 'The Flemings' are mentioned making bricks at 'Crokkernende' (Bond *et al.* 1980, 3–5). The medieval expression for moulded brick is 'hewentile' and there are references in the Kirby Muxloe accounts of the 1480s to 'breke leyers and hewers' for chimneys and vaulting (Hamilton-Thompson 1913–14, 205, 208). Since the bricks at Chalgrove were not found fixed in any structural context, their function is uncertain. It is possible that they were specially fashioned to provide a polychromatic and, therefore, contrasting edging to a fireplace or hearth. Their soft and crumbly surface would have made them unsuitable for any external use or any surface which was exposed to high temperatures. They are probably late medieval or early post-medieval in date.

ARCHITECTURAL STONE
(FIGS 4.3–4.4; TABLE 4.3)

[Editor's note. A total of 35 freestone fragments were identified by John Blair during and shortly after the

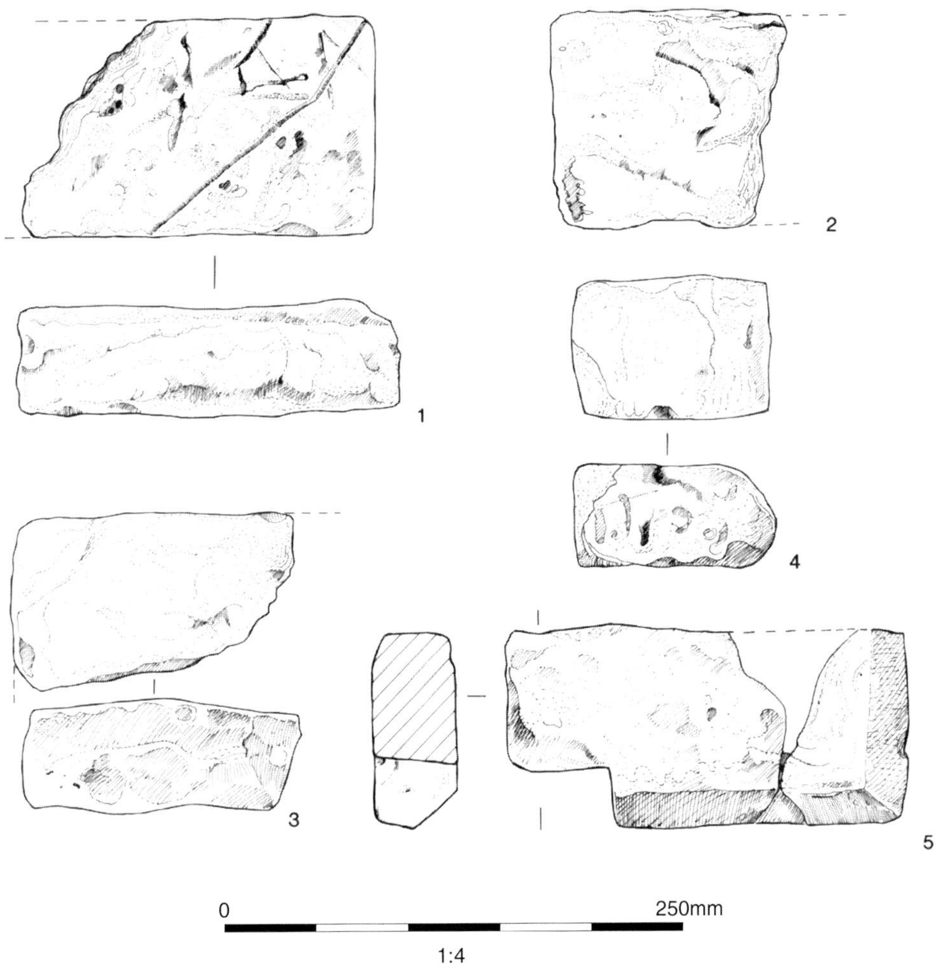

Figure 4.2 Medieval bricks.

end of the fieldwork. Of these, 17 were of particular interest and are discussed and catalogued below. The remainder have been listed by Kate Atherton in Table 4.3, together with other miscellaneous items of undiagnostic stone recorded in the archive.]

Architectural stone catalogue
by John Blair

Voussoirs from a Romanesque doorway (Figs 4.3–4.4, Nos 1–5, Fig. 4.4A–C)

Numbers 1–5 are five voussoirs from a doorway arch with a calculated width of *c* 1.20 m. Bands of chevron on the main face and soffit meet at the arris to form lozenges, each of which contains a small carved fleuron. This pattern of chevron ornament, Borg's type 4, was popular in Oxfordshire during the second half of the 12th century (Borg 1967, 135–6, 40). The voussoirs were found in a context associated with Building A12 (see above). A sketch reconstruction of the arch created by voussoirs 1–5 is presented in Figure 4.4A. Figure 4.4B presents a section at the centre of the voussoir and Figure 4.4C a section at the edge of the voussoir.

Catalogue

4.3.1 Romanesque **voussoir** WS 2 (Cxt 27, Ph 4, Building A12).
4.3.2 Romanesque **voussoir** WS 3 (Cxt 27, Ph 4, Building A12).
4.4.3 Romanesque **voussoir** WS 4 (in two pieces) (Cxt 27, Ph 4, Building A12).
4.3.4 Romanesque **voussoir** WS 5 (Cxt 27, Ph 4, Building A12).
4.3.5 Romanesque **voussoir** WS 9 (Ctx 27, Ph 4, Building A12).

Voussoirs from a Gothic doorway (Fig. 4.4D)

Three voussoirs were recovered, probably from a Gothic doorway; the calculated radius of the curve is *c* 0.60 m. The moulding profile comprises an arris roll with two side fillets flanked by hollows. These are probably 14th-century, but all were unstratified. A section is shown in Figure 4.4.D.

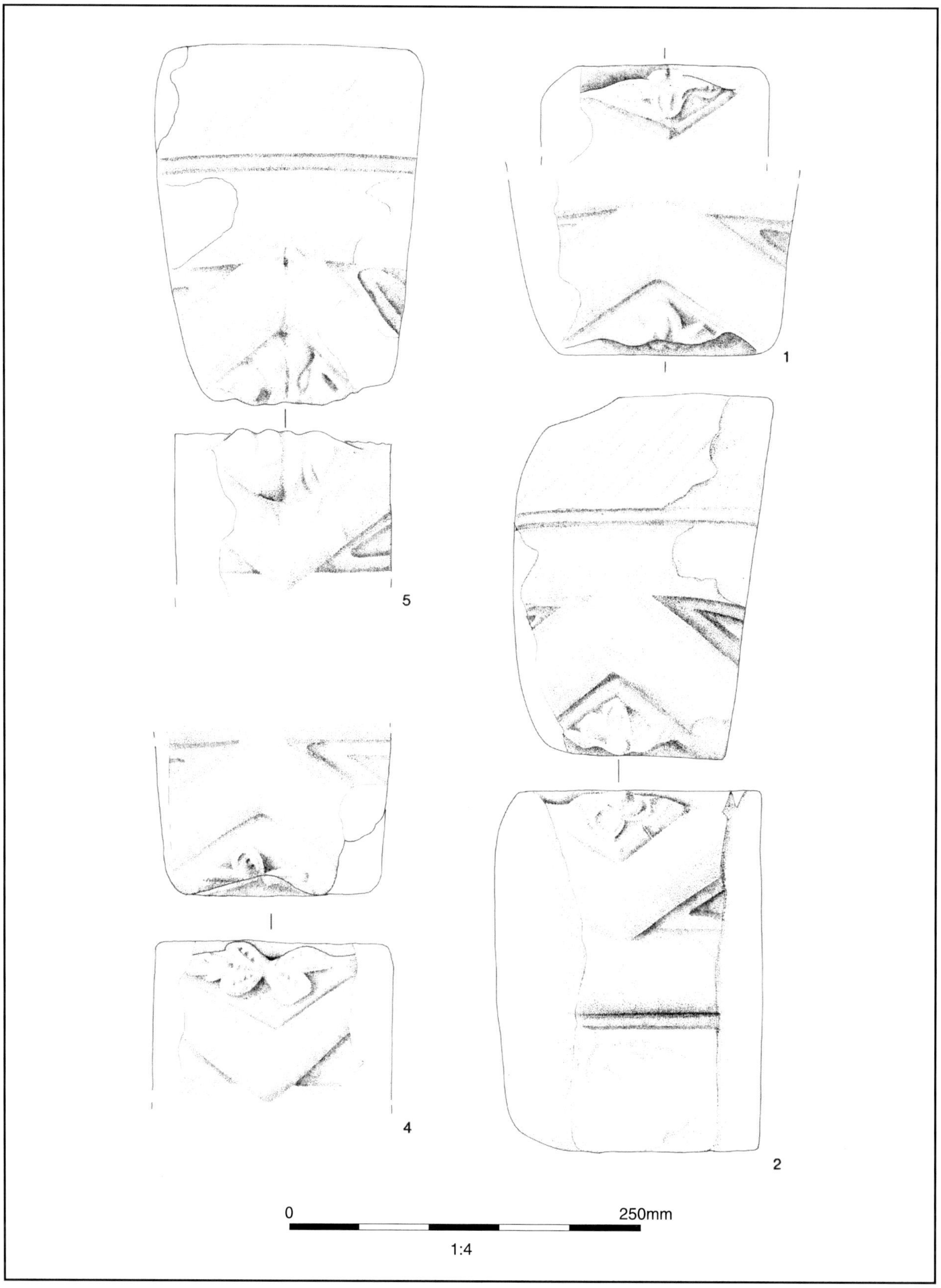

Figure 4.3 Architectural stone.

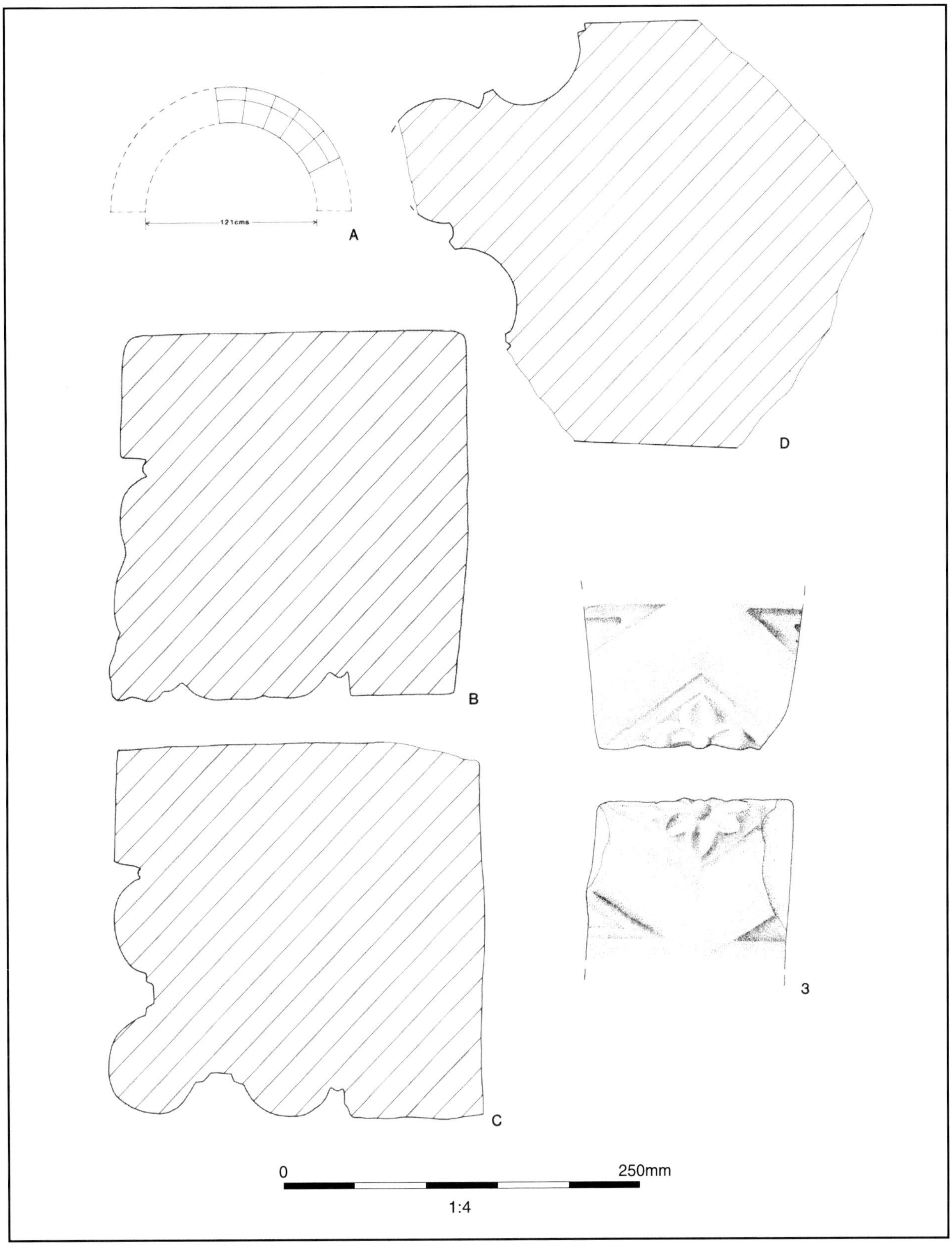

Figure 4.4 Architectural stone.

Table 4.3 Miscellaneous architectural worked stone (WS)

WS no	Context no	Phase	Building/ Room	Description
12	23	4	A12	Burnt limestone, secondary use of groove
16	132	5	A10	Chamfered door jamb?
20	57	U/S	U/S	Part of chamfered door jamb?
21	500	5	A9	Fragment
22	512	5	A9	Part of door jamb?
23	520	5	A9	Fragment
24	542	5	A1	Part of door jamb?
25	542	5	A1	Part of door jamb? Thinner than WS 24
26	591	4	A13	Fragment
27	599	5	A4	In two pieces
28	186	5	demolition	Fragment
29	267	4	T	Fragment
30	606	5	A14	Corner fragment
31	511	5	A9	Fragment
33	520	5	A9	Fragment
34	628	5	A3	Fragment
35	512	5	A9	Fragment from chamfered block stone
36	357	3	A10	Fragment
37	357	3	A10	Fragment
42	885	4	A1	Reddish sandstone with hole (joins WS 43). Natural?
43	885	4	A1	See above
44	966	1	Yard surface	Corner of squared block
45	600	3–5	A4	Chamfered block
50	1080	5	demolition	Fragment
51	1080	5	demolition	Fragment
–	U/S	U/S		Worked corner with projection; shelly limestone
–	186	5	demolition	Slab fragment; Th: 37 mm
–	527	5	demolition	5 worked limestone fragments
–	1209	2	moat upcast	Unworked burnt sandstone

U/S: unstratified contexts.

Catalogue

6 Gothic **voussoir** (NI), WS 6 U/S
7 Gothic **voussoir** (NI), WS 7 U/S
8 Gothic **voussoir** (NI), WS 8 U/S

Column-drum fragments

Four fragments (WS 38–40, 49) were found that would originally have been part of the outer casing of a plain circular pier or piers. The thickness of the casing is 0.10 m and the calculated diameter of the complete pier is *c* 0.61 m.

Catalogue

9. **Column-drum** fragment (NI), joins WS 39 to form quarter-arc of circle (WS 38, Ctx 962, Ph3, Room A9).
10. **Column-drum** fragment (NI), joins WS 38 (WS 39, Ctx 962, Ph3 Room A9).
11. **Column-drum** fragment (NI) (WS 40, Ctx 962, Ph3 Room A9).
12. **Column-drum** fragment (NI) (WS 49, Ctx 983, Ph2).

Miscellaneous moulding fragments

Numbers 15–17 come from an arch or window with a profile similar to the Gothic voussoirs (Nos 6–8) but about two-thirds the size.

Catalogue

13. **Scroll moulding** (NI). Straight 120 mm. Material not certain (WS 47, Ctx 1073, unstratified).
14. **Hollow moulding**, indeterminate fragment (NI) (WS 1, unstratified).
15. **Roll-moulding** (NI) D: 60 mm (WS 12, Ctx 26, Ph5 Building A12).
16. **Roll-moulding** (NI) (WS 14, Ctx 26, Ph5 Building A12).
17. **Roll-moulding** (NI) D: 55 mm (WS 19, unstratified).

STONE SLATES (TABLE 4.4)
by Philip Page and J Carlinge

A total of 78 pieces of slate were recovered from the excavation. These represent a minimum of 54 individual slates of which 21 were complete. These have been assigned to 2 different quarry sources by the authors in conjunction with Philip Powell of the Oxford University Natural History Museum. Fabric A is Forest Marble, the nearest source of which is at Filkins, Oxfordshire. Poulton, near Fairford in Gloucestershire, was known to produce slates from at least the 17th century. Fabric B is Stonesfield Slate from the north of Oxfordshire. Fabric C was not identifiable. The use of the three sources throughout the different phases of the site's history is quantified in Table 4.4.

Slates were recovered from almost all of the domestic buildings, Buildings J, I, H and Area F and around the courtyards. The largest number of slates, apart from the five found in the moat upcast, was a group of five from Phase 4 occupation deposits (contexts 7 and 535) of Building A12. Four fragments each were found in contexts associated with the occupation and demolition of Room A9 and

Table 4.4 Quantification of each slate stone type by phase

	Fabric A	Fabric B	Fabric C	Total
Phase 2	3	1	1	5
Phase 3		10	1	11
Phase 3–4		3		3
Phase 4	1	13		14
Phase 5	1	32	3	36
Unstratified		9		9
Total	5	68	5	78

Building H. A layer of slates (context 1148) noted between Buildings A1 and D may represent building debris from the construction of Building D during Phase 2. The demolition of the building in Phase 4 would probably also have provided the slate fragments found in the dump (573) that sealed the remains of the building. The majority of the slates, if they were not reused anywhere on the estate, are likely to have been sold, and this may help to explain the small size of the assemblage.

PLASTER, MORTAR AND DAUB (TABLE 4.5)
by S Smithson

Approximately 284 fragments of plaster were recovered from 35 locations at the site. Three fragments were painted red, two from Buildings A1 and A11, but no designs were evident. The majority of the structures produced faced plaster, including Building H. Some was also found in Area F, suggesting some redeposition was in progress. Unpainted plaster was found *in situ* on walls in Rooms A9 and A10. However, approximately 80% of the plaster came from Phase 5 demolition contexts and could, therefore, have come from any location. No plaster was found associated with the Phase 1 structures, although there were fragments in the building platform onto which the Phase 2 manor was built. It is likely that the majority of the structures were internally faced with plain plaster (as in Rooms A9 and A10) from Phase 2 onwards.

Mortar was evident in several locations around the site and only representative samples were taken. A total of 74 fragments of mortar were retained from 37 locations. These included samples from the Phase 2 wall of Building A1 (993) and from the Phase 3 walls of Room A4 (contexts 526 and 536). Samples were also taken from mortar floors where they survived, including a mortar floor in Building A1 (context 1017).

Among the deposits and layers of mortar recorded, but not kept, was a dump of mortar in the corner of Building J (context 368), a mortar floor in Structure A13 and the remains of a floor in Building A1, and Room A3 comprising pinkish mortar (context 1068). Pink mortar was also observed in a demolition context associated with Room A9 (context 512) and also with a Phase 3 occupation deposit from Area F (context 508). Mortar floors in Building A11 and Structure A13 were associated with floor tiles, unlike the floor in Building A1 which had no tiles. Unlike plaster, traces of mortar were found in Phase 1 deposits.

Three fragments of daub were found from three contexts. These were confined to Phases 1 and 2.

WINDOW LEAD (FIG. 4.5.22 A AND B)
by Barry Knight

[Editor's note. The window lead was identified and catalogued by Barry Knight. The catalogue has subsequently been arranged in phase order by Kate Atherton, with added information about the provenance of individual pieces. Most of the window lead consists of small decayed twisted fragments from demolition layers, and therefore does not convey much information about the chronology of the glazing of the house.]

Typology

Type A has thick diamond-shaped flanges and a prominent casting flash along the outside edge. It was cast in a hinged two-piece mould about 0.50 m long, as described by Theophilus in Book II, Chapters 24–5 (Hawthorne and Smith 1963, 67–9). One of the Chalgrove fragments (SF 520) is particularly interesting because it appears to have come from the bottom of the mould and has been discarded unused. Type B (not represented here) and Type C were made as Type A cast came and the casting flash was scraped off. This process is described by Theophilus in the last paragraph of Book II Chapter 26 (ibid., 70). The only difference between Types B and C is the amount of lead removed from the flange. Types A and C occur throughout the medieval period and do not, therefore, provide much chronological information. The absence of milled lead, perhaps introduced in the late 15th and early 16th centuries, accords with the documentary evidence for the abandonment of the site by this time.

Catalogue

SF 198 (NI).	2 twisted **fragments**, Type C. Possibly remains of 2 triangular quarries, 1 measuring *c* 50×45×70 mm. (Ctx 673 Ph4 Structure A14)
SF 526 (NI).	**Fragment**, Type C. (Ctx 561 Ph4 courtyard)
4.5.22a. (SF 203B).	**Remains of rectangular quarry**. Type C. Coloured glass remains (see Window glass No. 10), L: *c* 22, W: 45 mm. (Ctx 666 Ph5 Structure A14)
4.5.22b SF 66.	**2 small decayed fragments**. Type C, split in web. Remains of 2 rectangular quarries, L: *c* 35 and 23 mm. (Ctx 520 Ph5 Room A9).
SF 517 (NI).	**Fragment**, Type A, with casting flaws (bubbles) in web, L: 70 mm. (Ctx 26 Ph5 Building A12)
SF 518 (NI).	**Decayed fragments**, Type C. (Ctx 124 Ph5)
SF 519 (NI).	**2 tiny fragments**, split in the web, possibly Type C. (Ctx 125 Ph5 Building A11)
SF 520 (NI).	**2 joining fragments**, Type A. This piece appears to be unused; one end comes from the bottom of the mould and other has been cut off. Total L: 210 mm. (Ctx 186 Ph5)
SF 521 (NI).	**3 small fragments**, Type C. (Ctx 221 Ph5)
SF 522 (NI).	**1 small fragment**, split in web, Type C. (Ctx 520 Ph5 Room A9)
SF 523 (NI).	**1 small fragment**, split in web, Type A. (Ctx 542 Ph5 Building A1)
SF 524 (NI).	**1 small fragment**, split in web, Type C. (Ctx 549 Ph5 Building A1)
SF 525 (NI).	**1 fragment**, Type C. (Ctx 550 Ph5)
SF 527 (NI).	**1 fragment**, split in web, plus flat piece apparently melted, Type A. (Ctx 590 Ph5 Building A1)
SF 528 (NI).	**1 small fragment**, split in web, Type C. (Ctx 666 Ph5 Structure A14)
SF 243 (NI).	**1 fragment** comprising 2 pieces soldered together and split in web, Type C. Possibly used to tie a glazed panel to a window bar. L: *c* 50 mm. (U/S)

Table 4.5 Quantities of plaster, mortar and daub for each building by phase (number of contexts in parentheses)

Building	Phase 1	Phase 2	Phase 3	Phase 3–5	Phase 4	Phase 5	U/S	Total
Plaster								
Moat upcast		2 (1)						2 (1)
A1			2 (1)		13 (2)	65 (5)		80 (8)
A3				10 (1)		5 (2)		15 (3)
A4						13 (1)		13 (1)
A9						5 (2)		5 (2)
A10						99 (3)		99 (3)
A11						10 (2)		10 (2)
A14						1 (1)		1 (1)
Area F						2 (1)		2 (1)
H					1 (1)			1 (1)
Other		20 (2)	3 (2)		1 (1)	27 (4)	6 (3)	57 (12)
Total		22 (3)	5 (3)	10 (1)	15 (4)	227 (21)	6 (3)	285 (35)
Mortar								
Moat upcast		1 (1)						1 (1)
A1		1 (1:s)	17 (6, inc 2 s)		5 (3:s)			23 (10
A3			2 (1:s)					2 (1)
A4			2 (2:s)	6 (1:s)				8 (3)
A9					6 (2)	5 (2)		11 (4)
A10			1 (1:s)			3 (1)		4 (2)
A12						1 (1)		1 (1)
A14						2 (1)		2 (1)
D					1 (1)			1 (1)
F			3 (1)			1 (1)		4 (2)
W			2 (1)					2 (1)
Other	2 (2)				7 (4)	5 (3)	1 (1)	15 (10)
Total	2 (2)	2 (2)	27 (12)	6 (1)	19 (10)	17 (9)	1 (1)	74 (37)
Daub								
Yard	1 (1)							1 (1)
Moat upcast		1 (1)						1 (1)
Other		1 (1)						1 (1)
Total	1 (1)	2 (2)						3 (3)

s: sample from wall or deposit.
U/S: unstratified contexts.

SF 253 (NI). **1 fragment**, soldered joint split in web, probably Type C. L: 29 mm. (Ctx 900 cleaning reference Building D)

SF 529 (NI). **2 twisted fragments**, Type C. (U/S)

WINDOW GLASS (FIG. 4.5.7–8)
by Jill Channer

Introduction

[Editor's note. The majority of the window glass was identified and catalogued by Jill Channer shortly after the excavations (Nos 1–23 below). Two further fragments of window glass were identified by Jeremy Haslam amongst the vessel glass assemblage, and these have been added to the end of Jill Channer's catalogue and identified by their original Vessel Glass (VG) numbers. Further fragments present in the archive were noted by Kate Atherton and are listed at the end of the catalogue.]

The total amount of window glass, 42 fragments, recovered from the excavations was very small. The fragments formed an area of only approximately 300 square millimetres of which less than 13% was painted. Presumably most of the windows at the manor were removed when it was demolished. The glass was generally poorly durable, although not fire-damaged, and burial had caused deterioration. Some fragments were obviously corroded before burial, indicating that they were in windows for some time.

A small quantity of the glass is of 13th- or probable 13th-century date, and shows geometric designs. There are architectural designs from the 14th to 15th century, with an interesting fragment showing an angel's wing (Fig. 4.5.7) and a few fragments of

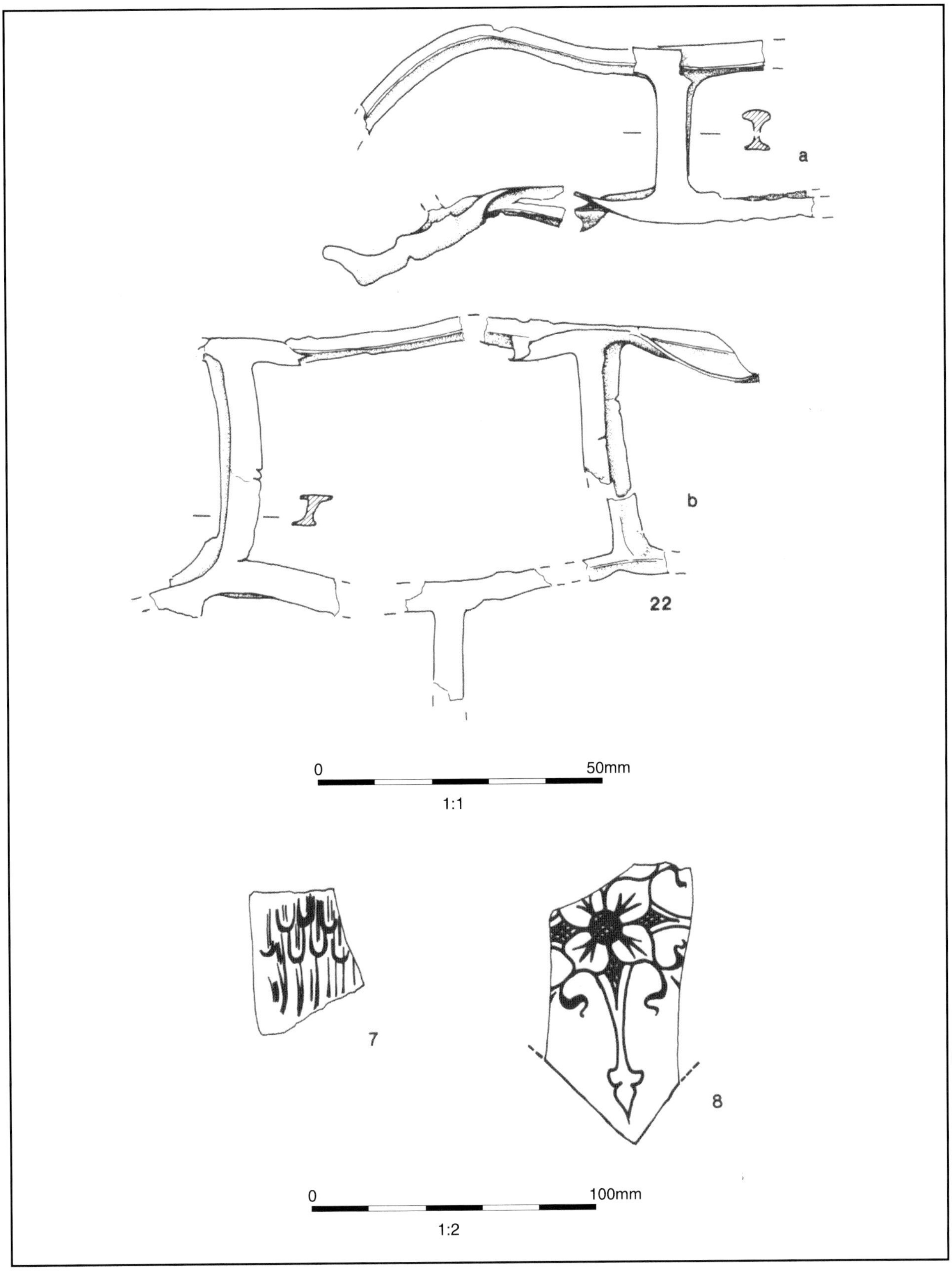

Figure 4.5 The window lead and glass.

15th-century quarry glazing. Fragment No. 4.5.8 is comparable with designs in a mid 15th-century window at Marsh Baldon Parish church, not far from Chalgrove.

Catalogue

13th-century glass (not illustrated)

1. **5 fragments**, cross-hatched background, geometric design and edge strip. Corroded before burial. Mid to late 13th century (SF 22, unstratified).
2. **Fragment**, originally white, Th: 4 mm. Formal geometric design, paint very decayed. Design picked out of matt wash, exterior pitted. 2 grozed edges (SF 47, Ctx 170, Ph3).

Possible 13th-century glass (not illustrated)

3. **Decayed fragments**, like 1, possibly 13th century (SF 215, Ctx 593, Ph4 Building A1).

14th/15th-century glass

4 (NI). **2 fragments**, devitrified crown glass, Th: 4 mm. No paint visible. Poorly durable, 1 grozed edge. Probably later than 14th century (SF 235, Ctx 748, Ph5 Room A8).

5 (NI). **Fragment**, edge of architectural design and serpentine trail, dots in interstices, no back painting. Design picked out of matt wash. 1 grozed edge, no lead shadow. Colour not discernible (SF 105, unstratified).

6 (NI). **Fragment**, possible architectural design, fragmentary paint. Very poorly durable, corroded on exterior before burial. Late 14th/early 15th century (SF 164, Ctx 140, Ph4).

4.5.7. **Fragment**, white glass, angel's wing picked out in ?matt wash. 1 grozed edge. L: 48, W: 38 mm. ?14th/15th century (SF 20, unstratified).

15th-century glass

4.5.8. **Fragment** showing quarry design, combining elements of quarry types 5 and 9. Both designs occur in a mid 15th-century window at Marsh Baldon parish church (Newton and Kerr 1979, Window J, As and 1a, 1b, 1c, 2a, 2c, 3a, 3c) (SF 102, Ctx 556, Ph5).

9 (NI). **2 fragments**, poorly durable quarry glazing (SF 96, Ctx 547, Ph5).

Glass of uncertain date (not illustrated)

10. **Small fragment**, coloured glass (not red) cemented into H-shaped lead came with a round head. Pre-16th century (SF 203A, Ctx 666, Ph5 Structure A14).
11. **One fragment** of white glass, remains of paint. Too fragmentary to discern design. One fragment of plain white quarry glass (SF 103, Ctx 549, Ph5 Building A1).
12. **Fragment**, originally green pot metal glass (*ie.* not flashed onto surface). 3 grozed edges, no paint visible (SF 86, Ctx 518, Ph5). 13. **Fragment**, poorly durable, originally white glass with line paint showing architecture or drapery (SF 87, Ctx 525, Ph5).
14. **Tiny fragment**, 1 painted line, 1 partly grozed edge (SF 118, Ctx 590, Ph5 Building A1).
15. **Fragment**, white, unpainted glass, possibly edge of quarry glass, not early (SF 202, Ctx 665, Ph5).
16. **Fragmentary painted glass**, perished and decayed (SF 532, Ctx 44, Ph4 Room A10).
17. **Fragment, painted glass**, stripes (SF 533, Ctx 44, Ph4 Room A10).
18. **Fragmentary plain glazing** (SF 535, Ctx 186, Ph5).
19. **Fragmentary painted glass**, perished or decayed (SF 536, Ctx 189, Ph5).
20. **Fragmentary plain glazing** (SF 537, Ctx 554, Ph3-4 Room A3).
21. **Fragment, plain white glazing** (SF 538, Ctx 584, Ph5 Room A3).
22. **Fragment, plain white glazing** (SF 540, unstratified).
23. **Fragment, plain white glazing** (SF 330, Ctx 573, Ph4).

VG 7 **Probable window glass**, completely decayed. ?Late medieval (SF 534, Ctx 134, Ph5 Building B).

VG 9 **Fragment**, much decayed, slightly curved, one edge possibly grozed. Late medieval (SF 544, Ctx 554, Ph3-4 Room A3).

Small fragment, decayed (SF 539, Ctx 596, Ph3-4 Room A3).

Small fragment, decayed (SF 33, Ctx 130, Ph3).

9 other fragments, some with geometric design (SF 292, Ctx 986, Ph4 Structure A13).

Chapter 5: Environmental Evidence

ANIMAL BONES AND SHELLS

by Bob Wilson with contributions by Enid Allison, Kate Atherton and Mike Wilkinson

Summary

The assemblage recovered is sufficiently large to enable a thorough analysis of spatial distribution patterns and species exploitation. In conjunction with related documentary evidence, it has also allowed some conclusions to be drawn about the economic regime practised by the arable manor.

Introduction

The material collected consisted of 11,105 bones of vertebrates and 2265 shells of marine molluscs, which were mostly hand-collected during the excavation. Small quantities of sieved soil yielded 1670 fragments of bone and shell. The general preservation of the bones was good, with the surfaces showing little sign of extensive leaching or encrustations of iron oxides or hydroxides. Cracking and whitening of bones deposited in the upper levels of the site indicate that leaching had begun but very few bones appeared to have disintegrated as a result of this factor. Some mechanical destruction from scavengers, such as dogs and rodents, was evident from gnawing marks.

The disparate classificatory groups of vertebrate bones and marine molluscan shells are treated together, since the bulk of the material is comprised of domestic and dietary refuse. Emphasis has been placed on variability in the distribution of waste from butchery, cooking and consumption within and around the domestic and farm buildings, based on a general model for the spatial distribution of bones developed for the Iron Age site of Mingies Ditch, Oxfordshire (Wilson 1993). Evidence for the farm economy is also discussed in order to facilitate comparison with the documentary evidence available for the organisation of medieval farms.

The faunal assemblage provides an opportunity to compare material from this relatively poorly-known medieval settlement type with that from other contemporary sites. Preliminary sampling during 1980 of the bones collected revealed potentially significant differences compared to other sites in the region. Pig was unusually well-represented (41%) while sheep (15%) was under-represented. Fallow deer and rabbit bones appeared to be more common than usual compared to other sites in the area. The frequency of general classes of bones and shells in the different phases of the site's use is presented in Table 5.1, that of fragments of different species in Table 5.2 (mammals), Table 5.3 (birds), Table 5.4 (fish) and Table 5.5 (marine molluscs). The author is grateful to Enid Allison and Mike Wilkinson who, respectively, identified the bird and fish bones and provided other interpretative information, and to Mark Robinson for identification of some of the molluscs.

Occurrence of species (Tables 5.2–5.6)

Most mammal bones were of domesticated and farm animals, with bones of pig unusually well represented and occurring more commonly than cattle, sheep and horse (Table 5.2). It is possible that wild pig occurs among the domesticated pig. Bones of fallow deer and rabbit were also relatively common. Red and roe deer bones were few but identifications were certain. No positive identifications of goat were made. An incomplete third phalanx from Phase 5 context 134 may be that of a donkey.

The small mammals present included black rat, house mouse and stoat but some of their skeletal remains could not be identified satisfactorily. The size ranges of black and brown rat are still uncertain but no rat bones were as robust as the author's comparative specimens of modern brown rat and no bones were attributed to this latter species. The least common species identified was a tibia of stoat *Mustela ermina* among the Phase 5 demolition debris of context 186. A tibia of hedgehog was noted among unstratified debris but was not recorded elsewhere.

Domestic fowl, goose and pigeon were abundant (Table 5.3), as well as probable occurrences of domestic duck; a bone of peafowl was also present. Modest numbers of wild bird bones included grey heron, mute swan, teal, tufted duck, peafowl, buzzard, partridge, moorhen, lapwing, golden plover, snipe, woodcock, barn owl, redwing and jackdaw. Chief species of interest among the identifications are quail *Coturnix coturnix* and the herring/lesser black-backed gull, which at the time of writing had not been previously recorded from excavations in Oxfordshire.

A variety of freshwater, migratory and marine species of fish were represented by small numbers of identifiable bones and greater numbers of unidentifiable elements or fragments, particularly fin rays (Table 5.4). Freshwater fish bones included tench, roach, chub and perch. Eel and salmon or trout were present. Seafish included spurdog, conger eel, cod, haddock and gurnard. Chief occurrences of note are those of bass (*Dicentrarchus labrax*), scad (*Trachurus trachurus*) and herring (*Clupea harengus*), which at the time of excavation not been recorded previously from archaeological contexts in Oxfordshire. Herring bones were later identified from Blackfriars, Oxford. The size range of bones within each species, and the number of species, in this small group of identified bones indicates that they represent only a fraction of the bones of fish which were originally present on the site. This was confirmed by the sieving results.

Table 5.1 Fragment frequencies of general classes of bones and shells at different phases (excluding sieved bones)

	Phase 1	Phase 2	Phase 3	Phase 4	Phase 3–5	Phase 5
Large and medium-sized mammal	12	227	275	783c	129	1333
Unidentified mammal	12	406	629	1474	217	2771
Total	24	633	904	2257	346	4104
% identified	50	36	30	35	37	48
Burnt bones		2	7	7		12
% burnt		0.3	0.9	0.3		0.4
Small mammal (ie, hare and rabbit)	1	4	11	38	2	65
Small mammal (chiefly rodent)		3	3	35c	6	163a
All birds recorded	9	33	366	630	92	860c
All fish recorded	1	2	20	204	3	98
Frog		14	1	8	3	32b
Marine molluscs	2	84	152	582	50	1392
Freshwater mussel *Anodonta* sp.						2

a: Including stoat (1).
b: Excluding toad (2).
c: Excluding skeletons.

Nearly all of the molluscan shells were marine in origin, with oysters, mussels, cockles and whelks present as expected (Table 5.5). Oyster shells were particularly abundant. Remains of edible crab (*Cancer pagurus*) were found in Phase 2 construction debris of Building A1 (892) and in Phase 5 demolition debris associated with Room A9 (512).

The abundance of selected mammal species as percentages of the total number of mammal bones in each phase group is presented in Table 5.6. In addition, remains of bird, fish, oyster and marine mussel are expressed as a percentage index of the number of mammal bones in each phase group. This facilitates comparison with species representation at other medieval sites in the region. It emerges that pig, fallow deer, rabbit, domestic and wild birds and oysters are relatively abundant while sheep is unusually less well represented. Some chronological changes in species representation are apparent, with possible increases in the abundance of sheep and oyster and a sudden decline in the frequency of pig bones at Phase 5. However, these results must be qualified to some extent by the variability of bone and shell debris across the site.

Table 5.2 Fragment frequencies of mammal bones from different phases (excluding sieved bones)

	Phase 1	Phase 2	Phase 3	Phase 4	Phase 3–5	Phase 5	Total
Cattle	1	85	81	259	47	532	1005
Sheep/goat	2	30	69	142	23	313	579
Pig	8	94	116	359	49	430	1056
Horse	1	9	1	3	3	18	35
Dog		3	5	6	1	11b	26
Cat		3		3b	3	10b	19
Red deer						4	4
Fallow		3	3	11	2	15	34
Roe					1		1
Rabbit	1	4	10	28	2	56	101
Hare			2	10		9	21
Stoat						1	1
Black rat		1	2	35b	5	22	65
Apodemus sp.					1	77	78
Mus sp.						9	9
Arvicola terrestris		1					1
Field vole		1				46	47
Shrew						6	6
Mole						2	2

a: No antler recorded for any species of deer.
b: Counts exclude part skeletons, except of rodents which were indeterminable.

Table 5.3 Fragment frequencies of bird bones from both sieved and unsieved deposits by species

	Phase 1	Phase 2	Phase 3	Phase 4	Phase 3–5	Phase 5	Sieved samples
Grey heron *Ardea cinerea* L.				2		8	
Mute swan *Cygnus olor* (Gmelin)				1 (?2)		?1	
Domestic/Greylag goose *Anser anser* (L.)	1	8	62	69	18	142a	8
Wild goose spp.	2	?1	?1			1 (2?)	
Indet. Goose						5	
Teal *Anas crecca* L.				4		4	1
Domestic/wild mallard *Anas platyrhynchos* L.			7	7		21	1
Pochard *Aythya ferina* (L.)						?1	
Tufted duck *A. fuligula* (L.)			1	?1			
Indet. duck sp.						1	
Buzzard *Buteo buteo* (L.)						1	
Domestic fowl *Gallus gallus* L.	6	15	130	273	28	348	50
Peafowl *Pavo cristatus* L.				1			
Partridge *Perdix perdix* (L.)			3	4 (5?)	1	13	
Quail *Coturnix coturnix* (L.)				1			1 (?3)
Moorhen *Gallinula chloropus* (L.)							2
Lapwing *Vanellus vanellus* (L.)			1	4			
Golden plover *Pluvialis apricaria* (L.)			1			1	
Snipe *Gallinago gallinago* (L.)				3		4 (?5)	1
Woodcock *Scolopax rusticola* L.			3	2			?1
Unidentified Scolopacid				1			
Indet, Wader sp.				1			
Herring/lesser black-backed gull *Larus argentatus* Pontoppidan/*L. fuscus* L.				1			
Domestic pigeon *Columba livia*	1	1	41 (?46)	33	4 (?5)	72	20
Barn owl *Tyto alba* (Scopoli)						4	
Blackbird/Fieldfare *Turdus merula* L./*T. pilaris* L.			1	1		4	4
Redwing *Turdus iliacus* Brehm						1 (?4)	
Song thrush *Turdus philomelos* Brehm			?1				?1
Unidentified small passerines				6		22	11
Jackdaw *Corvus monedula* L.						2	
Crow/rook *Corvus corone* L./*frugilegus* L.						5	
Indet. frags		8	102	213	40	194	169

a: Excluding 76 bones of one goose.
b: All bones identified by Enid Allison.

Intra-site distribution

Factors

A major objective of the study of the bone debris was to compare species abundance in particular areas of the manor. Distributions were studied in buildings, in rooms of the main building, in external areas and in peripheral areas. This would help to determine whether primary and secondary butchery and consumption of food occurred in the central area of the site or in more distant areas. Particular attention was therefore paid to internal and external building contexts, to particular structures and to deposits associated with other specific structures, such as ovens and hearths within a building. Centres of domestic activity would be identified by the presence of relatively high proportions of bones of most small or medium-sized species, particularly sheep, pig, rabbit, domestic fowl and all fish.

Certain potential complicating factors were recognised and have been considered in the results. Larger bones would tend to be removed from cooking and eating areas while smaller bones, and small fragments of large bones, would tend to be incorporated into deposits near to where food was prepared or where table refuse was cleared away. Therefore small bones would enter internal deposits such as postholes, pits, softer floor layers and even walls through rodent scavenging. Scavenging, trampling and weathering may also have destroyed small bones exposed in external contexts, such as courtyards.

A relative abundance of large bones would be an indicator of peripheral activity at the site although the factors outlined above would have an effect on their numbers. Scavenging would also tend to disperse larger fragments farther than small ones. Slaughtering and primary butchery of larger carcasses would take place some distance from the

Table 5.4 Frequencies of identified fish bones by phase (unsieved) and from sieved samples

	Phase 3	Phase 4	Phase 3–5	Phase 5	Total	Sieved samples P2–5 (see Table 22)
Freshwater species						
Tench *Tinca tinca*		1			1	1
Chub *Leuciscus cephalus*		1			1	
Roach *Rutilus rutilus*						1
Cyprinid sp.		14		2	16	20
Perch *Perca fluviatilus*		2		2	4	1
Freshwater/migratory species						
Salmon/trout *Salmo* sp.			1		1	1
Eel *Anguilla anguilla*	5		2		7	117
Marine species						
Spurdog *Squalus acanthias*			1		1	
Thornback ray/Roker *Raja clavata*						1
Elasmobranch			1		1	1
Herring *Clupea harengus*						156
Conger eel *Conger conger*	2	5	1	1	9	
Cod *Gadus morhua*		7	4	4	15	16
Haddock *Melanogrammus aeglefinus*		2		1	3	
Gadoid sp.			2	1	3	3
Gurnard sp.		1			1	
Bass *Dicentrachus labrax*				3	3	
Scad *Trachurus trachurus*						1
Flatfish sp.		1			1	1
Total	7	34	12	14	67	320

Results include 923 among sieved.
Results exclude unidentified fish remains which were not counted by identifier but incorporated in general results in Tables 5.1 and 5.7–5.13.
All bones identified by Mike Wilkinson.

kitchen and eating areas and these areas might not be easily locatable because of the intensity of scavenging or the intensive human use of larger bones for marrow, tallow or other products. There is a possibility that butchery and its associated waste disposal may have occurred outside the excavated area, such as outside the moat, at an adjacent farm or, as in the case of deer, in the chase.

Internal and external contexts

Although bones and shells were found in approximately equal quantities in internal and external contexts (Table 5.7), the bones of medium and small-sized animals, sheep, pig, rabbit, birds and fish, were relatively more abundant among deposits inside buildings (Table 5.8). Further evidence of this is given elsewhere (Wilson 1996, fig. 18; see also Wilson 1989). Unidentified bones are common in internal contexts which is to be expected considering that most unidentified bones are small. Sheep, rodents, fish and mussels are generally better represented in internal contexts but the figures display some variability which may be related to a variety of cultural factors, including changes of diet over time,

Table 5.5 Fragment frequencies of marine shells and minimum number of individuals (MNI)

		Phase 1	Phase 2	Phase 3	Phase 4	Phase 3–5	Phase 5	Total
Oyster *Ostrea edulis*	f	2	32	145	499	45	1243	1966
	MNI (a)	1	21	71	219	29	575	
Mussel *Mytilus edulis*	f		46	7	74	3	129	259
	MNI		10	4	29	2	64	
Whelk *Buccinum undatum*	f		1		11		11	23
	MNI		1		11		11	
Cockle *Cerastoderma edule*	f		5		1	2	9	17
	MNI		3		1	1	5	

a: MNI based on simple counts of adductor muscle scar. Estimates comparable to those of mammals might be equivalent to 110–130% of the figures given here.

Table 5.6 Percentage representation of bones and shells in different phase groups

Phase	Phase 1	Phase 2	Phase 3	Phase 4	Phase 5	All phases
No. of animal bones (n)	13	231	264	816	1398	2881
	%	%	%	%	%	%
Cattle	8	37	30	31	38	34.9
Sheep	15	13	23	17	22	20.1
Pig	62	41	40	44	31	36.7
Horse	8	3.9	0.4	0.4	1.3	1.2
Dog		1.3	1.9	0.7	0.8	0.9
Cat		1.3		0.4	0.7	0.7
Red deer					0.3	0.1
Fallow		1.3	1.1	1.3	1.1	1.2
Roe						+
Rabbit	8	1.7	3.8	3.4	4	3.5
Hare			0.4	1.2	0.6	0.7
Relative abundance of other groups of bones expressed as index % of n:						
Domestic fowl	46	6.5	44	33	25	27.8
Domestic goose		3.5	22	8.5	10	10.4
Other dom. spp. (max. est.)	8	0.4	18	5	6.7	6.7
Wild birds	16		3.4	3.8	7	4.4
Fish	8	0.9	3.8	25	4.4	11.4
Oyster	15	14	51	61	89	68.2
Marine mussel		20	3	9	9	9

and the destruction of domestic buildings and the alteration of habitats, such as of rodents.

Conversely, a higher percentage of cattle bones, and likewise of identified bones, is attested in external than internal deposits. Generally, bone debris from outside tends to be coarse in composition in the courtyard and farm areas and also in overlying destruction levels. One consideration is that smaller bones might be more vulnerable to degradation in external areas, although it is unlikely that this factor alone adequately explains the relative frequencies observed. The bones from Chalgrove are far less degraded than the bones from Mingies Ditch, Oxfordshire (Wilson 1993; Wilson 1985, 81–94) but nevertheless the data from there appeared to provide reliable indications of some cultural or ecological

Table 5.7 Frequencies of bones and shells in internal and external building contexts

	Internal							External				
	Phase 1	Phase 2	Phase 3/1	Phase 3/2	Phase 4	Phase 5	All phases (a)	Phase 2	Phase 3	Phase 4	Phase 5	All phases
Burnt			7		7	3	17	2			9	11
Horse	1	1	1		1	7	14	8			11	19
Cattle	1	22	49	3	76	138	336	63	29	150	394	636
Pig	8	51	86	11	192	129	526	43	19	137	301	500
Sheep	2	5	41	8	73	106	258	25	20	61	207	313
Deer			2		5	6	16	3	1	4	13	21
Dog			4		3	2	10	3	1	2	9	15
Cat		2			1	5	11	1		2	4	7
Rabbit & hare	1	4	11	1	28	27	74			3	38	41
Rodent		3	1		17	129	138		1	1	33	35
Domestic fowl	6	2	83	13	240	228	572	10		20	139	169
Domestic goose		2	90	5	64	78	239	7	2	4	45	58
Other bird	3	5	115	51	259	232	665	4	2	31	125	162
Fish	1		10		202	86	302	2		1	12	15
Oyster	2	6	122	10	307	407	899	26	13	187	836	1062
Mussel		10	7		73	103	196	36		1	26	63

a: Including bones from contexts of wider phase.

Table 5.8 Percentage comparisons of bones and shells in internal and external contexts of buildings

	Internal							External				
	Phase 1	Phase 2	Phase 3/1	Phase 3/2	Phase 4	Phase 5	All phases	Phase 2	Phase 3	Phase 4	Phase 5	All phases
% of identification	50	32	29	19	25	31	28.1	38	39	48	33	36.7
% of burnt bones			1		1	+	0.5	1			+	0.3
Total of cattle, horse, pig, sheep (n)	12	79	177	22	342	380	1134	139	68	348	913	1468
% of horse	8	1	1		+	2	1.2	6			1	1.3
% of cattle	8	28	28	14	22	36	29.6	45	42	43	43	43.3
% of pig	67	65	49	50	56	34	46.4	31	28	39	33	34.1
% of sheep	17	6	23	36	21	28	22.8	18	29	18	23	21.3
Other groups Index % of n												
Deer			1		2	2	1.4	2	2	1	1	1.4
Dog			2		1	1	0.9	2	2	1	1	1
Cat		2			+	1	1	1		1	1	0.5
Rabbit and hare	8	5	6	5	8	7	6.5			1	4	2.8
Rodent		4	1		5	34	13.8		2	+	4	2.4
Domestic fowl	50	3	47	59	70	60	50.4	7		6	15	11.5
Domestic goose		3	51	23	19	21	21.1	5	3	1	5	4
Other bird	25	5	65	232	76	61	26.6	3	3	9	14	11
Fish	8		6		59	23	26.6	1		+	1	1
Oyster	17	8	69	46	88	107	79.3	19	19	54	92	72.3
Mussel		15	4		21	27	17.3	26		+	3	4.3

processes. Therefore, the comparison of internal and external contexts appears to confirm that the internal contexts of buildings were functionally and spatially related to the cooking and consumption of food. The results from Chalgrove indicate that this took place in or near the principal building. Bones were subsequently dispersed by refuse clearance and disposal and scavenging. Refuse removal from the house, particularly of larger bones, contributed to the distribution of coarse debris in the farm and courtyards, with finer debris being more likely to be left behind and become incorporated into floor deposits.

Internal contexts (Tables 5.9–5.12)

The comparison of fragment frequencies and percentages (Tables 5.9, 5.10 and 5.11) according to the rooms of buildings in which the bones and shells were found does not allow for any differences between phase groups which may have pointed to chronological changes. However, such influences are not believed to significantly affect the results. Most bones occurred in the foundations of the domestic range A1–A14, although some rooms (A2, A6, A7, A11 and A14) yielded few bones for a variety of reasons. The most important of the modest deposits of the remaining parts of the site were found in Buildings B, H, T and W, and Area F. The buildings further away from the domestic range, Buildings G, J and K, yielded a small quantity of bones approaching the coarseness of those in the adjacent yards. Table 5.9 presents the overall quantities of debris and the species representation, which initially indicate that the most important areas of cooking and consumption refuse are A1, A9, A10 and A12, followed by a less important group consisting of A3, A4, A5, A13, A14, T, F and W.

The results were subsequently evaluated systematically for all buildings. Percentages and percentage indices of bones and shells for each building were ranked for each of nine criteria considered to be the most relevant of results given in Table 5.10 and according to whether the lowest or highest values indicated the greatest association with cooking and eating. Individual rankings of buildings are presented in Table 5.11. These rankings allow for the varying size of buildings and rooms and of the random variation due to small sample size of some building groups. These results found that Building A1 and Room A9 have the lowest totals of rankings, followed by Room A10 and three others of the domestic range. These rooms therefore contained the smallest and finest bones and fragments and the best representation of small animal species. This confirms the earlier indication that cooking and eating occurred in or near these rooms. The results also confirm the architectural and documentary evidence that the 'A' range was domestic in function.

Results presented in Table 5.12 show that the density of bones and shells in most buildings was low; less than five fragments per square metre of building area. Densities were greater, up to

Table 5.9 Frequencies of bones and shells in buildings and rooms (all phases)a

	A1	A2	A4	A5	A6	A9	A10	A11	A12	A13	A14	B	D	F	G	H	I	J	K	M	P	Q	R	T	W
No. of bones (b)	609	69	149	534	1	808	153	15	735	34	20	166	18	275	47	107	1	23	17	3	5	7	3	59	84
Burnt	2			2		1			2	2				6						1				1	
Horse and cattle	13	3	15	83	1	30	6	6	77	3	2	24	3	34	7	15		3	2	1	1	1		4	7
Pig and sheep	74	15	30	127		150	35	4	170	7	13	27	5	41	16	20		4	2		4	1	3	16	24
Deer				3		1		1	5		2	2		2											
Dog				2		1			1			1		3			1	1							
Cat	2			8												1									
Rabbit and hare	10		1	5		23	7		14		1	1		3		2					1				2
Rodent	3	5		125		9			9			3	1												
Domestic fowl	71	2	25	24		310	43		75	1	6	5	1	9		9	8							1	5
Domestic goose	18	4	11	17		94	56		37		4	5	1	4			1								3
Other bird	173	11	17	57		238	77		77		3	4		15	1	2									4
Fish	115			12		156	14		6		2	1		3			5								
Oyster	102		18	69		514	12	10	73	6	8	11	1	23		6	1	2	1			1	1	27	6
Mussel	15	4		6		112	18	1	31		1			1		1									

a: Lack of structural definition of buildings or absence of bone evidence excludes some rooms from consideration (eg. A2 A7, A8).
b: Number of identified and unidentified animal bones excluding those of rodent.

Table 5.10 Percentage comparison of bones and shells in buildings and rooms

	A1	A3	A4	A5	A6	A9	A10	A11	A12	A13	A14	B	D	F	G	H	I	J	K	M	P	Q	R	T	W
% of identification	14	25	29	39	100	22	27	67	34	29	75	31	44	27	49	33	100	30	24	33	80	29	100	34	37
% of burnt bones	0.3					0.1			0.3	5.9				22						33				1.7	
Total of cattle, horse, pig & sheep	87	18	45	210	1	180	41	10	247	10	15	51	8	75	23	35		7	4	1	5	2	3	20	31
% cattle and horse	15	17	33	40	100	17	15	60	31	30	13	47	38	45	30	43		43	50	100	20	50		20	23
% pig and sheep	85	83	67	60		83	85	40	69	70	87	53	62	55	70	57		57	50		80	50	100	80	77
Other groups Index % of n																									
Deer				1.4		0.6		10	2		13	4		0.3											
Dog				1		0.6			0.4			2		4			>100	1.4							
Cat	2.3			3.8												2.9									
Rabbit and hare	11.5		2.2	2.4		12.8	17.1		5.7		6.7	2.0		4		5.7					20				6.5
Rodent	3.4	28		60		3.3			3.6			5.9	13												
Domestic fowl	82	11.1	56	11.4		172	105		30	10	40	9.8	13	12		26	>800							5	16
Domestic goose	21	22	24	8.1		52	137		15		27	9.8	13	5.3			>100								9.7
Other bird	199	61	38	27		132	188		31		20	7.8		20	4.3	5.7									13
Fish	132			5.7		87	34		2.4		13	2.0		4			>500								
Oyster	117		40	33		286	29	100	30	60	53	22	13	31		17	>100	29	25			50	33	135	19
Mussel	17	21		3		62	44	10	13		7			1		3									

Table 5.11 *Rank order of frequencies, % and % indices given in Tables 5.9 and 5.10 to determine rooms/buildings most associated with cooking*

	A1	A3	A4	A5	A6	A9	A10	A11	A12	A13	A14	B	D	F	G	H	I	J	K	M	P	Q	R	T	W
No. of bones (highest=1)	3	11	8	4	24	1	7	19	2	14	16	6	17	5	13	9	24	15	18	22	21	20	22	12	10
% identified (lowest=1)	1	4	7	17	23	2	5	20	14	7	21	11	18	5	19	12	23	10	3	12	22	7	23	14	16
% burnt (highest=1)	5	8	8	8	8	7	8	8	5	2	8	8	8	3	8	8	8	8	8	1	8	8	8	4	8
% sheep & pig (highest=1)	3	5	13	15	23	5	3	22	12	10	2	19	14	18	10	16	23	16	20	23	7	20	1	7	9
% rabbit and hare	4	13	11	10	13	3	2	13	7	13	5	12	13	9	13	7	13	13	13	13	1	13	13	13	6
% domestic fowl	4	12	5	12	17	2	3	17	9	14	6	15	10	11	17	8	1	17	17	17	17	17	17	16	9
% domestic goose	7	6	5	12	14	3	1	14	8	14	4	10	9	13	14	14	2	14	14	14	14	14	14	14	11
% fish	1	9	9	5	9	2	3	9	7	9	4	8	9	6	9	9	9	9	9	9	9	9	9	9	9
% oyster	3	20	7	9	20	1	13	4	12	5	6	16	19	11	20	8	20	13	15	20	20	7	9	2	17
Ranking totals	31	88	73	92	151	26	45	126	76	88	72	105	117	81	113	91	123	115	117	131	119	115	116	91	95
Order of rankings	2	8	5	12	25	1	3	23	6	8	4	14	19	7	15	10	22	16	19	24	21	16	18	10	13

Rooms or buildings most associated with cooking and eating in rank order: A9, A1, A10, A14, A4, A12, F, A3, A13, H, T, A5, W, B, G, J, Q, R, D, K, P, I, A11, M, A6

General notes

a: Total number of bones indicate the greatest long term accumulation of bones near eating and cooking areas.

b: % of burnt bones may indicate rooms associated with cooking.

c: The low % of identified bones, the high % of sheep and pig, and the high % indices of rabbit and hare, domestic birds, oyster and fish indicate highest % of small sized bones and fragments in or near rooms associated with cooking and eating.

approximately twelve fragments per square metre, in A1, A10, A12, F and T. Bones were very abundant in A5 and most of all in A9, with approximately fifty fragments per square metre. However, deposits in A9 were slightly deeper than in other buildings in the domestic range. The depth of deposits in the farmyard buildings was affected by deeper topsoil stripping. As yet such figures make no distinction, however, between deposits associated with the primary use of the buildings and those derived from their construction or destruction.

Internal and external contexts by phase

Tables 5.13a and b and 5.14a and b examine the largest groups of bones and shells from different phases and feature types, from within buildings and from the most significant of the external contexts. Only the results from Building A1, A12 and B, and Rooms A5 and A9, are worth splitting into phase groups. Building A1 gives consistent results for the medium and large mammal bones in Phases 2 to 5, although the presence of smaller bones varies. The relative absence of coarse debris of the bones of medium-sized species is only exceeded by those of Phase 4 in Room A9. However, the overall densities of bones in A9, and the relative abundance of bones of small animal species, greatly exceeds those of Building A1 in their respective phases, except where finely fragmented bird bones give a high value for A1 in Phase 4. Floor or occupation deposits therefore yielded the finest eating or cooking refuse, characterised with a relative abundance of pig, rabbit with hare, domestic fowl, fish and oyster. The results also indicate the clearance of coarse refuse from the floors of these buildings and this explanation can be applied to the interpretation of more variable results in other buildings.

The demolition phase of Room A5 contains a predominance of cattle bones but this does not preclude the possibility that such debris also accumulated during the earlier occupation of the building. The same is also true of the Phase 5 debris of Building A12. In this room coarse debris is particularly common in the robber trenches, suggesting that the debris was incorporated following the abandonment and demolition of A5. Building B differs in that the bone from Phase 4 is coarser than that from Phase 5, but this building should be treated as a more peripheral building away from the domestic range and where coarser debris is not unexpected.

Coarse debris of cattle and horse bones in external features is most evident for bones of Phase 5 in the sump 504 and gully 518 of the courtyard enclosed by Rooms A4, A9, Buildings A12, W and Area F. Similar debris occurred in the Phase 4 drain 115 between Buildings A11 and A12 and in the moat infill. Less coarse debris occurred in the Phase 2 moat upcast, in the Phase 4 dump 573 near Building E, and in the general Phase 5 demolition layers, 186, 189 and 119. The least coarse debris in external contexts occurred in the Phase 4 courtyard layer 519 and this should possibly be regarded as an extension

Table 5.12 Densities of bones and shells per square metre of deposits in rooms and buildings

	A1	A3	A4	A5	A6	A9	A10	A11	A12	A13	A14	B	D	F	G	H	I	J	K	M	T	W
Area of room/ building m^2	105	46	42	20	12	42	28	33	24	98	43	41	15	46	110	87	15	67	266	23	14	52
Densities of bones or shells																						
All mammal (a) exc. rodent	5.8	1.5	3.6	27	0.1	43	5.5	0.5	10	0.4	0.5	4.1	1.2	6	0.4	1.2	0.1	0.3	0.1	0.1	4.2	1.6
Rabbit and hare	0.1		+	0.3		0.6	0.3		0.2		+	+	+	0.1		+						0.1
Domestic fowl	0.7	+	0.6	1.2		7.4	1.5		1	+	0.1	0.1	0.1	0.2		0.1	0.5				0.1	0.1
Fish	1.1			0.6		3.7	0.5		0.1		0.1	+		0.1			0.3					
Oyster	1		0.4	3.5		12	0.4	0.3	1	0.1	0.2	0.3	0.7	0.5		0.1	0.1	+	+		1.9	0.1
Burnt	+			0.1		+			+					0.1							0.1	

a: Includes unidentified fragments.

of the fine debris found within the domestic range. A similar interpretation is likely for the higher values of bird bones in the sump and gully (518) of the courtyard.

Ovens and hearths yielded small quantities of bone and 8% of these were burnt. Other areas or layers containing material such as charcoal or ash yielded little evidence of burnt bones. Bones appear rarely burnt by accident unlike those at some prehistoric sites.

Distribution of skeletal elements

Objectives

The collection of data regarding the distribution of skeletal elements was restricted to an examination of the most productive contexts. The aim was to discover the composition of debris in deposits associated with the domestic area where food was cooked and consumed. Study of skeletal elements might indicate whether butchery had taken place in any of the buildings and what form it took and whether the bones mainly represented refuse left behind after eating.

Sheep were considered the most worthy species of investigation because proportions of skeletal elements were known to vary more than those of pig or cattle in urban medieval and post-medieval deposits. This allowed a crude division of the process of butchery and consumption into several stages. The first stage was primary butchery, involving the initial slaughtering, skinning and some dismemberment of the carcass. Secondary butchery consisted of the division of the main meat carcass by a commercial butcher (not at the site) or within the household prior to cooking. The third stage was the consumption and dismemberment of cooked joints at the meal table, followed by the breaking up and boiling of the bones as butchery or other waste for the extraction of tallow, glue and so on. Several smaller species were also selected, which might reveal butchery patterns different to those of sheep, and whose bones might be less susceptible to rubbish clearance than those of larger mammals. Rabbit and hare were obvious choices, although their bones were not numerous. The abundance of domestic fowl also offered an opportunity to discover whether the skeletal element distributions were determined by cultural factors other than rubbish clearance.

Rooms with the largest deposits of bone were chosen. Room A9 was selected because it appeared to be the main centre for deposition associated with cooking and consumption and was, perhaps, related to the preparation of food in the kitchen. Building A1, the hall, was of interest because its refuse might indicate the type of debris left after most waste from the table had been cleared away. Finally, Room A5 was chosen because this room stood away from the main centre and might indicate other kinds of dumped rubbish. In addition, several external contexts appeared to offer useful comparative information, such as the moat upcast (Phase 2), the dump debris 573 and drain 115 (Phase 4). Features from the demolition Phase 5 would yield information of less certain value because the sources of this debris are less easily determinable.

Skeletal elements of sheep (Table 5.15)

Sample sizes were small but a distinctive trend in the representation of skeletal elements is shown in Table 5.15. Skeletal elements of the body (eg the upper limb bones and especially vertebrae) are disproportionately abundant in Rooms A9 and A10, correlating with the concentration of refuse associated with food preparation and consumption. Head and foot debris became more common further away from this area. The number of body elements of sheep, compared to head and foot elements, was greater in Rooms A9, A10 and Building A1. They occurred in lesser quantities in external contexts and in Rooms A12 and A5, and in Buildings B, W and Area F (an intermediate distance from A9) and were found less frequently in Buildings H, I, J and K (the most distant group). The exact reverse was the case for the occurrence of head and foot elements which increased in abundance with distance from Room A9.

This pattern indicates that refuse from the primary butchery of the carcass was disposed of separately

Table 5.13a and b Frequencies of bones and shell among larger groups from internal and external contexts

Table 5.13a Internal contexts

Phase	A1 2–3	4	5	A5 2	3–5	5	A9 3/1	4	5	A12 4	5	B 4	5	Ovens 3–4
No of bones (a)	105	307	167	224	145	164	181	407	208	459	276	78	76	102
Burnt		2				2		1		2				8
Horse	1					1					5		1	
Cattle	4	5	3	20	26	36	13	2	14	36	36	18	4	6
Pig	16	19	11	48	32	27	37	54	26	84	25	7	1	5
Sheep	9	12	7	4	4	12	12	7	10	36	25	5	13	8
Deer					3		1			3	2	2		
Dog					1	1	1			1		1		
Cat		1	1	2	3	3								
Rabbit and hare	1	7	2	4	1		1	13	9	5	9		1	
Rodent	1	b	2	3	1	121		3	6	9	1	3		
Domestic fowl	3	36	20		27	13	33	143	124	51	24	3	2	2
Domestic goose	3	5	8		18	7	34	30	26	19	18	3	1	1
Other bird c	6	93	24		45	25	19	91	133	63	14		3	
Fish	11	77	27	5	1	6		110	51	6		1		1
Oyster	11	68	23	10	9	50	102	200	212	18	55	1	10	6
Mussel		7	8			6		31	81	27	4			1

Table 5.13b Contexts over buildings

Phase	Moat upcast 2	Courtyard 3	Courtyard 4	Drain 115 4	Dump 573 4	Sump 504 4	Gully 518 4	Demo. 119 5	Demo. 186 5	Moat (infill) 5+	Topsoil 1
No of bones (a)	205	107	170	105	214	195	546	324	872	78	443
Burnt	1					1					
Horse	3						1	1	4	3	
Cattle	36	12	18	26	65	31	99	43	116	19	62
Pig	30	11	55	11	34	9	31	46	83	8	35
Sheep	16	14	11	7	16	6	24	25	115	3	28
Deer	1	1	1	2	1		2		7		
Dog	1				1			2	3	1	
Cat			1b		1		2	1	2b	1	
Rabbit and hare			1	1			6	9	8	1	
Rodent					1		1		32		
Domestic fowl	6	1	11	2		9	22	7	65	4	15
Domestic goose	7		2			2	8	2	21		9
Other bird c	4	1	19	7	3	3	23	7	66		13
Fish					1		5		3		
Oyster	2	7	51	7	22	1	185	34	282	6	196
Mussel			1	1	1		11		6	34	5

a: Number of identified and unidentified bones of mammals except rodents.
b: Excluding part skeleton.
c: Including unidentified bird bones.

and further away from the refuse from kitchen preparation and consumption, as represented by body elements. Bone debris in Room A9 and its vicinity appears to represent waste from cooking and, primarily, consumption.

An index of bone degradation was calculated as a crude measure of the extent to which sheep bones had been degraded by processes such as leaching, scavenging or trampling (Table 5.15). This consists of the percentage presence of four skeletal elements (mandible, radius, tibia and loose teeth) in groups of sheep bones. A low percentage indicates that bones are well preserved and a high percentage indicates highly degraded bones. For those contexts in which

Table 5.14a and b Percentage comparisons among larger feature groups of bones and shells from internal and external contexts

Table 5.14a Internal contexts

	A1			A5			A9			A12		B		Ovens
	Mixed Features			Layers		Layer/pit	Floor/occupation layers		Mixed features	Occup. layers	Robber trenches	Layer	Robber trenches	
Phase	2–3	4	5	2	3–5	5	3/1	4	5	4	5	4	5	2–3
% of identification	29	12	13	32	43	46	34	16	24	34	33	39	25	13
% of burnt bones	–	0.7	–	–	–	1.2	–	0.3	–	0.4	–	–	–	7.8
Total of cattle, horse, pig & sheep	30	36	21	72	62	76	62	63	50	156	91	30	19	19
% of horse	3	–	–	–	–	1	–	–	–	–	6	–	5	–
% of cattle	13	14	14	28	42	47	21	3	28	23	40	60	21	32
% of pig	53	53	52	67	52	36	60	86	52	54	28	23	5	26
% of sheep	30	33	33	6	7	16	19	11	20	23	28	17	68	42
Index % of n														
Deer	–	–	–	–	5	–	2	–	–	2	2	7	–	–
Dog	–	–	–	–	2	1	2	–	–	1	–	3	–	–
Cat	–	3	5	3	5	4	–	–	–	–	–	–	–	–
Rabbit & hare	3	19	10	6	2	–	2	21	28	3	10	–	5	–
Rodent	3	–[b]	10	4	2	159	–	5	12	6	1	10	–	–
Domestic fowl	10	100	95	–	44	17	53	277	248	33	26	10	11	11
Domestic goose	10	14	38	–	29	9	55	48	52	12	20	10	5	5
Other bird[c]	20	258	114	–	73	33	31	144	266	40	15	–	16	–
Fish	37	214	129	7	2	8	–	175	102	4	–	3	–	5
Oyster	37	189	110	14	15	66	165	318	424	12	60	3	53	32
Mussel	–	36	38	–	–	8	–	49	162	17	4	–	–	5

[a] Number of identified and unidentified bones of mammals except rodents.
[b] Excluding part skeleton.
[c] Including unidentified bird bones.

Table 5.14b External contexts

	Moat upcast		Courtyard		Drain	Dump	Sump	Gully	Above buildings		
									Yard	Domestic	Farm
					F115	F573	F504	F578	F119	F186	F189
Phase	2	2	3	4	4	4	5	5	5	5	5
% of identification	42	42	35	49	42	54	24	28	35	36	29
% of burnt bones	–	0.5	–	–	–	–	0.5	–	–	–	0.5
Total of cattle, horse, pig & sheep	33	85	37	84	44	115	46	155	115	318	130
% of horse	9	4	–	–	–	–	–	1	1	1	4
% of cattle	58	42	32	21	59	57	67	64	37	37	48
% of pig	24	35	30	66	25	30	20	20	40	26	27
% of sheep	9	19	38	13	16	14	13	16	22	36	22
Index % of n											
Deer	–	1	3	1	5	1	–	1	–	2	2
Dog	3	1	–	–	–	1	–	–	2	1	–
Cat	3	–	–	1[b]	–	1	–	1	1	1[b]	–
Rabbit & hare	3	–	–	1	2	–	–	4	8	3	2
Rodent	–	–	–	–	–	1	–	1	–	10	–
Domestic fowl	12	7	3	13	5	–	20	14	6	20	12
Domestic goose	–	8	–	2	–	–	4	5	3	7	4
Other bird[c]	–	5	3	23	16	3	7	15	6	21	10
Fish	–	–	–	–	–	1	–	3	–	1	–
Oyster	18	2	19	61	16	19	2	119	30	89	151
Mussel	103	–	–	1	2	1	–	7	–	2	4

Table 5.15 Percentage of grouped skeletal elements of sheep from selected context groups

	Internal							External				
	A9	A10	A12	A1	A5	BFW	G–K	MU	CY	Dump 573	Demo. 186	Demo. 189
Phase	3–5	3	4–5	2–5	2–5	3–5	3–5	2	4	4	5	5
n	30	9	58	27	21	45	20	19	30	15	78	28
	%	%	%	%	%	%	%	%	%	%	%	%
Head	4	22	19	11	29	33	50	16	17	33	27	29
Foot	13		10	11	19	13	15	11	10	20	19	7
Body	83	78	71	78	52	53	35	74	73	47	54	64
Mandible	3		9	4	10	13	10		10	13	8	18
Loose teeth		22	7		5	7	30	11	3	13	13	7
Vertebrae	43	22	12	11	5	4		5		7	5	11
Small bones	7		5	7		11					3	4
Metapodials	7		5	4	19	2	15	11	10	20	17	4
% index of degradation a	20	40	48	33	24	51	65	58	63	60	42	54

MU: Moat upcast.
CY: Central courtyard.
a: Percentage of loose teeth and fragments of mandible tibia and radius.

bones are highly degraded (*cf.* 72–93% of bones at Mingies Ditch, Oxfordshire) the percentage index is considered to be related to both the type of deposit and the depth to which the bones were buried in the ground (Wilson 1985 and 1993). Similar results with less degraded material (34–72%) were obtained at Mount Farm (Wilson 1995).

The percentage index at Chalgrove ranges from 20–65% and confirms that the bones from this site are relatively well preserved. Sheep bones from inside buildings (20–65%), especially Room A9 (20%), tend to be better preserved than those from external deposits (42–63%). The variable pattern from individual buildings parallels the distribution of fine and coarse debris (see above). One way to bypass the extent to which differential degradation affects the observed pattern of skeletal element distribution is to study elements which are known to be particularly resistant to degradation (see below).

Skeletal elements of pig (*Table 5.16*)

A different pattern emerges with pig, including a marked difference between Room A9 and neighbouring contexts. Higher percentages of loose teeth, partly indicating greater disintegration, contribute to a larger amount of head debris than occurred generally for sheep. Metacarpals and metatarsals occurred in relatively high quantities in A9 and, in contrast to sheep, bones from head and limb extremities generally predominate over body elements. However, the head, neck and trotters of pig offer more edible tissues than the same parts of sheep and it is therefore not surprising that bones from these parts of pigs feature more prominently in debris from food preparation and consumption.

Skeletal elements of cattle (*Table 5.17*)

Bones of cattle show a different distribution pattern with few elements in and around the centre of food preparation and consumption. Parts of foot and head were most common in external contexts, notably 504, 518, 573 and 115. This patterning could derive from practices of rubbish clearance or from scavenging, with large bones being more likely to be redistributed outwardly after butchery or cooking. In addition, boneless meat was probably brought to the places of cooking and eating with most bones disposed of elsewhere.

Table 5.16 Percentage of grouped skeletal elements of pig from selected context groups

	Internal						External	
	A1	A9	A10	A12	BFW	G–K	Dump 573	Demo. 189
Phase	2–5	3–5	3–5	4	3–5	3–5	4	5
n	45	113	22	85	42	11	34	35
	%	%	%	%	%	%	%	%
Head	56	26	41	59	55	64	60	46
Foot	11	44	23	11	12	9	3	11
Body	33	30	36	31	33	27	47	43
Mandible	11	4	5	15	24	18	18	9
Loose teeth	33	14	32	27	26	27	9	26
Vertebrae	7	9	9	6	10		3	9
Small bones	9	12	9	7	5	9	3	6
Metapodials	2	32	14	4	7			6

Table 5.17 Percentage of grouped skeletal elements of cattle from selected context groups

	Internal			External		
	A9	BFW	G–K	504 & 518	573 & 115	189
Phase	3–5	3–5	3–5	4	4	5
n	29	30	61	125	67	62
	%	%	%	%	%	%
Head	21	23	20	15	36	21
Foot	24	18	17	13	24	18
Body	55	54	63	72	40	61
Mandible	14	8	5	9	24	6
Loose teeth	3	8	10	6	6	11
Vertebrae	28	15	10	24	10	21
Small bones	14	11	10	8	11	13
Metapodials	10	7	7	5	7	5

Skeletal elements of rabbit and hare (Table 5.18)

Cranial and metapodial debris of rabbit and hare was generally uncommon, while bones from the main meat carcass were relatively abundant. Table 5.18 indicates a trend for the metapodial and head elements to be found away from the centre of food preparation and consumption where the vertebrae and upper limb bones predominate. This is significant because any mandibles and metapodials should have been more prominent among the small bones of Building A1. Since this contradicts the general pattern whereby small bones occur in the centre of the site, it suggests that, as for sheep, the dumping of feet and head parts took place outside the central buildings. Therefore, as for sheep carcasses but in contrast to pig, the heads and feet of rabbit and hare appear to have been separated from the carcass and dumped elsewhere before most of the bones reached Room A9. Heads and paws might have been removed at the same time as the skin and this most probably took place in the kitchen prior to cooking.

Fewer rabbit bones survive compared to sheep and cattle but the complete humeri and femuri recovered nevertheless outnumber those from the larger species. This suggests (though not conclusively because cattle and sheep bones may have been rendered further for tallow, glue and so on) that owing to its small size the main meat carcass of rabbit was disjointed little before cooking.

Table 5.18 Percentage of grouped skeletal elements of rabbit and hare from selected context groups

	Internal				External
	A1	A9	A10	A12	573 & 189
Phase	2–5	3–5	3–5	4–5	4–5
n	12	23	7	15	9
	%	%	%	%	%
Head	8				11
Foot	17		29		33
Body	75	100	71	100	56
Mandible					11
Loose teeth	8				
Vertebrae	8	26	14		11
Small bones			14		
Metapodials	8		29		33

Skeletal elements of domestic fowl (Table 5.19)

Results presented in Table 5.19 show that, as for rabbit and hare, the head elements of domestic fowl are scarcely represented, and that the bones from the head and feet tended to occur more frequently in external contexts and with distance from room A9. The evidence again suggests that the bones in A9 and nearby are refuse from food processing and consumption.

Site distribution of mandibles (Table 5.20)

Mandibles and teeth of the larger mammals are relatively resistant to bone degradation, although at Chalgrove there is a tendency for some pig and sheep mandibles and maxillae to have disintegrated. To minimise the possibility of bias arising from such disintegration, the presence of certain teeth was used as a control. The presence across the site was plotted of individual mandibles, loose fourth deciduous premolars and loose third molars where these could not be assigned to mandibles from the same feature. The teeth showed very little sign of mechanical damage or leaching and mandibles of immature animals, even if disintegrated, should therefore each be represented by a single deciduous tooth and those of mature animals by the third molar. Too few mandibles were recovered to enable comparison between the buildings, but there were sufficient for the examination of frequencies of cattle, sheep and pig mandibles in external and internal contexts.

Statistical testing indicates that the distribution of mandibles is anomalous and the frequencies of

Table 5.19 Percentage of grouped skeletal elements of domestic fowl from selected context groups

	Internal				External		
	A1	A5	A9	A12	504 & 518	186	189
Phase	2–5	3–5	3–5	4–5	4	5	5
n	43	24	289	74	27	41	15
	%	%	%	%	%	%	%
Head		4					
Foot a	7	13	5	8	22	15	13
Body b	93	83	95	92	78	85	87

a: Metatarsus and phalanges.
b: Excluding ribs.

Table 5.20 Frequency by context of complete mandibles, 4th deciduous premolars or 3rd molars of other mandibles

	Cattle	Pig	Sheep
Internal			
A9	(2)	3	
A12		4	1
A1		1 (1)	
A3		1 (1)	
A4	(2)		
A5	(3)	1 (4)	
A14			(1)
F		3	1
G			(1)
H		(1)	1
W		1	
Total	0(+7)=7	14(+7)=21	3(+2)=5
External			
Phase 2	3	4	1
Phase 3	1	3	2
Phase 4	7	6	4
Phase 5	9	10	5
Phase 5 (186)b	3	2	5
Phase 5 (119)b	3	4	5
Total	26	29	22
Indeterminate	4	6	2

a: Bracketed figures include records which may represent intrusive debris during construction/demolition of buildings.
b: Contexts 186 and 119 are demolition debris layers.

Table 5.21 Fragment frequencies of bones and shells from sieved debris a

Phase	Moat infill (279) Phase 2	A9: 639 and 512 Phases 4 and 5
Cattle	2	
Sheep	2	2
Pig	2	15
Hare	1	1
Rabbit	1	1
House mouse		4
Black rat	1	
Unident. Mammal	66	438
Domestic fowl	8	33
Domestic goose	1	7
Domestic pigeon	1	9 (?10)
Quail		1 (?3)
Snipe		1
Woodcock		1?
Passerine		14
Unident. Bird	7	162
Shark or ray		1
Thornback ray		1
Herring		156
Eel		117
Salmon/trout	1	
Tench		1
Roach		1
Cyprinid sp.	2	16
Cod	1	15
Gadoid		3
Perch		1
Scad		1
Flatfish		1
Unident. fish	nc.	nc
Oyster		*c* 265 (frag.)
Mussel	15	*c* 210 (frag.)
Cockle		7
Eggshell (bird)	*c*5	36

a: Each group of results is from the sieving of between 1–2 buckets of soil (10–20 litres).

mandibles in particular indicate a relative deficiency of cattle and sheep mandibles in internal deposits, as indicated in the trends of Tables 5.15 and 5.17. Although the percentage of cattle mandible fragments in Room A9 (Table 5.17) is anomalously high, few mandibles are actually represented there. As might be expected, the frequencies of mandibles in internal and external deposits vary most for cattle and sheep, and least for pig.

Some of the mandibles present in internal contexts appear derived from construction debris, or from intrusive debris following abandonment and demolition. This implies that the number of mandibles found in internal contexts, especially of cattle, were over-represented. However, some of the demolition debris from Phase 5 contexts 186 and 119 (Table 5.20) might have been derived from later activities within the buildings.

Bones from sieved samples (Tables 5.21–5.23)

Deposits were not extensively sieved, however, some useful information was obtained by the sieving of material from the moat infill (279) and from two contexts in Room A9, namely, occupation layer 639 (Phase 4) and Phase 5 floor layer 512. This enables further comparison between external and internal deposits.

The frequencies of bone fragments in these samples is shown in Table 5.21. Bones of smaller species, small unidentifiable bones and broken marine shells were more abundant in the samples from A9, though less frequent in the demolition phase than in the earlier occupation deposit. The percentages of animal bone and shell representation by weight are shown in Table 5.22 and again, although the samples are small, the smaller animals are best represented in samples from Room A9. The weights of marine mussels indicate that this species is under-represented by routine collection because their shells are more fragile than oyster shells. The fragment size distributions of mammal bones are shown in Table 5.23. Material from the moat is relatively coarse compared to that from Room A9, although debris from demolition 512 is coarser than that from occupation deposit 639.

Table 5.22 Weight of sieved bones from internal and external contexts

	Moat 279 Phase 5	A9: 639 and 512 Phases 4 and 5
Total weight	0.181 kg	0.131 kg
% by weight	%	%
Cattle	21.8	
Sheep	6.4	0.5
Pig	5.5	6
Rabbit and hare	0.2	1.5
Rodent	+	0.2
All mammal	95.5	63.6
All bird	2.1	17.6
All fish	2.4	18.8
Index % of shell weight compared to bone weight	%	%
Oyster		38.7
Mussel	3.5	20.9
Cockle		0.8
Eggshell (bird)	+	0.5

The evidence from the sieved samples confirms that the representation of bones of smaller species and unidentifiable bones is greater in sieved deposits than in unsieved material. In the former, foetal or juvenile pig bones, herring and freshwater fish species are quite prominent. The differences observed among the sieved material confirm conclusions that material from internal deposits is finer and smaller than that from external deposits.

Articulated bones and skeletons

Skeletons

Articulated remains, and relatively complete bones, of the larger mammals were not common, probably because most were broken up by butchery, scavenging and other processes during the occupation of the site. However, five part skeletons from smaller mammals were recorded, in addition to a goose skeleton that was found in association with rodent bones (see below). The bones of the goose showed no signs of butchery, indicating that the animal was probably a domestic goose that died of natural causes. More unusual material included a pelvis and an os penis from a dog.

Semi-articulated debris and relatively complete crania are disproportionately associated with the few pits on the site, with Rooms A4 and A5, and perhaps also with Phase 5. The distribution suggests that bones deposited in pits and in these rooms were less disturbed by depositional processes or by other activities than bones from other contexts. This is partly confirmed by the presence of clusters of rodent bones and the goose skeleton among the demolition debris. In layer 726, the rodent bones were found over the crania of cattle and pig.

Table 5.23 Fragment size distribution of all mammal bones in sieved samples a

Context No	Location	Phase	0–1	1–2	2–3	3–4	4–5	5–6	6–7	10–11
279	Moat	5	13	12	9	6	3	1	1	
639	A9	4	197	129	18	6	2	1		1
512	A9	5	11	49	10	4	1			

a: Excluding new breaks.

Part skeletons

Cat: 7 newly broken vertebrae, 13 rib pieces, 3 limb bones, small-sized; ti. GL 95 mm (Ctx 561, Ph 4)
Cat: 11 limb bones with fused epiphyses except of prox. hu. Medium-sized individual: ti. GL 109, ra. GL 89, hu. Bd 16.5 mm. (Ctx 186, Ph5)
Puppy: 7 vertebral and 23 rib fragments. (Ctx 228, Ph3)
Black rat: crushed cranium, 20 vertebrae, 9 limb bones. Molars erupted but slightly worn. All epiphyses unfused except for dis. hu. (Ctx 548, Ph4 Building A1)
Black rat: Articulated hu., ra. and ul. of immature individual. (Too few bones to be noted in Table 5.2) (Ctx 512, Ph5)
Domestic goose: 76 bones of a mature or old goose. One cervical vertebra shows eburnation on the articular surface. Bone proliferation on skull, some vertebrae, dis. ul., prox. metacarpals and on posterior phalanges. (Ctx 186, grid reference 787/290, Ph5)

Crania

Cattle: unfused elements from juvenile. (Ctx 935 Ph3–5 Room A5)
Cattle: matching mandibles (Ctx 980 Ph3, Room A5)
Cattle: much of a half cranium, divided in the midline by butchery. (Ctx 726, Ph5 Room A5)
Pig: half cranium divided in the midline (Ctx 120 (grid reference 770/280), Ph4)
Pig: much of a whole cranium lacking mandibles, probably male. MWS of maxillae teeth is 35. Measurements (45) 124, (40) 30, (21), 57.5, (31 Length of M3) 31 mm (Ctx 726, Ph5 Room A5)
Sheep: (Ctx140, Ph4)
Sheep: (Ctx 124, Ph5)

Thoracic vertebrae

Pig: (Ctx 600 Ph3–5 Room A4)

Pelves

Horse: unfused portions of left and right pelves which must be from same juvenile individual (Ctx 206 and 207, Ph2 – also layer 204, Ph1)

Limb bones

Cattle: mc-phl (Ctx189, Ph5)
Pig: matching ulnae (Ctx717, Ph5 Room A5)
Sheep: Hu-ra-ul (Ctx 599 Ph5 Room A4)

Other rodent bones (Table 5.24)

Among the diffuse scatter of rodent bones recovered from the site, several clusters of their bones were found with other fine debris. The most prominent concentrations of bones came from a demolition layer (186, grid reference 787/290) and from a charcoal layer in Room A5 (126), both Phase 5. Retrieval of bones from these deposits was biased in favour of large rodent bones, especially the tibia of field or wood mouse (*Apodemus* sp.), and this tends to distort the counts of fragments, as does the inability to identify all skeletal elements (Table 5.24). Frog bones were common in these two deposits, as were bones of small passerines, especially in context 726. The same context also produced a humerus of a male buzzard (GL 98.1 mm). The rodent bones in demolition layer 186 were closely associated with the bones of one goose (see above).

The rodent bones are mainly complete and were from both mature and immature individuals. They do not appear to have been eaten or digested by predators unless the bones were regurgitated whole. It is possible that the bones represent detritus from owl or buzzard droppings deposited near roosts among the ruins of the buildings. It is also possible that the remains are caches of food made by larger carnivores. A third alternative is that the rodents burrowed intensively among the demolition and rubbish deposits or occupied gaps between tumbled debris. The latter two factors might also explain the presence of frog bones. The activity of predators might also account for the bones of passerines, or they may simply have roosted and died amongst the ruins.

Rabbit

The probability that some rodent bones represent later intrusions into medieval deposits raises the question of whether other bones are also intrusive. The status of rabbit bones, therefore, may affect the interpretation regarding the role of rabbit as part of the diet of the inhabitants.

Rabbit-sized burrows were not observed during the excavation and no whole skeletons were found to indicate that rabbits had died in their burrows, as did at least some of the rodents. Rabbit bones were not conspicuously associated with the rodent bones and their occurrence did not indicate any successive occupation of previously dug animal burrows or other holes. The distribution of rabbit bones is consistent with the distribution of small, fragmented rubbish and with anomalies in the presence and absence of skeletal elements. It indicates that the bones were from butchered carcasses and are therefore contemporary with the other medieval bones.

Minimum Number of Individuals (MNI)
(Table 5.25)

The minimum number of individuals was estimated from age estimate records of Mandible Wear Stages (MWS, see below) and other data of mandible and loose teeth presence following, in principle, the comparative method of Chaplin (1971, 69–75). This method did not entail re-examination of the mandibles themselves as a separate group, except where information was incomplete for the minor species. The method was not applied to unstratified remains.

The results, with percentages of species in the total, are presented in Table 5.25. The most obvious source of bias is the absence of any mandibles of fallow and roe deer. Compared with the percentages of bone fragments in Phase 5 (Table 5.6), cattle are underestimated by MNI (35% against 27%) while the less common species, except fallow and rabbit, are

Table 5.24 Abundance of rodent bones in two similar deposits (186 and 126)

	No of fragments	No of mandibles
Black rat	10	1
Apodemus sp.	76	11
House mouse	9	5
Field vole	46	12
Shrew	6	3
Mole	1	
Also present		
Frog (24)		
Small passerine birds (23)		
Buzzard (1)		
Other scattered bones		
Domestic goose remains (context 186)		

Table 5.25 Minimum number of individuals (MNI) estimated from mandible data and loose teeth (Phases 1–5)

	MNI	%	Fragments/Individual
Cattle	19	27.1	33.5
Sheep	16	22.9	19.6
Pig	27	38.6	18.5
Horse	2	2.9	10.5
Dog	3	4.3	5
Cat	2	2.9	3.5
Rabbit	1	1.4	c34
Total	70	100.1	

Red, roe and fallow deer, hare and stoat are all represented by skeletal elements other than mandibles. Rabbits and hare almost certainly under represented by MNI. Rodent bones are not considered here (see Table 5.24).

better represented by MNI. Percentages of pig and sheep are very similar.

Age information from mandibles and comparison with other sites (Figs 5.1–3)

Eruption and wear stages of the mandible teeth of cattle, sheep and pig were recorded. The Mandible Wear Stages (MWS) were calculated following the method of Grant (1982), with the exception that MWS were not estimated for broken mandibles where there is a degree of uncertainty of more than two places of the most probable MWS. The frequencies of age-staged mandibles are given in Figures 5.1–5.3.

Ageing of sheep (Fig. 5.1)

The data indicates that nearly all of the sheep were killed after MWS 30, by which stage the third molar was in wear. Many of these sheep would have matured skeletally. Their mandibles range between Stages E to I of Payne's scheme (1973). The sample of mandibles is small (15) but their age-stage distribution is probably typical of the kill-off pattern of the site. Twenty-four third molars between stages E–I and eighteen between F–I were recorded, compared to two p4 of a lamb and a hogget. A small sample with a similar distribution of old mandibles is recorded for 12th-century Middleton Stoney, Oxfordshire, and of somewhat younger mandibles, for sizeable groups from the 12th- to 16th-century site of the Hamel, Oxford, and a 16th- to 19th-century group from Church Street and other sites in Oxford (Rahtz and Rowley 1984; Wilson and Bramwell 1980; Wilson and Locker 1989).

Although the sample sizes are not entirely satisfactory, most of these medieval distributions differ statistically (Siegal 1956: Kolmogorov-Smirnov test, Ho p-.0.5) from those from the Iron Age and Romano-British periods at other local sites such as Ashville, Barton Court Farm, Abingdon, and Mount Farm (Wilson *et al.* 1978; Wilson 1986; Wilson 1995). In these earlier samples many sheep were killed at much younger ages than during the medieval period. This difference with the earlier sites is true for both rural and urban medieval sites, suggesting that the medieval pattern may be best explained by the keeping of older sheep for wool and less by marketing strategies for meat. However, a greater abundance of relatively immature sheep were marketed from farms to towns (Wilson 1994).

Ageing of cattle (Fig. 5.2)

Figure 5.2 shows the distributions of age data of cattle for Chalgrove compared to unpublished evidence from medieval and post-medieval sites in Oxford. Over half of the cattle at Chalgrove were slaughtered at late age stages, when the third molar was well worn. However, approximately one quarter died, or were slaughtered, as calves before or as the first molar began to erupt (TWS V–E).

The presence of a high proportion of calf mandibles is characteristic of post-medieval urban deposits (Fig. 5.2), although it is probable that this urban pattern results from the domestic consumption of calf heads and the dumping of the crania of older cattle in uncommon but dense concentrations associated with tanneries, fellmongers or other industrial concerns. Nevertheless, the presence of the calf mandibles in post-medieval deposits and at Chalgrove,

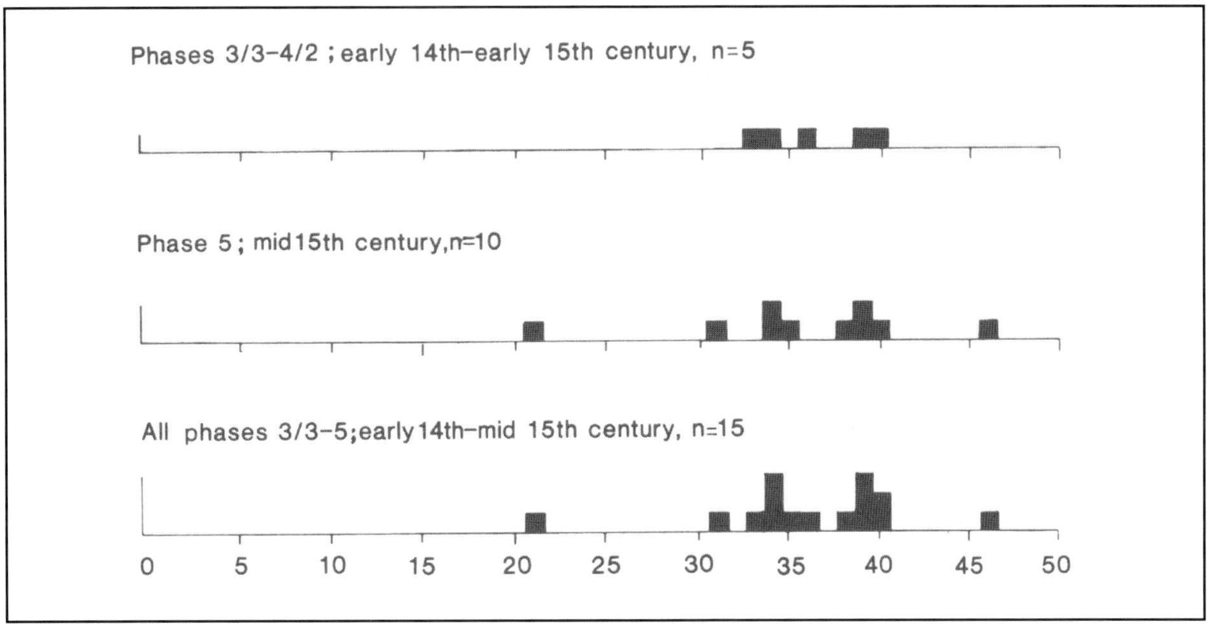

Figure 5.1 Mandible Wear Stages of sheep.

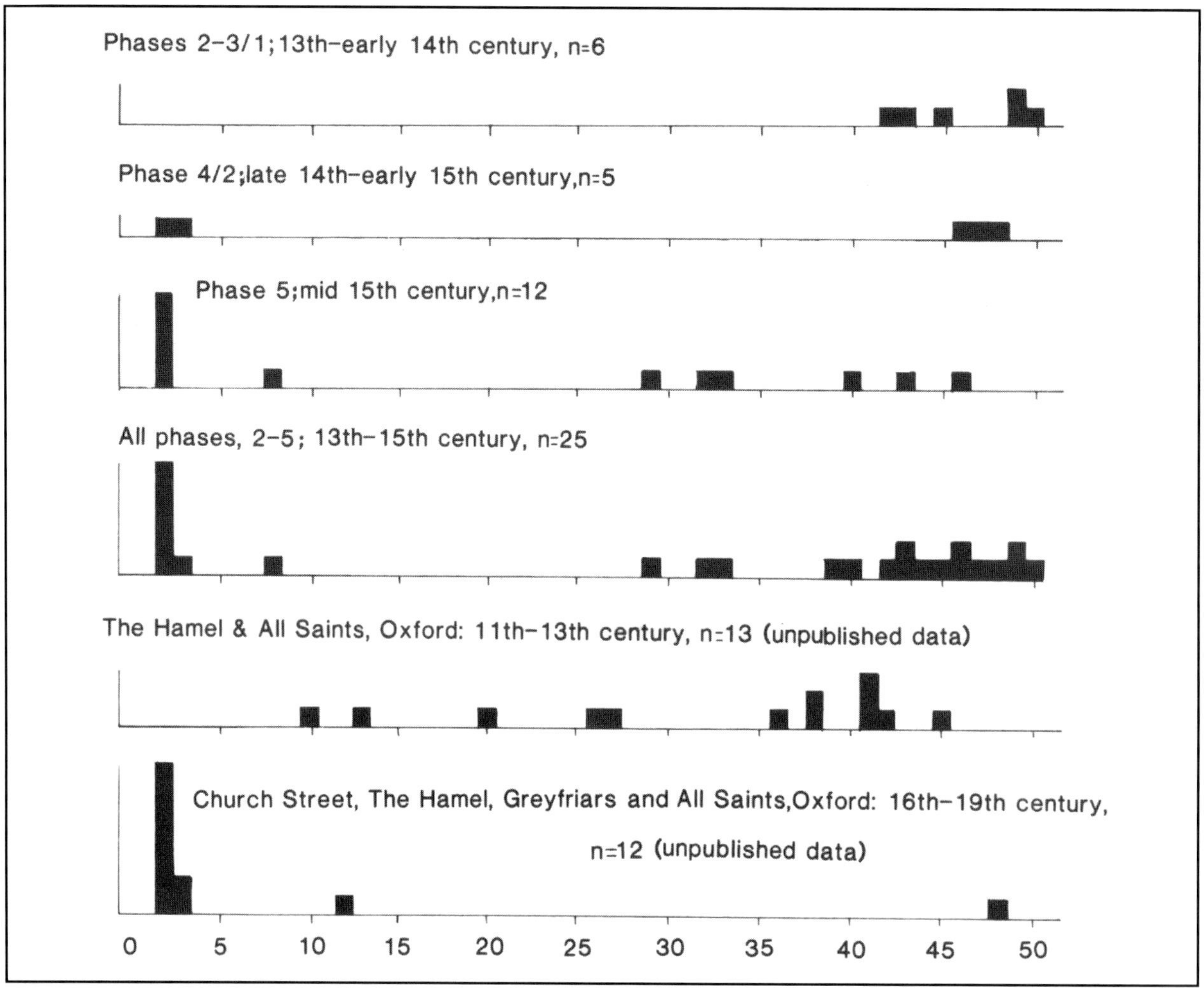

Figure 5.2 Mandible Wear Stages of cattle.

particularly in the destruction and later deposits, suggests that there is some similarity and continuity of farm husbandry between these groups which differs in some degree from that during the earlier medieval period when calf remains are less apparent. Further evidence of this trend is seen among medieval mandibles from Church Street, Oxford (Wilson and Locker 1989). The presence of calf mandibles is indicative of a milking economy, stimulated by the birth of calves, males of which were frequently killed young. This type of husbandry may, therefore, have had greater emphasis during the late medieval and post-medieval periods.

Mandibles of the oldest cattle (MWS 39–50) probably represent oxen and dairy cows. These animals tend to predominate at the earlier medieval period. Three intermediate aged mandibles (MWS 28–33) were probably of immature castrates. In the medieval group of mandibles from urban Oxford, immature cattle (MWS 10–30) are more evident than at Chalgrove. This observation is supported by the data from medieval Church Street (Wilson and Locker 1989). The presence of these immature cattle indicates steers, unwanted bulls or sterile cows which were sent from farms to market and butchers in Oxford. Such marketing could explain the few immature cattle (excepting calves) being butchered at Chalgrove. Another possible explanation is that economic or environmental pressure severely constricted animal husbandry and farm prosperity at Chalgrove.

Sample sizes of cattle mandibles from other sites in the region are usually too small to test against the modest Chalgrove sample. Although the Romano-British sample (64) from 3rd- to 4th-century AD Barton Court Farm, Abingdon, is not statistically different to that of Chalgrove, those from Iron Age sites certainly have a greater proportion of younger animals present overall. On the earlier sites, particularly Barton Court Farm, a greater proportion of calves were kept to greater ages but short of maturation before being slaughtered, presumably with the relatively successful aim of maximal meat production (Wilson 1986). This deduction may imply that both the economy and husbandry of medieval sites was much more constricted than on earlier ones.

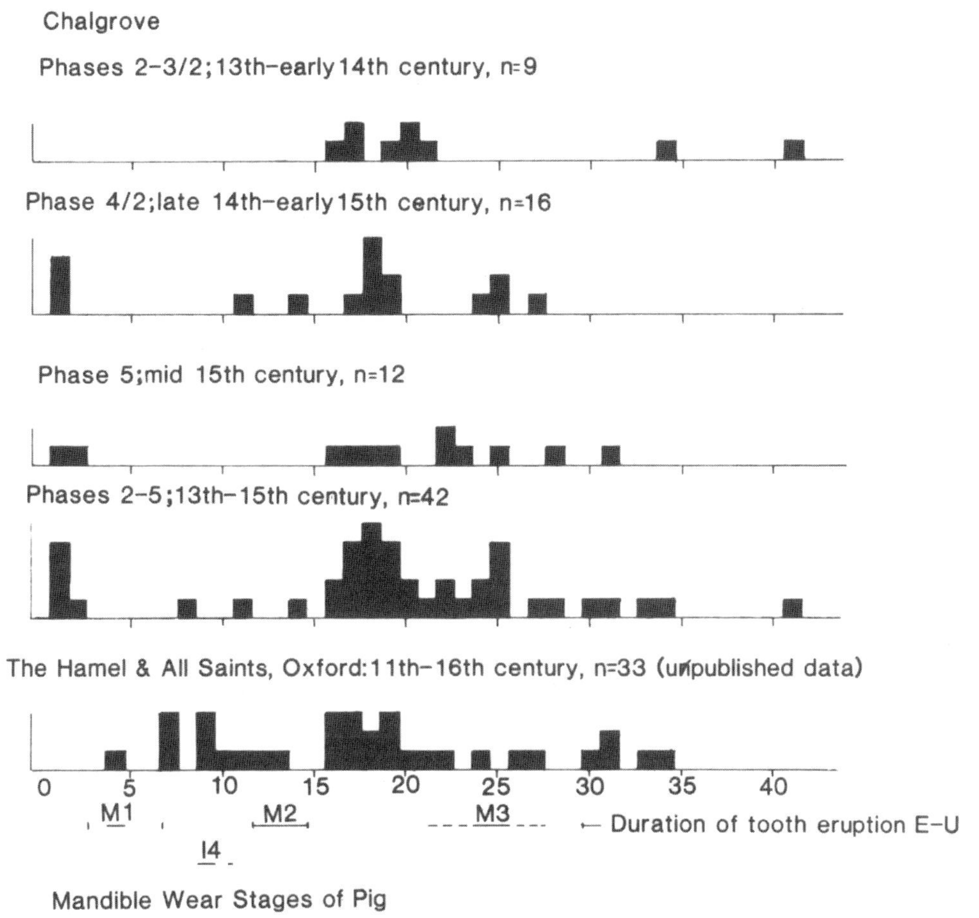

Figure 5.3 Mandible Wear Stages of pig.

Ageing of pig (*Fig. 5.3*)

Figure 5.3 compares data from pig mandibles at Chalgrove with unpublished data from medieval Oxford. The two kill-off patterns are similar and a significant difference in the results is unlikely. These patterns also resemble those of local Iron Age and Romano-British sites. There is little evidence of marketing patterns.

Age information on domestic birds (*Table 5.26*)

The frequencies and percentages of immature and fully ossified bones of domestic birds are presented in Table 5.26. Domestic goose and duck were mainly eaten as old birds and, to a lesser extent, this is also true of domestic fowl. Domestic pigeon, however, were eaten immature as squabs, presumably from a dovecote.

Table 5.26 Frequency and percentage of immature and ossified bones of domestic bird species

Phase	1–3 Imm	Oss	% of adults	4–5 Imm	Oss	% of adults
Fowl	60	92	61	196	452	70
Goose	5	65	93	15	277	95
Duck/mallard		7	100	4	24	86
Pigeon	1	42	2	106	1	1

Bone measurements: size and sex
(Tables 5.27–31)

A selection of the more common skeletal elements were measured and the results are summarised in Tables 5.27–31 which also include some information on other regional sites. Although nearly all of the measurements are specified with reference to the work of von den Driesch (1976), they correspond closely to those taken on other regional sites. General evidence of size differences between urban and rural sites, and the observation of size decreases in animals during the early medieval period, suggests environmental causes such as the general deprivation of human and animal populations in or near towns, as opposed to rural populations, reflecting also differences in social status.

Table 5.27 Selected measurements of sheep bones (mm)

	n	r	x̄	s
Width of distal humerus (Bd)				
CHHF	13	28–33	29.54	1.71
OX12–15 (a)+A29	37	25–31	29.16	1.42
Width of distal tibia (Bd)				
CHHF	27	22–26	23.33	2.4
OX12–15	33	22–27	24.3	1.29
Width of distal metacarpal (Bd)				
CHHF	6	21–26	23.67	(1.86)
OX12–15	31	21–26	24.09	1.39
Length of metacarpal (GL)				
CHHF	4	104–130	114.5	
Ox12–15	8	107–126	115.9	
Width of distal metatarsal (Bd)				
CHHF	4	21–23	22	
OX12–15	28	21–24	22.46	0.95
Length of metatarsal (GL)				
CHHF	5	117–124	121.4	(2.88)
OX12–15	3	114–132	124.3	
Width of distal radius (Bd)				
CHHF	6	24.29	26.5	(1.64)
OX12–15	11	24.29	25.86	1.22
Length of radius (GL)				
CHHF	4	129–146	137.3	
OX12–15	2	128–143	135.5	

a: Data from the Hamel (OXH) and All Saints (OXS) Oxford (Wilson 1980). Period refers to 12–15th centuries.

Sheep (Table 5.27)

Ranges, means and standard deviations indicate a general similarity in the size of sheep bones to those found in medieval Oxford (Table 5.27). They are smaller than Romano-British and Saxon sheep bones. In the Chalgrove group, the raw data from the more abundant elements, such as distal tibia, do not show polymodal peaks indicative of sexual differences in bone size. Any potential bimodal trend may have been obscured by the effects of castration on males, or possibly by their early slaughtering, although there is little evidence of the latter.

Two medium-sized horn cores, with outer circumference lengths of 75 and 90 mm, were found in addition to a large, robust, curved and broken horn, probably from a ram or wether, which measured 123 mm long and 122 mm around the base. No polled crania were noted although they might have been present in a larger sample overall.

Cattle (Figs 5.4–5.5; Table 5.28)

The bones of the Chalgrove cattle are larger, particularly in their distal widths, than those from medieval Oxford (Table 5.28), and some approach the size of large Romano-British stock. Sexual dimorphism is more evident among cattle bones, however, and the comparison of data between sites may be biased therefore by quite different proportions of larger and smaller sexes and as a result of differences in animal husbandry. Few complete bones survived to measure at Chalgrove but some interesting points emerge.

Figures 5.4–5.5 are scattergrams of data from metapodials at Chalgrove against a background plot of data from medieval Oxford. The bones of calves, or the recently fused bones of immature cattle, are not represented. Clustering of data appears to be restricted to the denser scatter of measurements of relatively small bones which, in Iron Age and Romano-British samples, appear to represent cows. The diffuse spread of data from larger bones probably derives from steers, oxen or bulls. This interpretation is supported by the presence of larger

Table 5.28 Selected measurements of cattle bones (mm)

	n	r	x̄	s
Width of distal humerus (Bd)				
CHHF	2	76–92	84	
Width of distal tibia (Bd)				
CHHF	6	51–63	57.5	(5.61)
OX11–16	13	55–66	56.15	4.62
Width of distal metacarpal (Bd)				
CHHF	8	56–63	60.63	(2.18)
Ox12–16	12	44–67	53.33	6.27
Length of metacarpal (GL)				
CHHF	1	184		
OX 12–16	1	205		
Width of distal metatarsal (Bd)				
CHHF	13	48–58	53.07	3.94
OX12–16 (a)	19	42–62	49.3	4.95
Length of metetarsal (GL)				
CHHF	4	192–220	205.5	
OX12–16	2	204–209	206.5	
Length of radius (GL)				
CHHF	6	57–67	62	(4.20)
OXH12–16	11	56–62	58.6	2.06

a: Previously unpublished data from the Hamel, Oxford.

Table 5.29 Selected measurements of pig bones (mm)

	n	r	x̄	s
Width of distal humerus (Bd)				
CHHF	3	36–44	40.7	
OXA 12 (a)	15	33–49	37.8	4.11
Length of astragalus				
CHHF	6	38–48	43.3	(3.78)
OXH 12–16	8	35–40	39.6	(2.50)
Length of 3rd metacarpal (GL)				
CHHF	4	73–80	75.3	(3.20)
OXA 11–15 (a)	5	64–89	75.8	(11.10)
Length of 4th metatarsal (GL)				
CHHF	2	98–101e	99.5	
OXA 11-14 (a)	8	75–92	84.9	(6.03)

a: Previously unpublished data from medieval Church Street, Oxford.

Table 5.30 Selected measurements of bones: Fallow, rabbit, cat, stoat and black rat (mm)

	n	r	x̄	s
Fallow				
Astralagus GLI	2	36–38	37	
tibia dw	1	32		
Rabbit (GL)				
humerus	6	58–65	61.5	(2.26)
femur	4	79–85	81.3	
tibia	1	89		
Cat a				
Humerus Bd	2	16–17	16.5	
Stoat				
tibia GL	1	37		
Black rat (GL)				
humerus	2	25–26	25.5	
femur	2	31–33	32	

a: See also measurements of cat skeletons.

bones showing deformations (see below), indicating the presence of draught oxen which are normally expected to be castrated males.

The evidence suggests that at least some, and possibly most, of the largest cattle at Chalgrove were draught oxen and castrates. Examination of fragmentary pelves indicated that three were of castrates or possibly bulls and one other was female. The metapodial samples are small but indicate that castrates and intact males outnumbered females. It is possible that some of the small cattle represented in the urban Oxford group are not cows, but steers or bulls which were given less favourable feeding and shelter than oxen and consequently their growth was stunted. However, it is suspected that these small Oxford animals were mainly cows, which suffered poorer environmental conditions than cattle at Chalgrove.

Table 5.31 Selected measurements of bird bones (mm)

	n	r	x̄	s
Domestic fowl (GL)				
humerus	22	61–88	71	5.54
femur	11	67–90	78.5	6.47
tibiotarsus	8	85–117	102.8	(10.85)
metatarsus	9	62–85	76.8	(8.53)
Domestic goose (GL)				
femur	5	80–86	82.6	(3.13)
metacarpus	4	90–103	96.3	
metatarsus	1	93		
tibiotarsus	1	102		
radius	1	148		
Mallard/domestic duck (GL)				
metacarpus	3	59	59	
metatarsus	2	47–50	48.5	
Domestic pigeon (GL)				
femur	1	44	44	

Pig, rabbit and cat (*Tables 5.29–5.30*)

As with cattle, and compared to sites in medieval Oxford (Table 5.29), pig bones tend to be larger at Chalgrove, with two very long metatarsals, one unfused, in evidence in Phase 5. The measurements for other domesticated species, when compared with unpublished data from Oxford (Table 5.30), suggest that they were slightly larger in size at Chalgrove. For medieval urban samples, a decline in the size of bones of cat, and other extant species, is evident following the late Saxon period.

Bird bones (*Figs 5.6–5.7; Tables 5.31–5.33*)

The results for selected measurements of bird bones are presented in Table 5.31 and in Figure 5.6 which gives additional information on sex. Figure 5.7 compares metatarsal measurements of bones from Chalgrove with some of known sex from black leghorn cross bantams. Contrary to West (1982), the metatarsi which show spur scars are considered to be of males that were killed before the spur had become fully ossified and fused to the shaft. The largest bones, therefore, appear to be from males as cocks or capons. Slightly fuller evidence of sex from complete and incomplete bones is presented in Tables 5.32–5.33 which indicate a predominance of males in the samples and possibly during the later phases (information from Enid Allison).

Pathology

Several bird and mammal bones showed slight abnormalities of little pathological significance. These mainly consisted of slight outgrowths of bone and worn bones and teeth. One sheep, probably castrate, horncore had slight depressions in the surface which are possibly indicative of nutritional deficiencies during life. Most of the abnormalities are related to minor injuries or to long term mechanical stress on the bones of old or working animals. Some pathology, particularly of the mouth, was more evident than among sheep bones at Church Street, Oxford (Wilson and Locker 1989).

Butchery

No systematic study was made of the butchery marks on bones but some observations were made. One dog pelvis (from a Phase 4 context in the vicinity of Building A12) showed an oblique chop through the ilium and other parallel cuts which indicate that either dog meat was eaten or that dog carcasses were cut up and boiled or rendered for other purposes, such as for fat. Cutting marks were observed on the ulna of a black rat (535, a Phase 4 occupation layer of Building A12). This suggested at least the skinning, and possibly the cooking, of this animal. Many small fragments of bird bones, possibly of goose, were found in clusters, for instance Phase 3 context 1009,

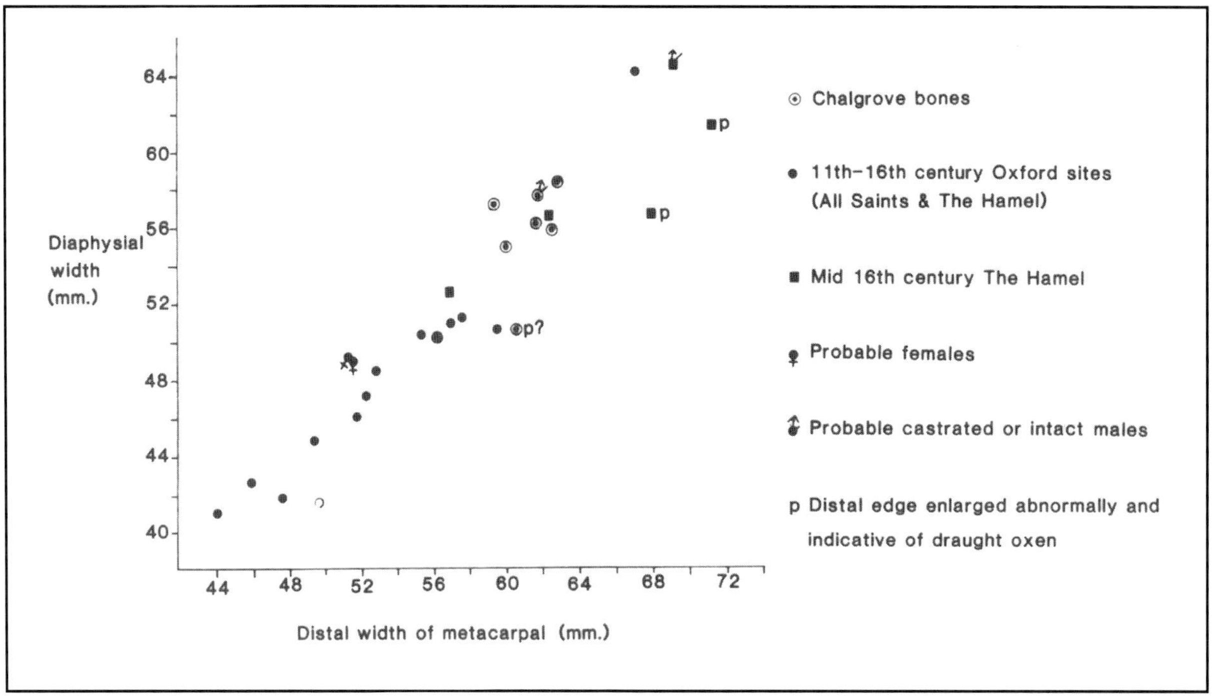

Figure 5.4 Scatter diagram of measurements of cattle metacarpals.

and it is possible that some of these bones were deliberately broken and boiled for fat. Alternatively, they may have been crushed by trampling. Butchery marks were also noted on fowl metatarsi, suggesting that the aim of cutting was to remove the feet from the rest of the carcass.

Discussion

Abundance of species

Pig was the most abundant mammal represented in terms of MNI estimates, although many did not live

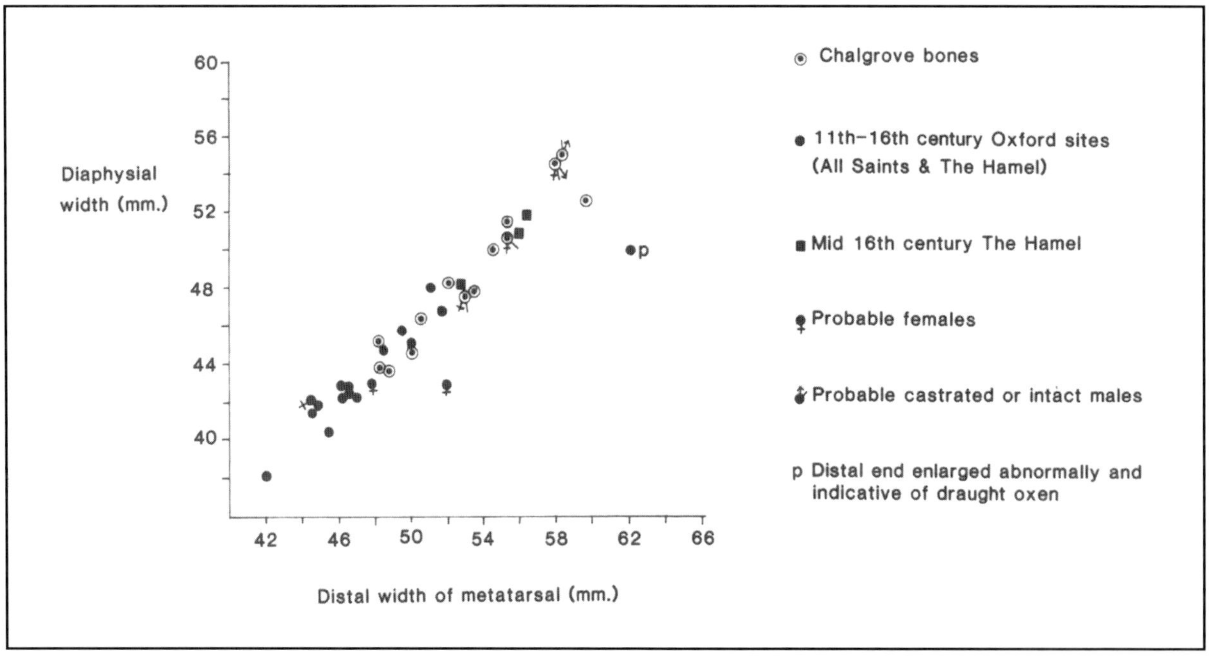

Figure 5.5 Scatter diagram of measurements of cattle metatarsals.

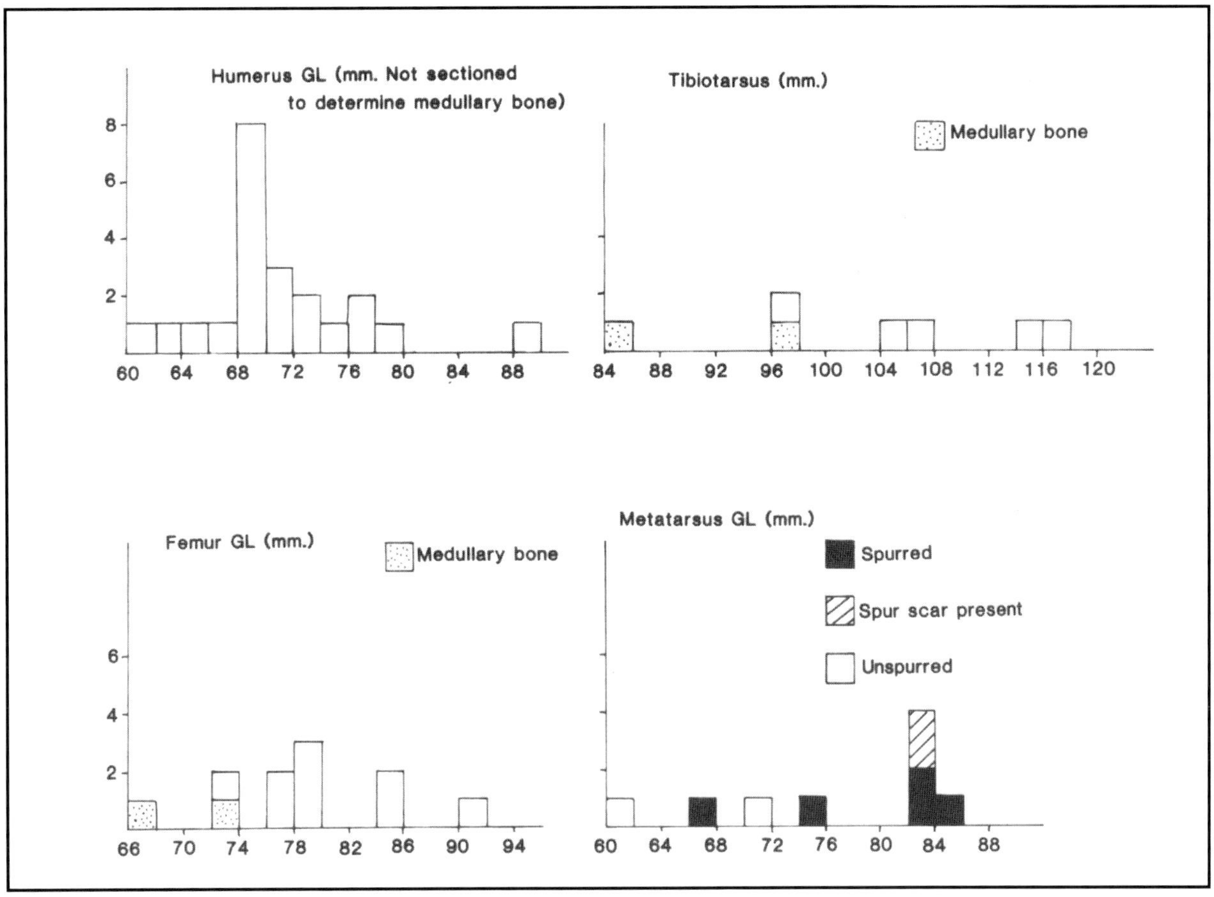

Figure 5.6 Measurements of domestic fowl bones and evidence of the sex of birds.

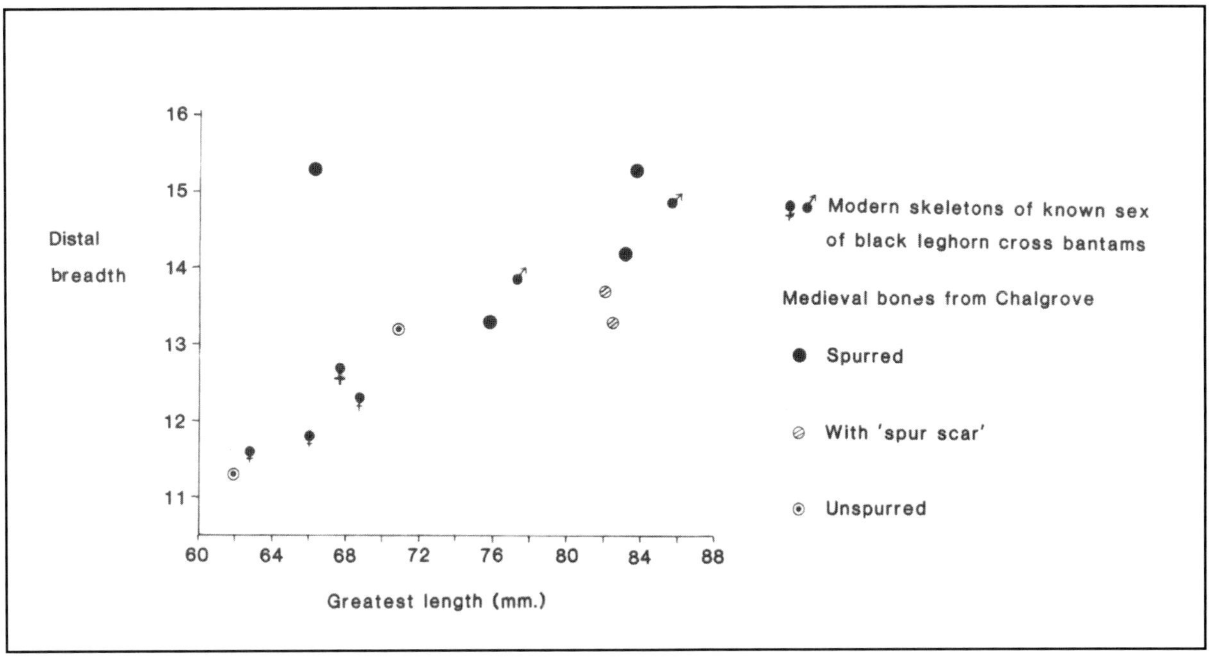

Figure 5.7 Comparison of measurements of Chalgrove metatarsi with those of modern Black Leghorn Cross bantams of known sex.

Table 5.32 Presence of medullary bone in domestic fowl

Phase	Femur Present	Absent	% present	Tibiotarsus Present	Absent	% present
P1–3	2	4	33	3	9	25
P4–5	3	25	11	5	50	9

long. Cattle were the second most abundant mammal species but they may be under-represented if dumps of bone extended much beyond the excavated area. Unusually, sheep were less common than cattle or pig. Individuals were relatively small and were generally slaughtered as mature or old individuals. Wether and ewe sheep appeared equally abundant, if pelves of sheep sent from manors to market are a good guide (Wilson and Locker 1989).

Small and large dogs were present. The cat bones indicate small to medium-sized animals. Domestic fowl of bantam size, geese and ducks were abundant and tended to be killed off as mature or old birds. Domestic pigeons were killed immature.

Diet

Although relatively more pork was eaten at Chalgrove than was usual at medieval sites, especially urban ones, the amount of beef consumed would still be much greater than pork. Less mutton was consumed than usual, while the consumption of venison, rabbit and domestic birds, including pigeon squabs, is better attested here than at many sites. Marine and freshwater fish, wild fowl and fowl eggs were also eaten. Marine shellfish were commonly eaten, especially oyster, but also mussel, whelk and cockle.

Fragments of edible crab are of interest, as is a butchered pelvis of dog, though fat extraction may have been the intention of the butchery. No butchery marks were seen on horse or cat bones. At times food may have been in short supply, either for the servants or for the entire household. The quantity of meat consumed relative to dairy products and to the arable harvest is difficult to determine, but a consideration of animal husbandry (see below) suggests that both cereal and dairy produce were important.

The diversity of species that were eaten is not unusual for the medieval period but implies an increased level of exploitation of animal resources compared with previous periods. The greater consumption of pork, ham or bacon, venison and rabbit and the diversity of birds and fish imply a diet of high quality compared to most urban households in Oxford, or at least a greater degree of access to less common food sources.

Table 5.33 Evidence of spurred metatarsal a of domestic fowl

Phase	Spurred	With scar	Unspurred	% male
P1–3	2	2		100
P4–5	6	3	5	62

a: Fully ossified bones only.

Animal husbandry and use

Management of cattle was the most important element of animal husbandry at the site. Although their meat yield was the largest of all the animal species, cattle were more important for other purposes. There is limited evidence of steers or bulls being raised and killed at optimal ages for meat production, although some such individuals may have been sent to market. Keeping cattle until they were mature or old indicates that husbandry was directed toward the maintenance of the herd for dairy production and the keeping of draught oxen. It appears that draught oxen were more abundant than cows and also horses (see below). The economy appears, therefore, to have centred on arable farming rather than pastoralism. However, the abundance of calves slaughtered during the final phase may indicate some change away from arable production to a greater emphasis on dairying.

Ewes and wethers appeared to be present in approximately equal numbers, and were kept until maturity or old age. This suggests that sheep were mainly kept for wool production. Occasionally lambs were slaughtered but the kill-off is not comparable to that of young calves, and dairying of sheep would appear insignificant beside the productivity of cows. The kill-off patterns also indicate that some younger sheep were marketed.

Certainly the rearing of pigs for meat was more important than at other sites, though the kill-off pattern indicates that less pork, ham or bacon was eaten than the abundance of bones might at first suggest. Pigs may well have been kept at the manor, although no pigsties have been identified. The abundance of pig need not necessarily imply that they were kept in woodland, since rough wet land would suit their feeding. The presence of fallow deer suggests the exploitation of some woodland terrain.

Horse comprises a low percentage of the identified bones, indicating that it figured less prominently as a beast of burden and transport at medieval Chalgrove than elsewhere, for example at the Romano-British villa at Barton Court Farm, Abingdon, which yielded a several fold higher percentage of horse (Wilson 1986 fiche).

The rabbit bones are thought to represent primary rather than intrusive deposition, and the rabbits were probably obtained from locally kept warrens. A comparable find is of 52 well-stratified bones recovered from a 12th-century garderobe at Middleton Stoney, Oxfordshire (Levitan 1984, 108–24). The historical consensus is that rabbits were commonly associated with the post-conquest houses and estates of the nobility (Lever 1977, 62–75).

Modestly abundant remains of fallow deer and the scarcity of red and roe deer suggest that most venison was obtained from emparked herds of fallow deer, and that red and roe deer were rarely kept in any local parks. Deer may occasionally have strayed over greater distances. In order to keep and hunt deer, or to receive venison, substantial connections with royalty were required (see Blair above; Bond 1984, 125–27). In general, both red and roe deer bones become very scarce in urban Oxford deposits after the 12th and 13th centuries, while bones of fallow persist in low numbers (Wilson 1980, 198, F08–F11; Wilson *et al.* 1983, 68–69; Wilson 1984, 1989). Red deer did survive in some abundance up to around the 12th century in the vicinity of Ascot D'Oilly near Wychwood and at Middleton Stoney, both in Oxfordshire. Documentary evidence indicates that emparkment protected and conserved this species at Wychwood, Woodstock and, to a lesser extent because it had to be restocked, at Middleton Stoney (Bond 1984, 125–27; Levitan 1984, 108–24; Jope 1959, 269–70). Hare was also almost certainly hunted for sport and food.

Domestic fowl, geese, pigeon and duck were probably common farmyard animals. Although hens appear less common than cockerels or capons among the dietary refuse, eggshell indicates the importance of egglaying by hens. The presence of a dovecote is probable since nearly all of the pigeons or doves were eaten as squabs. The latter would most conveniently be taken from the pigeonholes.

Freshwater fish like roach, chub, perch and tench were fished, presumably from the moat, stream and local fishponds, but probably most of the fish eaten were imported as marine or migratory species.

Change of husbandry and economy

The arable economy of the site appears to have undergone some modification towards a greater emphasis on the dairying of cattle. Pig was partially replaced by sheep, which is a trend evident in urban Oxford from an earlier period (Wilson 1980, 198, F08-F11; Wilson *et al.* 1983, 68–9, Wilson 1984). This change reflects an increased interest in wool production. The general trend towards a deterioration in the level of subsistence identified for the medieval period does not seem to be in evidence at Chalgrove (Robinson and Wilson 1987, 68–70).

Site and environment

The abundance of pig and deer indicates a greater degree of exploitation of woodland or scrub than is usual for sites in the Thames Valley, although a variety of cultural factors may, of course, determine species presence and abundance. Some of this woodland probably took the form of deer parks, and was perhaps much altered by management. Woodland species are not abundantly represented among the bird bones so these parks may not have been large and could have been some distance away from the site. The extent of any 'woodland' associated with pig keeping may have been reduced by its conversion to pasture when sheep replaced pigs in the later medieval period.

Wet or dampland grazing appears to have been prominent, to judge from the abundance of cattle, pig and the wetland birds, and this may help to explain why sheep played a smaller part in the economy. A similar pattern of medieval environment and land use is evident further north at Sadlers Wood, Lewknor, and Tetsworth (Marples 1973, 161; Pernetta 1973, 112–14) and seems to have been related there to the presence of heavier ground. Such environmental factors probably influenced the type of husbandry practised when such marginal sites were first occupied. However, the changing relative frequencies of sheep and pig, noted above, indicate that social and economic factors influenced land use and animal husbandry, so that environmental factors did not wholly prevail.

In general, the indications from evidence of animal bone size, diet, and social and environmental conditions are somewhat more favourable for Chalgrove than for urban Oxford and elsewhere during the medieval period.

Besides being a pest and carrier of disease, the black rat seems to have had the further ecological effect of virtually excluding water vole from the vicinity of this low-lying site. Water vole is relatively common on rural sites of earlier periods. As the buildings on the site were abandoned or demolished, field voles and field mice appear associated with the reversion of the settlement to a field. House mouse occurred less commonly and most probably dispersed to other human habitation. Bones of small passerines, barn owl, buzzard and jackdaw also occurred in the last deposits and such birds may have roosted or nested in the abandoned and possibly overgrown buildings before their final demolition.

Trade and marketing

The best evidence for trade is provided by the marine fish, shellfish and crab imported deep into the centre of England. They may have been the only meat purchased since other exotic items, such as venison, might have been brought in by other forms of exchange, for example as gifts.

Some live animals or animal products were probably exported, but this is difficult to demonstrate. Immature animals might have been sent to other manor farms, or sold to butchers along with older animals. There is some evidence that more immature cattle and sheep were slaughtered at medieval urban sites in Oxford than at Chalgrove, and this indicates a regional trend of selling younger animals to towns. However, the emphasis of the manor animal economy seems to have been on the production of arable and secondary animal products, and the export of surplus animals was probably limited. The small size of flocks and herds would also tend to limit the surplus of dairy products, wool and other items, though the emphasis on arable farming would have provided the manor with a substantial income. The relative increase in the abundance of sheep suggests that wool increased in value and implies the production of a larger wool clip in the later period.

A virtual absence of cattle horn cores indicates that these were set aside, probably with the skins, and were sold for leather and horn working. An absence of antlers indicates similarly that such material was not worked here. Some or most of this material would be sold to craftsmen in towns like Oxford where antler fragments are found. However, the owners, keepers, or other people associated with the deer herds who benefited from the sale of antler may not have lived at the manor.

Status and prosperity

The relative abundance of pig and deer bones is related not only to a varied meat diet and some prosperity in marketing farm produce, but also to the relative abundance of these species at regional sites of high social status (Levitan 1984, 108–24; Jope 1959, footnote 11; Pavry and Knocker 1960, 177–78). This is despite the general impression that the medieval period is not a prosperous one for English society as a whole (Robinson and Wilson 1987, 68–70).

The economy of the manor in a historical context

The manor is the first site in the region to be excavated which has its acreage of landuse documented. In 1279 the manor is recorded as having 311 ¼ acres of arable land, 30 acres of meadow and 30 acres of pasture (see Blair above).

The 30 acres of grass pasture allowed at around 1–3 acres per cattlebeast indicates that the farm livestock included 10–30 cattle. The pasture would cover their feeding for much of the year and the meadow would provide summer grazing and winter hay. However, the higher estimate of cattle needs to be reduced to allow for the grazing of other species, namely horse and sheep. The acreage of arable land indicates that at least two plough teams of up to eight animals would be required. Thus around half to all of the cattle present would have been draught oxen, chiefly as castrates. The remainder of the herd would mainly have been cows for dairying, breeding and completing the plough teams if necessary.

The numbers of cattle required to support an arable farm economy and the limited acreage of pasture available would restrict the numbers of sheep and pigs which could be kept, even with the availability of additional browsing. Grass and hay requirements for the ruminants would largely preclude pigs from using and damaging these resources, and suggest that they were kept in sties and/or on woodland or rough pasture elsewhere.

Evidence from the wild bird bones suggests that they were hunted in a wide landscape and that the environment was open and not much wooded. Damp or wetland birds predominate, though they may be over-represented in comparison with those of the relatively uniform and sparse arable habitat. While wetland indications are appreciable, the acreage of arable land shows that any wetness or heaviness of ground was not sufficient to preclude an emphasis on cereal cropping.

The nearby manor of Cuxham is a well documented parallel for the 13th and 14th centuries (Harvey 1965, 17–19, 57, 96). There was a larger acreage of arable land at Cuxham than at Chalgrove. A quarter of the estate consisted of pasture or meadow and this was greater than the one sixth at Chalgrove, yet extra hay was purchased, oats were fed to the horses and cattle, and livestock was also taken elsewhere to stubble feed or pannage. The arable economy predominated at Cuxham, producing five to eight times as much income from corn as from sales of livestock and animal products such as wool, cheese and hides. The activities of the villagers and their livestock were incorporated into it, as well as those of the manor household.

The manor at Cuxham employed two to three plough teams which sometimes included horses and even a bull, as well as oxen. One to four other horses were used as cart animals. Most oxen and horses were bought elsewhere. Cows retained were usually fully grown and less numerous than oxen, and calves were often sold in their first year. Sheep numbers fluctuated greatly from none to around 150. They were used to produce cheese and wool, but sometimes the entire flock appears to have been sold when it is absent from the manor records. At least once it suffered badly from murrain. A variety of economic and environmental factors seem, therefore, to have determined the presence of sheep. Some pigs were always present, mainly as porkers bred from a few sows and sold between one and three years of age. Domestic fowl, geese, ducks, and pigeons were kept and there was a dovecote which provided many squabs. Fish such as roach and bream were used to stock the 'vivorium'.

Such documentation yields many enlightening details and provides a more reliable socio-economic context for discussion of the faunal remains. Economic factors appear to have been more important than environmental ones in the management of the manors, although this emphasis depends on the level at which the organisation of medieval society is examined.

We may conclude that the orientation of animal husbandry at Chalgrove, especially that of cattle, was directed towards cereal production. Pasture left over from this process was used largely for producing secondary products from cattle, sheep and domestic birds and this livestock was sold or slaughtered after their usefulness was diminished. Only the rearing of pigs, pigeon squabs and perhaps rabbits was undertaken primarily for meat production, and much of this was probably destined for home consumption.

These factors, the fecundity of pigs and their killing at early age stages, should explain the high percentages of their bones at the manor. It is ironic that the abundance of pig at the site must be interpreted within the context of an arable economy, rather than as evidence primarily for the exploitation of woodland or wetland resources, though the latter were used where possible. More flexible explanatory principles are required in the interpretation of bones where history stays silent.

ENVIRONMENTAL EVIDENCE
by Mark Robinson

Sampling for preserved environmental remains was limited in scope, concentrating on the examination of the fill of the large moat for plant and molluscan remains. Other significant conclusions are drawn from analysis of charcoal deposits from the final period of the manor's occupation.

Invertebrate and seed remains from the moat (Tables 5.34–5.37)

The preservation of organic remains in the moat was poor and was only recorded in a sample from the very bottom of the moat (moat infill 279). The sample, which consisted of grey, and somewhat organic, sandy silt with some gravel, charcoal fragments, *Mytelus* (mussel) shell fragments and pieces of rotten wood, was sieved to 0.2 mm and sorted under a binocular microscope.

Insect preservation was poor but included an example of *Xestobium rufovillosum*, the death watch beetle. Seeds from 31 species of plants and trees were identified, among which were walnuts, plums and grapes. Fifteen species of land and freshwater mollusca were present. The results are shown in Tables 5.34–5.37, with the exception of the insect remains.

Interpretation

The non-marine mollusca (5.37) are mostly aquatic species which presumably lived in the waters of the moat, along with a few terrestrial species which probably fell into the deposit. The aquatic species *Bithynia* spp and *Valvata piscinalis* are species of streams, rivers and lakes which require relatively clean, oxygenated water (Boycott 1936, 139–41). Their presence suggests that the moats, which were not very wide or deep, were fed from a diverted stream. Table 5.34 includes seeds of aquatic species but none of them are from substantial plants, *Lemna* spp. (duckweed) being the most abundant. It is possible that the moats were kept weeded of the large emergent species which would otherwise have choked them.

The other seeds are from plants from a range of terrestrial habitats. Some scrub or trees seem to have been present in the vicinity of the manor. The identified agricultural weeds included *Agrostemma githago* (corn cockle) and *Anthemis cotula* (stinking mayweed). The evidence for the arable crops of wheat and field/broad bean, each represented by a

Table 5.34 Quantification of seeds by species

Species	Common name	No
Brassiceae gen. et sp. indet.		3
Agrostemma githago L.	Corn cockle	1
Stellaria media gp.	Chickweed	2
Chenopodiaceae gen. et sp. indet.		1
Vitis vinifera L.	Grape vine	1
Filipendula ulmaria (L.) Maxim.	Meadow-sweet	1
Rubus fruticosus agg.	Blackberry	4
Prunus domestica L.	Plum	1
Anthriscus sylvestris (L.) Hoffin	Cow parsley	2
Polygonum aviculare agg.	Knotgrass	1
Rumex sp.	Dock	3
Urtica urens L.	Small nettle	1
U. dioica L.	Stinging nettle	132
Juglans regia L.	Walnut	1
Corylus avellana L.	Hazel	1
Fraxinus excelsior L.	Ash	2
Solanum cf. dulcamara L.	Woody nightshade	1
Lycopus europaeus L.	Gypsy-wort	9
Stachys sp.	Woundwort	1
Labiatae gen. et sp. indet.		1
Sambucus nigra L.	Elder	10
Anthemis cotula L.	Stinking mayweed	7
Arctium sp.	Burdock	2
Carduus or *Cirsium* sp.	Thistle	2
Sonchus oleraceus L	Sow-thistle	6
S. asper (L.) Hill	Sow-thistle	1
Alisma sp.	Water-plantain	1
Zannichellia palustris L.		1
Juncus sp.	Rush	10
Lemna sp.	Duckweed	23
Carex sp.	Sedge	1
Total		233

Table 5.35 Other plant remains

Other plant remains
Bud scales
Deciduous tree leaf fragments
Leaf abscission pads
Rosa (rose) prickle
Salix (willow) capsule
Wood and twig fragments

Table 5.36 Carbonised seeds

Species	Common name	No
Vicia faba L.	Field/broad bean	1
Triticum sp.		1
Total		2

Table 5.37 Land and freshwater molluscs

Species	No
Valvata cristata Mull.	1
V. macrostoma Morch	2
V. piscinalis (Mull.)	1
Bithynia tentaculata (L.)	3
Bithynia sp.	14
Carychium sp.	1
Planorbis planorbis (L.)	1
Bathyomphalus contortus (L.)	1
Cochlicopa sp.	1
Discus rotundatus (Mull.)	2
Limax or *Deroceras* sp.	2
Clausilia bidentata (strom)	1
Trichia hispida (L.)	5
Pisidium sp.	2
Total	37

single carbonised seed, was only to be expected, but there were also some more interesting cultivated species. Walnuts, plums and grapes were either grown on the estate or imported by the manor.

The poor preservation of organic remains in the moat system may have resulted from the moat having been drained after the abandonment of the site. Subsequently, the water table of the site was raised, probably above the medieval level. A possible cause of the high modern water table was the construction, probably in the 18th century, of the overshot watermill at Mill Lane.

Death watch beetle tends to infest large hardwood structural timber such as oak and is likely to have been derived from one of the major buildings.

The charcoal (Table 5.38)

Forty hand-excavated fragments of charcoal were examined from selected contexts. The vast majority of the fragments were of beech. Oak, elm, ash and another unidentified species were also represented.

Only one of the unidentified fragments (context 279) was definitely not from beech, oak, elm or ash. Almost all the beech charcoal was of slow-grown

Table 5.38 Quantification of charcoal by phase and type

Context	Phase	*Fagus* Beech	*Quercus* Oak	*Ulmus* Elm	*Fraxinus* Ash	Unident
1022/1015/600	3–5	13	2			
535	4	5			1	
508	3					1
509	3	3	1		1	1
279	5	1		2		1
534	2	2				
518	5	5				1

contorted branch-wood, even allowing for the shrinkage caused by drying, aged between about 12 and 24 years. For example, one sample (context 600) contained a 13-year-old charcoal, 12 mm in diameter, and a 21-year-old charcoal, 50 mm in diameter. In contrast another sample (context 535) had a charcoal 12 years old which was 100 mm in diameter. The oak, elm and ash charcoal included fragments from both substantial timbers and small-diameter slow-grown branches.

Most of the charcoal from the manor represents wood brought to the site as firewood. Few of the fragments were from timbers substantial enough for structural use and the slow-grown small diameter pieces were probably from branches too crooked for use as stakes or wattles. It is interesting that the assemblage is dominated by beech rather than oak and this probably represents a regional variation owing to the proximity of the Chilterns beech woods. The absence of charcoal from understorey species, such as hazel, is also noticeable.

It is probable that the firewood consisted mostly of the trimmings from felled standards in a wood dominated by beech, the timber going elsewhere, or the pollarding of elderly parkland trees, or that it was the result of the clearance of badly grown beech scrub. If it had come from a well-managed pollard wood or coppiced trees, there ought to have been more rapidly grown pieces, with the character of the charcoal described above from context 535.

Chapter 6: Discussion

INTRODUCTION

The archaeological evidence from the accumulated fieldwork, in addition to the documentary evidence sheds considerable light on the development of the moated manor, from the excavation of the moat, through periods of modernisation to abandonment and demolition towards the end of the 15th century.

The following discussion initially examines the manor's structural development in the light of the archaeological evidence, and with reference where pertinent to the documented manorial history. Consideration follows of the economy and environment of the manor as shown by the artefactual and environmental evidence. The final section considers the archaeological and documentary evidence for the abandonment and eventual demolition of the manor.

STRUCTURAL DEVELOPMENT

Before the moated manor (late 12th – early 13th century) (Fig. 2.1)

Anglo-Saxon pottery sherds and two 9th-century strap ends (Figs 3.8.15–16) recovered from various deposits on the site suggest some Saxon occupation in the vicinity of Harding's Field. However, the sum of material archaeological evidence for pre-Conquest settlement in Chalgrove as a whole remains meagre (see Hind, Chapter 1). The best that can be said is that the material evidence, alongside the inferences drawn from the topographical evolution of the village, tentatively suggest that there was a late Saxon settlement close to the site of the church, which may have extended as far as the area of the excavation.

The earliest definite structural evidence for occupation on the site was represented by the truncated remains of at least one, and possibly three buildings linked by a common yard surface, and sealed by the later moat upcast. The dating for this occupation suggests a brief period in the late 12th- early 13th century.

Ironically, the most completely understood building of this early period (Building P) was constructed of the least durable and identifiable material – cob – and also was heavily disturbed and truncated by later building. The evidence appears to show a large rectangular building with a chalk, flint and clay floor and successive open central hearths close to the west end. No other internal features were identified. The pottery from the few securely dated contexts associated with Building P seemed largely of a domestic nature, supporting the suggestion that the building was possibly a kitchen. A yard surface to the south of the building was also identified.

Cob commonly consists of a mix of clay with flint or gravel and straw. By its very nature it is very difficult to identify once the form of the wall has been lost or destroyed. At the time of the excavation, only a few examples of cob-walled buildings of the medieval period had been identified in the region. The most complete example was a rectangular three-roomed building of similar date and size (8.5 m by 12.5 m) revealed in the backfilled moat of Wallingford Castle, 8 km to the south of Chalgrove (Webster and Cherry 1973, 159–61). In the years since the excavation, more examples have been found in the region. A line of cob-walled tenements was constructed in Oxford's extra-mural suburb of St Thomas' in the 13th century, possibly as an investment by Osney Abbey (Hardy 1996, 267–70; Roberts 1996, 222–4). Another example is the cob walled structure at Dean Court Farm, Cumnor (Allen 1994, 422), which is perhaps more relevant to the situation at Chalgrove, as it preceded a stone building associated with the moated grange of Dean Court. While it is clear from the examples of cob building found in recent decades that no easy presumption of the status of the building can be made on the basis of the use of cob, it does seem in this instance as though the building was of utilitarian function.

The other structures of this phase (R and S) displayed shallow stone rubble footings, presumably for timber or possibly cob superstructures, although too little of either structure was exposed to give a clear idea of their footprints or their function.

Given the proximity of the putative original core of settlement round the church to the east, could this group of structures merely be early expansion to the west, marginalised when the focus of the settlement shifted to the axis of the High Street, and suppressed by the early 13th-century manor imposition? There is a local example of such expansion at Seacourt, Berkshire (Bruce-Mitford 1940; Biddle 1961–62). However, the absence of archaeological activity detected in fields immediately surrounding the site does not support this idea, and seems to indicate that the occupation was restricted to the Hardings Field site only. Therefore, despite the incomplete excavation of this phase of activity, it is tempting to suggest that the structures may represent elements of an early manor complex, a direct predecessor to the Phase 2 moated manor of the later 13th century. A number of aspects of the evidence support this hypothesis.

While none of the structures discovered showed signs of high status in their fabric, the five 12th-century voussoirs from a doorway, re-used in a later structure, could suggest the presence somewhere in the vicinity of a 12th-century building of some elaboration, although it is accepted that the voussoirs could have come from a building some distance from the site. The presence of wall plaster and some slates in the moat upcast (see below) could also suggest that a building or buildings of some sophistication stood on the site in Phase 1.

The characteristics of the structures, and their apparent linking by a cobbled surface, show similarities with other sites. Similar associated buildings were found among the pre-moat occupation at Ashwell, Hertfordshire (Hurst and Hurst 1967, 65), and at Northolt Manor, Middlesex (Hurst 1961, 215).

If the site was part of the original curia that was developed by Hugh Malaunay in 1199 and inherited by the Barentin family in 1233 (see Blair Chapter 1), why was the manor complex not more fully developed by the early 13th century? It is important to note that the Phase 1 activity coincides with a period when, although the separation of the manor of Chalgrove into two equal parts was a fact, the tenure of the manor was still unstable. So while a manorial residence may have been established, there may well not have been enough stability of tenure to encourage the investment and commitment required by a major building programme.

If this phase of activity represented a manorial residence, there was no evidence to suggest that it was surrounded by a precursor to the later moat, although the north and east arms of the Phase 2 moat may follow earlier ditched land divisions.

The moated manor (Phase 2 – mid to late 13th century) (Fig. 2.2)

The moats

The evolution of moat building

The phenomenon of moat construction in the context of manorial or sub-manorial residences has been examined in great detail in recent decades, both regionally, nationally (Aberg 1978) and in a north-western European context (Aberg and Brown 1981). Its motivation has been attributed variously to emulation of castle moats (and thereby aggrandisement by association), an embryonic desire for a social separation between the lord and his subjects, a practical response to environmental conditions, a defence, and a source of fish.

Moats served to underline the separateness of the lord's role in the community and would have acted as a psychological barrier (Steane 1985, 59). Moats in the context of manor houses were not great barriers of defence in a practical sense, but they could act as a deterrent against marauders and casual trespassers. The period of popularity of moats coincides with a time, in the 13th and early 14th century, of social and political unrest; the sense of security would almost certainly have been a factor in the excavation of a moat. Moats would protect not only the family and the manor house but also the ancillary buildings and stock which were integral parts of a manor.

The practical benefit of moats should not be overlooked; moats could also be useful for water supply, waste disposal, and as fishponds (Clarke 1984, 56–7), although the latter is generally seen as a later medieval development, particularly in a monastic context. It is unlikely that moats alone could have been used for breeding fish on any significant scale but they could be used to provide occasional pike or bream on feast days.

The dating of the moats at Harding's Field

The dating of the construction of the moat around the building complex is principally determined from the artefactual evidence found within the material dumped as a platform over the north-east part of the site, sealing the demolished buildings of the first phase. Although it cannot be demonstrated unequivocally, it is reasonable to assume that this material derived from the moat excavation – principally of the north and east arms, but also possibly from the widening of the natural watercourse as well.

The excavation of the moat entailed the adaptation of an existing natural water course rather than the creation of a completely new landscape feature surrounding the chosen area. The curving western arm of the moat is formed by the natural stream course, which was widened and deepened. A substitute stream course was excavated to the west (where it survives today) leaving a wide margin of land outside the moat. The northern and eastern moat arms were possibly existing ditch boundaries which were enlarged, although as neither was accessible for detailed archaeological investigation, this remains unconfirmed.

The principal moat was not apparently accompanied by any sort of earthwork, either inside or outside the moat, and furthermore, while the width of the moat is, in places, substantial, its depth is meagre, based upon the sections cut through it (see Fig. 2.7). This would argue against there being a seriously defensive motive in the moat's conception.

The molluscan samples taken from the moat silts indicate that it held free-flowing and well-oxygenated water (see Robinson, Chapter 5). This could mean that the natural water flow was of sufficient quantity and regularity both to provide a constant level of flowing water in the moat, and supply the diverted stream to the south. It would be unusual if a form of water control – a sluice gate – was not utilised, but its location was not identified, and may well have been sited well beyond the excavated area (Bond pers. comm.).

Whether the larger and smaller moats are contemporary is open to question. With no dating evidence recovered from the small moat, and no structural or occupation evidence recovered from the two trenches excavated on the small island, one is forced back to topographical considerations. It could be argued that the diverted stream channel at Harding's Field appears to have been cut to skirt both moated islands, and therefore the small island is part of the original design. An alternative, and equally plausible, scenario has the natural channel diverted in such a way as to provide a margin of land to the west of the large island; only later was the small moat and island created out of the northern part of that margin.

The construction of moated islands containing no buildings is generally accepted as a later phase of the moat building phenomenon, and seems to have had more to do with the elaboration of the sentiment of exclusivity and status, although Clarke suggests that a number of empty second moats nationally were motivated more by economic aspirations (Clarke 1984, 59). Small moated islands could often be secure enclosures for animals, and the remains of a slight earthwork, possibly a nominal gesture towards increased security, were identified around the edges of the secondary island at Harding's Field. Alternatively, small moated islands could be devoted to orchards or select cultivation, reflecting the evolving interest of the new 'knightly' class in pleasure gardens. It is possibly significant that a document of 1600 records an orchard at the site (see Blair Chapter 1).

The historical context

The documentary evidence indicates that the Barentin family acquired the only manor building in the village when the manor was divided equally between themselves and the de Plessis family in 1233 (see above). The de Plessis manor was probably constructed in the 1240s and is likely to have been moated from its inception. It is not known why the Barentin family decided to replace the earlier structures with a moated complex in *c* 1255 but it is interesting to note that this action followed shortly after the construction of the de Plessis manor.

There are numerous examples of manors being moated around this time and into the 14th century. The 12th-century timber hall at Thorpe Lodge, Ellington, was demolished *c* 1250–1300 and almost immediately replaced by a moated platform (Tebbutt *et al.* 1971, 31). Similarly in Wintringham, a moated hall replaced the late 12th-century building in *c* 1250 (Beresford 1977, 205). The excavation of moats and the replacement of structures would have caused considerable expense and inconvenience and can often be associated with the rise in status of the family, or of the family's decision to use the site as their principal residence, as they became more directly involved with direct or demesne farming from the 13th century

The shape of the main Harding's Field moat is untypical, dictated as it is by the natural watercourses. The majority of moats appear to be single, quadrilateral enclosures, encompassing an area in the range of 0.3 to 0.8 hectares (0.74 to 1.97 acres) and this shape predominates in Worcestershire and Essex. However, survey work by C C Taylor in Cambridgeshire and Lincolnshire has shown that investigation in the field often reveals a more complex pattern of earthworks than may be discernible from a map. Moated sites in eastern England tend to be more complicated, with many more subsidiary features than those in the west, south or south-west Midlands. There is an overwhelming predominance of simple moats in Warwickshire, Worcestershire and Oxfordshire and even fairly straightforward double moats like Harding's Field are very much in the minority (Bond pers. comm.). As has been suggested above, the unusual shape of the Harding's Field moat may be seen as support for the idea that Phase 1 activity was the original manorial residence.

Access to the island

The evidence of a small bridge spanning the north side of the moat is not conclusive, but at least plausible. With archaeological investigation of either the moat itself at this point or the northern bank denied, confirmation of the hypothesis either in the form of an opposing abutment of rubble limestone, or any evidence of a support in mid-stream was unobtainable. The narrowness of the identified abutment implies that this could only have been a footbridge with a superstructure probably of timber rather than stone. Spanning a channel *c* 10 m wide, it would qualify as a 'short bridge' by the definition used in Rigold's classification of structural types (1975, 56–59).

The purpose of such a bridge is open to some cautious speculation. The position of the bridge appears to correspond with a boundary line between two fields behind the High Street frontage (evident on the 1822 map – Fig.1.2 and Pl.1.3), so a path over the bridge could have led to the main road. Alternatively, the bridge could have led into another enclosure belonging to the manor.

The location of the bridge suggests that it was not the main entrance to the manor, and may well not have survived throughout the manor's life. As no significant excavation was possible along the line of the eastern arm of the moat, only conjecture, based upon the topography of the site, the disposition of the buildings, and the relationship of the manor to the church and the village, can be employed to suggest alternative locations for the manor's main access.

The disposition of the buildings strongly suggests that the most likely position for the main crossing and entrance to the manor complex would have been over the eastern moat arm, between buildings B and C. This would have given access to the central courtyard, and provided the most impressive elevation of the manor house for visitors. Presumably the crossing took the form of a bridge, although whether built of stone or wood (or both) is unknown.

In addition, the contour survey of the moat earthworks identified a possible causeway across the southern corner of the large moat, which could have represented an alternative access to the agricultural buildings and yards at the southern end of the island. Two machine-dug evaluation trenches (Trenches V and VI – see Fig. 1.5), situated close to the southern corner of the moat, did not reveal any significant deposits to clarify this possibility, but the plausibility of a such an access remains.

The mid-13th century manor buildings

The archaeological evidence points to the rebuilding of the manorial complex in the mid 13th century. Support for this date can be seen in the documentary evidence which records the royal gifts of a total of 19 oaks to Drew Barentin between 1232 and 1256, a strong indicator of a major building programme.

The extant Chalgrove Manor, at the west end of the village, is a timber framed building on stone plinth foundations, built in the 15th century, replacing the original de Plessis manor. Was the 13th century manor at Hardings Field also timber framed?

On the one hand the location of the site is not near any source of building stone. The principal medieval building stone source was some distance to the north and/or west – well beyond Oxford. Timber in the county was not in short supply, and the documentary evidence does highlight the gift of oaks from the King to Drew Barentin in the 13th century. From a general perspective, then, there would have been clear financial advantages in building in wood.

As has been described in Chapter 2, the archaeological evidence of the buildings is almost entirely composed of *in situ* stone footings or, in some instances, the robbed-out foundation trenches that originally contained stone footings. The size and depth of the footings varies considerably – those of the agricultural buildings are generally slight and shallow, those of the main hall and cross-wing much more substantial.

Plinth walls intended for a timber-built superstructure would not need to be much wider than the timber they were supporting. The largest elements of timber framing were typically no more than *c* 0.25 m thick; the slight footings of the agricultural buildings and most of the ancillary domestic buildings could have been, and probably were, for timber-framed structures constructed on stone plinth footings. In contrast, the 1 m wide footings of the main domestic range and cross-wing would seem extravagant for timber-framed superstructures, and surely must have supported stone walls. It appears that, at least as far as the main domestic range was concerned, the inconvenience of the resource was outweighed by the desire to make a clear and public statement of wealth and status.

The disposition and broad orientation of the redesigned manor buildings appears to have been principally influenced by the shape of the island. The main hall was situated towards the northern (and highest and driest) part of the island, with ancillary domestic buildings attached or close by. The central part of the island became an open courtyard, with agricultural buildings and associated structures bordering the south and west sides of the island.

The evolution of medieval domestic planning has been the subject of considerable study in recent years; the results have demonstrated a more convoluted and subtle development than was once accepted. Blair (1993) argues persuasively that the integrated medieval dwelling of the later medieval period, with a cross passage and two service rooms at the lower end of the hall, combined with chambers above, evolved from the earlier arrangement of associated – but physically separate – hall, chamber and service block.

It is clearly possible that there could have been a manorial complex at Harding's Field consisting of separate hall, chamber and services in the late 12th century (Phase 1), but it is by no means demonstrable on the basis of the limited excavated evidence. Not only was the majority of the early stratigraphy left intact and unexposed, but it is also entirely possible that the stone footings of the later hall and cross wing were superimposed on earlier structural footprints.

Further refinement in our understanding of the evolution of later medieval house design has come from Gardiner (2000), who has sought to trace the evolution of further subdivisions, developing the distinct 'service' end of the hall at the opposite end to the private chamber. Thus by the mid 13th century the rectangular hall contained three or four distinct physical and functional spaces. The entrance would be at the middle of a long side, usually giving onto the first space – the cross entry or cross passage which often led to an entrance on the opposite side. On one side of the passage would be the hall, the principal formal and social space within the house, open to the roof and (at least initially) provided with a central hearth. On the opposite side of the passage was the service area, devoted to the storage and preparation of food. In larger houses this area was divided into two and sometimes bisected by a through passage leading to an external kitchen. The fourth space was originally the separate chamber block, which by the 13th century was accommodated within the overall footprint, and situated sometimes beyond the hall on the ground floor, or on the first floor, over the services.

More is comprehensible with regard to the layout of the Phase 2 domestic range, but a degree of caution must still be employed. Building A1 could be seen as a three bay structure, with the eastern bay devoted to the services, the building bisected by a cross passage, and the central and western bay forming the hall. In this scenario the chamber (if an attached part of the whole) must have been over the service end, as the small western chamber A3 is a later addition.

That by the mid 13th century the plan of manorial and sub-manorial houses had become notably standardised is arguably a reflection of the development of a maturing social hierarchy, with a consensus about the use of social space, and a clear separation of the gentry and those who served them (Gardiner 2000, 179).

Building A1

The archaeological evidence for the hall in its first manifestation (Fig. 2.8) is so fragmentary that conclusions about its structural details will be inevitably subject to qualifications. The overall dimensions suggest that it was a three-bayed aisled building, with the middle and western bays forming the great hall and the eastern bay forming the service end. The solar would presumably have been situated over the eastern service area, accessible by a staircase, although no archaeological evidence survived to directly support this. However, it could be argued that the substantial post-settings later obscured by the rebuilt cross wall (see below) imply an upper storey over the services.

The superstructure

As has been suggested above, the size of the footings implies that the hall was stone-built. Fragments of window glass were found in the debris from the demolition of the west wall (646, 1069). Shutters are perhaps more likely than glass in a window of this date but glass in domestic contexts was beginning to be more widely used during the 13th century (Wood 1965, 351–2). At Cogges Manor Farm, a 13th-century window has pivots for shutters as well as a thickened and pierced central mullion between two lights for security bars (Rowley and Steiner 1996, pl. 7).

The evidence for internal structural elements in the hall was slight but one reasonably convincing aisle postpad (1045) was located 2.0 m out from the side wall and 6.2 m from the west end of the building. This could suggest the presence of an aisle, or conceivably a gallery or staircase giving access to the upper chamber.

The length of the west bay at 6.2 m seems to have been almost standard for this type of building. Aisled halls are common in south-east England, and a local example is timber-framed Lime Tree House, Harwell, which had four bays and measured 13.7 m by 7.6 m with a nave span of 4.6 m (Fletcher and Currie 1979, 182). The Harding's Field hall measured 19.2 m × 10.2 m wide (external) and with posts set 2.0 m out from the walls the nave width would have been narrow at *c* 3.8 m. As a comparison, the aisled hall of Saxilby, Lincolnshire, measured 15.24 m by 7.62 m externally (Whitwell 1969, 129).

The length of the middle bay can only be inferred because of the later insertion of the wall (819) between the hall and service bay. The two sub-circular pitched stone features (81 and 865) of Phase 3 could represent consolidation over the post-settings or postholes of the original cross wall. The construction of wall 819 would have destroyed any evidence of a spere truss, such as that at Lampetts, Fyfield in Essex (Smith 1975, 34–5). In this example the hall bays were of apparently uneven length owing to the presence of the spere walls. If this was also the case at Harding's Field, the doorways at the opposite ends of the cross-passage would have been approximately 1.5 m to the east of the partition represented in Phase 3/1.

Presumably the hall and service end, with solar above, would have been separated by a cross-passage, with opposing doorways, and from this passage one or two doorways would have given access to the service area or areas.

It is worth considering the likely configuration of the roof of the building at this point. The excavated evidence does not indicate whether the eastern bay represented a 'cross-wing', which was roofed separately from the hall, or a 'compartment', which was roofed with the hall. It is perhaps more likely that it was enclosed as part of the hall roof since a transverse roof would imply a more substantial divide between the solar block and the hall than there was evidence for. However, a simple pitched roof could have limited the headroom in the solar. At Warnford, Hampshire, this was overcome to some extent by lowering the floor level of the service rooms (Wood 1965, 71), although this was clearly not the case at Harding's Field.

It is difficult to understand the function of the length of wall footing (robber trench 1084 and footing 1135 – Fig. 2.8) in the context of the Phase 2 hall. Perhaps the most likely possibility is that it represents an aborted extension to the east of the hall range.

Building D

A clear interpretation of the function or character of this building (Fig. 2.9) presents problems, not least because the structure was heavily damaged during the topsoil stripping. The shallow stratigraphy within the building, and its relatively short lifespan (when compared to the main range) mean that there is little material evidence surviving to consider in addition to the structural evidence. In addition the situation of the building does not easily fit with conventional manorial layouts.

The dating evidence for the construction of the building is meagre, but in two aspects it is clear that it post-dates the moat construction. The footings were cut into the platform material, and along the northern edge of the building the wall was reinforced by two exterior buttresses on the edge of the moat.

There is some evidence of domestic or craft activities taking place in the building, attested by the presence of two or three open hearths, and the recovery of two fragments of stone mortars from the building's occupation and demolition layers. The indented western end of the building (720) may be the remains of a hearth setting against the wall, as in the 14th-century kitchen at Wintringham, Huntingdonshire (Beresford 1977, 241–245). A similar setting was found in a building at South Witham, Lincolnshire, which was interpreted as a smithy (Mayes 1968, 236–7).

At the site of the medieval manor at Cogges, near Witney, a substantial stone building, of probable 13th century date, is situated north of the west end of the hall. Although in its post-medieval guise it became a dairy, and there is some evidence to suggest it may have been a brewhouse in the late medieval period, the quality and size of the footings examined suggest it was a substantial, two-storey structure. (Rowley and Steiner 1996, 15). This is unlikely to be the case with Building D. In this context it is important to remember that the service rooms at Cogges were at the west end of the hall, not, as at Chalgrove, at the east end.

It is not impossible that Building D could have been a kitchen, or a dairy, although these were almost always situated close to the service end of the hall (as indeed are the later recognised kitchens at Harding's Field). Perhaps the best suggestion for the function of Building D is a bakehouse or brewhouse, which would require hearths and, furthermore, easy access to water. Its relatively short lifespan would be consistent with the evidence of the later medieval development of the north side of the moat, requiring the removal of utilitarian buildings.

Building E

The excavator's interpretation of this building (Fig. 2.9) was a dovecote, and, primarily because of its shape in plan, such an interpretation is tempting. However, the obvious interpretation is worth a critical examination.

Although there is plenty of evidence for the keeping of doves in the Roman period, there is no evidence that the practice was maintained by the Saxons, and only after the Conquest was the keeping of doves reintroduced, although permission to do so was reserved for manorial lords, monastic houses and parsons. Few failed to exercise this prerogative (Bond 1973, 20); it was a fiercely guarded privilege and a mark of social status that was supported by the threat of severe punishment for those who harmed or raided the birds.

A number of manorial or monastic dovecotes have been excavated, or survive as upstanding structures, and most had (or have) internal diameters of 6.0 m or more. Two standing late medieval Oxfordshire dovecotes, at Duns Tew Manor and Minster Lovell Manor, have internal diameters of 6.0 m or more (Bond 1978b, 72), and another (also probably late medieval) in the grounds of the Old Rectory at Kidlington, Oxon has an internal diameter of 5.6 m (Bond 1982, 103). By comparison the Harding's Field structure has an internal diameter of just 3.1 m. The only surviving stone-built circular medieval dovecotes with an internal diameter under 4.0 m are all in the far west, in Pembrokeshire and Cornwall, and all have the form of a domed corbelled stone roof as is normal in those parts of Britain. The usual midland form is a conical timber-raftered roof with a central lantern, which would be difficult to achieve on a structure this small (Bond, pers. comm.).

Perhaps the closest – in both senses of the word – structural parallel, is the circular dovecote at Dean Court Farm, Cumnor, which had an original internal diameter of *c* 5.0 m, and was later rebuilt, possibly after the collapse of the original, with a diameter of 3.6 m (Allen 1994, 433). The original dovecote was probably constructed in the 14th century, the smaller rebuild is undated.

That doves were eaten (and presumably kept) at Harding's Field is supported by the assemblage of pigeon bones recovered, particularly those from young birds or squabs (birds not yet fledged). However, doubts over the function of Building E remain, chiefly because of its small size.

An alternative explanation of Building E's function may be suggested by a small circular structure at Sydenhams Moat, Warwickshire, which had an internal diameter of *c* 2.5 m and stone walls *c* 0.9 m thick. It was initially interpreted as a dovecote (Perry 1980, 61), but subsequently reinterpreted as a store for malted grain (Smith 1989–90, 51). In this context it may not be a coincidence that Building E is close to the possible bakehouse or brewhouse, Building D.

Buildings N, O, Q and U

Fragmentary remains of the stone footings of a number of buildings (Fig. 2.2) were revealed in the southern part of the large island. None was associated with evidence of domestic occupation. The area was later reorganised and developed as a complex of farm buildings and yards, so it is reasonable to see these four buildings as an earlier phase (or possibly two) of agricultural structures.

It cannot be confirmed beyond question, however, that they necessarily belong with the first phase of activity after the moat construction, as this area lies beyond the extent of the dumped platform material. Very little dating evidence was recovered in association with any of the buildings. The material from a hollow in the floor of building Q, for instance, although dating to between the late 13th and 14th century, could equally derive from activity associated with the later building on the same site. Ultimately therefore, their inclusion in this phase should be accepted with caution.

The modernisation of the manor (Phase 3 – early 14th century) (Fig. 2.3)

The archaeological evidence indicates that early in the 14th century extensive alteration of the buildings and their layout took place.

Although it cannot be definitely proved to be at his instigation, these alterations broadly coincide in date with the acquisition of the manor by Drew Barentin II and such changes as were made would have reflected the increased standards of prestige and comfort that a man of his standing would have expected (see Blair Chapter 1). There is evidence throughout England of a general remodelling of domestic and agricultural buildings in the first decades of the 14th century, in part the result of the success and profitability of demesne farming during the 13th century (Platt 1978, 47).

The main range of the manor at Harding's Field was radically altered. The decision to demolish the entire old service bay, rather than add to it, may to some extent reflect the idea of separateness that was developing with regard to separation of the hall and the chambers or rooms that serviced it. There are examples of other halls being completely rebuilt at this time, as at Brome in Suffolk (West 1970, 95–7) and at Wintringham in Huntingdonshire, where a new house was built *c* 1300 (Beresford 1977, 192).

The plan of the service area at ground level was now typical of many medieval houses of this date with two service rooms (typically a buttery and pantry) divided by a corridor or leading to an external kitchen. At Haddon Hall, Derbyshire, built *c* 1300, the rooms were of almost identical dimensions to those at Harding's Field and were also in the same position relative to the hall (Faulkner 1975, 107, fig. 28). At Harding's Field the corridor to the kitchen was central and the rooms on either side were unequal in size because the more northerly room extended into the ground floor of the new cross-wing. This was the case at Warnford Manor House, Hampshire (Wood 1965, 36). Two doorways gave access from the hall to the buttery and the pantry and a central door led through the corridor to the kitchen on the east side of the island.

While the interior of the new wing contained little or no construction debris from this rebuilding, a layer of construction debris was noted around the southern corner of the house. The rubble appeared to have been covered with a layer of loam (170 and 228), presumably to created a raised bed, and possibly to give the effect of a raised platform in front of the main elevation of the house.

Room A1

The construction of the dividing wall (819) between the main building (A1, Fig. 2.10) and the cross-wing (Fig. 2.11) would have meant that the bays were of uneven length. It is possible that the opportunity was taken to replace the original roof structure by a base cruck construction. The thrust of the roof, previously taken through aisle posts onto the floor, was thereby transferred to the walls. This may explain the two small buttresses (560 and 895 – see Fig. 2.10), which were added on either side of the hall. The result was that the hall was divided into two equal bays, each of which was the same length as the new service bay. A similar conversion took place at Lime Tree House, Harwell, Oxfordshire, with the construction of a base cruck roof in 1297–8 (Currie 1992, 139–40).

Rooms A9 and A10

The interpretation of the function of the two rooms in the cross-wing service area (Fig. 2.11) was supported by the recovery of several artefacts from the floors of the rooms (although it should be noted that most of the artefacts were found in the later deposits within the buildings). The remains of glass vessels were found in each of the rooms (see Chapter 4). The pottery forms, such as jugs and a bottle, found in the larger room (A9) were not incompatible with those that would be used in a buttery and the large number of small bones included the remains of fish, birds and smaller mammals. Finds from Room A10 included two knives, one of which was possibly a bench knife.

No evidence was found for external doorways in either room, and therefore access must have been restricted to the doorways leading off from the cross passage, or the two doors accessing the hall. There was also evidence of a threshold providing access from Room A9 into the chamber beyond (A4).

Post-settings in the centre of the two rooms may have supported timbers running lengthways across the bay, from north-west to south-east, in the form of a spine beam. The construction of the corridor walls (354 and 359) would have made use of the timber uprights (in settings 113 and 357) in the middle of the bay and of their cross-beams.

Room A4

The function of the ground floor room A4 (Fig. 2.11) is somewhat unclear. The floor deposits indicate a fair amount of wear, periodically repaired by patches of cobbling. As with other rooms in the domestic range, the potential of the artefactual material recovered to determine the room's function is limited, as most was undiagnostic and found within upper layers or the Phase 5 demolition material.

With no evidence for a hearth, it is unlikely to have served as a parlour or private living room for the lord's family, and more by default than by positive evidence one may suggest that it could have been a store, or a wardrobe. The wardrobe was used as a store for valuable items and was, therefore, often stone-walled to provide a secure, fireproof environment. The proximity of the garderobe (A5 – see below) could have been beneficial, as the likely stench of ammonia from the garderobe would have been a deterrent to moths.

The upper floor

Typically, by the 14th century, the solar was situated over the high end of the hall for convenience, and the rooms above the service bay were used for guests, a son's family or for staff such as a bailiff. Unusually, this does not appear to be the case at Harding's Field and the lord's solar remained over the service end of the hall. The possibility of a grand window behind the high table is one of the advantages and attractions of this alternative arrangement. There are a few other examples, such as the Treasurer's House at Martock in Somerset where this is the case (Wood 1965, fig. 28).

Staircases

The location of the necessary access to the upper floors of A9 and A10 is unclear. The excavator speculated that two spiral staircases were incorporated into wall 819, which separates the hall A1 from the rooms A9 and A10. Footings 81 and 893 were interpreted as footings for the stairs. However, the footings are barely 1.5 m in diameter, implying a stair width of around 0.5 m which is unfeasibly narrow. Contemporary examples of spiral staircases (such as Old Soar, Plaxtol in Kent) were at least 2 m in diameter, and usually situated in a corner to provide extra structural support (Wood 1965, fig. 26). The footings 81 and 893 are much more likely to represent consolidation over the settings for postholes of the Phase 2 bay division.

A much more likely candidate as a base for a staircase serving the upper floor of the service wing would be the small near-square room A8 (Fig. 2.11), situated in the angle of the north side of Room A1 and the west side of Room A9. Further support for a staircase at this point is indicated by the substantial footings of A8 and the infill of clay and flint, almost devoid of finds, within the structure.

A staircase giving access only from the main hall gives some indication of the function of the upper floors of A9 and A10 (and by implication A4 and A5). The possible external chimney base, which would have served a fireplace, adds further support to the likelihood that the upper floor was a suite of rooms exclusive to the lord of the manor. Thus it is possible that on the first floor counterparts to A9 and A10 were one room – the solar, and A4 represented the bedchamber, with the first floor garderobe beyond to the north.

Room A3

A short bay was added to the high end of the hall A1 (Fig. 2.10). Its position suggests that it was a parlour, a separate room to which the family could retire from the high table. Parlours were commonly converted from what would have been the solar basement but at Harding's Field the solar was at the other, low end of the hall and there was no evidence for a second storey at the high end. The presence of a small central hearth with a base of limestone slabs (796) within the parlour suggests that the room was open to the roof. The demolition of what was originally the high end of the hall would have resulted in the removal of any window, and fragments of window glass were found in the later floor make up of this new room.

There was no evidence of a door between the new room and the main hall, so presumably the opening would have been screened by a curtain when necessary. Parlours or withdrawing rooms were a result of the increasing desire for privacy that developed during the 14th century (Wood 1965, 91). Other examples of this trend exist; at Wintringham, Huntingdonshire, a room called a 'bower' was built *c* 1300 at the dais end of the hall (Beresford 1977, 224).

Room A5

The evidence (Fig. 2.11) appears to represent the foundations of a garderobe or privy, serving the private chambers of the first floor. No evidence of a latrine pit as such was identified, so it is assumed that there would have been a clearance arch, as at Old Soar, Paxtol in Kent, in the northern wall to allow the waste to run out into the moat (Wood 1965, 380). A stone wall divided the ground plan of the garderobe into two parts, and the ground in the northern part was cess-stained in a slight pit (935). The southern half was not stained, implying that the actual privy shaft serving the upper chamber was separated from the structural north wall of the ground floor chamber, presumably to prevent seepage back into the lower chamber.

Building A6

The evidence (Fig. 2.10) appears to represent a porch facing onto the courtyard. The side walls were represented by robber trenches slightly shallower than those of the main building. The front of the porch appeared to be open, or have a wooden rather than a stone front, which suggests that the porch was probably not a full two-storey construction with an upper room, as is found in a number of examples, for instance Woodlands Manor, Mere (Wood 1965, plate IX). A small quantity of stone slate was found within the material excavated from the porch, which may indicate the roof covering.

Building A7

The wall footings of a small rectangular building (Fig. 2.14) were attached to the south-east corner of the service block, with a possible linking wall to the west side of Building B. There was little evidence to indicate the character or function of the building, and any internal floor or other deposits were removed by the construction of the later building A11 (see below). It is possible that it was a small storehouse, maybe serving the kitchen. An outbuilding adjoining the kitchen at Kent's Moat, Sheldon, Warwickshire, was interpreted as a possible coal store (Dornier 1965, 50).

Building W

The evidence (Fig. 2.12) is interpreted as a detached kitchen to the east of the service range, the traditional place for a kitchen in a manorial complex. King John's Hunting Lodge at Writtle, Essex, had a series of kitchens to the east of, and in series with, the hall (Rahtz 1969). At other sites at this time, such as Wintringham, Huntingdonshire (Beresford 1977, 205), kitchens were rearranged, rebuilt or furnished with more formal ovens and hearths. It was still conventional for the kitchen to be detached from the main building range to reduce the risk of fire. The dating of the construction of Building W is less than secure, given the degree of later rebuilding and use. Therefore it is possibly significant to note that the line of the west wall of this building lies directly alongside the eastern end of the extension (1135) to the north wall of Phase 2 Building A1, which could suggest that Building W was built before the construction of the Phase 3 cross-wing.

The wall footings of Building W were slight compared to those of the main range, implying that the building was timber-framed. Although monastic kitchens were usually built of stone by this time, timber-framed examples in a manorial context were not uncommon. Provided the roof was high and cooking was restricted to a central open hearth, the fire risk was acceptable. Fireplaces incorporated or added to the structure would be brick- or stone-built, with chimneys. Internally Building W was simply arranged, with one large open hearth in the centre, surrounded by a beaten earth floor. There was no evidence of internal ovens or fireplaces at this stage. At Northolt Manor, a large kitchen of 1300–1350 was a timber-framed building, with a central hearth (Steane 1985, 265). Significantly, most of the cooking at Northolt appears to have been done in a cobbled yard outside the kitchen. The same arrangement may have applied at Harding's Field, with the juxtaposition of Building W and Area F (see below).

Area F

The north-east corner of the main island appears to have evolved into a working area (Fig. 2.12), ultimately separated by a fence or wall from the domestic ranges. It is likely that the dimensions of the area were dictated by the east wall of the north-south range and the north wall of Building W, which suggests that it post-dates the major redevelopment of the manor. The dating of the establishment of this area is difficult to fix precisely from the artefactual evidence; a small assemblage of pottery and a few metal objects suggest an early 13th century date, although the open nature of the area throughout its life undoubtedly exacerbated the degree of intrusion by later material. The area eventually contained ovens, a yard surface and possibly a small roofed building. The variations in the construction details of the three ovens suggest that a number of activities may have been undertaken at any one time, possibly a combination of bread-making and malting. A bread oven with similar dimensions to one of the three ovens in Area F (509) was excavated at Penhallam Manor, Cornwall (Beresford 1974, 111–112).

Neither the stratigraphy nor the artefactual assemblage recovered from Area F can elucidate the internal development of the area or indeed its longevity. There is some empirical evidence that the area may have become disused before the rest of the domestic complex in the relative scarcity of later pottery fabrics – for instance Fabrics 60–9 (see Table 3.3) – in comparison to the later kitchen, Building A12. However, this could equally well be a consequence of changing activities within the area.

The water supply to the manor

The source of potable water for the manor requires some consideration at this point. Curiously, no archaeological evidence was found for a well at any point (or in any phase) in the building complex. Are we to assume that they drew water straight from the moat? Most rural sites contain wells or water pits, which would be a source of water less prone to pollution than a moat (particularly if the moat is, as seems to be the case at Harding's Field, also in use as a sewer).

Given the abbreviated excavation strategy, it is perhaps most prudent to suggest that a well (or wells) may remain undetected under undisturbed deposits on the site.

Building B

The lightly founded three-bay building (Fig. 2.16) to the south of Building W revealed few artefactual clues to its function, and again consideration is centred on its internal layout and relative position in the building complex. It appears to have been a timber-framed building, judging by the insubstantial footings, with a fireplace against one interior wall. The building's proximity to the kitchen and the service area could suggest that it was accommodation for manorial staff. A contemporary parallel is documented at Belchamp St Paul, Essex (Le Patourel 1980, 40–1), which housed manorial servants on the first floor, over a ground floor dairy. There is some evidence that the upper floor of the later dairy at Cogges Manor Farm, Oxfordshire, was fitted out as living quarters (Rowley and Steiner 1996, 74). It is possible that the same combination applied at Harding's Field, although no artefactual evidence for the dairy function was produced.

Building J

The function of building J (Fig. 2.17), set apart from the main domestic buildings, is difficult to determine. The demolition debris from the building (337) included sherds of 14th-century fine tableware, two decorated sherds and a bronze buckle. It is possible that the building was used as accommodation for fairly senior manorial staff. The building overlooks the farmyard which would be a suitable location for the house of the domestic steward or bailiff.

Building I

Building I (Fig. 2.17) was attached to the southern wall of Building J and its function is possibly related. A key element (at least in the building's original guise) must have been the stone-lined pit (341) in the south-west corner of the structure. A larder at Penhallam had a small pit, partly lined with stone, which was interpreted as a cool storage pit (Beresford 1974, 114) and a similar feature in a town house in Lincoln was also interpreted as a larder (Colyer and Jones 1979, 64–65, fig. 5). Another possibility is suggested by two stone-lined tanks recorded in the late 14th- to 15th-century phase of the kitchen at Dean Court Farm (Allen 1994, 430–4). These were interpreted as fish tanks which were important enough for the kitchen to be redesigned around them. It was also considered that they may have been used as part of the brewing process.

However, these tanks were much larger than the Harding's Field example; furthermore, the lack of stone lining on one side of the pit seems to argue against it being water-filled.

Fresh meat was probably less difficult to obtain in the winter than has been previously thought but as a matter of prudence a certain amount of meat would have been kept pickled or salted in most aristocratic or gentry households of the period. Therefore, the likelihood seems to be that building I was a store or larder. The pit in one corner could have been used for storage (or possibly for ice) and could be supervised by the occupant of the adjacent building (J).

The central courtyard

There was no evidence that the courtyard was divided in any way during this phase. The courtyard surface (396) provided a stratigraphic link between buildings B, I, J, the porch A6 and the farm building K, all of which it abutted. The yard also appeared to respect a line between the eastern corner of building J and the western corner of the porch, and another line between the western corner of the porch and building B on the east side of the island. In Phase 4, these lines were marked by walls which probably contained gardens to the north and it is quite likely that walls, or another kind of barrier, existed during this earlier phase. The courtyard was not traced to the edge of the eastern moat immediately south of Building B, although it is not clear whether this was due to later truncation or the presence of a boundary wall along the moat edge. In the southern corner of the island the courtyard surface was lost due to truncation.

The agricultural buildings (Phase 3 – early–mid 14th century)

The irregular scatter of farm buildings in the southern half of the main island were replaced by an orderly arrangement of barns, byres and stables. There are many examples of similar reorganisation, for instance at Sydenham's Moat, Solihull, Warwickshire (Smith 1989–90, 47) and at the Knights Templars moat at South Witham, Lincolnshire (Mayes 1968, 236), and they seem to be a signal of a developing and prospering agricultural organisation.

The overall disposition and phasing of the agricultural buildings

While the overall reorganisation of the southern half of the island at Harding's Field is obvious, the sequence of building is uncertain, and the precise functions of individual buildings are open to question. By their nature archaeological remains of agricultural buildings are usually insubstantial, and contain few datable artefacts. These factors were exacerbated by the limited excavation undertaken over the southern half of the island. Thus the phasing of Building C before the range G and H is open to some question – there is a suggestion that the north wall of building G originally extended to the east, and was shortened to accommodate Building C. Equally, however one could argue that the logical sequence of building would have been first the two buildings K and C at the south and east edges of the moat, followed by the range G and H, effectively dividing the farmyard into two discrete areas. It is from the interrelationship of the buildings, both to each other and to the entire manorial complex itself, that the most plausible identification for the buildings' functions can be formed.

Building K

The building (Fig. 2.18), measuring nearly 42 m × 7.5 m in plan, was positioned on the edge of the moat, and was almost completely devoid of finds except for small miscellaneous sherds of pottery, an iron staple and strip and a piece of lead from the overlying (demolition?) material. The only clue to its function is the plan of the building itself.

One possible interpretation of Building K is a stable block. The great length of the building appears excessive for the stabling of horses for recreational use or hunting in a relatively modest manorial establishment. Except for the partitions at either end there was no evidence for mangers or drains, or a run of internal partitions, essential in stables. There is also only one entrance which would not be desirable in a stable block of this length. Additionally, if the building had been used as a stable, a more substantial flooring might have been expected, as was found in the pitched limestone flooring in the 15th-century barn of the manorial house at Minster Lovell, Oxfordshire (Bond pers. comm.).

An alternative function for Building K is accommodation for draught animals. Wilson suggests (see Chapter 5) that perhaps 16 oxen would have been required on the manor to supply two plough teams. Again, the lack of evidence of a substantial floor could argue against this use.

It is perhaps more likely that the building was used as a cowshed or a sheepcote, both of which would require less segregation of the animals than in a stable, so few if any partitions would be necessary. Building XII at Waltham Abbey, which had a domestic hall and solar at one end but was otherwise interpreted as 15th-century housing for 32 animals, measured approximately 50 m in length excluding the domestic portion (Huggins 1972). This exceeds the length of building K but most manorial byres or cowsheds were significantly smaller than the Harding's Field building. A new byre was built by Glastonbury Abbey at Street in 1343 with its dimensions recorded as 63 feet by 20 feet (*c* 19.2 m by 6.1 m) (M Thompson pers. comm.).

Sheepcotes were used during the later medieval period for the overwintering of flocks, for the storage of fodder and as a source of manure, and their considerable length is one of their most distinctive characteristics, varying from 23 m to 65 m in length

Plate 6.1 Artist's reconstruction of Barentin's manor in the late 14th century.

and 6 m to 8 m in width (Dyer 1995, 136–139). They are further identified by having one entrance only and by the close proximity of one long wall to major walls or boundaries such as a moat (ibid. 139). They were usually built of timber on stone sill walls and would have had considerable roof space for storage. Sheepcotes were often permanent and substantial structures because of the high income provided by sheep farming during the wool boom of the 13th and 14th centuries.

Building C

A large, lightly founded building interpreted as a barn (Fig. 2.18), with a porch on its western side, was built to the south of Building B, post-dating the laying of the courtyard surface. The remains of the walls suggest that the structure was timber-framed on stone sills. No finds were recovered from the building to assist in dating its construction. Assuming the porch was located in the centre of the building the original length of the barn can be estimated at *c* 33 m, of which there was archaeological evidence for 30.5 m. One substantial internal post pad (394) was identified indicating that it was an aisled or quasi-aisled structure.

The porch itself measured approximately 4.5 m by 4 m, which would be suitable for a cart porch and is generous in size compared to extant examples attached to medium-sized or small medieval barns elsewhere. The size of the carts able to enter the barn was limited by the width of the doorway and this was 3.2 m to 3.4 m on the four surviving Somerset barns of Glastonbury Abbey (Bond and Weller 1991), 3 m at Shippon and possibly as little as 2.5 m at Tadmarton on the Abingdon Abbey estates (Bond 1979). Even at Great Coxwell the original doorways were only about 3 m wide and these served until the 18th century when larger openings were made in the two gable ends. However, although Building C seems to have been given a generously large porch, the east side of the barn abuts the line of the edge of the moat which would make an opposing doorway and therefore a through passage for carts impossible. Wagons would have had to back out of the barn or be turned inside the barn once they were offloaded. This would not have been an ideal arrangement, and one may speculate that the large porch was an attempt to alleviate this problem by allowing more turning space within the building.

Chalgrove lies within the western limits of the area in which medieval aisled barns are common, such as the larger barn at Great Coxwell, Berkshire, with a width of 11.6 m internally (Bond pers. comm.). The estimated length of the Harding's Field barn (33 m) places it well within the 'middle-sized' range of medieval barns so characteristic of manorial sites, as distinct from the large barns on monastic granges which would store grain from several manors. Monastic barns were typically more than 40 m in length and 'small' barns less than 25 m (*cf.* Bond and Weller 1991). The Harding's Field barn compares in length with two surviving manorial barns on the Glastonbury Abbey estates, at Pilton (33 m by 8.4 m internally) and Doulting (29 m by 8.2 m), both of which are narrower because they have cruck roofs. Arguably arable production on a midland open-field manor such as Harding's Field would probably have been greater than in the rather mixed economy of Somerset and therefore it may not be unusual that the Harding's Field barn was of substantial size.

The western side of the main island

The topsoil stripping and the evaluation trenches excavated along the western edge of the main island (Fig. 2.19) did not reveal any structural evidence, and it is considered that this area was maintained as an open area – possibly pasture. The probable pond (320) located by Trench II, could also suggest that poultry were kept here. A scatter of material (319), including 42 sherds of pottery and a circular iron buckle, was identified *c* 20 m to the north-west of building J, close to the edge of the moat. In conjunction with the oyster shell dump located close to the western side of Structure T, it suggests that the area (or parts of it) was also occasionally used as a midden.

Later structural development (Phase 4 – late 14th century) (Fig.2.4)

The central theme of the various structural developments in the manor complex is the adaption of the existing buildings to suit the changing aspirations of the knightly class, especially the desire for a clearer separation of the lord's living quarters from the areas devoted to service or work.

Building A11

Although the building (Fig. 2.14) overlay the footprint of the Phase 3 Building A7, such is the difference in the nature of the surviving footings that it seems unlikely that the two had the same function. Internal deposits associated with Building A11 suggest that the floor was raised, which might explain why no evidence of an entrance threshold was identified. The only recovered artefacts that may give a clue to the building's function were a few fragments of encaustic inlaid floor tiles (see Chapter 4). Such tiles are ubiquitous in monastic contexts, particularly in claustral buildings such as the chapter house. While their presence in deposits within building A11 is by no means conclusive proof that they were originally laid there, it is suggested that this evidence, albeit meagre, could mean that A11 was a private chapel.

An episcopal licence was issued during Thomas Barentin II's lifetime, confirming the presence of an oratory on the site in 1370 (see Blair above) and the situation of Building A11 is the most likely location, given that the lord's chambers were above the service wing. The chapel at Charney Bassett Manor House, Oxfordshire, is attached to the solar in the same way as at Harding's Field with the access at first-floor level (Wood 1965, fig. 69).

In the 14th century there was a preference for two-staged or first-floor chapels, although ground floor chapels, such as the mid 14th-century ground floor chapel at Stonor House, Oxfordshire (Wood 1965, 245), are known. A 15th-century development was to have a chapel on the ground floor with a chancel the height of two floors (ibid, 237). An example of this arrangement can be found at Champs Chapel, East Hendred, Berkshire, and could have been the arrangement for Harding's Field. Thus the lord would enter the chapel from his first floor chamber above Room A10, while the manorial staff would enter from the ground floor. This fitted in with the separation of the lord and his family from his servants which had already occurred in the separation of the parlour from the hall. The lord and his servants would worship in the same building, but separately.

Room A1

The post-setting (618) in the centre of the hall (A1, Fig. 2.10) is a possible indication that efforts were made to update the hall itself. The post would have supported a crossbeam bearing a floor jettied out over almost the whole of the eastern part of the hall. This could be seen as an attempt to modernise an old house by reducing the roof space, without the expense of inserting a chimney and a fireplace. By flooring over part of the hall, an extra first-floor chamber was created while the roof space was reduced effectively to a large smoke bay. A number of standing examples of this alteration have been examined, particularly in Kent (Pearson 1994) and there is an example in a house dating from *c* 1500 in Watlington, Oxfordshire (J Steane, pers. comm.).

The curving feature (865), leading from the post-setting 618 to the north wall is difficult to explain. Though it has similarities with a drain, it is difficult to see why a drain would be needed at this point, let alone a curving one. Just possibly it was a slot to secure the lower edge of a lightweight screen or curtain, suspended from the jettied floor described above.

There are several alternative interpretations for the three postholes (862, 867, 868) on the north side of the hall. Their spacing makes it unlikely that they represent the foundations for a gallery providing access from the hall to a first floor room in A3. There is no evidence that a first floor was inserted within A3, since the central hearth was never replaced by a wall fireplace. An alternative interpretation is that they supported a staircase that led to the first floor room inserted into the eastern bay of the hall. Clearly a staircase in this position would only have been possible if the side bench of the hall had gone out of use by this time. Another theory is that the posts may have represented some sort of elaborate canopy over the bench especially as medieval furniture was commonly built into a room, rather than being free-standing.

It is possible that the step or dais in front of the opening into Room A3 was renewed at this time (622), with evidence of a tile-on-edge revetment (799) found to the north-west of the hearth.

Hearth development

A plinth of limestone flags (885) was placed against the south-east side of a new hearth (563) and was perhaps used as a stand for vessels, to keep food warm or to stack wood ready for the fire. One of the stones in the plinth had a conical hole worked through it and this, together with the burning on the underside of the stone, suggests that it may have originally been a tuyère block from a smelting hearth. A hearth of similar dimensions was excavated within the Manor of the More, Hertfordshire (Biddle *et al.* 1959, pl. XIXA).

Building A12

A further development of the sophistication of the services of the manor is implied by the rebuilding of the kitchen (A12, Fig. 2.13). Although this new kitchen had similar dimensions (9.0 m by 6.0 m) to its predecessor (Building W), it was attached to the hall by a corridor or pentice (18, 114) which would have provided covered access to the corridor between the buttery and pantry. Such pentices were characteristic of the growing conglomeration of medieval manorial and palatial buildings (Wood 1965, 336). They ensured that moving between buildings was in relative comfort and (where necessary) privacy. There is an order in the Liberate Rolls to make an aisle between Queen Eleanor's new chapel and chamber at Woodstock 'so that she may go and return from the chapel with a dry foot'. A passageway with open sides led from the hall to the kitchen at Weoley Castle and a number are known to have connected the rambling buildings of the royal palace of Clarendon, Wiltshire.

The interior of the new kitchen was more complex, the main cooking area containing a series of stone-lined ovens or fireplaces against the east wall, augmenting the large central hearth. The concentration of ovens and hearths in such a small area suggests that the rebuilt kitchen may have been stone-built, unlike its predecessor, although it is clear that the building's foundations were not appreciably deeper. The northern part of the building was separated by a partition wall, and possibly served as a woodstore, judging by the socketed axe-head (SF95) found within it.

The distribution of animal bones (see Wilson, Chapter 5) indicate that, although the cooking appeared to take place in Building A12, the preparation of the cooked meat for the table tended to take place in Room A9.

Other artefacts found within the main part of the kitchen included copper alloy cauldron and vessel feet, and a cauldron handle (SFs 472, 474, 478 and 7). However, although it is quite likely that cauldrons were used in the kitchen, it should be noted that they had been partially melted down and they may instead have been associated with the later metal-working on the site (see below).

Courtyards and gardens (Figs 2.19–20)

The fashion for ornamental pleasure gardens for relaxation and entertainment, paralleled by an aesthetic interest in plants, grew during the 14th century and complemented the development of comfortable houses (Steane 1985, 213–4; Harvey 1981, 94). The precise conventions surrounding this fashion would not evolve for another century or two, and the example at Harding's Field should be seen in the context of Steane's observation (ibid., 214) that these developments are manifestations of impulsive and unplanned acquisitiveness, reflecting an emerging leisured middle class but not yet a social code to go with it.

Traces of a curtain or garden wall were identified (692), extending north from the western end of the main domestic range, and following the northern moat edge to the western side of the garderobe A5, thus enclosing a large area over the footprint of the demolished Phase 2 buildings D and E. The enclosed area was bisected by a lightly founded structure (A13 – see below)

Medieval gardens were commonly walled and could also include timber rails, turf seats, gravel paths and water features (Harvey 1981). The Harding's Field walled garden contained an area of gravel and flint courtyard (732) and a small rectangular enclosure (572) which could represent a raised flowerbed. These were common features in gardens of this date (McLean 1981, 160).

Structure A13

The insubstantial structure bisecting the garden area north of the main range (Fig. 2.20) is best interpreted as a pentice, or open-sided walkway. The structure incorporated a mortar floor forming the bedding for decorated floor tiles, two of which survived *in situ*. The tiles had been laid in a diagonal pattern and comprised four different designs (see Chapter 4). The pentice enclosed a small cloister-like courtyard of gravel and flint which may have been a small-scale emulation of a monastic cloister (Wood 1965, 336). The courtyard was probably entered from a doorway in the north-east facing wall of the pentice, which may help to explain the lack of evidence for a wall at that point.

Structure A14

A small rectangular structure (Fig. 2.20) was constructed against the west end of Room A3, incorporating the garden wall (670) to form its south side. No evidence of a doorway was found between A14 and A3, and no material was found within A14 to explain its function. Structure A14 itself was augmented by a further small extension to the west, and one may surmise that both of these structures were utilitarian buildings – possibly store sheds relating to the garden.

Structure T

The very lightly founded Structure T (Fig. 2.19), situated between building J and the garden wall to the north was possibly an enclosure rather than a roofed building. Artefactual evidence was scarce – two horseshoes and an arrowhead were recovered from deposits within the structure, but these do not necessarily give a clear indication of the structure's function. It could represent a small paddock or pen, possibly for poultry, with the moat and the possible pond (320) situated close by to the west.

The agricultural buildings

The increase in the number of farm buildings was clearly dictated by the changing economic requirements of the estate. Either the estate was increasing in size and needed further farm buildings or, as is perhaps more likely, there was a changeover to a dominance of animal husbandry. The division of the farmyard would have benefited stock control. Greater profits could be made from stock rearing and the buoyant market in English wool made sheep rearing commercially attractive, in suitable parts of the country, like Oxfordshire (Steane 1985, 180).

Buildings G and H

These two buildings (Fig. 2.18) were constructed, apparently as a pair, effectively dividing the farmyard into inner and outer yards. The gap between the two buildings had a well-metalled surface which was edged on one side by a limestone kerb.

The narrow footings of building G would probably have supported a timber framed superstructure. Although smaller than building K, G still appears too large to be stables and no evidence was found for internal partitions, which would be expected in stables. Its proximity to the barn, convenient for the supply of threshed straw as feed and litter suggests that it may have been a cattle byre. The pitched stone hardstanding in front of the building may have had a role in the watering and feeding of cattle.

Building H seems to have been an altogether more substantial stone building, probably with a tiled roof, judging by the number of fragmentary tiles in the overlying deposits. Its north-western end was partly partitioned and drained and therefore it is possible that at least some of the building functioned as stables. The south-eastern end of the range comprised open-fronted bays and it may have served as a carthouse, as did one of the buildings at Cuxham (Harvey 1981, 36). Another example was the carthouse built in 1343 onto the end of the byre at Street, Somerset, measuring 30 feet by 20 feet (M Thompson pers. comm.).

Thus it seems likely that the function of the range G and H would have been linked to activities at least partially involving the lord and his family – for instance stables. The more utilitarian activities – grain storage or sheep and cattle shelters would be 'out of sight' to the south of the central range, accommodated by buildings C and K respectively. In addition, animal access to the open area along the west side of the island, or across the possible bridge or causeway in the southern corner of the island would be easy from the yard in front of Building K.

Building I

The construction of Building H seemed to prompt the refitting of Building I (Fig. 2.17); the stone-lined pit in the south-west corner appears to have been infilled. A new floor was laid and a small central hearth was constructed. Although the building may have been modified during this period, it was still likely to be functionally linked to Building J.

The abandonment of the manor (Phase 5 – mid to late 15th century)

The documentary evidence reveals that Reynold Barentin inherited the Oxfordshire manor of Haseley Court, Little Haseley, from his wealthy uncle Drew Barentin in 1415. By the middle of the 15th century Haseley Court had replaced the manor house at Harding's Field as the main Barentin residence (see Blair Chapter 1). Corroborative archaeological evidence for the date of the abandonment of the site as a residence was provided by the coinage, none of which was deposited later than the 15th century. However, this does not imply that either the domestic ranges, or the agricultural complex were necessarily deserted by the middle of the century.

It was certainly not unusual for a moated manor site to be abandoned by the owner at this time. By the 16th century moated manors were no longer constructed and many were abandoned (Platt 1978, 196; Steane 1985, 61). It was not uncommon for the residence to be moved elsewhere and the moated site retained for agricultural use, as at Harding's Field and also at Brome, Suffolk and at Cogges, Oxfordshire (Wilson and Hurst 1968, 103; Rowley and Steiner 1996, 46). The hall at Brome was possibly reduced in status to become a bakehouse or brewhouse (West 1970, 100). The 15th and 16th century also witnessed the extinction of some family lines, through confiscation or death, as was the case at Brome and at other sites, including Ellington (Tebbutt *et al.* 1971, 33), and Moat Hill, Anlaby near Hull (Thompson 1956–58, 70).

The demolition of the manor

It is difficult to be precise about the date of the demolition of the manor, or indeed how long that process lasted. The documentary evidence offers some persuasive evidence that it was a somewhat drawn-out affair. Blair argues that the manor house was finally demolished on completion, in 1485, of the transfer of the property from the financially troubled John Barentin II to the newly endowed Magdalen College, via Bishop Wayflete's agent Thomas Danvers. Furthermore, the apparent dispute with Abingdon Abbey in the 1480s over the sale of timber and roof tiles suggests that the superstructure of at least some of the buildings at Harding's Field was intact well into the last quarter of the century. However, by the middle of the 15th century the evidence suggests that Haseley Court had become the family's principal residence, although Blair suggests that there is some evidence of services being held in the Harding's Field chapel as late as 1451, which implies at least the occasional presence in Chalgrove of members of the family.

There is no archaeological evidence to contradict these documentary inferences, and it seems perfectly plausible for the manorial complex to have survived until the late 15th century as a working agricultural centre, even if the domestic range was gently decaying through neglect.

Once the process of demolition began in earnest, the buildings would have been swiftly stripped of usable building materials and fittings, leaving derelict shells standing. These shells would have their own uses to locals. Evidence, principally in the form of layers of charcoal and some ash, was found for some small-scale metalworking on the site in the form of a hearth or furnace constructed within the garderobe chamber (A5), presumably to recycle the lead recovered from the demolished window fittings. The lack of ash associated with the charcoal suggests that the material was brought into the room as charcoal and not as firewood. Fragments of furnace lining material and ironworking slag were also found in the immediate vicinity. The location of the furnace suggests that the walls were still standing to a height suitable for a sheltered furnace. The charcoal, some of which had spread into the derelict Room A4, was all beech, derived from trees aged 12 and 14 years which may suggest management by coppicing but are more likely to represent lopping of felled standards or clearance (see Robinson, Chapter 5).

The agricultural buildings

The farm buildings may have continued in use for some time after the demolition of the manor house. A rectangular timber-framed structure (Building M) was constructed on the demolition debris of Building H and probably reused the stone sill foundations. This may be the culver house or dovecote referred to in a document of 1520 (see Blair Chapter 1), although no archaeological evidence was found to support this hypothesis. A 1520 document records that John Quartermain owed rent for the site of a former manor and for a barn, in addition to the culver house mentioned above. The most likely candidate for the barn in this document is building C, the demolition of which certainly post-dated that of buildings G and H. The two buildings are still extant in a document of 1600 but are not mentioned in a document of 1675, suggesting that they had by then been demolished.

The moats

There is no evidence that the moats were backfilled once the site was abandoned. They appear to have been allowed to silt up naturally, which does not suggest that the abandoned site was in great demand for re-use in the early post-medieval period. The small assemblage of 16th-century material recovered from the upper fills of the moat attests to the low level of activity in the area at the time. By 1822 the moats appear to be no longer visible as significant earthworks, to judge by the estate map (see Pl.1.3).

THE MATERIAL CULTURE OF THE MANOR

In general the degree by which understanding of the manor's development and how it operated is enhanced by the artefactual and environmental evidence is disappointing. The reasons for this are various. As detailed in Chapter 1, the nature of the excavation and the necessary strategy played a part; their details will not be reiterated here. However, given the character of the site, it is arguable whether a more thorough excavation covering the same area would have produced much more in the way of sealed – or in other ways viable – environmental or artefactual assemblages. Manors were similar to monasteries – by their nature they were (usually) organised and efficient complexes of buildings linked by open spaces. Rubbish and occupational debris – both within the buildings and in external areas – would be disposed of away from the occupied area for health and aesthetic reasons. Such material remaining would inevitably be at risk of repeated redeposition, reducing its value both as a dating mechanism and as an indicator of function. Nevertheless, some conclusions regarding the manor's origin, development and demise can be tentatively deduced by considering aspects of the material culture against the background of the structural development.

The pottery

The few sherds predating the moat construction give little indication of high status, although as most came from what is suggested to be a kitchen, or cooking area, this lack of exotic wares may be misleading. As Page and Tremolet say, much of the pottery from Phase 3 contexts, particularly those within the main domestic buildings, was recovered from dumped make up layers, and therefore cannot be considered as accurate indicators of the activities at any one place or time. However, one may suggest that if there is any general trend, it is that the manor looked to the south and west (to Wallingford, Abingdon and Nettlebed) rather than north and west to Oxford for its local pottery source. The occurrence of rare French pottery in the 14th-century phases of activity is a reflection of the lord's status or at least contacts with import centres like London.

The metalwork and other small finds

The overall assemblage has produced few surprising or unexpected items. The general picture is one of a community lifestyle encompassing typical farm-related activities such as leather and woodworking, animal husbandry, and latterly, dairying. A considerable quantity of horse equipment was also recovered suggesting an emphasis on the role the horse played in the life of the manor, although this is more likely to have been as much for high status transport or recreation as general traction.

The personal items are typical in a manorial family context, with notable items such as the 12th- or 13th-century enamelled figure of a saint, and the two bone chess pieces. A notable assemblage of vessel glass reinforces the suggestion given by the continental pottery that there was a strong personal connection with London.

Artefactual use and distribution in the hall and service ranges in the 14th century

Following the structural changes of Phase 3, little evidence was found for the use of room A3 prior to its demolition. As with the other rooms, and at other sites (Hurst 1971, 99), constant cleaning left scarce evidence for floors and associated occupation debris and the artefacts that did survive were mixed in date. Few sherds of pottery were recovered but these included a high proportion of Tudor type tablewares, as might be expected from a lord's dining room. Similar pottery was also found in the demolition layers of the room in addition to numerous copper alloy pins, fragments of glazed window glass and plaster.

The hall (A1) itself yielded an assemblage of material that could be construed as indicative of its more public and formal role in the life of the manor, principally a number of coins, buckles and utilitarian dress objects such as lace tags. The presence of the large hearth was not an indication of its routine use as a cooking area.

Rooms A4 and A5 similarly contained thin, fragmentary layers from this period but their date range was even wider than that for room A3 and covered a period from Phase 3/1 to Phase 5. At least some of the layers within these two chambers belonged to the early part of Phase 5 during which time it is likely that metalworking took place (see below). The evidence for the cleaning out of the domestic rooms was particularly apparent within room A4 where it had resulted in a definite depression in the centre of the room. This effectively meant that the thin stratigraphy could not be traced across the chamber but survived as discrete islands against the walls.

Fragmentary patches of mortar (600/10, 1071, 1022/6) may have been part of a mortar floor associated with a layer of occupation debris (600/11, 600/9, 1022/5). However, all of the subsequent layers above the mortar were much more reminiscent of construction debris (507, 599, 600/2, 600/4, 1021, 1023). This would suggest either that the floor layers had been completely lost or that the construction debris was simply trodden down into the underlying surface and used as a floor. The occupation layers within the latrine A5 were even less informative. The pottery included material which may have been contemporary with that of Phase 2. Two cooking pots, a shallow dish and an abraded face mask, typical of types found in London, were also recovered. It is quite possible that the cooking pots had a secondary use as chamber pots.

The building materials

It is not surprising that the quantities of worked stone recovered from the site were disappointingly small. It is assumed that once the buildings were demolished, the usable stone – whether mouldings, plain ashlar blocks, or rubble was sold or scavenged. Although Haseley Court has a medieval core (Sherwood and Pevsner 1974, 685–7), there is no evidence on the basis of existing knowledge that the Harding's Field buildings were 'cannibalised' to provide architectural features for the inherited property. Therefore, it does appear that, aside from evidence of fairly plain gothic doorways and windows, the manor complex was never over-embellished with architectural elaboration.

Other architectural material suggests that most, if not all the main range, and some of the outlying buildings, were roofed with clay tile – possibly, in some cases, a replacement for stone slate. Little can be deduced about the internal decoration of the manor house. Evidence suggests that the main rooms were plastered, and in some cases this was painted, although no details of the design were identifiable. Curiously, the floor of the hall (Room A1) seems never to have been given a solid floor of flagstones or tiles. Indeed, the evidence for even a mortar floor beyond the immediate surrounds of the successive central hearths is inconclusive. One could suggest that it reflects on the increasingly marginalised role played by the hall in the lifestyle of a manorial lord, in his formal, private or leisured role. This contrasts significantly with the evidence of the tiled flooring of the possible chapel (A11) and the pentice (A13), the one signalling the continued strong role played by active religious worship, and the other reflecting the growing appreciation of leisure – aesthetically and as a statement of position in society.

The animal bone

While the animal bone assemblage is also constrained by the same circumstantial factors from providing a secure and complete assemblage for analysis, it is sizeable, and has allowed a number of lines of enquiry, providing possibly the best avenue by which to consider the manor, in its economic and environmental context (see Wilson – Chapter 5). The salient points are briefly rehearsed here.

Unsurprisingly, the three main domestic animals were prevalent, although pig is far more common than sheep or cattle. Pigs were bred for meat, whereas the cattle were mainly bred for traction or, increasingly in the late 14th century, for dairy products. Sheep were bred for their wool. This general regime accords with known (and documented) manors like Cuxham, Oxfordshire, or the archaeological evidence from the manorial areas of the Benedictine Grange at Dean Court Farm (Allen 1994, 440–2). Other bones suggest a wide diversity of diet, including geese and ducks, and pigeons, which were certainly kept, even if the identity of the medieval dovecote is uncertain. Imports to the manor included a wide variety of dietary supplements, including marine fish, oysters and crabs. Oysters are fairly ubiquitous over medieval sites, surviving as background scatters in general deposits – particularly in an urban or monastic context. Occasionally, as seems to be the case at Harding's Field, they are found as discrete dumps, apparently the refuse from a single feast (Hardy *et al.* 2003, 431).

Exports from the manor of Harding's Field are, of course, difficult to demonstrate archaeologically, but are implied by the make up of the animal bone assemblage in conjunction with the documented holdings of pasture in relation to arable land. Trade appears to have centred around secondary animal products and grain. Latterly there are signs of increasing proportions of sheep and cattle at the expense of pig, and an increase in the killing off of calves. This reflects the increasing regional specialisation of sheep farming (for wool) and dairying in the 14th and 15th centuries (Steane 1985, 180).

Reasons for the abandonment of the manor

Some aspects of the process of the abandonment of the manor have been touched upon above; the motivation for its demise is a more speculative area, although some areas of the archaeological evidence may help to eliminate some factors and suggest others.

It is accepted that the climate in England began to deteriorate significantly from the late 13th century (Steane 1985, 174–6), with lower temperatures and increasing rainfall. However, there is no evidence that living conditions in the manor at Harding's Field were materially affected. The moats were never particularly deep, and show no signs of being enlarged to accommodate more water; nor is there any evidence that the building platform was raised or protected by increased barriers. If waterlogging was becoming a problem through the latter part of the 14th century, one might expect evidence of the construction of extra drainage around the buildings, which was not the case. The documentary history indicates that the manor at Haseley was inherited by Reynold Barentin in 1415, yet it was not until 1485 that his great-grandson John Barentin II sold the Harding's Field property. Until that time, even though successive lords were living at least part of the time at Haseley, the Barentin manor at Chalgrove appeared to be still functioning as a working farm.

Overall, a good case can be made that the seeds of the manor's demise lie in the increasing difficulty of reconciling the topographical restraints of the site to the sophisticated domestic demands of the late medieval period. While the manorial home and the working farm were one and the same unit, the confines of the moat were acceptable. As the desire for a physical separation of the two elements grew, coupled with aspirations for more internal and external leisure areas for the lord and his family, so the restrictions of the moat would have become more and more apparent. Blair suggests that financial problems added a spur to break the link between the Barentins and Chalgrove. The opportunity provided by the inherited (and unmoated) house at Haseley would have been welcomed as a simple solution to both problems. A few years after the final sale of the Chalgrove manor, John Leland admired 'the right fair mansion place' at Haseley 'and marvellous fair walkes, topiarii operis, and orchardes and pools' (see Blair Chapter 1). Clearly these features, so popular among the emerging landed middle class, would have been very difficult to achieve on the moated site at Harding's Field without major redevelopment of the whole complex.

CONCLUSION

Inevitably the perspective on the archaeological study of moated medieval manors has evolved since the excavations at Harding's Field. The excavators were faced with problems and uncertainties, in the context of an 'old fashioned' rescue dig, which nowadays (hopefully!) would be accommodated and addressed before the excavation began. Within the context of what was possible at the time, the emphasis on recovering an overall building plan of as much of the main island as appeared to be developed was the only worthwhile approach that could be taken, and in the light of that, it is undeniable that the excavations at Chalgrove, despite the circumstantial constraints, produced a valuable body of information on a moated manorial site.

The value of such a project lies as much in the information not recovered as in the data collected. Although the project in Harding's Field has shown (principally by the structural remains) the development over two centuries of a manorial complex, and how that complex reflected the evolution of a 'knightly' class and their evolving aspirations, the value of the evidence relating to the understanding of how the manor operated, and in what sort of environment, both physical and economic, should not be overestimated. It has demonstrated – as other excavations, particularly on monastic sites have also demonstrated – that ideally the scope of excavation should be much wider than the footprints or immediate vicinities of the buildings, to encompass the peripheries of the occupied area and the potential areas of occupational debris deposition. Furthermore, the use of geophysical survey, fieldwalking and – in controlled circumstances – metal detecting can add significantly to the wider picture. In other words, understanding of manorial sites requires a much wider scope of investigation than can be achieved by close examination of just the principal buildings.

Bibliography and Abbreviations

BL. Add. Chs.	British Library Additional Charters
Black Prince's Reg.	*Black Prince's Register*
Bodl. MS Oxon. Ch.	Bodleian Library, Oxfordshire Charters
Cal. Fine R.	*Calendar of Fine Rolls*
Cal. Inq. P.M.	*Calendar of Inquisitions Post Mortem*
Calendarium Inq. P.M. Sive Esceat	*Calendarium Inquisitorium Post Mortem Sive Esceat*
Cal. Liberate R.	*Calendar of Liberate Rolls*
Cal. Pap. Reg.	*Calendar of Papal Register*
Cal. Pat. R.	*Calendar of Patent Rolls*
Cal. Chart. R.	*Calendar of Charter Rolls*
Cal. Close R.	*Calendar of Close Rolls*
Excerpt. Rot. Fin.	*Excerpta e Rotuli Finium*
PRO	Public Record Office
Rot. Chart.	*Rotuli Chartorum*
Rot. Hund.	*Rotuli Hundredorum*
Rot. Lit. Claus.	*Rotuli Litterarum Clausarum*
VCH 1939	*Victoria History of the County of Oxfordshire*, **1**

Bibliography

Aberg, F A (ed.), 1978 *Medieval moated sites*, CBA Res. Rep. **17**

Aberg, F A and Brown, A E (eds), 1981 *Medieval moated sites in North-West Europe*, BAR **121,** Oxford

Addyman, P V and Goodall, I H, 1979 The Norman church and door at Stillingfleet, North Yorkshire, *Archaeologia* **106**, 75–105

Allen, T G, 1994 A medieval grange of Abingdon Abbey at Dean Court Farm, Cumnor, Oxfordshire, *Oxoniensia* **59**, 219–447

Allen Brown, R, Colvin, H M and Taylor A J, 1963 *The History of the King's Works* **2**

Arkell, W J, 1947 *Oxford stone*, Wakefield

Armstrong, P, 1977 *Excavations in Sewer Lane, Hull*, East Riding Archaeologist **3**

Ashmolean Museum, 1886 *Catalogue*, Oxford

Barnard, F P, 1916 *The casting counter and counting board*, Oxford

Beresford, G, 1974 The medieval manor of Penhallam, Jacobstow, Cornwall, *Medieval Archaeology* **18**, 90–145

Beresford G, 1977 Excavation of a moated house at Wintringham in Huntingdonshire, *Archaeol J* **134**, 194–286

Berry, G, 1974 *Medieval English jettons*, London

Biddle, M, 1961–62 The deserted medieval village of Seacourt, Berkshire, *Oxoniensia* **26–27**, 70–201

Biddle, M, 1990a *Object and economy in medieval Winchester*, Winchester 7. **i** and **ii**, Oxford

Biddle, M, 1990b Copper alloy vessels and cast fragments, in Biddle 1990a, 947–59

Biddle, M, Barfield, L and Millard, A, 1959 Excavation of the Manor of the More, Rickmansworth, Hertfordshire, *Archaeol. J.* **116**, 136–99

Biddle, M and Elmhirst, L, 1990 Sewing equipment, in Biddle 1990a, 804–17

Blair, J, 1993 Hall and Chamber: English Domestic Planning 1000 – 1250 in G Meirion-Jones and M Jones (eds) *Manorial Domestic Buildings in England and Northern France*, Society of Antiquaries Occasional Paper **15,** 1–21

Bond, C J, 1973 The estates of Eynsham Abbey: a preliminary survey of their medieval topography, *Vale of Evesham Hist. Soc. Res. Pap.* **4**, 16–18

Bond, C J, 1978a Moated sites in Worcestershire, in Aberg 1978, 71–77

Bond, C J, 1978b Notes on dovecotes at Manor Farm, Minster Lovell and Duns Tew Manor, CBA Group 9 *Newsletter* **8** (1978), 72–5

Bond, C J, 1979 The reconstruction of the medieval landscape: the estates of Abingdon Abbey, *Landscape History* **1**, 59–75

Bond, C J (ed.), 1981 *Moated Sites Research Group* 8

Bond, C J, 1982 Dovecote at the Old Rectory, Kidlington, CBA Group 9 Newsletter **12** (1982), 103–4

Bond, C J, 1984 The Documentary Evidence in Rahtz and Rowley 1984, 125–27

Bond, C J, 1986 The Oxford region in the Middle Ages, in Briggs *et al.* 1986, 135–59

Bond, C J, Gosling, S and Rhodes, J, 1980 *Oxfordshire brickmakers*, Oxon. Museums Service Publications 14, Woodstock

Bond, C J and Weller, J B, 1991 The Somerset barns of Glastonbury Abbey, in *The archaeology and history of Glastonbury Abbey* (eds L Abrams and J P Carley), 57–87, Woodbridge

Borg, A, 1967 The development of chevron ornament, J. *Brit. Archaeol. Assoc.* 3rd ser. **30**, 122–40

Boycott, A E, 1936 The habitats of fresh-water mollusca in Britain, *J. Animal Ecology* **5**, 139–141
Briggs, G, Cook, J, and Rowley, T (eds), 1986 *The archaeology of the Oxford region*, Oxford University Department for External Studies, Oxford
Brooks, F W, 1939 A medieval brickyard at Hull, *J. Brit. Archaol. Assoc.* 3rd ser. **4**, 155–56
Bruce-Mitford, R L S, 1940 The excavations at Seacourt, Berkshire, 1939, *Oxoniensia* **5**, 31–41
Carter, W F, 1936 *The Quartermains of Oxfordshire*
Chalgrove Local History Group, 1980 *Chalgrove: an Oxfordshire village*
Chambers, R A, 1978a Chalgrove, Harding's Field, moated site, CBA Group 9 *Newsletter* **8** (ed. D N Hall), 110–112
Chambers, R A, 1978b Kidlington, Moat Cottage, CBA Group 9 *Newsletter* **8** (ed. D N Hall), 114–6
Chambers, R A, 1982 Chalgrove, CBA Group 9 *Newsletter* 12 (ed. D N Hall), 119, 121
Chambers, R A, and Meadows, I, 1981 Kidlington, Moat Cottage, CBA Group 9 *Newsletter* **11** (ed. D N Hall), 127–8 and figure 34, 114–6
Chaplin, R E, 1971 *The study of bones from archaeological sites*, London
Charleston, R J (ed.), 1968 *Studies in glass history and design*, Sheffield
Charleston, R J, 1972 The glass, in *Finds from excavations in the refectory at the Dominican Friary, Boston*, Lincolnshire History and Archaeology **1:7**, 45–8, 52–3
Charleston, R J, 1975 The glass, in Platt and Coleman-Smith 1975, 204–26
Cherry, J, 1982 The Talbot casket and related late medieval leather caskets, *Archaeologia* **107**, 131–40
Clarke, H, 1984 *The archaeology of medieval England*, London
Clarke, H and Carter, A, 1977 *Excavations in King's Lynn 1963–1970*, Soc. Medieval Archaeol. Mono. Ser. **7**
Colyer, C and Jones, M J (eds), 1979 Excavations at Lincoln, second interim report: excavations in the Lower Town 1972–8, *Antiq. J.* **59**, 50–91
Cook, P J, 1960 Moated settlements in the Blackwater region of Essex, unpublished thesis, St Hugh's College, Oxford
Cowgill, J, de Neergard, M and Griffiths, N, 1987 *Knives and scabbards: medieval finds from excavations in London*, London
Currie, C R J, 1992 Larger medieval houses in the Vale of the White Horse, *Oxoniensia* **57**, 81–244
de Watteville, H G, 1897 Monumental brasses in the churches of Stadhampton, Chalgrove and Waterperry, Oxon., *J of Oxford University Brass-rubbing Society* I (iii) (December 1897)
Dodgshon, R A, 1975 Land-holding foundations of the open-field system, *Past and Present* **67** (May), 3–29
Dodgshon, R A, 1980 *The origin of British field systems: an interpretation*, London
Dornier, A, 1965 Kent's Moat, Sheldon, Birmingham, *Trans Birmingham Archaeol Soc* **82**, 45–57
Duby, T, 1790 *Traite des monnaies des barons* **i**, Paris
Dunning, G C, 1977 Mortars, in Clarke and Carter 1977, 320–347
Durham, B D, 1977 Archaeological investigations in St Aldate's, Oxford, *Oxoniensia* **42**, 83–203
Dyer, C, 1995 Sheepcotes: evidence for medieval sheep farming, *Medieval Archaeology* **39**, 139–164
Eames, E, 1968 *Medieval tiles: a handbook*, London
Eames, E, 1980 *A catalogue of the lead-glazed earthenware tiles in the British Museum*, London
Egan, G, 1989 Bone, ivory and antler objects from Church Street (Site A), in Hassall *et al* 1989, 231–3
Ellis, B, 1995 Spurs and spur fittings, in J Clarke, *The Medieval Horse and its Equipment*, Museum of London, Medieval finds from excavations in London **5**, 124–56
Emery, F, 1974 *The Oxfordshire landscape*, London
Essex Arch. Soc. 1913–28 *Feet of Fines for Essex* **ii**
Fairbrother, J R, 1990 *Faccombe Netherton: excavation of a Saxon medieval manorial complex*, 2 volumes, British Museum Occasional Paper No 74, London
Farley, M, 1979 Pottery and pottery kilns of the post-medieval period at Brill, Buckinghamshire, *Post-Medieval Archaeology* **13**, 127–152
Faulkner, P A, 1975 Domestic planning from the 12th to 14th centuries, in Swanton 1975, 97–117
Fingerlin, I, 1971, *Gurtel des hohen und spaten Mittelalters*, Berlin
Firman, R J and Firman, P E, 1967 *A geological approach to the study of medieval bricks*
Fletcher, J M with Currie, C R J, 1979 The Bishop of Winchester's medieval manor house at Harwell, Berkshire, and its relevance in the evolution of timber-framed aisled halls, *Archaeol. J.***136**, 173–192
Fowler, W J, 1971 Lilley Farm moated site, CBA Group 9 *Newsletter* **1** (ed. R T Rowley), 25
Freese, S, 1957 *Windmills and Millwrighting*, 102–7, pl. 28b, c
Gardiner, M, 2000 Vernacular buildings and the development of the later medieval domestic plan in England, *Medieval Archaeol* **44**, 159–79
Gasparetto, H A, 1968 Les relations entre l'Angleterre et Venise aux XVI et XVII siecles et leur influence sur les formes verrieres Anglaises, in Charleston 1968
Gelling, M, 1953 *The place-names of Oxfordshire* **1**
Gibbons, A, 1888 *Early Lincoln wills*, Lincoln
Goodall, A R, 1980 Objects of copper alloy, in A Vince, Bartholomew Street, Newbury: a preliminary report on the archaeological excavations of 1979, Newbury District Museum
Goodall, A R, 1990 Objects of copper alloy and lead, in Fairbrother 1990, 425–436
Goodall, I H, 1976 Metalwork, in Excavations at Oxford Castle, 1965–1973 (T G Hassall), *Oxoniensia* **41**, 298–302
Goodall, I H, 1977 Iron objects, in Clarke and Carter 1977, 291–298
Goodall, I H, 1990a Locks and keys, in Biddle 1990a, 1001–36

Goodall, I H, 1990b Arrowheads, in Biddle 1990a, 1070–74

Grant, A, 1982 The use of tooth wear as a guide to the age of domestic animals, in Wilson *et al.* 91–109

Greening Lamborn, E A, 1942, *Notes and Queries* (26 September 1942), 190–92

Haberley, L, 1937 *Medieval English paving tiles*, Oxford

Haldon, R, 1977 The pottery, in Durham 1977, 111–139

Hamilton-Thompson, A, 1913–14 *The building accounts of Kirby Muxloe Castle, 1480–4*, Leicestershire Archaeol. Soc.

Hardy, A, 1996 Archaeological excavations at 54–55 St Thomas's Street, Oxford, *Oxoniensia* **61**, 225–273

Hardy, A, Dodd, A and Keevill, G D, 2003 *Aelfric's Abbey. Excavations at Eynsham Abbey, Oxfordshire 1989–92*, Oxford Archaeology Thames Valley Landscapes Monograph **16**

Harvey, J, 1981 *Medieval gardens*, London

Harvey, P D A, 1965 *A medieval Oxfordshire village: Cuxham 1240–1400 AD*, Oxford Hist. Ser. 2nd series

Harvey, Y, 1975 The small finds: the bone, in *Excavations in medieval Southampton 1953–69, volume 2* (C Platt and R Coleman Smith), 271–275, Leicester

Haslam, J, forthcoming Medieval glass from London

Hassall, T G, Halpin, C E, and Mellor, M, 1989 Excavations in St. Ebbes, Oxford, 1967–1976: Part I: Late Saxon and medieval domestic occupation and tenements, and the medieval Greyfriars, *Oxoniensia* **54** 1989, 71–277

Hawthorne, J G and Smith, C S, 1963 *Theophilus, On divers arts*, Chicago University Press

Hedges, J, 1978 Essex moats, in Aberg 1978, 63–70

Hinton, D A, 1973 *Medieval pottery of the Oxfordshire region*, Oxford

Hinton, D A, 1990a Two- and three-piece strap-ends and belt-plates, in Biddle 1990a, 503–505

Hinton, D A, 1990b Belt-hasps and other belt-fittings, in Biddle 1990a, 539–542

Hinton, D A, 1990c Copper alloy appliqués for leather and textile, in Biddle 1990a, 1086–88

Hinton, D A, 1990d Copper alloy, lead and pewter rings, in Biddle 1990a, 1095–97

Hinton, D A and Biddle, M, 1990 Copper alloy bells, in Biddle 1990a, 725–27

Hohler, C, 1942 Medieval paving tiles in Buckinghamshire, *Records of Bucks* **14**, 1–49

Huggins, P J, 1972 Monastic grange and outer close excavations, Waltham Abbey, Essex 1970–72, *Trans. Essex Archaeol. Soc. 3rd ser.* 4,30–127

Hurst, J G, 1961 The kitchen area of Northolt Manor, Middlesex, *Medieval Archaeology* **5**, 211–299

Hurst, J G, 1971 A review of archaeological research (to 1968), in *Deserted medieval villages* (eds M Beresford and J G Hurst), London

Hurst, D G and Hurst, J G, 1967 Excavations of two moated sites: Milton, Hampshire and Ashwell, Hertfordshire, *J. Brit. Archaeol. Assoc.* 3rd series, **30**, 48–86

James, S, Marshall, A and Millett, M, 1984 An early medieval building tradition, *Archaeol. J* **141**, 182–215

Jarvis, M G, 1973 Soils of the Wantage and Abingdon group, sheet 253, *Memoirs of the soil survey of Great Britain*

Jope, E M, 1951 The development of pottery ridge-tiles in the Oxford region, *Oxoniensia* **16**, 86–88

Jope, E M, 1956 The tinning of iron spurs: a continuous practice from the 10th to 17th century, *Oxoniensia* **21**, 35–42

Jope, M, 1959 Animal bones, in E M Jope and R I Threlfall, The 12th-century castle at Ascot Doilly, Oxfordshire: its history and excavation, *Antiq. J.* **34,** 269–70

Keevill, G D, 1995 *In Harvey's House and in God's House: excavations at Eynsham Abbey 1991–3*, Oxford Archaeology Thames Valley Landscapes Monograph **6**

Kingsford, C L, 1919 *The Stonor Letter and Papers*, ii (Camden 3rd ser. **xxx**)

Lever, C, 1977 *The naturalised animals of the British Isles*, London

Levitan, B, 1984 The vertebrate remains, in Rahtz and Rowley 1984, 108–163

Le Patourel, H E J, 1978a Memoranda submitted to the Department of the Environment; points to be considered when selecting moated sites for rescue excavation, in Aberg 1978, 6

Le Patourel, H E J, 1978b The excavation of moated sites, in Aberg 1978, 36–45

Le Patourel, H E J, 1980 Within the moats or beyond, *Moated Sites Research Group Report* **7**, 40–42

McCormack, J, 2002 Manors and seigneurial pretensions in the Channel Isles, in G Meirion-Jones, E Impey and M Jones (eds), *The Seigneurial Residence in Western Europe AD c 800–1600*, BAR Int. Ser. **1008**, Oxford, 113–30

McLean, T, 1981 *Medieval English gardens*, London

Macray, *Calendar of Magdalen College Deeds*, typescript in Magdalen College Library, Oxon.

Margary, I, 1976, *Roman Roads in Britain*

Margeson, S, 1993 *Norwich households: the medieval and post-medieval finds from Norwich Survey excavations 1971–1978*, East Anglian Archaeology **58**, Norwich Survey

Marples, B J, 1973 The animal bones, in A deserted medieval farmstead at Sadlers Wood Lewknor (R A Chambers), *Oxoniensia* **38**, 160–161

Mayes, P, 1968 South Witham, *Current Archaeology* **9** (July), 232–237

Mellor, M, 1980 The pottery, in Palmer 1980, 124–225 and fiche

Mellor, M, 1982 Nettlebed: Soundess Field, OAU *Newsletter* 9:6 (December)

Mellor, M, 1994 A synthesis of middle and late Saxon, medieval and early post-medieval pottery in the Oxford region, *Oxoniensia* **59**, 17–217

Midgley, L M, 1942 Minister's accounts of the earldom of Cornwall 1296–1297, *Camden Soc.* 3rd series, **66**, 98

Miles, D, 1977 Aerial reconnaissance in Oxfordshire, CBA Group 9 *Newsletter* **7** (eds D N Hall and W J Fowler)

Moor, C, 1929 *The knights of Edward I*, i, Harl. Soc. **80**

Moorhouse, S, 1971–72 A late medieval domestic rubbish deposit from Grove, near Wantage, Berkshire, *Berkshire Archaeological J.* **66**, 117–120

Moorhouse, S, 1977 Finds from Basing House, Hampshire (*c* 1540–1645) Part 2, *Post-Medieval Archaeology* **5**, 35–76

Morris, J (ed.), 1978 *Domesday Book: Oxfordshire*

Murray, H, 1913 *History of chess*, Oxford

Newton, P A, and Kerr, J, 1979 *Corpus vitrearum medii aevi; The County of Oxford; a catalogue of medieval stained glass*, Oxford

Oakley, G and Harman, M, 1979 The other finds: worked bone, in *St Peter's Street, Northampton excavations 1973–1976* (J H Williams), 308–318, Northampton

OAU 1976 *Newsletter*, December

Oswald, A, 1975 *Clay pipes for the archaeologist*, BAR **14**

Ox. Arch. Soc. Report 1909, transcript of Magdalen College Deed Chalgrove 41A, 32

Page, P S, 1976 Moated sites in Oxfordshire, unpublished survey, Chalgrove Hardings Field archive

Palmer, N, 1980 A Beaker burial and medieval tenements in the Hamel, Oxford, *Oxoniensia* **45**, 124–255

Parker, J H, 1853 *Some account of domestic architecture in England from Edward I to Richard I*, Oxford

Parker, J H and Burges, W, 1860 On mural paintings in Chalgrove church, Oxfordshire, *Archaeologia* **38**, 431–38

Parrington, M, 1975 Excavations at the Old Gaol, Abingdon, *Oxoniensia* **40**, 59–78

Pavry, F H, and Knocker, G M, 1960 The Mount, Princes Risborough, *Rec. Bucks* 16, Appendix 3

Payne, S, 1973 Kill-off patterns in sheep and goats: the mandibles from Asvan Kale, *J. Anatolian Studies* **23**, 281–303

Pearson, S, 1994 *The medieval houses of Kent: an historical analysis*, RCHM

Pernetta, J, 1973 The Animal Bones, in Excavations at Copt. Hay Tetsworth, Oxfordshire (M A Robinson), *Oxoniensia* 38, 112–15

Perry, J G, 1980 Interim report on the excavation at Sydenham's, Solihull, 1972–8: a moated site in the Warwickshire Arden, *Trans. Birmingham and Warwickshire Archaeol. Soc.* **90**, 49–64

Pinder-Wilson, R H and Brooke, C N C, 1973 The reliquary of St Petroc and the ivories of Norman Sicily, *Archaeologia* **104**, 261–305

Platt, C, 1978 *Medieval England*, London

Platt, C and Coleman-Smith, R, 1975 *Excavations in medieval Southampton 1953–1969, Vol. 2: The finds*, Leicester

Plot, R, 1677 *The natural history of Oxford-shire*, Oxford

Preece, P, 1987 Firewood from the Oxfordshire Chilterns, *Arboricultural J.* **11:3**, 227–235

Preece, P, 1987–8 Woodmen of the Oxfordshire Chilterns, 1300–1800, *Folk Life* **26**, 70–77

Preece, P, 1990a Medieval woods in the Oxfordshire Chilterns, *Oxoniensia* **55**, 55–72

Preece, P, 1990b Wood products from the Oxfordshire Chilterns before 1830, *Local Historian* **20:2**, 73–79

Rackham, O, 1980 *Ancient woodland: its history, vegetation and uses in England*, London

Rademacher, H, 1933 *Die Deutschen Glaser des Mittelalters*, Berlin

Rahtz, P A, 1969 *Excavations at King John's hunting lodge, Writtle, Essex, 1955–57*, Soc. for Medieval Archaeol. Mono. **3**

Rahtz, S and Rowley, T, 1984 *Middleton Stoney: excavation and survey in a north Oxfordshire parish 1970–72*, Oxford

Reddaway, T P and Walker, L E M, 1975 *The early history of the goldsmiths' company, 1327–1509*, London

Rigold, S E, 1970 Six copper-alloy objects from St Augustine's, Canterbury, *Antiq. J.* **50**, 345–47

Rigold, S E, 1975 Structural aspects of medieval timber bridges, *Medieval Archaeology* **19**, 48–91

Roberts, M R, 1996 A Tenement of Roger de Cumnor and other archaeological investigations in Medieval North Osney, Oxford *Oxoniensia* **61**, 181–224

Robinson, M A and Wilson, R, 1987 A survey of environmental archaeology in the South Midlands, *Environmental Archaeology: a regional review* 2 (ed. H Keeley), HBMC Occasional Paper **1**, 68–70

Roden, D, 1968 Woodland and its management in the medieval Chilterns, *Forestry* **41**, 59–71

Rowley, R T and Steiner, M, 1996 *Cogges Manor Farm, Witney, Oxfordshire*, Oxford

Salter, H E, 1930 *The Boarstall Cartulary*, Oxford Hist. Soc. **88**

Salzman, L F, 1967 *Building in England down to 1540*, 2nd edition, Oxford

Sherwood, J and Pevsner, N, 1974 *The buildings of England: Oxfordshire*

Siegal, S, 1956 *Non-parametric statistics for the behavioural sciences*, Tokyo

Smith, J T, 1975 Medieval aisled halls and their derivatives, in Swanton 1975, 27–44

Smith, J T, 1989–90 Sydenham's Moat: a 13th-century moated manor-house in the Warwickshire Arden, *Trans. Birmingham and Warwickshire Archaeol. Soc.* **96**, 27–68

Sosson, J P, 1972 Pour une approche economique et sociale du batiment, l'example des travaux publiques à Bruges aux XIV et XV siècles, *Bulletin de la Commission Royales des Monuments et des Sites* T2, 129–53

Steane, J M, 1985 *The archaeology of medieval England and Wales*, London

Sturdy, D, 1959 Thirteenth-century and later pottery from the Clarendon Hotel and other sites, *Oxoniensia* **24**, 22–36

Swanton, M J, 1975 *Studies in medieval domestic architecture*, Royal Archaeological Institute Monograph

Tait, H, 1979 *The golden age of Venetian glass*, London

Tebbutt, C F, Rudd, G T and Moorhouse, S, 1971 Excavation of a moated site at Ellington, Huntingdonshire, *Proc. Cambridge Antiquarian, Soc.* **63**, 31–73

Thompson, M W, 1956–8 Excavation of a medieval moat at Moat Hill, Anlaby near Hull, Yorkshire, *Yorkshire Archaeol J.* **39**, 67–85

Thorpe, W A, 1935 *English glass*, London

Toulmin Smith, L (ed.), 1907 *The itinerary of John Leland* i, London

VCH 1939 *Victoria History of the Counties of England, Oxfordshire* **1**

von den Driesch, A, 1976 *A guide to the measurement of animal bones from archaeological sites*, Peabody Museum Bulletin **1**, Cambridge, USA

Walton, D, 1978 Archaeomagnetic intensity measurements using a SQUID magnetometer, *Archaeometry* **19**:2, 192–200

Ward-Perkins, J B, 1949 A medieval harness-mount at Termoli, *Antiq. J.* **29**, 1–7

Weaver, J R H and Beardwood, A (eds), 1958 *Some Oxfordshire wills*, Oxon. Rec. Soc. **39**

Webster, L E and Cherry, J (eds), 1973 Interim reports on Wallingford castle, Berkshire and Owermoigne, Dorset, *Medieval Archaeology* **17**, 159–161 and 174

Wedgewood, J S and Holt, A D, 1936 *History of Parliament: biographies of members of the Commons House*, London: HMSO

West, S E, 1970 Brome, Suffolk: the excavation of a moated site, 1967, *J. British Archaeol. Assoc.* 3rd series, **33**, 89–112

West, B, 1982 Spur development: recognising caponised fowl in archaeological material, in Wilson *et al.* 1982, 255–61

Whitwell, J B, 1969 Excavations on the site of a moated medieval manor house in the parish of Saxilby, Lincolnshire, *J. British Archaeol. Assoc.* 3rd series, **32**, 128–144

Williams, A, 1986 Cockles Amongst the Wheat: Danes and English in the Western Midlands in the First Half of the Eleventh Century', *Midland History* **xi**, 1–22

Wilson, D M and Hurst, D G (eds), 1968 Interim reports: Brome, Suffolk and Horley, Surrey: Court Lodge Farm, *Medieval Archaeology* **12**, 193–196

Wilson, R with Allison, E and Jones, A, 1983 Animal bones and shell, in Late Saxon evidence and excavation of Hinksey Hall, Queen Street, Oxford (C Halpin), *Oxoniensia* **48**, 68–9

Wilson, R, 1984 Medieval and post-medieval animal bones and marine shells, in Excavations in St Ebbes, Oxford, part II, 1967–76 (B Durham, C Halpin and M Mellor), *Oxoniensia* **49**, Fiche 6

Wilson, R, 1985 Degraded bones, feature type and spatial patterning on an Iron Age occupation site in Oxfordshire, England, in *Palaeobiological investigations: research methods, design and interpretation* (eds N R J Fieller, D D Gilbertson and N G A Ralph), BAR Int. Ser. **266**, 81–94

Wilson, R, 1986 Bone and shell report, in *Archaeology at Barton Court Farm, Abingdon* (D Miles), CBA Res. Rep. **50**, fiche, Oxford

Wilson, R, 1989 Fresh and old table refuse: the recognition and location of domestic activity at archaeological sites in the Upper Thames Valley, England, *Archaeozoologia* III, **1.2**, 237–60

Wilson, R, 1993 Reports on the bone and oyster shell, in *The prehistoric landscape and Iron Age enclosed settlement at Mingies Ditch, Hardwick with Yelford, Oxfordshire* (T G Allen and M A Robinson), Oxford Archaeology Thames Valley Landscapes: The Windrush Valley **2**, 123–134

Wilson, R, 1994 Mortality patterns, animal husbandry and marketing in and around medieval and post-medieval Oxford, in *Urban-rural connexions: perspectives from environmental archaeology* (eds A R Hall and H K Kenwood), Symposia of the Association for Environmental Archaeology **12**, Oxbow Monograph **47**, 103–115

Wilson, R, 1995 The animal bone, in Mount Farm, Dorchester-on-Thames (A Barclay and G Lambrick), unpublished OAU document for submission to English Heritage

Wilson, R, 1996 *Spatial patterning among animal bones in settlement archaeology*, Brit Archaeol Report, British Series **251**, Oxford

Wilson, R and Bramwell, D, 1980 Animal bone and shell, in Palmer 1980, 198 and fiche F08–F11

Wilson, R, Grigson, C and Payne, S, 1982 *Ageing and sexing of animal bones from archaeological sites*, Brit Archaeol Report, British Series **109**, Oxford

Wilson, R, Hamilton, J, Bramwell, D and Armitage, P, 1978 The animal bones, in *The excavation of an Iron Age settlement, Bronze Age ring-ditches and Roman features at Ashville Trading Estate, Abingdon (Oxfordshire) 1974–76* (M Parrington), OAU Rep. 1, CBA Res. Rep. **28**, 110–139, London

Wilson, R and Locker, A, 1989 Medieval animal bones and marine shells from Church Street and other sites in St Ebbes, Oxford, in Excavations in St Ebbes, Oxford, 1967–76. Part 1: late Saxon and medieval domestic occupation and tenements and the medieval Greyfriars (T G Hassall, C E Halpin and M Mellor), *Oxoniensia* **54**, 258–268

Wood, M E, 1965 *The English medieval house*, London

Youngs, S M, Clark, J, & Barry T B 1982 'Medieval Britain and Ireland in 1982' *Medieval Archaeology* XXVII 1982, 161–229

Index

Page numbers in *italics* refer to figures and plates.